CW01095561

Probate
and
The Administration of Estates:
A Practical Guide

Second Edition

AUSTRALIA
The Law Book Company
Brisbane • Sydney • Melbourne • Perth

CANADA
Ottawa • Toronto • Calgary • Montreal • Vancouver

Agents:
Steimatzky's Agency Ltd, Tel Aviv;
N.M. Tripathi (Private) Ltd, Bombay;
Eastern Law House (Private) Ltd, Calcutta;
M.P.P. House, Bangalore;
Universal Book Traders, Delhi;
Aditya Books, Delhi;
MacMillan Shuppan KK, Tokyo;
Pakistan Law House, Karachi, Lahore

Probate
and
The Administration of Estates:
A Practical Guide

Second Edition

by
Philip S. A. Rossdale
M.A., Ll.M. (Cantab.)
of the
Inner Temple and Lincoln's Inn, Barrister

With a foreword by
The Rt. Hon. Sir Robert Megarry,
formerly the Vice-Chancellor

London
Sweet & Maxwell
1996

First Edition 1991
Second Edition 1996

Published by Sweet & Maxwell Limited of
South Quay Plaza, 183 Marsh Wall, London E14 9FT
Computerset by P.B. Computer Typesetting,
Pickering, N. Yorks
Printed and bound by Butler & Tanner Ltd, Frome and London

A catalogue record
for this book is available
from the British Library

ISBN 0–421–562–706

No natural forests were destroyed to make this product.
Only farmed timber was used and saplings were re-planted.

No part of this publication may be reproduced or transmitted
in any form or by any means, or stored in any retrieval system
of any nature without prior written permission, except for
permitted fair dealing under the Copyright, Designs and Patents
Act 1988, or in accordance with the terms of a licence issued by
the Copyright Licencing Agency in respect of photocopying and/or
reprographic reproduction. Application for permission for other
use of copyright material including permission to reproduce extracts
in other published works shall be made to the publishers. Full
acknowledgment of author, publisher and source must be given.

©
Philip S.A. Rossdale
1996

"I have learnt much from my teachers,
more from my colleagues than from my teachers,
and from my pupils more than from anyone".

R. Chaninah
quoted in *Taan.* 7a

FOREWORD

By Rt. Hon. Sir Robert Megarry, formerly the Vice-Chancellor

This is a somewhat unusual book. In its 45 chapters it covers a wide range of subjects. The style is concise, the language is clear (and often informal), and the whole approach is essentially practical. The text deals with many points of importance that are not to be found readily (if at all) in the larger books on the subject, and the author has not hesitated to express his views on a wide range of questions that are devoid of authority. The book will plainly be a useful addition to the library of very many solicitors' offices. An appendix of some nine pages expounds the basic system of the law of England and Wales that is relevant to the subject; and this, coupled with the direct style of the text, will make the book both accessible and useful to foreign lawyers who become concerned with the administration of assets in this country. Correspondingly, solicitors here who are administering an estate with substantial assets abroad would be well advised to ensure that a copy of this book is in the hands of any foreign lawyers assisting them. The book seems to me to accomplish its chosen object admirably, and I warmly commend it.

Lincoln's Inn   R.E.M.
June 1, 1991

PREFACE TO THE SECOND EDITION

This edition is designed to bring the book up to date. My object in writing it and the potential readers to whom it is addressed are stated in the Preface to the First Edition, printed below. I hope that this edition too is clear, both to lawyers in England and Wales and to others.

First and Second Appendices

I have revised the former Appendix and re-named it the "First Appendix". The Second Appendix contains a list of further alterations in the law that are desirable.

The statutory system[1] governing the incidence of liabilities and of legacies under the Administration of Estates Act 1925 First Schedule, Part Two as judicially interpreted, is "notoriously obscure", and has given rise to "numerous judicial decisions, some of which are not readily reconcilable"[2]: it ought to receive the attention of the Law Commission.[3] This, I think, remains the area in need of statutory revision. In paragraph 26–04 I suggest a short and simple statutory solution to this "riddle".[4]

Reported cases

The Court of Appeal's decision *Sen v. Headley* [1991] Ch. 425 (where an appeal to the House of Lords was compromised) extends the scope of a deathbed gift not made by will (*donatio mortis causa*): see paragraph 22–04. The doctrine can be used to advance an unmeritorious claim. Now that a witness's written statement may stand as evidence, and not be subject to the searching process of being elicited orally ("in chief"), the result can be to force a compromise of such a claim. The abolition of the doctrine is desirable; as, according to Lord Eldon, it was[5] in 1827.

---

[1] See Chapter 26.
[2] *Re Taylor* [1969] 1 Ch. 254 at p. 249.
[3] *ibid* at p. 253.
[4] *ibid* at p. 253.
[5] See the citation in para. 22–04.

The decision of the Court of Appeal that the "right to buy" does not survive the purchasing tenant's death, *Bradford Metropolitan City Council v. McMahon* [1994] 1 W.L.R. 52 (see paragraph 20–06), will probably not in practice induce unenthusiastic local authorities to act more speedily on such sales.

Statutes

The Law of Property (Miscellaneous Provisions) Act 1994 has introduced new hazards for personal representatives when making covenants for title; especially when selling a leasehold; but these hazards can be avoided: see paragraph 23–05.

The Landlord and Tenant (Covenants) Act 1995 is principally an alteration in the law of landlord and tenant; it complicates the position of personal representatives of a landlord or of a tenant. The 1995 Act cannot be excluded. I have only included a short summary of its potential effect on personal representatives: paragraph 25–09.

The Criminal Appeals Act 1995, s.7 has abrogated *R. v. Kearley* [1994] 2 A.C. 414 (holding that the Court of Appeal was unable to hear personal representatives appeal against a financial penalty on a deceased offender); the decision is briefly mentioned in paragraph 25–07, as the point might arise elsewhere in the Commonwealth.

The need to account on intestacy has been abrogated in respect of deaths from January 1, 1996, by the Law Reform (Miscellaneous Provisions) Act 1995, s.1.

The Private International Law (Miscellaneous Provisions) Act 1995 Part Two operating from January 8, 1996 deals with the position in the U.K. of those with overseas polygamous marriages. It appeared too late to be included in Chapter 27 here; but is covered in an Addendum.

Other points added in this edition

The revised paragraph 1–01 was very kindly suggested by the late James Elliott, formerly the Belfast Coroner.

I have added a few other points not in the first edition, that have been suggested to me.

One of them is the consequence of a minor or a person without capacity attesting a will: paragraphs 12–09 and 12–10. To this passage there applies the remark about prescription by the late Michael Bowles[6]:

> "I think it can fairly be said that any lack of clarity in this ... reflects the present state of the law on the subject."

---

[6] Preface to Gale, *Easements* (13th ed., 1959).

The birth of a child to a woman aged 59 has been reported; and so I have also added observations on the position of personal representatives who might be presented with such a birth: paragraph 27–14.

Chapter headings

A list of the paragraphs in each chapter has been inserted.

Index

The Index has been enlarged.

Precedents

I have been asked why no precedents are included. They would have increased the size, and so the cost, of the book; without, I think, really improving its usefulness. Ordinary cases only need printed forms readily available from law stationers: an unusual case requires documents specially prepared for it.

The Publishers

I should like to thank Sweet & Maxwell for encouragement and help that I have had in writing this edition. They have also dealt carefully with the altered references and cross-references, and other necessary alterations in the text.

Solicitors Journal

I am grateful for permission to repeat here material that appeared as articles in the *Solicitors Journal*.[7]

Date of the law

The law is stated as on August 11, 1995 with a few later additions made in the proofs.

P.S.A. ROSSDALE
10 Old Square
Lincoln's Inn

November 24, 1995

---

[7] Financial penalties on deceased offenders (1994) 138 Sol. Jo. 1157; when a grant of representation should be renounced (1995) 139 Sol. Jo. 10; dealing with delay in probate or in administration of an estate (1995) 139 Sol. Jo. 424; traps for personal representatives (L.P.A. 1994) (1995) 139 Sol. Jo. 747.

PREFACE TO THE FIRST EDITION

"Matters of administration [of estates] are settled by practice which reflects common sense or, what is to my mind the same thing, reason tempered by convenience": Uthwatt J. in *Re Bradberry* [1943] Ch. 35 at p. 40.

This book offers a succinct summary of the procedure to obtain probate and of the ordinary administration of estates in England and Wales after a death.

Those not accustomed to the administration of estates may feel perplexed about property rights after a death. Difficulties can arise; but difficulties do not normally arise. Contrary to what is sometimes thought, there is no need for delay in dealing with an estate. Someone concerned, as executor or administrator or as a beneficiary, is not alone: advice is readily available from solicitors or from counsel; when necessary, a question can be referred to a judge informally for authority to act on counsel's opinion; or can be referred to a judge for a formal decision on written evidence (by affidavit) after hearing argument: as explained in Chapter 42.

Readers with knowledge of the law of England and Wales

The administration of estates concerns those professionally engaged in it: solicitors and their staff (judges and barristers concerned with the subject are familiar with most of what is said here); officials of banks and other trust corporations; accountants and their staff; and lawyers elsewhere than in England and Wales, especially in continental Europe. Students, of law and of other related subjects, are also concerned to understand this system. Read with the footnotes, this book is intended to assist them.

Citation of authority

Only a few sections of Acts of Parliament are reprinted here; I assume that those concerned have access to the current statutes.[1] The

---

[1] See Sweet & Maxwell's *Property Statutes* and Sweet & Maxwell's *Family Law Statutes*.

footnotes, when possible, cite recent and accessible judicial authorities; and I have cited a few Commonwealth authorities, that throw light on the law of England and Wales. Those who wish to consult all the authorities on a point will find them in other books.

Readers without technical knowledge of the law of England and Wales

Read without the footnotes, this book is intended to offer help at each stage to anyone concerned in an estate, who is unfamiliar with the law.

The Appendix

For those unfamiliar with the English legal system, I have added an Appendix[2] describing the civil legal system here (so different from that on the continent of Europe). The Appendix is intended to be read before the rest of the book by anyone to whom the legal system is unfamiliar. It is too early to take into account there the future effects of the Courts and Legal Services Act 1990.

Arrangement

The topics are arranged in approximately the order in which they are likely to occur in practice; but with an attempt to keep related subjects together: to avoid having very short chapters, I have in one or two places run together what were originally two successive chapters.

I have put towards the end two subjects that do not normally arise: Insolvent Estates and Acting as a Personal Representative without Authority; and have concluded with Proceedings in Court: in most estates an application to the court is the last thing that anyone desires.

Short points that occur in more than one context appear in each context; for longer ones, I have used a cross-reference.

Practical points

The book covers practical points that tend to arise; including:

---

[2] Pages [321] to [331]; based with kind permission on the format used in Pugh, *The Administration of Foreign Estates*.

1. When a grant should not be accepted (a question sometimes overlooked until after a grant has been unwisely accepted), Chapter 5;
2. What steps to take when a will or a codicil is missing, Chapter 15 and paragraph [1–09];
3. What a personal representative should do when faced with a claim by letter that a will already proved is invalid, without the claimant bringing legal proceedings (a frequent occurrence), paragraph 10–06;
4. What to do when the deceased has (as elderly people do) lost or accidentally destroyed a land certificate, title deeds or share certificates, paragraphs 20–04 and [20–09];
5. The questions that face the personal representatives of someone who had been in partnership until his death, paragraphs 20–14 to 20–19;
6. What to do when the deceased had liabilities that are not being asserted by the creditor, paragraph 25–05;
7. What personal representatives should do when (as often happens) urged by beneficiaries to ring legal proceedings that the personal representatives think unwise, paragraph [42–20];
8. Individual status, as far as relevant when administering an estate, Chapter 27. For example the questions arising when someone leaves two or more wives whom he had lawfully married overseas in a polygamous union, and at his death the law of England and Wales applies to the devolution of his property.

It is difficult to state correctly the statutory incidence of liabilities and of legacies, in the light (although that is not the right word) of the courts' decisions on the First Schedule to Administration of Estates Act 1925; see Chapter 26. In practice it is usual, in my experience, to adopt a rough (if not ready) solution as less costly than exploring this labyrinth; that represents "reason tempered by convenience". A clear and workable schedule should have been substituted by legislation long ago.

Rules

I assume that the Non Contentious Probate Rules 1987 and the Rules of the Supreme Court are available; and so they are not reprinted here. I have mentioned a few desirable amendments of the Rules of the Supreme Court: see paragraphs 44–02 and 19–05.

Matters only summarised

Inheritance Tax. Inheritance tax on obtaining a grant is summarised; but not the detailed questions that may arise in estates which, after exemptions and reliefs, exceed £140,000 formerly £128,000 (not devolving on a surviving spouse or a charity): those questions are answered in books on revenue law.

Litigation. This book deals only briefly with litigation concerning an estate; litigation, whether brought or only threatened, necessitates detailed legal advice in the circumstances of each case.

Matters omitted

This book does not cover specialist subjects that may arise in an administration: such as claims for damages for personal injuries causing the death and, back duty claims for income tax after a death; nor claims by dependants for reasonable financial provision under the Inheritance (Provision for Family and Dependants) Act 1975.

This is not a book on the construction of wills. Few wills nowadays occasion the questions of construction that formerly arose; when such questions arise, they can be answered from Jarman, *Wills*, (8th ed.), or Theobald, *Wills* (14th ed.). The boundaries between administering an estate and construing a will are not fixed. Thus the right of a posthumous child to share on intestacy is a matter of administration, paragraph 31–12; but the question (discussed in Theobald, *Wills* (14th ed.) at pp. 378–379) when the language of a particular will includes or excludes a posthumous child is one of construction, outside the ambit of this book.

I have not discussed points that seem not to arise in practice: not even the interesting question of the right of personal representatives to appeal to the Court of Appeal against directions given at first instance with which they are dissatisfied; it seems only to have arisen on two occasions; these two authorities are however cited, discussing another point, in a note to paragraph 36–06.

Acknowledgments

It is a pleasure to acknowledge the help that I have been generously given.

The late Joseph Wolfe and the late Hubert Rose, whose pupil I was successively, each in his own way initiated me into the outlook and practice of the Chancery Bar as he had received it from his teachers. The long line of tradition through teacher and pupil is a happy feature of the Bar.

Over the years, I have had much help from my colleagues, my clients and my pupils; especially in drawing my attention to actual problems, and suggesting their inclusion here.

At an early stage James Arbuthnot M.P. generously found time to read the typescript, and made numerous suggestions. I gratefully adopted them all. The errors that remain are my own.

My wife read the typescript, to identify sentences which needed to be rewritten so as to be clear to someone without legal experience; and I rewrote them.

It is most gratifying to express my thanks to Sir Robert Megarry for his generosity in reading the entire book in page proofs, and writing his kind introduction: those who know him, as author or judge, will no doubt agree that anything I write would be inadequate in the circumstances.

I have been able to write this book, because of the cheerful unfailing support of the staff here; especially my Clerks, Frank Wright and Chris Reade.

The help and encouragement of my publishers Sweet & Maxwell has been an important factor in my writing this book. The connection between them and these Chambers gives me special pleasure: for Sweet & Maxwell all three editions of Gover, *Capital and Income* (1901, 1910 and 1933) written here.

Date of the law

The law is stated as on September 19, 1990; but a few subsequent additions have been made within the scope of the typescript and proofs.

P. S. A. ROSSDALE
10 Old Square
May 22, 1991   Lincoln's Inn

ADDENDUM

Polygamous Marriages Abroad

Private International Law (Miscellaneous Provisions) Act 1994

The recognition or non-recognition under English law of a marriage affects the revocation of wills and the status at the death of those who survive.

A polygamous marriage cannot be solemnised in the United Kingdom.[1] When one party or both parties to a marriage are domiciled here, and marry abroad in a country that allows polygamy, the Private International Law (Miscellaneous Provisions) Act 1995, Part Two ("the Act") distinguishes between *potentially* polygamous marriages and *actually* polygamous marriages.

The Act commenced on January 6, 1996 (s.16(2)) but does not apply to rights under a will, codicil or intestacy where the death was before its commencement (s.6(6)). In other respects the Act governs a marriage before its commencement (s.6(1)); with exceptions mentioned below.

Potentially polygamous marriages and actually polygamous marriages. A "potentially polygamous marriage" is one celebrated under the law of a country that allows polygamy (or perhaps polyandry), where in fact neither party has another spouse. An "actually polygamous marriage" is one solemnised under the law of a country that allows polygamy, where one party (usually the husband) actually continues to be married to someone else too.

Application of the Act. The Act does not apply to polygamous marriages when both parties are domiciled abroad; nor to an actually polygamous marriage, when one party is domiciled here. The Act applies only to potentially polygamous marriages where at least one party is domiciled here, celebrated in a country that allows polygamy. Two such types of ceremony that are apt to occur come within the Act.

---

[1] See para. 27–04, note 9.

First, someone domiciled here may go abroad to marry someone domiciled abroad under the local law, in a country that allows polygamy. *Secondly*, both parties domiciled here may go for a few days to a country with a better climate to marry under the local law there; without considering that such local law would potentially allow polygamy and so might affect the validity of their marriage in England and Wales on their return.

Section 5. Section 5(1) is as follows:

> **"Validity in English law of potentially polygamous marriages**
> 5.(1) A marriage entered into outside England and Wales between parties neither of whom is already married is not void under the law of England and Wales on the ground that it is entered into under a law which permits polygamy and the either party is domiciled in England and Wales."

Accordingly the law here recognises as valid a potentially polygamous marriage when one party or both parties are domiciled here.

Subsection (2) provides (in short) that subsection (1) does not affect the determination of the validity of a marriage under the law of another country with jurisdiction to do so.

Exception to s.5. Section 5 does not apply to an earlier polygamous marriage that has meanwhile before the commencement of the Act been followed by a later valid marriage (s.6(2)).

Section 5 does not apply to a marriage annulled or declared invalid by a court having jurisdiction to do so, before the commencement of the Act of afterwards in proceedings begun before its commencement (s.6(3), (4) and (5)).

The Act does not apply to marriages in the Royal Family (s.8(1) and s.15(2)); nor to rights of succession to a hereditary title (s.6(6)(d)).

Practical effect of the Act. Accordingly a marriage validated by the Act may revoke a will[2] or create the status of surviving spouse or lawful child.[3]

Commentary on the Act. There is a detailed commentary on the Act in *Current Law Statutes 1995*; which should be consulted.

---

[2] See para. 14–02.
[3] See para. 27–19.

Budget 1995

Under the November 1995 Budget, on deaths on or after April 5, 1995 the threshold for Inheritance Tax is increased to £200,000 and the business and agricultural relief is increased to 100 per cent in some cases. Details will appear in the consequent Finance Act. Paragraphs 4–03 and 4–05 should be read subject to this.

CONTENTS

TABLE OF CASES

TABLE OF STATUTES

TABLE OF STATUTORY INSTRUMENTS

TABLE OF RULES

TABLE OF RULES OF THE SUPREME COURT

TABLE OF COUNTY COURT RULES

ABBREVIATIONS

A.E.A.	Administration of Estates Acts 1925 and 1971
A.J.A.	Administration of Justice Acts 1977, 1982 and 1985
C.C.A.	County Courts Act 1984
C.C.R.	County Court Rules
C.G.T.A.	Capital Gains Tax Act 1979
F.A.	Finance Acts 1983, 1986 and 1995
F.L.R.A.	Family Law Reform Act 1987
J.T.A.	Judicial Trustees Act 1896
L.C.A.	Land Charges Act 1972
L.P.A.	Law of Property Acts 1925, 1989 and 1994
L.R.A.	Land Registration Act 1925
L.R.R.	Land Registration Rules 1925
L.R.R.	Land Registry Rules 1990
M.C.A.	Matrimonial Causes Acts 1965 and 1973
N.C.P.R.	Non-Contentious Probate Rules 1987
R.S.C.	Rules of the Supreme Court
S.C.A.	Supreme Court Act 1981
S.L.A.	Settled Land Act 1925
T.C.G.A.	Taxation of Chargeable Gains Act 1992
T.M.A.	Taxes Management Act 1970
V.T.A.	Variation of Trusts Act 1958

Part One: Death and Grant of Representation

1. The body and the funeral

1–01 Registration. The first step after a death is to register the death.[1] The persons who have a duty to register the death depend on whether or not the death occurs in a "house."[2] When a person dies in a house the following are qualified to give information concerning the death; and within five days[3] of the death one of them is bound to give the registrar of deaths such information and to sign the register[4]:

(a) any relative of the deceased person present at the death or in attendance during the last illness;

(b) any other relative of the deceased residing or being in the sub-district where the death occurred;

(c) any person present at the death;

---

[1] Under the Births and Deaths Registration Act 1953, Pt II. The exact date of death need not be ascertained: *Re Long-Sutton* [1912] P. 97 (drowned body found, leave to swear death not required). There are statutory provisions for registration of the deaths of members of the armed forces and merchant seamen.

[2] Defined in s.41 as including a public institution. The word "house" is not further defined in this Act. The question what is or is not a "house" for this purpose is unlikely to arise for decision. In practice a flat and a shop are treated as a "house" for registration purposes without regard to the technical questions that arise under other Acts referring to a "house."

[3] Which may be extended to 14 days by giving written notice of the death to the district judge within the five days: s.18.

[4] 1953 Act, s.16.

3

(d) the occupier of the house if he knew of the happening of the death;

(e) any inmate of the house who knew of the happening of the death;

(f) the person causing the disposal of the body.

Where the death is not in a "house," those qualified to give information one of whom is likewise bound to do so are[5]:

(a) any relative of the deceased who has knowledge of any of the particulars required to be registered concerning the death;

(b) any person present at the death;

(c) any person finding or taking charge of the body;

(d) any person causing the disposal of the body.

In the normal case, there is a medical certificate of the cause of death.[6] When necessary, a coroner's certificate is supplied instead.[7] (The law concerning coroners' inquests is outside the scope of this book).

Under the Coroners Act 1988, ss. 5, 6, 7 and 8, the coroner within whose district the body lies (or the deputy coroner) holds an inquest when:

(a) the deceased has died a violent or an unnatural death;

(b) has died a sudden death of which the cause is unknown;

(c) has died in prison or in such a place or in such circumstances as to require an inquest under any other Act.

1–02 Disposal of the body. It is then the duty of the executor[8] (if any) appointed by the deceased's will to dispose of the body, at the cost of the deceased's estate.[9]

There is no legal property in a dead human body; in all ordinary circumstances, where there is no suspicion of crime, the executor has a right to possession of the body for disposal.[10]

If someone, such as a friend or relative or a hospital, in possession of the body withholds it, the executor can obtain an order for

---

[5] s.17
[6] Under s.22.
[7] s.23.
[8] See definition in para. 2.02.
[9] *Rees v. Hughes* [1946] K.B. 517; the obligation is primarily that of the executor.
[10] *Williams v. Williams* (1882) 20 Ch.Div. 659.

delivery of the body[11]: there appears to be no reported example of that being necessary.

Until modern times, the usual method of disposing of a body was by burial; it was only as recently as 1884 that it was first held that burning a body, if not done so as to constitute a public nuisance, is not a crime at common law.[12] In recent years cremation has become usual, except in those communities that believe an individual does not own his or her body and that to burn a body is wrong.[13]

1–03 Medical use of a body. The medical use of the body after the death may be authorised by the person lawfully in possession of the body when authorised by the deceased, either: in writing at any time; or orally during his last illness in the presence of two witnesses when there is no reason to believe that the request was subsequently withdrawn.[14] For this purpose many people carry what are called "donor cards" authorising medical use of their body. When the deceased has authorised medical use of his body, the wishes of a surviving spouse or relative are not taken into account.

When the deceased has not authorised the medical use of his body, the medical use after the death may be authorised by the person lawfully in possession of the body if, after making reasonable inquiry, there is no reason to believe that the deceased had expressed an objection to it (which had not been withdrawn) and no reason to believe that the deceased's surviving spouse, or any surviving relative, objects to the body being so dealt with.[15] Religious scruples may arise about such use, as they do about cremation (see above). Those who object to such use sometimes carry a card recording their objection to the medical use of their body after death.

1–04 The deceased's directions and the family's wishes about disposal of the body. Apart from these statutory restrictions on medical use, the deceased's directions about his body have been held, in actions for damages, not to be legally binding on the living. Thus

---

[11] Under R.S.C., Ord. 29, r. 1. To establish the executorship, the plaintiff has to give evidence of the will: when necessary, a will can be admitted in evidence before probate: *Whitmore v. Lambert* [1955] 1 W.L.R. 495, although the general rule is that a grant of probate is required to establish the status of executor. An undertaking would be required from the executor to apply promptly for a grant of probate. Probate is not normally granted within seven days of a death: r. 6(2).

[12] *R. v. Price* (1884) 12 Q.B.D. 247. Cremation has long been regulated by statute: Cremation Act 1902, Cremation Act 1952.

[13] In practice in those faiths that disapprove of cremation, there is a divergence of view. The Church of England holds that cremation is lawful but unless there is good and lawful reason to the contrary the ashes should be interred: Canon B.38, para. 3. Some denominations of Christianity disapprove of cremation; traditional Judaism and Islam disapprove of it. Information on this is collected in *Encyclopaedia Britannica* (1968 ed.), Vol. 9 "Funerary Rites and Ceremonies."

[14] Human Tissue Act 1961, s.1.

[15] s.1.

personal representatives who infringed the deceased's clear directions about the disposal of the body were held not liable to recoup the costs and expenses of someone who actually performed such wishes.[16] On the other hand a living person may obtain damages for breach (by other use) of a contractual right of exclusive burial.[17] Both these cases concerned a claim for damages, not a claim for an injunction. If there was clear evidence of the deceased's actual wishes about the disposal of his body, an injunction might nowadays be granted at the suit of someone with an interest in the estate to restrain the personal representatives from disposing of the body in a manner contrary to the deceased's wishes.[18]

Care should be taken by personal representatives, especially by professional persons or a trust corporation, to ascertain and to observe the deceased's wishes about the body and the family's wishes. A departure, however well-intentioned, from such wishes is apt to create resentment (especially when such wishes are based on religious beliefs) and to form the basis of suspicion throughout the administration.

1–05 The funeral and its cost. Reasonable funeral expenses are the first charge on the estate[19]; even when the estate is insolvent.[20] They are allowed as a deduction for inheritance tax.[21]

The sum allowable for funeral expenses is the reasonable cost. The reasonable cost of a stone over the grave is part of the funeral expenses, but only the reasonable cost,[22] when the actual cost was greater. The sum allowable depends on the circumstances of each case. In a case in 1960[23] some £195 was claimed and £40 was allowed. In an insolvent estate in Canada where only $1,000 was got in, part of the funeral expenses was disallowed, $71.30 expended on a tombstone was disallowed; and the disallowed sums fell on the personal representative personally.[24]

---

[16] *Williams v. Williams* (1882) 20 Ch.Div. 659; holding that there is no property in a dead body and that the deceased's directions about his body cannot be legally enforced.

[17] *Reed v. Madon* [1989] 2 Ch. 408; where *Williams v. Williams* above was not cited.

[18] Under the Supreme Court Act 1981, s.37, which is widely applied nowadays; and R.S.C., Ord. 85, r. 2(1) and r. 5(1).

[19] *Rees v. Hughes* [1946] K.B. 517, abrogating the former common law rule that a widower is primarily liable for his wife's funeral expenses.

[20] Administration of Insolvent Estates of Deceased Persons Order 1986 (S.I. 1986 No. 1999) made under the Insolvency Act 1986, s.421.

[21] Inheritance Tax Act 1984, s.172.

[22] *Goldstein v. Salvation Army Assurance Society* [1917] 2 K.B. 291, where the defendant had issued a policy of assurance for funeral expenses; *Hart v. Griffith-Jones* [1948] 2 All E.R. 729 (funeral expenses recovered as damages for tort); *Stanton v. Youlden (Ewart F.)* [1960] 1 W.L.R. 543 (a similar case).

[23] *Stanton v. Youlden* above.

[24] *Hutzal v. Hutzal* [1942] 2 W.W.R. 492 (CAN.).

1–06 Recovery by a stranger of the reasonable costs of burial or cremation. When those primarily responsible for disposing of the body are inaccessible or unknown, and so a stranger disposes of the body, the stranger seems to be entitled to recover such expenses from the personal representatives. Before the emancipation of married women,[25] a stranger could in such a case recover suitable funeral expenses from the husband of a deceased married woman, who was then primarily liable[26]; it appears to follow that a stranger can recover such expenses now from the personal representatives, who are primarily liable (see previous paragraph).

1–07 Absence of a body. In the absence of the body and of clear evidence of the death, it is necessary for an applicant for a grant to obtain from the district judge leave to swear to the death (see paragraph 3–07 below).

1–08 Death as the basis of the jurisdiction. The jurisdiction to administer an estate is based on the death of its owner. This jurisdiction is not to be confused with the different and quite distinct powers of the courts when someone is alive: such as the power to administer the property of a living person who is mentally disordered[27]; or to supervise the exercise, after the donor's loss of capacity, of an Enduring Power of Attorney[28]; or to appoint a receiver, for example for a living person who is inaccessible and unable to deal with his own property,[29] such as someone who has been taken hostage.[30]

FINDING OR OBTAINING THE WILL AFTER THE DEATH

1–09 Finding the will after a death. The safest place to deposit a will is at the Probate Registry.[31] This facility has been available since 1857[32] and it deserves to be used more frequently.

---

[25] Under the Married Women's Property Act 1882, replaced by the Law Reform (Married Women and Tortfeasors) Act 1935.

[26] *Jenkins v. Tucker* (1788) 1 H.Bl. 90; *Tugwell v. Heyman* (1812) 3 Camp. 298; *Ambrose v. Kerrison* (1851) 10 C.B. 776; *Bradshaw v. Beard* (1862) 12 C.B. (N.S.) 344; all cited and approved in *Rees v. Hughes* above at pp. 524 and 528.

[27] Under the Mental Health Act 1983, exercised by the Court of Protection.

[28] Under the Enduring Powers of Attorney Act 1985.

[29] Under S.C.A. 1981, s.37(1).

[30] Which can be done in chambers without publicity: R.S.C., Ord. 30, r. 1(1).

[31] Under the Administration of Justice Act 1982, s.23. The deposit is in a sealed envelope, indorsed with the relevant information and it may be withdrawn during the testator's lifetime. After the death, the district judge opens the envelope on production of a death certificate: Wills (Deposit for Safe Custody) Regulations 1978.

[32] Under the Court of Probate Act 1857, s.91 and its successors.

Another safe place for the deposit of a will is at a bank or at a solicitor's office. There will then be a record of any withdrawal of the will and it is unlikely to be tampered with.

It is dangerous, but not unknown, to keep a will at home (perhaps in a cupboard or under a bed), or at a place of business. There is a risk of its accidental loss or destruction[33]; or of its deliberate destruction, either during the testator's last illness or after the death by someone disappointed by its provisions. Dishonestly destroying, defacing or concealing a will is a criminal offence under the Theft Act 1968, s.20.[34] This fraud is frequently suspected, and is occasionally proved by admissible evidence (when a copy is admitted to probate: see paragraph 15–01).

Inquiry as to any will should be made at the Principal Registry, and at the deceased's known banks and solicitors. A thorough search should be made of every place where a will is likely to be found.

1–10 Finding a copy will. When such inquiries produce, as often happens, a *copy* of a will at a solicitor's office or elsewhere, it is necessary to consider whether the original is to be taken to have been revoked; if not, the copy may be entitled to probate: see paragraph 15–01 below.

1–11 Enforcing disclosure and production by examination. It is usual to disclose any knowledge someone has of a will of a deceased person. If disclosure is not forthcoming, an order may be made[35] for any person of whom there are reasonable grounds to believe has knowledge of a testamentary document to attend to be examined in court about such knowledge and to bring in any document[36]; but not about collateral matters.[37] This is an effective remedy; a proposal to adopt it tends to yield information.

1–12 Enforcing disclosure and production. A *subpoena* may be issued,[38] requiring the person named to bring a testamentary document into the registry.[39] This is useful when possession of the document is admitted.

---

[33] As happened to the will of Lord St. Leonards, a former Lord Chancellor who died on January 13, 1870, aged 93 years; it had been kept at his home in a locked box, to which there were four keys. At first instance Hannen P. spoke of the "false security" of the deceased's and the family's belief "that this will was secure from the hands and eyes of either the curious or the dishonest": *Sugden v. St. Leonards* (1876) 1 P.D. 154 at p. 204.

[34] See *Archbold* (1994 ed.) vol. 2, para. 21–199.

[35] By a district judge on summons under N.C.P.R. 1987, r. 50; or if a probate action is proceeding by the Master under Ord. 76, r. 13.

[36] S.C.A. 1981, s.122.

[37] *Evans v. Jones* (1867) 16 L.T. 299; decided on the similar words of the Court of Probate Act 1862 s.24.

[38] As before, footnote 36.

[39] S.C.A. 1981, s.123.

A *subpoena* is not a satisfactory first step when possession of the document is not admitted. Such a *subpoena* is issued without a previous determination that the person against whom it is issued possesses the document; and so, although he may file an affidavit saying it is not in his control,[40] it cannot be a contempt if he takes no notice of the *subpoena*.[41] On an application (if made) to commit him for contempt of the *subpoena*, before there is a determination that he has the document, all that the court can do is to make an order for him to attend to be examined.[42]

---

[40] N.C.P.R. 1987, r. 50(2).
[41] *Re Emmerson* (1887) 57 L.J.P. 1, C.A.; In *Re Austin*, March 16, 1988, unreported, Waite J. applied *Re Emmerson* and dismissed with costs a motion to commit for contempt in disregarding such a *subpoena*.
[42] *Re Emmerson*, p. 3.

2. Need for a United Kingdom grant of representation and its effect: definition of legal terms

GRANTS MADE IN ENGLAND AND WALES

2–01 Need for a grant in the United Kingdom.[1] The law of England and Wales requires a "grant of representation" to be made by the court to the executor/s or to administrators of a deceased person, who are thereby authorised to administer the estate. This is different from the position in continental countries.

---

[1] For the recognition in England and Wales of grants made in Scotland and Northern Ireland, see para. 2–11 below.

The only evidence of the devolution of the deceased's property ordinarily accepted in legal proceedings (except for interlocutory relief: see paragraph 2–12 below) is a grant of representation made in the United Kingdom. The need for such a grant cannot be avoided by seeking to appoint a new trustee in place of the person in whom the estate is vested pending a grant.[2]

2–02 Definitions. *Personal representatives.* The personal representatives of a deceased person are the persons or person or company entrusted with the administration of the estate of that deceased person. There are two classes of personal representatives, an executor/executrix, or an administrator/administratix.

Executor. An executor is someone appointed by the deceased's will (or codicil) to administer the deceased's estate, almost always the entire estate. A *special executor* is one appointed for only part of the deceased's property (such as the deceased's literary property; or settled land[3] settled in his lifetime).

Executor according to the tenor. An executor according to the tenor is someone appointed by will or codicil to act as executor by implication, not expressly. It is a question of construction of each will, whether someone is or is not an executor according to the tenor, decided nowadays by the district judge and not reported. In the days when such a question was brought before a judge, the reported cases show a tendency to treat expressions in a will referring to the estate's administration by a named person, as the appointment of that person executor according to the tenor.[4] Once probate is granted to an executor according to the tenor, he is in the same position as an executor nominated in the will.

Executor by representation. The grant of probate to an executor renders him the *executor by representation* of any earlier testator of whom the deceased was himself the sole executor or the sole surviving executor. This is so by the aptly named "chain of representation", which is broken only by an intestacy, a failure of a testator to appoint an executor, or a failure to obtain probate of a will.[5] This burden of continuing the administration of an estate, about

---

[2] *Re Deans* [1954] 1 W.L.R. 332, refusing such an order. It follows that such an appointment may not be made by deed.
[3] The Settled Land Act Trustees are deemed to be so appointed as regards settled land under the S.L.A. 1925 remaining settled at the death: Administration of Estates Act 1925, s.22.
[4] *Re Lush* (1887) 13 P.D. 20; *Re Leven and Melville (Earl)* (1889) 15 P.D. 22; *Re Russell, Re Laird* [1892] P. 380; *Re Way* [1901] P. 345; *Re Cook* [1902] P. 114; *Re Kirby* [1902] P. 188.
[5] A.E.A. 1925, s.7.

which little might be known, is often a good reason for an executor to renounce probate.

Administrator. Any personal representative who is not an executor is an administrator.

Executor de son tort. Anyone (other than an executor who afterwards obtains probate) who administers assets in England of a deceased person without holding a grant of representation made in the United Kingdom is acting wrongfully. A person who acts in this way is held liable to the deceased's creditors, true personal representatives, or beneficiaries, as *executor de son tort* or "executor in his own wrong."[6] It should be noted that a grant or its equivalent outside the U.K. does not operate in the U.K.[7]

Legatees, devisees, beneficiaries. Those to whom property is given by will or codicil or on intestacy are beneficiaries. Strictly a gift of personalty (anything except a freehold) is a *bequest* to a *legatee*, and a gift of a freehold is a *devise* to a *devisee*; but the two forms of wording are interchangeable.[8]

Heir. The word *heir* correctly applies nowadays to a successor at death to land entailed under the S.L.A. 1925; the incorrect use of the word "heir" is a recipe for litigation, the result of which is difficult to foresee.[9]

2–03 Form and description of grant of representation. A grant of representation to an executor is a grant of probate.

Anyone else to whom representation is granted is an *administrator*, not an executor. If the deceased left a valid will, there is a grant of letters of administration with the will annexed.[10] Otherwise there is a grant of letters of administration.

There are practical differences, mentioned below, between an executor and an administrator, because of the difference in the vesting of the deceased's property, and of the relation back of a grant. These differences have their roots in history[11] and can create confusion or difficulty nowadays. They have not been abolished by assimilating the position of the two sorts of personal representatives by Act of Parliament.

---

[6] A.E.A. 1925, s.28; *Re Lovett* (1876) 3 Ch.Div. 198; *New York Breweries v. Att.-Gen.* [1899] A.C. 62; *I.R.C. v. Stype* [1982] Ch. 356. See Chap. 40 below.
[7] *Finnegan v. Cementation Co.* [1953] 1 Q.B. 688; *Whyte v. Rose* (1842) 3 Q.B. 493.
[8] *Re Gibbs* [1907] 1 Ch. 465; *Re Bailey* [1945] Ch. 191.
[9] See Jarman, *Wills* at pp. 1543–1571; and the subsequent case *Re Bourke's Will Trusts* [1980] 1 W.L.R. 539.
[10] N.C.P.R. 1987, r. 20.
[11] Traced in *Hewson v. Shelley* [1914] 2 Ch. 13.

2–04 Vesting of property on death; service of notices and registration after a death.

Executor. At death, the deceased's property in the United Kingdom, (other than property devolving by survivorship under a joint tenancy[12]), vests in someone else. When probate is granted to an executor, the property is held to have vested in the executor as from the death.[13] Accordingly, notice served on the executor after the death and before the grant of probate is effective.[14]

No executor. The Law of Property (Miscellaneous Provisions) Act 1994, s.14[15] has solved the difficulties[16] that arose under the Administration of Estates Act 1925, s.9 about the vesting of property on death when there is no executor. Section 14 replaces section 9 of the A.E.A. 1925; vesting in the Public Trustee the estate of a deceased person, where there is an intestacy or no executor. The Public Trustee is one of the proper recipients[17] of notices required to be served on the deceased's personal representatives, when the death is known and there is no subsisting grant of representation.[18] Examples of such notices are a notice to quit a tenancy[19] or a notice to be served under an option or under a partnership agreement.

After the death intestate (as far as is known) of the owner of dangerous animals or of dangerous or defective structures, those damaged can obtain relief in the courts, by procuring the estate to be represented for litigation purposes.[20] There is also occasionally the right to self help at common law.[21]

2–05 Notices after a death.

Death unknown. Under the Law of Property Act 1994, s.17 a notice is effective if it is served by someone who has no reason to believe that the person purported to be served is dead.

Death known. Under L.P.A. 1994, s.18 when the death is known and before a grant of representation has been filed, a notice may validly be served by serving it on "the personal representatives" of

---

[12] See para. 22–07.
[13] *Chetty v. Chetty* [1916] 1 A.C. 603; *Whitmore v. Lambert* [1955] 1 W.L.R. 495; *Re Masonic and General Life Assurance Co.* (1885) 32 Ch.Div. 373.
[14] *Kelsey v. Kelsey* (1922) 91 L.J.Ch. 382.
[15] Which came into force on July 1, 1995: S.I. 1995 No. 1317.
[16] See para. 2–04 of the previous edition of this book.
[17] See para. 2–05 below.
[18] See para. 2–01 above for the way to ascertain this.
[19] *Smith v. Mather* [1948] 2 K.B. 212; *Mackley v. Nutting* [1949] 2 K.B. 55; *Fred Long & Sons v. Burgess* [1950] K.B. 115.
[20] See para. 2–11 below, under *Ad litem grant.*
[21] See *Clerk and Lindsell on Torts* (17th ed.), paras. 29–22 to 29–25.

the named deceased at the deceased's last known place of residence or business in the U.K. and a copy similarly addressed is served on the Public Trustee[22] who must keep a register of such notices, which may be searched.[23]

2–06 Fees to the Public Trustee. Under L.P.A. 1994, s.19(5), the Public Trustee is entitled to charge fees by reference to the Public Trustee Act 1906, s.9 for exercising his functions in respect of documents sent to him.

2–07 Land charges. Similarly a land charge may be registered now after the death of the person against whom it is to be registered: the L.P.A. 1925, s.15.

2–08 Relation back of *probate*. Probate relates back to the death so proceedings by an executor brought before the date of the grant of probate are valid. If proceedings are heard before there is a grant of probate, they will be stayed or adjourned pending a grant,[24] or may be dismissed without prejudice to subsequent proceedings.[25] A mere application for probate is not enough to support legal proceedings.[26] The court insists of its own motion, notwithstanding the other party's admission, on a grant and will usually allow an adjournment for the purpose of obtaining a grant.[27] This requirement is not, therefore, only a question of evidence which can be met by a party's admission.

2–09 Operation back of *letters of administration*. A grant of letters of administration (whether with a will annexed or on intestacy) has a different effect: it operates from its own date, but with relation back for the benefit of the estate to the date of the death.[28] This relation back does not however justify a writ issued before the date of the grant of letters of administration; and so the strange result of this outmoded distinction is that, at common law, a writ issued by an administrator before the date of the grant is invalid.[29] There is now an escape from this trap; it is within the court's power to allow pending proceedings to be amended to be brought in a capacity subsequently acquired.[30] Thus the personal representative was substituted as plaintiff where a writ was served after the death of the

---

[22] *Practice Direction* [1995] 1 W.L.R. 1120.
[23] S.I. 1995 No. 1330.
[24] *Pinney v. Hunt* (1877) 6 Ch.Div. 98; *Tarn v. Commercial Bank of Sydney* (1884) 12 Q.B.D. 294; as under the previous law: *Webb v. Adkins* (1854) 14 C.B. 401.
[25] *Re Crowhurst Park* [1974] 1 W.L.R. 583.
[26] *Hadijar v. Pitchey* [1894] A.C. 437.
[27] *Re Crowhurst Park* above at p. 591; and *Lall v. Lall* [1965] 1 W.L.R. 1249.
[28] *Re Pryse* [1904] P. 301 at p. 305; *Fred Long & Sons v. Burgess* [1950] K.B. 115; *Mills v. Anderson* [1984] Q.B. 704.
[29] *Ingall v. Moran* [1944] K.B. 160; *Hilton v. Sutton Steam Laundry* [1946] K.B. 65.
[30] R.S.C., Ord. 20, r. 5(4), applicable in a county court: C.C.R., Ord. 15, r. 1.

person named as plaintiff and before letters of administration to his estate had been granted.[31] The principle of relation back has been held to apply only to a person *claiming* in right of an estate; but to be no answer by a defendant who had made a wrongful claim on behalf of an estate without exercising the right to obtain letters of administration.[32]

Another practical (and equally unfair) effect is that someone who, as administrator (not executor), makes an unwise agreement on behalf of the estate before obtaining a grant of letters of administration is able afterwards to assert that the agreement does not bind the estate.[33]

2–10 Nature of the interests of the personal representatives and of the beneficiaries in the estate of the deceased. Until the estate has been fully administered, the assets are held by the personal representatives and a beneficiary does not have an interest in any specified assets of the estate, but only a right to have the estate duly administered.[34] This principle, arising from the common law, is different from the position in equity under a trust.

An application of the principle that a beneficiary does not, during the administration, have an interest in any specified assets of the estate is that personal representatives, when agreeing valuations with the Revenue, should consider the interest of the estate as a whole and are not under the duty (imposed on *trustees*) to hold an even balance between the beneficiaries.[35] This principle is not however imposed when it is inappropriate. Two relaxations of the principle have occurred. A bequest of shares in a company operates as a bequest of the outstanding right to receive those shares on distribution in the administration of the estate of a previous testator,[36] or intestate. Relief may be given under the Forfeiture Act 1982[37] in respect of rights in an estate not yet fully administered.[38] Other relaxations of the principle may occur in the future.

2–11 Special forms of grant. *Ad colligenda bona.* The estate may be in need of immediate protection (especially houses liable to trespass). A grant may be made on the order of a district judge,

---

[31] *Fielding v. Rigby* [1993] 1 W.L.R. 1355.
[32] *Loudon v. Ryder (No. 2)* [1953] Ch. 423; *Hadjiar v. Pitchey* above was not cited.
[33] *Mills v. Anderson* [1984] Q.B. 704; for relation back applies only for the *benefit* of the estate.
[34] *Sudeley v. Att.-Gen.* [1897] A.C. 11; *Dr Barnardo's Homes v. Income Tax Special Commissioners* [1921] 2 A.C. 1; *Commissioner of Stamp Duties (Queensland) v. Livingston* [1965] A.C. 694; *Cunliffe-Owen v. I.R.C.* [1953] Ch. 545; *Marshall v. Kerr* [1995] 1 A.C. 148.
[35] *Re Hayes* [1971] 1 W.L.R. 758.
[36] *Re Leigh's Will Trusts* [1970] Ch. 277.
[37] See para. 18–08.
[38] *Re K.* [1986] Ch. 180.

supported by affidavit evidence,[39] appointing a suitable person to look after the estate and specifying the powers conferred. Notwithstanding the misleading Latin name, suggesting that it only applies to goods, a grant *ad colligenda bona* applies to goods, land and any other property (unless expressed to be limited).

De bonis non grant. When the last surviving personal representative of a deceased person has died and the estate is not fully administered, there may be a chain of representation (paragraph 2–02 above) constituting the executor of the deceased executor, and the executor of the original testator. If not, a new grant is necessary to enable the estate of the first deceased person to be duly administered; it is known as a grant *de bonis non*, that is to say, as to the property not yet administered including land.

Attorney administrator. When the person entitled to a grant wishes to appoint an attorney to take the grant (as is frequent if the person entitled to a grant resides abroad), a grant is made to the attorney.[40] Once appointed, the attorney-administrator acts under the grant, as long as the grant to him remains unrevoked, as the personal representative in his own right not merely as agent for the person who appointed him.[41]

Minors, or mental illness. Provision is made in the rules[42] for grants on behalf of minors to the parent or guardian, and for no renunciation to be made of that right during the minority. The rules[43] also make provision for the case where the person entitled suffers from mental illness.

Grants of administration in case of minority or of a life interest. When a beneficiary is a minor or there is a life interest, a grant of letters of administration (as distinct from *probate* of a will to executors) is only made to a trust corporation or to two individuals, as administrator/s, unless the circumstances make the appointment of only one administrator expedient.[44] The kind of circumstances that might satisfy a district judge that the appointment of only one administrator is expedient are, for example, that the proposed administrator is a solicitor or a chartered accountant; that the proposed administrator is the surviving spouse and the estate almost

---

[39] Under N.C.P.R. 1987, r. 52, and S.C.A. 1981, s.116.
[40] N.C.P.R. 1987, r. 31.
[41] See *Re Lorillard* [1922] 2 Ch. 638, *Re Manifold* [1962] Ch. 1 and *Re Weiss* [1962] P. 13.
[42] N.C.P.R. 1987, rr. 32, 33, and 34.
[43] See N.C.P.R. 1987, r. 35.
[44] S.C.A. 1981, s.114.

entirely devolves on him or her; or sometimes that the children will very soon attain majority.[45]

Settled land. There are provisions for special grants where there is land that is "settled land" within the S.L.A. 1925.[46] Settled land is however often allowed to devolve on the general personal representatives, who can then deal with it in the correct manner under a general grant.[47]

Ad litem grant. A grant of letters of administration may be made by a district judge, limited to bringing legal proceedings on behalf of the estate ("*ad litem*"). The need for such a grant limited to defending legal proceedings has been much reduced by the power of the court to appoint a representative of the estate as defendant.[48]

Grant in common form; grant in solemn form. See paragraphs 6–01 and 6–05 for an explanation of these technical terms.

2–12 Interlocutory relief to overcome the absence of a grant. *Receiver.* The absence of a grant of representation has never prevented a person interested in the estate from obtaining interlocutory relief by the appointment of a receiver before a grant.[49] A receiver may be appointed on summons before the Master, after obtaining an appointment; or, more speedily, on motion before the judge.[50] Remuneration may be awarded to a receiver so appointed.[51] An independent professional person is often appointed and he may act on the order.

Grant pendente lite, during the pendency of an action. When a probate action is pending in the Chancery Division, there is an alternative form of relief: that is, to obtain an order for the appointment of an administrator pending the determination of the action, "*pendente lite*."[52] The rule requires the appointment to be sought on summons: but in a case of urgency, the speedier procedure

---

[45] A risky decision for the district judge to take: a child who has recently attained majority is particularly subject to improper pressure to sign away legal rights: see *Re Pauling's Settlement Trusts* [1964] Ch. 303 where this happened and the children afterwards, unusually, brought litigation to set aside the transactions.

[46] N.C.P.R. 1987, r. 29; the settled land in a continuing settlement should devolve on the S.L.A. trustees as special personal representatives: A.E.A. 1925, s.22.

[47] *Re Bridgett & Hayes's Contract* [1928] Ch. 163 at p. 168; treating the grant of representation as an order of the court within L.P.A. 1925, s.204.

[48] S.C.A. 1981, s.87(2); R.S.C., Ord. 15, r. 6A and r. 15.

[49] See *Ingall v. Moran* above, where the authorities are collected at pp. 169 and 171–172.

[50] S.C.A. 1981, s.37; Ord. 30, r. 1.

[51] Ord. 30, r. 3.

[52] S.C.A. 1981, s.117; Ord. 76, r. 14.

by motion can be adopted in lieu of a summons.[53] The person appointed cannot act on such an order but still needs to obtain a grant under it. This additional step, and the time it can occupy, makes the appointment of a receiver a better remedy. Under the terms of a grant *pendente lite*, the powers of the administrator end at judgment in the probate action; leaving a gap until a grant is obtained following the judgment.

A temporary grant can be made under the same authority pending an appeal.

2–13 Grant in England and Wales to person entitled abroad. A grant of letters of administration may be made here to the person so entitled by the law of the deceased's domicile[54] or to his duly appointed attorney.[55]

GRANTS MADE OUT OF ENGLAND AND WALES

2–14 Grants made in other parts of the United Kingdom and in a colony. A grant made in Scotland or in Northern Ireland is effective in England, without being resealed.[56] A grant made in a colony needs to be resealed in England, when it becomes operative here.[57] The procedure to obtain re-sealing of a colonial grant is similar to the procedure for obtaining a grant when the deceased had a foreign domicile: see paragraph 3–15 below.

2–15 Grant outside the United Kingdom. Any other grant outside the United Kingdom[58] (including one in the Channel Islands or the Isle of Man) is by itself ineffective as regards property in the United Kingdom.[59] If there is no grant here, anyone acting on the basis of an overseas grant is acting wrongfully (as executor *de son tort*).

2–16 Exception. Recognising an overseas grant. There is one apparent exception to the non-effect here of a foreign grant: it is that in a proper case the court may authorise personal representatives duly appointed here to pay over to a foreign administrator[60]; or may refuse to authorise it.[61] In some circumstances personal

---

[53] *Re Manmac Farmers* [1968] 1 W.L.R. 572, following a dictum in *Heywood v. B.D.C. Properties* [1964] 1 W.L.R. 971.
[54] N.C.P.R. 1987, r. 30.
[55] N.C.P.R. 1987, r. 31.
[56] A.E.A. 1971, s.1 and s.4.
[57] Colonial Probates Act 1892.
[58] See para. 2–01 above.
[59] *Finnegan v. Cementation Co.* [1953] 1 Q.B. 688; *Whyte v. Rose* (1842) 3 Q.B. 493.
[60] *Re Achillopoulos* [1928] Ch. 433.
[61] *Re Manifold* [1962] Ch. 1.

representatives here may make such payment without an order of the English court,[62] but it is safer to obtain the court's authority.

---

[62] *Re Weiss* [1962] P. 136.

3. Obtaining a grant

3–01 Issue of a grant. A grant of representation is issued by a probate registry, being either the Principal Registry in London, or a district registry.[1] A district judge (formerly known as a district registrar[2]) may refer an application to the Principal Registry,[3] so that an application likely to occasion difficulty is best made in London. The application may be made by a solicitor[4] or by an applicant in person.[5] The application must be accompanied by any will or codicil of which probate is sought, and by an oath in a standard printed form, available for various circumstances (to be sworn or affirmed), setting out the relevant facts and undertaking duly to administer the estate.[6] The application must also be accompanied by the relevant

---

[1] S.C.A. 1981, ss.105 and 106.
[2] Courts and Legal Services Act 1990, s. 74. A *district* judge, formerly a registrar, should not be confused with a circuit judge sitting as the judge of a County Court; but probably will be.
[3] N.C.P.R., r. 7.
[4] N.C.P.R., r. 4.
[5] N.C.P.R., r. 5; as to r. 5(3)(a) see n. 40 and 41 below.
[6] N.C.P.R., r. 8.

papers dealing with inheritance tax (see para. 4–02 below); and by the fee payable for the grant. The fee is assessed on the net value of the deceased's estate,[7] with a further fee when the application is made in person.[8]

3–02 Persons who may apply. An application for Probate may, subject to conditions stated there, also be made[9] by:

(a) a barrister;
(b) a notary public;
(c) the Public Trustee;
(d) the Official Solicitor;
(e) an authorised bank;
(f) an authorised building society;
(g) an authorised insurance company;
(h) a subsidiary company of such a bank, building society or insurance company.

Those applications seem not to rank as personal applications under rule 5.

3–03 Time for issue of grant. A grant is not issued while there is more than one application pending.[10] A grant of probate is not issued within seven days after a death, and letters of administration are not issued within 14 days after a death, except by leave of a district judge.[11] In appropriate cases, expedition may be allowed for a grant on an application by letter, explaining the need for it.

3–04 Priority for a grant of representation where there is a will. An executor appointed under a will or a codicil has priority to take a grant of probate,[12] unless he renounces probate.[13] Where there is no surviving executor, or the executors renounce probate, the

---

[7] Non-Contentious Probate Fees Order 1981 (S.I. 1981 No. 861) Sched. I, para. 1 imposes them on the value of the estate as follows:

value up to	£10,000	nil
	£25,000	£40
	£40,000	£80
	£70,000	£150
	£100,000	£2.50 per £1,000 or part thereof
exceeding	£100,000	£250

and for every additional £100,000 or part thereof a further £50.
[8] Para. 2 thereof: if the assessed value of the estate does not exceed £500 a fee of £1; does not exceed £1,000 a fee of £2; does not exceed £5,000 a fee of £5; if exceeding £5,000 a fee of £1 for each £1,000 or part thereof.
[9] Courts and Legal Services Act 1990, s. 74.
[10] See S.C.A. 1981, s.107.
[11] N.C.P.R., r. 6(2).
[12] N.C.P.R., r. 20.
[13] Under N.C.P.R., r. 37(1).

rules state the order of priority.[14] When the person entitled is a minor, the minor's parents or guardians may obtain a grant until he or she is 18 years old[15]; or the other executors may obtain a grant with power for the minor to apply when of full age.[16] Someone not described in the will by the word "executor" but appointed to perform all or some of the functions of an executor, is called the "executor according to the tenor" and may take a grant of probate on satisfying the district judge that, as a matter of construction, he *is* the executor according to the tenor.

3–05 Priority on intestacy. On intestacy the order of priority for a grant[17] is as follows:

(a) the surviving husband or wife;

(b) the children of the deceased and the issue of any deceased child who died before the deceased;

(c) the father and mother of the deceased;

(d) brothers and sisters of the whole blood and the issue of any deceased brother or sister of the whole blood who died before the deceased;

(e) brothers and sisters of the half blood and the issue of any deceased brother or sister of the half blood who died before the deceased;

---

[14] N.C.P.R., r. 20, reading as follows:

  (a) the executor (but subject to rule 36(4) (d) below;

  (b) any residuary legatee or devisee holding in trust for any other person;

  (c) any other residuary legatee or devisee (including one for life) or where the residue is not wholly disposed of by the will, any person entitled to share in the undisposed of residue (including the Treasury Solicitor when claiming bona vacantia on behalf of the Crown), provided that—

    (i) unless a district judge otherwise directs, a residuary legatee or devisee whose legacy or devise is vested in interest shall be preferred to one entitled on the happening of a contingency, and

    (ii) where the residue is not in terms wholly disposed of, the district judge may, if he is satisfied that the testator has nevertheless disposed of the whole or substantially the whole of the known estate, allow a grant to be made to any legatee or devisee entitled to, or to share in, the estate so disposed of, without regard to the persons entitled to share in any residue not disposed of by the will;

  (d) the personal representative of any residuary legatee or devisee (but not one for life, or one holding in trust for any other person), or of any person entitled to share in any residue not disposed of by the will;

  (e) any other legatee or devisee (including one for life or one holding in trust for any other person) or any creditor of the deceased, provided that, unless a district judge otherwise directs, a legatee or devisee whose legacy or devise is vested in interest shall be preferred to one entitled on the happening of a contingency;

  (f) the personal representative of any other legatee or devisee (but not one for life or one holding in trust for any other person) or of any creditor of the deceased.

[15] N.C.P.R., r. 32.

[16] N.C.P.R., r. 33.

[17] Under N.C.P.R., r. 22.

(f) grandparents;
(g) uncles and aunts of the whole blood and the issue of any
     deceased uncle or aunt of the whole blood who died before
     the deceased;
(h) uncles and aunts of the half blood and the issue of any
     deceased uncle or aunt of the half blood who died before
     the deceased.

After them comes, when applicable, the Treasury Solicitor in right
of *bona vacantia*. A grant may also be made to a creditor; or to a
person with a beneficial interest only on an accretion to the estate; or
to the personal representatives of someone entitled to a grant. The
personal representatives of a deceased person specified in paragraphs
(b) to (h) are preferred to the personal representatives of a spouse
who had died without taking a grant.

3–06 Passing over. These are not rigid rules. Those with priority
may be passed over in "any special circumstances."[18] That is
frequently done. It is a matter of the court's discretion depending
nowadays on the facts of each case.[19] The court passed over an
executrix serving a sentence of life imprisonment[20]; and passed over
the personal representative of an executed murderer.[21] A person who
has "unlawfully aided abetted counselled or procured the death"[22]
would also be passed over.

3–07 Deposing to the death. In the ordinary way, there is no
difficulty in deposing to the death. The exact date of the death need
not be ascertained when the fact of the death is certain.[23] When there
has been a disappearance (either unexplained or presumably in a
known disaster, such as a maritime collision or the destruction of an
aircraft), the district judge gives[24] leave to swear the death, on
affidavit evidence. This is permission for the deponent to depose to
the death[25]; it does not prove anything and is not to be confused with
a declaration (in an action) presuming someone dead.

---

[18] S.C.A. 1981, s.116. As in *I.R.C. v. Stype* [1982] Ch. at pp. 456–457.
[19] The discretion was refused to be exercised on the application of persons with no
interest in the estate in *Re Edwards-Taylor* [1951] P. 24, where the adult entitled was
immature for her age.
[20] *Re S.* [1968] P. 302 where the executrix had been convicted of the testator's murder,
explaining *Re Crippen* [1911] P. 108.
[21] *Re Crippen* [1911] P. 108.
[22] Forfeiture Act 1982, s.1(2).
[23] *Re Long-Sutton* [1912] P. 97, where a dead body was found and it was held
unnecessary to obtain leave to swear the death.
[24] Under N.C.P.R., r. 53.
[25] *Re Jackson* (1902) 87 L.T. 747.

3–08 Uncertainty about the order of deaths. When it is "uncertain" which of two or more deceased persons died first, there is a statutory presumption that they died in order of age; that is to say that the younger survived the elder.[26] This presumption is applied in the absence of evidence of survivorship; deaths are not treated as simultaneous.[27] The presumption affects the entitlement to a grant of representation and the devolution of the estate: see paragraph 28–03, discussing section 184. There is one statutory exception: uncertainty as to which of two spouses died first does not now affect beneficial rights as between the estates of deceased spouses on *intestacy*.[28]

3–09 Wills in the Welsh language. The Welsh language has, within Wales, status as an official language.[29] A will made in Welsh is granted probate with an official translation into English. This may be obtained through any registry, but it is best sought through the Probate Registry of Wales, where there are Welsh-speaking members of staff; any other registry will refer the application there for translation of the will.

3–10 Wills in other languages. A will made in any language other than English or Welsh should be submitted for probate with a translation certified by a notary public. A number of residents here nowadays make wills in the language they speak, sometimes occasioning difficulties.[30]

3–11 Further information. The district judge issues the grant, if satisfied. The district judge usually is satisfied. He may require further information or inquiries[31]; in particular as to a will's execution,[32] its condition[33] and any apparent attempt to revoke it.[34]

3–12 Appearance before the district judge. In order to be satisfied with the application, the district judge may require the applicant, or the applicant's solicitor, to appear before him. This may be done *ex*

---

[26] L.P.A. 1925, s.184.
[27] *Hickman v. Peacey* [1945] A.C. 304.
[28] A.E.A. 1925, s.46(3), as amended.
[29] Welsh Language Act 1993; the history back to 1362 is stated in *Re Trepca Mines* [1960] 1 W.L.R. 24 at pp. 26–27 (decision later reversed on a different point of law).
[30] In one case a will was made in a continental language which had the same expression for a joint interest and an interest in common—unlike English: see para. 20–31 below.
[31] N.C.P.R., r. 6(1).
[32] N.C.P.R., rr. 12 and 16; and as to a blind illiterate testator or a will signed by another for the testator or other indications of doubts: N.C.P.R., r. 13.
[33] N.C.P.R., r. 14.
[34] N.C.P.R., r. 15.

parte, that is, without any other party being given notice of the application. Some frequent occasions for this are listed below.[35] If there is a likelihood of a serious question arising, the district judge directs a summons to be issued, to enable those with a contrary interest to be served[36] and heard. The matter is then decided on affidavit evidence by a district judge or by a judge.[37]

3–13 Matters to be considered by the district judge, or if necessary at a hearing before a district judge. Some circumstances which are frequently found and which call for affidavit evidence and consideration before the issue of a grant of representation, are mentioned in the Non-Contentious Probate Rules 1987, as follows:

(1) Where the due execution of the will or codicil appears to be in doubt[38];

(2) Where the will was not duly executed and the registrar is asked to mark it as refused probate accordingly[39];

(3) Where the testator appears to have been blind or illiterate[40];

(4) Where there are alterations on the will or an apparent attempt to revoke it[41];

(5) Where a question arises about foreign law,[42] or the deceased had a foreign domicile[43];

(6) Where there is an application to prove a copy will or a reconstruction of a will[44] or to rectify a will,[45] and a probate action has not been brought.[46]

The matter is brought before a district judge when it is sought to pass over the person primarily entitled to a grant,[47] and when it is necessary to obtain leave to swear to the death.[48]

3–14 Position of an applicant in person before the district judge. There is a strange rule going back to 1862 (not enforced in practice) that a personal applicant "may not be attended by any person acting

---

[35] para. 3–12.
[36] N.C.P.R., r. 66.
[37] N.C.P.R., r. 61.
[38] N.C.P.R., r. 12.
[39] N.C.P.R., r. 12(1).
[40] N.C.P.R., r. 13.
[41] N.C.P.R. rr. 14, 15 and 16.
[42] N.C.P.R., r. 19.
[43] N.C.P.R., r. 30; see para. 3–15 below.
[44] N.C.P.R., r. 54.
[45] Under the A.J.A. 1982, s.20(1).
[46] N.C.P.R., r. 55.
[47] See para. 3–06 above.
[48] N.C.P.R., r. 53; see para. 3–07 above.

or appearing to act as his adviser."[49] This is in conflict with the common law, that allows such assistance to a litigant in person,[50] and with the discretionary powers exercised by the court when hearing a litigant in person.[51] If challenged, this rule is likely to be held to be beyond the powers (*ultra vires*) of the rule-making body. There is also a rule[52] prohibiting a *personal* application from proceeding if it is necessary to bring the matter before the court by action or summons. The rule is of equally doubtful validity. It has recently been held by the Court of Appeal, reversing the decision of the Divisional Court, that as part of the requirement of fairness a party is entitled to reasonable facilities in *open* court in the exercise of his or her right of audience, including the assistance of a "friend" to give advice and to take notes, unless the court otherwise ordered in the interests of justice or to maintain order.[53] The Court of Appeal approved (at pages 288, 291 and 292) a previous decision[54]; where the Court of Appeal had upheld the refusal of a judge in chambers as a matter of discretion to allow a solicitor not on the record to assist an unrepresented father in this way in a confidential infancy matter. The *ratio decidendi*[55] of each of these cases appear to support the view that the sweeping provisions of N.C.P.R. 1987, r. 5(2) or r. 5(3)(a) are invalid: those rules are not expressed only to exclude an applicant's adviser when such exclusion is for the purposes of justice, or to maintain order or to maintain necessary confidentiality.

3–15 Grant in England and Wales when the deceased died with a domicile outside the United Kingdom. A grant of representation in the U.K. is necessary for property of the deceased situated here to be dealt with after the death[56]; except where there is a grant in Scotland or Northern Ireland.[57] Under rules 30(3)(a) when the deceased died domiciled outside England and Wales, a grant of probate may be issued here to an executor, or to an executor according to the tenor.[58] Under rule 30(3)(b) where the whole or substantially the whole of the deceased's estate in England and Wales consists of immovable property, a grant may be issued in accordance with the

---

[49] N.C.P.R., r. 5(2); previously 1954 Rules, r. 4(2); originally the 1862 Rules, r. 3 (printed in Mortimer, *Probate* (2nd ed.), at p. 863).

[50] *Mackenzie v. Mackenzie* [1971] P. 33 where the Court of Appeal (consisting of three former judges of the P.D.A. Division) applied, in divorce *Collier v. Hicks* (1831) 2 B. & Ad. 663 at p. 669 *obiter*.

[51] *Re Trepca Mines* [1960] 1 W.L.R. 24; *Re Fuld (No. 2)* [1965] 1 W.L.R. 1336.

[52] N.C.P.R. 1987, r. 5(3)(a); r. 4(3)(a) of the 1954 Rules.

[53] *R. v. Leicester Justices ex p. Barrow* [1991] 2 Q.B. 260 (proceedings for non-payment of the community charge).

[54] *Re. G.* (unreported) no. 679 of 1991.

[55] For the meaning of this phrase, see the First Appendix, para. 02.

[56] See para. 2–15 above.

[57] Recognised here; or a re-sealed grant: see para. 2–14 above.

[58] See para. 2–02 for the meaning of this expression.

law that would have been applicable had the deceased been domiciled in England and Wales.[59] Otherwise under rule 30(1) and (2) a grant may be made here to: (a) the person entrusted with the administration of the estate by the court having jurisdiction at the place where the deceased died domiciled; or (b) where there is no such person to someone beneficially interested under the law of the place where the deceased died domiciled; or (c) to such other person or persons as the district judge directs. An addidavit of foreign law is required made by someone suitably qualified; or a notarial certificate.[60] The application for the grant is made to a district judge.[61]

---

[59] Since immovable property in England and Wales devolves under the law of the place where it is situated: para. 11–02 below.
[60] Rule 19.
[61] Rule 30; and see para. 3–12 below.

4. Inheritance tax on applying for a grant of representation; capital gains tax on estates; income tax on personal representatives

4–01 Scope of this chapter. On applying for a grant, the applicant must pay and account for inheritance tax; this liability is summarised in this chapter. In any case where the position is not straightforward, specialist advice is needed. Capital gains tax and income tax on the estate arise later; for convenience these two topics are also summarised in this chapter.

4–02 Inheritance tax on applying for a grant of representation. Inheritance tax is imposed by the Inheritance Tax Act 1984[1] (formerly called the Capital Transfer Tax Act 1984) as extensively amended; consisting of 278 sections and 16 Schedules. For present purposes, it is enough to mention the liability at death, the principal exemptions and the principal reliefs. The details are to be found in revenue textbooks.

---

[1] Cited as amended, down to para. 4–08 by sections without repeating the name of the Act.

29

Inheritance tax (below "IHT") is charged on the deceased's assets at death,[2] unless the death was from active military service.[3] IHT must be dealt with on applying for a grant of representation.[4] This is done, when not dispensed with,[5] by delivering an account[6] and paying what, if anything, is due. IHT is levied at 40 per cent on net assets transferred at death, after allowing for deductions,[7] exemptions and reliefs,[8] in so far as those net assets exceed £150,000.[9] This figure is raised each year in accordance with the fall in the value of the £. Settled property in which the deceased had an interest for life is added in to the calculation[10] when assessing the tax; so is property given away by the deceased in the last seven years of his life,[11] with a relief after three years; and property given away more than seven years before the donor's death where the deceased reserved a benefit to himself from the gift.[12]

4–03 Dispensing with an account for inheritance tax. The delivery of an account is dispensed with by Regulations[13] provided that: (i) the estate passing at death is entirely under the deceased's will or intestacy, or a nomination, or by survivorship as a beneficial joint tenant (that is to say there was no settled property); (ii) the total gross amount of the estate for tax purposes does not exceed £125,000 (for deaths on or after April 6, 1991); (iii) there is not more than £15,000 out of the U.K.; (iv) the deceased died domiciled in the U.K.; (v) and made no lifetime gifts chargeable to inheritance tax. The Inland Revenue remains entitled even in such a case to call for an account; and an account must afterwards be delivered if it turns out in the course of the administration that these conditions were not met.[14]

---

[2] s.4.
[3] s.154, which is widely interpreted: *Barty-King v. Ministry of Defence* [1979] 2 All E.R. 80, where a wound in 1944 contributed towards cancer causing death in 1967; decided under the previous law.
[4] s.200; and S.C.A. 1981, s.109.
[5] See para. 4–03 below.
[6] s.216.
[7] Funeral expenses: s.172; and any income tax and capital gains tax due at the death: s.174; other liabilities: s.412).
[8] See below for exemptions and reliefs.
[9] On deaths on or after March 10, 1992, the figure is £150,000: F.A. No. 2 1992 s.72 (superseding Inheritance Tax (Indexation) Order 1992, S.I. 1992 No. 625 between April 6, 1991 and March 10, 1992 it was £140,000: Inheritance Tax (Indexation) Order 1991, S.I. 1991 No. 735.
[10] s.49.
[11] s.3A.
[12] See para. 4–04.
[13] Made under s.256: Inheritance Tax (Delivery of Accounts) Regulations 1991, S.I. 1991 No. 1248. For deaths between April 1, 1990 and April 5, 1991 it was £115,000: Inheritance Tax (Delivery of Accounts) Regulations 1990, S.I. 1990 No. 1110; superseding the Inheritance Tax (Delivery of Accounts) Regulations 1989 (S.I. 1989 No. 1078).
[14] The same Regulations.

4–04 Principal exemptions from inheritance tax at death. Examples of exemptions from inheritance tax include: transfers made (whether at death or by a lifetime transfer) between spouses domiciled in the U.K.,[15] gifts to charities,[16] and other favoured institutions[17]; modest amounts by way of wedding presents[18]; lifetime gifts at any time of £3,000 in each year[19]; gifts of not more than £250 to each person in a year[20]; gifts (known as "potentially exempt transfers") made after March 18, 1986,[21] and more than seven years before the death[22] to individuals or to an "accumulation and maintenance trust"[23]; and trusts for the disabled.[24] These exemptions are conditional on the deceased not having reserved a benefit to himself from the gift.[25] It is, however, not necessary[26] for the donor to be excluded from benefit if the gift was exempt from inheritance tax as being to the deceased's spouse, a small gift, a marriage gift, a gift to charity, a gift to a political party, a gift for national purposes, etc., a gift for the public benefit, or to a maintenance fund for historic buildings or to an employee trust.

4–05 Principal reliefs from inheritance tax. There is a relief of 100 per cent or of 50 per cent for business property[27] passing on death, whether the business is incorporated or not,[28] provided that it was held for two or more years[29] by the deceased or by the spouse of the deceased.[30] There is a similar relief for agricultural property,[31] including the agricultural property of a limited company,[32] occupied by the deceased for agriculture for two years before the death or

---

[15] s.13.

[16] s.23.

[17] For example, political parties: 1984 Act, s.24; but limited to £100,000 in the last year of life; national purposes: s.25; public benefit, as defined for this purpose: s.26; and gifts of land to a housing association; s.24A. (The omission to include political parties within the statutory definition of "public benefit" is an example of legislative humility.)

[18] s.22; the limits in 1990 were £5,000 from parents of the bride or bridegroom; £2,500 from other ancestors; £1,000 from others; special provisions for marriage settlements are found in subsection (4). Relationship by step-parentage, adoption or legitimation is enough: s.22(4).

[19] s.19.

[20] s.20.

[21] Transfers made before that date are taxed under the previous law.

[22] s.3A.

[23] That is to say, a trust for beneficiaries at an age up to 25 years, complying with statutory requirements (s.71).

[24] s.84 or s.79.

[25] The F.A. 1986, s.102 and Sched. 20.

[26] The F.A. 1986, s.102(5).

[27] Being a business profession or vocation if carried on for gain: s.103(3).

[28] s.104.

[29] s.106.

[30] s.108(b).

[31] s.116. This relief applies to agricultural property in the U.K., the Channel Islands and the Isle of Man: s.115(5).

[32] s.122.

owned by the deceased for seven years before the death and occupied (whether by the deceased or another) for agriculture,[33] (including in the deceased's period of occupation the occupation of the deceased's spouse.[34]) Inheritance tax on growing trees owned for five years or more may be postponed until sale.[35] There is a conditional exemption for what are in the Treasury's opinion objects, land and buildings, and land and objects associated with them of special interest.[36] It is conditional on the subject-matter being kept in the United Kingdom, preserved and made reasonably accessible to the public. If any of these reliefs might apply, detailed advice and consideration is needed.

4–06 Reliefs depending on the date of death. *Quick succession relief.* Where the deceased's estate had been increased by a transfer chargeable to inheritance tax during the last five years of his life, the inheritance tax at death is reduced by quick succession relief.[37]

Relief on loss of exemption for potentially exempt transfers. When the death is within seven years after a "potentially exempt transfer",[38] inheritance tax is charged on the subject-matter, but at a reduced rate.[39] It is open to the Revenue to collect such inheritance tax from the transferee or from the deceased's personal representatives.[40] If the personal representatives are compelled to pay such inheritance tax, they should be able to recover it from the transferee; under the principle that whoever has the benefit should bear the burden.[41]

Survivorship unknown. When it cannot be known which of two or more persons who have died survived the other/s they are assumed for inheritance tax purposes only to have died at the same instant.[42] This may operate in the case of a common disaster and in other circumstances.[43]

---

[33] s.117.

[34] s.120(1)(b).

[35] ss.125 and 126.

[36] s.31 setting out five categories of such things.

[37] s.141. The relief depends on how soon after the first transfer the death occurred: if it is within one year there is relief at 100 per cent, between one and two years 80 per cent, between two and three years 60 per cent, between three and four years 40 per cent, between four and five years 20 per cent.

[38] See para. 4–04 above.

[39] s.7; the rates depend on the date of the transfer: between three and four years before the death: 80 per cent, between four and five years before the death: 60 per cent, between five and six years before the death: 40 per cent, between six and seven years before the death: 20 per cent.

[40] s.199(2).

[41] *Tito v. Waddell (No. 2)* [1977] Ch. 106 (the *South Sea Island* case), at pp. 290–303, particularly p. 302B; the previous cases are fully cited there.

[42] s.4(2).

[43] See para. 28–03 below, discussing L.P.A. 1925, s.184.

4–07 Payment by instalments. Inheritance tax may be paid by 10 equal yearly instalments, if desired in special circumstances. These apply when it is due in respect of land; or in respect of a business or an interest in a business or in woodland[44]; or when it is due in respect of shares or securities in an unquoted company that is controlled by the shares, or where (without such control) payment otherwise than by instalments would incur undue hardship, or involve 20 per cent or more of the tax due at the death.

4–08 Variation or compliance with the testator's wishes. A variation of a will duly effected within two years after the death may for inheritance tax purposes be attributed to the deceased[45]; and so may compliance with a non-binding wish expressed by the testator[46]; but not a similar wish expressed by an intestate.

CAPITAL GAINS

4–09 No capital gains tax at death. On death, the assets of which the deceased was competent to dispose are treated for capital gains tax purposes as reacquired by his personal representatives at their market value, and so there is no capital gains tax by reason of the death.[47] Anyone who acquires the deceased's assets from his personal representatives as "legatee"[48] does not incur capital gains tax on that acquisition and is treated as if the personal representatives' acquisition of it at the death had been the legatee's.[49] It follows, that the legatee only pays capital gains tax on the gain in value as from the death, on the legatee's own subsequent disposal of the asset.[50] As with inheritance tax, a variation of the devolution of what the

---

[44] ss.227, 228 and 229.
[45] s.142.
[46] s.143.
[47] Taxation of Chargeable Gains Act 1992, s.62.
[48] s. 62(4); "legatee" is widely defined in s.64(2) and (3) as follows:
> (2) In this Act, unless the context otherwise requires, "legatee" includes any person taking under a testamentary disposition or on an intestacy or partial intestacy, whether he takes beneficially or as trustee, and a person taking under a donatio mortis causa shall be treated (except for the purposes of section 62) as a legatee and his acquisition as made at the time of the donor's death.
> (3) For the purposes of the definition of "legatee" above, and of any reference in this Act to a person acquiring as asset "as legatee", property taken under a testamentary disposition or on an intestacy or partial intestacy includes any asset appropriated by the personal representatives in or towards satisfaction of a pecuniary legacy or any other interest or share in the property devolving under the disposition or intestacy.

[49] s.62(4).
[50] 1992 Act Pt. 1 and 2.

deceased was competent to dispose, made within two years after the death, may be attributed to the deceased.[51]

On the other hand, anything disposed of by the personal representatives on sale during the administration is liable to capital gains tax[52] on the gain since the date of death, in so far as it exceeds £5,500 (variable with the value of the £) in each of the first three years since the death.[53] After the first three years, the liability is on the gain since the death in so far as it exceeds half that amount.[54] Personal representatives with assets that have appreciated so as potentially to come within this liability, should carefully consider which assets to sell and which assets to pass to legatees. A transfer to a legatee may have different tax consequences from a sale of the same assets to a legatee; the personal representatives should in some circumstances consider selling the asset. Fiduciary powers should properly be exercised so as to reduce tax if practicable.[55] The notes to the Taxation of Chargeable Gains Act 1992 in *Current Law Statutes 1992*, Volume 2, page 12 quote from the description of the Bill that became this Act by Lord Wilberforce in the second reading debate in the House of Lords:

> "Legislation of unimaginable complexity ... absolutely impossible for the ordinary citizen to understand ... impossible for many accountants to understand ... as I know from personal experience ... also impossible for officials of the Inland Revenue to understand. Sections are piled upon sections and schedules are piled upon schedules in order to deal with supposed cases of evasion ... We now have a monster tax which ... has outgrown the possibility of being handled ... the unfortunate taxpayer and his advisers are landed with a Frankenstein's monster that they must use."

Personal representatives faced with a potential question of Capital Gains Tax should obtain advice.

4–10 Income tax. Personal representatives[56] are liable to pay income tax at the basic rate on income received during the administration, but not tax at the higher rate.[57] The personal

---

[51] s.62(6); but not when the variation is made for extraneous consideraion in money or money's worth: s.62(8), replacing C.G.T.A. 1979, s.49(8).

[52] s.65 (as amended by F.A. 1995, s.114) and s.62(3).

[53] s.3(7), s.65.

[54] Sched. I, para. 2(3).

[55] *Pilkington v. I.R.C.* [1964] A.C. 612 at p. 632; *Re Collard's Will Trust* [1961] Ch. 293 at p. 302.

[56] If any is resident or is domiciled in the U.K.: F.A. 1989, s.111.

[57] *I.R.C.* v. *Longford* [1928] A.C. 252. The position of the beneficiaries receiving such income, already taxed in the hands of the personal representatives, is enacted in the Income and Corporation Taxes Act 1988, ss.695–701. It is not part of the administration of the estate.

representatives are not entitled to *personal* allowances. An allowance is, however, made in respect of one year's interest on a loan for the payment of inheritance tax.[58]

[58] Income and Corporation Taxes Act 1988, s.364.

5. Acceptance of a grant or renunciation

5–01 Points to be considered. An executor, or the person entitled to obtain letters of administration, should consider whether it is desirable to obtain a grant of representation or to renounce the position. Apart from personal circumstances, there may be legal grounds to make it prudent to renounce. Some of frequent occurrence are mentioned below.

5–02 The rule against self-dealing. A basic overriding rule of equity[1] prevents anyone acting for others, (such as executor, administrator or trustee) from being a party to a binding contract with himself, even if others are parties to the transaction.[2] There are potential exceptions to the rule,[3] but any personal representative who seeks to rely on one of the exceptions to the rule exposes himself to the risk of suspicion or of misunderstanding; and perhaps of litigation. When someone entitled to a grant of representation has an

---

[1] See Chap. 34.
[2] *Industrial Developments Consultants Ltd v. Cooley* [1972] 1 W.L.R. 443; *Re Thompson* [1986] Ch. 99, citing authorities back to 1802; and *Tito v. Waddell (No. 2)* [1977] Ch. 106 at pp. 240–243 (the *South Sea Island* case).
[3] See paras. 34–06 to 34–10.

interest which may require dealing between himself and the estate, he should normally renounce the right to a grant. It is not prudent to rely on mutual confidence; that may change. The same confidence might not be felt by successors (such as personal representatives of those concerned, or those administering their assets in the event of insolvency).

5–03 Contract with the deceased. A grant should be renounced by anyone who was in contractual relations with the deceased: as vendor or as purchaser under an uncompleted contract; as landlord or as tenant; under an option; or under any other continuing contractual relationship.

5–04 Tort. The same applies if there is any subsisting claim on either side as regards a tort.

5–05 Partnership. A person conducting business in partnership often appoints one or more of his partners as executors. A surviving partner should usually renounce his right to a grant with a view to facilitating winding up the estate and settling the partnership affairs.[4]

5–06 Trust. When the deceased was a beneficiary under a trust that remains to be wound up, agreement and a release will be needed between the trustees and the deceased's personal representatives. A trustee of the trust should renounce any right to a grant in a beneficiary's estate.

5–07 The deceased a sole trader. If the deceased was a sole trader or a sole survivor of partners, the administration of the estate is likely to be complicated. This could involve the interests of three classes, that is to say, the business creditors at the death, the creditors under contracts made while winding up the business, and the beneficiaries.[5] The estate of a solvent sole trader is best administered by a trust corporation, or by an accountant accustomed to act as a receiver. The estate of an insolvent sole trader should be administered in bankruptcy under the Insolvency Act 1986, s.421.[6]

5–08 The deceased was himself an executor. Probate of a testator's will renders the executor, the executor by representation of any earlier testator of whom the second testator was himself the sole or sole surviving executor.[7] This "chain of representation" (as A.E.A. 1925, s.7 aptly calls it) is only broken by an intestacy, a failure of a

---

[4] See paras. 20–14 to 20–19.
[5] See paras. 20–20 to 20–26.
[6] See para. 39–03.
[7] A.E.A. 1925, s.7.

testator to appoint an executor or, if the deceased was domiciled in Northern Ireland, a failure to obtain probate of the will in England and Wales.[8] Probate granted in Northern Ireland forms part of the chain of representation in England[9]; but a grant in Scotland does not form part of the chain of representation[10]; nor does a grant elsewhere.[11] The executor of the second testator must therefore take on both administrations or neither; he may not, except by leave of a district judge, renounce probate as executor and then seek a grant in another capacity.[12] It may be better to renounce probate rather than become involved in a contentious continuing administration of the estate of a previous testator.

5–09 Remuneration. A personal representative must act without fees for his work, like any other person in a fiduciary position,[13] unless authorised to charge remuneration. Those in a professional position or trust corporations, who are prepared to accept a grant only if so authorised, should consider this at the outset.[14]

5–10 Tax risks. It is sometimes feared that the deceased may have engaged in transactions that the Crown[15] might think incurred unmet fiscal liability. When all the deceased's assets are in the United Kingdom this is not a serious risk for a personal representative. When there are substantial assets outside the United Kingdom, there may be a risk to the personal representatives themselves. The risk is that the courts of the country with control of such overseas assets might prevent their use for payment of United Kingdom fiscal liabilities[16]; and yet the personal representatives might according to English enactments perhaps he held liable here to the Crown in respect of assets overseas.[17] It is prudent from the point of view of the executor (if not of those beneficially interested), to refuse a grant

---

[8] s.7(3).
[9] A.E.A. 1971, s.1(4).
[10] s.1(3) there.
[11] *Re Gaynor* (1869) 1 P. & D. 723; and see *Burns v. Campbell* [1952] 1 K.B. 15.
[12] N.C.P.R., r. 37(1) and (2).
[13] See Snell, *Equity* (28th ed.) at p. 253.
[14] See paras. 37–08 to 37–12.
[15] The phrase is a convenient way to refer to those exercising governmental powers; although the "Crown as an object is a piece of jewelled headgear under guard at the Tower of London": Lord Simon in *Town Investments v. Department of the Environment* [1978] A.C. 359 at p. 397.
[16] As recognised in *Government of India v. Taylor* [1955] A.C. 491 at pp. 504–505 and 514–515, most countries refuse to enforce tax laws of other countries. In the estate of Sir Charles Clore there was an injunction in Jersey that had the effect of prohibiting Jersey assets being used to meet English Capital Transfer Tax: *I.R.C. v. Stype Investments (Jersey) Ltd* [1982] Ch. 456 at p. 471B.
[17] Taxes Management Act 1970, s.74; Taxation of Chargeable Gains Act 1992, s.69; Inheritance Tax Act 1984, s.204. This is probably not the law; but cases in respect of overseas residents might be relied on by the Crown in this connection: *I.R.C. v. Stannard* [1984] 1 W.L.R. 1039, the 2nd point; *I.R.C. v. Stype Trustees* [1985] 1 W.L.R. 1290.

in such a situation, and to let a Crown nominee take a grant of letters of administration.[18]

5–11 The person entitled to a grant a debtor to the estate. When the person entitled to a grant owes money to the estate, and might have a defence of limitation under the Limitation Act 1980 against the personal representatives, he should renounce the right to a grant. If he accepts a grant he may be unable to enjoy the defence of limitation.[19]

5–12 Method of renunciation. A person entitled to a grant of representation either as executor[20] or administrator may renounce the right to a grant. The renunciation must be made in writing, witnessed,[21] and lodged at the registry, with any will or codicil of the deceased to which the person renouncing has access. The renunciation takes effect only when it is filed at the registry and may be withdrawn before being filed.[22]

5–13 Effect of renunciation. A renunciation by an executor has a different effect from a renunciation by someone entitled to become administrator. (For the difference between an executor and an administrator see Chapter 2.) A renunciation by an executor only causes his rights to cease "in respect of the executorship"[23]; and so an executor who has renounced probate may still obtain a grant of letters of administration in some other capacity unless that right is expressly renounced too[24]; as it usually is. On the other hand, a renunciation of administration by someone entitled to a grant of letters of administration, otherwise than as an executor, prevents the person renouncing from obtaining a grant (except by leave) in another capacity.[25] (This distinction has long been outmoded; and should have been abrogated when the rules were revised.) An executor who renounces probate has no right to a formal release on handing over documents that have come into the executor's possession.[26] It follows that someone who renounces a right to letters of administration has no such right.

---

[18] As in *I.R.C. v. Stype Investments (Jersey) Ltd* [1982] Ch. 456.
[19] See para. 25–01 below.
[20] A.E.A. 1925, s.5; unless the executor has begun to administer the estate when he may be disabled from renouncing probate: see para. 7–04 below.
[21] See Mortimer, *Probate* (2nd ed.) at p. 495. There seems to be no authority for this requirement, although it is the practice in all registries.
[22] *Re Morant* (1874) 3 P. & D. 151.
[23] A.E.A. 1925, s.5.
[24] N.C.P.R. 1987, r. 37(1).
[25] N.C.P.R. 1987, r. 37(2).
[26] *Tiger v. Barclays Bank* [1951] 2 K.B. 556 at pp. 560–562; where there had been terms of compromise: this point did not arise in the Court of Appeal, [1952] 1 All E.R. 85.

5–14 Withdrawal of renunciation. A renunciation that has been filed at the registry[27] may afterwards be withdrawn or retracted with leave of a district judge. After a grant has been made to someone else, it may however only be withdrawn in exceptional circumstances.[28]

---

[27] It has no effect before it is filed: *Re Morant*, n. 21 above.
[28] N.C.P.R. 1987, r. 37(3) and (4).

6. The effect of a grant of representation: obtaining notice of or before any grant

6–01 Grant in common form. A grant in common form is one issued on an unopposed application (as most grants are), or one issued after a summons under the Non-Contentious Probate Rules 1987.

A grant in common form ranks as an order of the court[1]; accordingly, even when it is afterwards set aside, what was done under it is effective and lawful.[2] Although it may turn out to be voidable (liable to be set aside by the court), such a grant is never void (wholly invalid).[3] Nevertheless personal representatives with notice that there is a claim to set aside the grant, cannot safely make payments to beneficiaries while such a claim is outstanding.[4]

6–02 Revocation or amendment of a common form grant. A common form grant may be revoked or amended by the court.[5] This

---

[1] *Hewson v. Shelley* [1914] 2 Ch. 13; *Re Bridgett & Hayes Contract* [1928] Ch. 163; L.P.A. 1925, s.204(1).
[2] A.E.A. 1925, ss.27 and 37.
[3] *Hewson v. Shelley* above; *McFarland v. Conlon* [1930] N.I. 138.
[4] *Guardian Trust and Executors Co. of New Zealand v. Public Trustee of New Zealand* [1942] A.C. 115.
[5] S.C.A. 1981, ss.25(1)(b), and 121.

is normally done by an order of the district judge[6] with the consent of the holder of the grant or in "exceptional circumstances," without it.[7] Frequent occasions for this power to be exercised are the finding of a later will or codicil, or the death or incapacity of a personal representative. It may also be varied as a result of an application, made in the Chancery Division,[8] to remove personal representatives.[9] A grant in common form may also be revoked as a result of a probate action in the Chancery Division, determining the devolution of the estate.

6–03 Effect of a grant in common form, recital of domicile. The recital of the deceased's domicile in the grant is not conclusive on domicile; whether it is made without inquiry, or even when it is made after a judicial determination not essential to the decision and not amounting to an estoppel.[10] (Those who are not lawyers frequently find this point perplexing.)

6–04 Effect of a grant in common form, recital of entitlement. On an intestacy, a grant of letters of administration to one or more of a class described in the grant as entitled on intestacy, even when described in the grant as the "only persons" entitled, does not prevent another member of the same class from making a claim to participate[11]; that is to say without the grant being revoked or varied. On the other hand a grant of letters of administration on intestacy to one of a specified class of next-of-kin is conclusive, as long as the grant stands, that there is no one in a class taking on intestacy in priority to the class of which the grantee is a member: anyone who challenges the claim of the person with such a grant must therefore being a probate action to revoke the subsisting grant.[12]

6–05 Grant in solemn form. A grant in solemn form is a grant made after a probate action. The grant bears a note that it was so made or confirmed (as the case may be). It is a grant in solemn form even when the order is made by compromise.[13] A grant in solemn

---

[6] With an appeal to a judge: r. 65; or sometimes a reference to the judge without a decision by the district judge: r. 61.

[7] N.C.P.R. 1987, r. 41.

[8] Ord. 93, r. 20.

[9] Under A.J.A. 1985, s.50.

[10] *Bradford v. Young* (1884) 26 Ch. Div. 656; affirmed without dealing with this point, (1885) 29 Ch. Div. 617; also *Concha v. Concha* (1886) 11 App. Cas. 541, affirming the same case reported as *de Mora v. Concha* (1885) 29 Ch. 268; where there had been an earlier finding as to domicile that was held not essential to the decision, and not binding.

[11] *Re Ward* [1971] 1 W.L.R. 1376, distinguishing *Re Ivory* (1879) 10 Ch. Div. 372 and applying *Concha v. Concha* above.

[12] *Re Ivory* (1879) 10 Ch. Div. 372. See Chapter 41 and Chapter 13.

[13] *Re Barraclough* [1967] P. 1.

form (as its name suggests) has a greater effect. When made on a contest, it binds: the parties to the action and those taking under them[14]; those cited by notice of the action[15]; and also those who knew of the action and did not take part in it.[16] It does not, however, bind someone with no right to intervene on his then state of knowledge.[17]

6–06 Grant in solemn form after a compromise of a probate action. A compromise of a probate action, however, only binds those who assent to it.[18] Accordingly a compromise ought to be made with all concerned; or to provide for anyone not a party to the action to receive the most such a person is entitled to on any outcome (for example where there are various wills, giving pecuniary legacies of varying amounts to persons not parties to the compromise).

6–07 Setting aside a grant in solemn form. A judgment for a grant in solemn form may, in theory, be set aside if obtained by fraud; but a successful claim on this basis is rare.[19] It would also be set aside on discovery of another will, not known at the time.[20]

6–08 Standing search. To obtain from the registry notice of any grant of representation within the previous 12 months, anyone may enter a standing search.[21] It requires renewal after six months.

6–09 Caveat. It may be desirable to prevent a grant being issued before notice is given, to ensure that there is an opportunity to object to it. For this purpose, anyone who wishes to object to the sealing of a grant may enter a caveat,[22] and is then known as the "caveator." A caveat is in force for six months and may be renewed; while it is in force no one else may obtain a grant of representation to the estate, except a grant limited to collecting the assets.[23] The entry of a caveat is a convenient way to delay a grant while the position is investigated.

---

[14] *Beardsley v. Beardsley* [1899] 1 Q.B. 746; *Re Barraclough* above; *Re Langton* [1964] P. 163.

[15] *Newell v. Weeks* (1814) 2 Ph. 224; the notice is under Ord. 15, r. 13A.

[16] *Ratcliffe v. Barnes* (1862) 2 Sw. & T. 486; *Re Langton* above.

[17] *Young v. Holloway* [1895] P. 87.

[18] *Wytcherley v. Andrews* (1871) L.R. 2 P. & D. 327; and on the other side *Re Barraclough* above.

[19] See *Birch v. Birch* [1902] P. 62, 130 and *Re Langton* above; where allegations of such fraud were struck out as vexatious.

[20] Mortimer, *Probate* (2nd ed.), at p. 240; no reported case of this seems to have occurred.

[21] Under N.C.P.R. 1987, r. 43, by lodging with the district judge, or sending by post, form 2 to the Non-Contentious Probate Rules, 1987.

[22] N.C.P.R. 1987, r. 44.

[23] By lodging or sending by post, form 3 to the rules at any probate registry.

6–10 Proceedings under a caveat: rule 44. Any one with an interest in the estate adverse to that of the caveator (that is to say under some other will or an intestacy) may serve a warning on the caveator; the caveator must enter an appearance to the warning; and the devolution of the estate can then be determined, usually in a probate action (discussed below). If the caveator does not dispute the devolution of the estate, but wishes to show that a grant ought for a valid reason not to be made to the person who has warned the caveator, he should have a summons for directions issued; the question to whom a grant should be made is then decided on affidavit evidence.

6–11 Cesser of caveat: rule 44. A caveat ceases to have effect if when warned, the caveator neither issues a summons for directions, nor enters appearance; if the caveator withdraws the caveat before entering appearance to the warning; or if on hearing the summons for directions, the district judge so orders. A caveat can also be cleared off by consent by an order of the district judge after an appearance to the warning.

6–12 Security for costs on a caveat. It has been held in England that a caveator cannot be odered to give security for the costs arising from the caveat.[24] In Ireland a caveator may be ordered to give such security.[25]

---

[24] *Re Emery* [1923] P. 184; *Rose v. Epstein* [1974] 1 W.L.R. 1565; where *Dobler* v. *Walsh* [1950] N.I. 150 was not cited.

[25] *Dobler v. Walsh* above. The judgment of Andrews C.J. seems convincing, but in England the result of *Rose v. Epstein* above is that the point is only open in the House of Lords.

7. The remedy for delay before a grant is made: citation

7–01 Citation; history
7–02 The remedy for delay; citation
7–03 Citation to accept or refuse a grant
7–04 Citation to take probate
7–05 Citation to propound a will
7–06 No citation to propound a codicil
7–07 Procedure under a citation
7–08 Subsequent steps
7–09 No citation after a grant in common form
7–10 Citation and Legal Aid

7–01 Citation; history. In the Court of Probate under the Court of Probate Act 1857, contentious proceedings were begun by citation.[1] On the creation of the High Court of Justice and the transfer of probate jurisdiction to the Probate, Divorce & Admiralty Division by the Judicature Acts 1873[2] and 1875, the procedural requirement to issue a writ was interposed; it was issued after a citation,[3] if there had been one. Accordingly a citation ceased to be essential; since a probate action could be brought by writ without or with a previous citation. This may nowadays have a significant effect in respect of Legal Aid: see para. 7–10 below.

7–02 The remedy for delay; citation. Delay on the part of the executor or other person entitled to a grant[4] causes inconvenience; as does delay in asserting his claim, by someone claiming that a will is valid. There is a swift and effective remedy putting an end to such

---

[1] Contentious Probate Rules 1862 as amended rules 13 and 14.
[2] ss.16 and 34.
[3] Judicature Act 1875, s.18 and Sched. 1, Ord. 2, para. 1.
[4] Under N.C.P.R. 1987, r. 20 when there is a will and N.C.P.R. 1987, r. 22 when there is an intestacy.

delay, before there is a grant of representation (but not after a grant has been made).[5]

The remedy before there has been a grant, for delay on the part of an executor or other person entitled to a grant, is a citation to accept or to refuse a grant.[6] The remedy for delay in asserting a claim to prove a will is a citation to propound that will.[7] There is therefore no need to suffer delay in obtaining a grant. There is also a little used citation to take probate.[8]

A citation is a formal court document issued, on affidavit evidence, by a probate district judge[9] on the application of the citor (the person seeking the citation) against the citee (the person cited).

7–03   Citation to accept or refuse a grant.   The remedy for delay on the part of a person entitled to a grant is for whoever is next entitled to a grant to obtain as citor, a citation[10] requiring the person cited ("the citee") to accept or to renounce the right to a grant; usually within eight days.

A citation to accept or to refuse a grant has nothing to do with the question of the validity of any will.

7–04   Citation to take probate.   A citation to *take* probate is a different matter. It compels an *executor* who has begun to administer an estate to take a grant of probate.[11] (This form of citation is not available against someone entitled to letters of administration.) Such a citation results in getting the estate administered by a citee who may be hostile to the citor. That is not desirable.[12]

After obtaining a citation to take probate, the citor may still ask the court to pass over the executor[13]; and to make a discretionary grant of representation to someone else.[14]

7–05   Citation to propound a will.   Delay may be caused before a grant of representation has been made, by a claim that there is another will in existence, made by someone who takes no positive

---

[5] See para. 7–09 below. After a grant has been issued, the remedy is to bring a probate action to revoke the grant, or to seek the removal of the personal representatives, or the appointment of a judicial trustee: see Chaps. 41 and 43 below.

[6] See para. 7–03 below.

[7] See para. 7–05 below.

[8] See para. 7–04 below.

[9] Under N.C.P.R. 1987, rr. 46 to 48.

[10] Under N.C.P.R. 1987, r. 47.

[11] Under N.C.P.R. 1987, r. 47(3).

[12] This form of citation appears to have become largely obsolete as long ago as 1927, see Mortimer, *Probate* (2nd ed.), at p. 509, relegating this procedure to a footnote.

[13] Under S.C.A. 1981, s.116.

[14] *Re Biggs* [1966] P. 118, applying *Re Potticary* [1927] P. 202 and *Re Leguia* [1934] P. 80.

step to justify the claim. Anyone with an interest contrary to those who make such a claim may obtain a citation to propound such alleged will, against the executors and the beneficiaries under it.[15]

If any citee enters appearance to the citation to propound, a probate action is begun and the question is then decided, or compromised. If, however, there is no appearance to a citation to propound, the court may issue a grant in common form on the basis that the will mentioned in the citation was invalid.[16] This procedure has been in use for many years[17]; it results in a will being disregarded in the registry, without judicial investigation: this procedure will not be extended:

> "I ask if consent cannot unmake a will, how can failure to appear to a citation unmake one?"[18]

Accordingly a citation to propound a will can only be issued against *all* the executors and *all* the persons interested thereunder[19]; or if any are without capacity, then against those who represent them.[20] Caution is, quite rightly, exercised in the registry before allowing such a citation to be issued.

This procedure is useful when the claim is not likely to be seriously asserted. Otherwise it only adds an extra stage to an inevitable probate action. If the claim is likely to be seriously asserted, it is better therefore to issue a probate writ impugning the disputed will.[21]

Like any other grant in common form, a grant made after a citation to propound can afterwards be impugned in a probate action.[22]

7–06 No citation to propound a *codicil*. An executor under a will, to which there is a doubtful codicil (a frequent state of affairs) is not permitted to issue a citation to propound the *codicil*. The proper course is for the executor to bring a probate action to prove the will in solemn form and to join those interested under the codicil.[23]

7–07 Procedure under a citation. Before seeking a citation, the citor must enter a caveat [24] and either procure the relevant will to be

---

[15] Under N.C.P.R. 1987, r. 48.
[16] Under N.C.P.R. 1987, r. 48(2).
[17] *Morton v. Thorpe* (1863) 3 Sw. & T. 179; *Re Dennis* [1899] P. 191; *Re Bootle* (1901) 84 L.T. 570, where Jeune P. "did not altogether like the form."
[18] *Re Muirhead* [1971] P. 263, Cairns J. at p. 269.
[19] N.C.P.R. 1987, r. 48(1).
[20] Under R.S.C., Ord. 80.
[21] See Chap. 41.
[22] *Re Jolley* [1964] P. 262.
[23] *Re Muirhead* above: the executor's duty if accepting probate is to perform all the deceased's wishes in any duly executed testamentary document. It is not always clear whether a document is a will or a codicil: if that doubt arises, *Re Muirhead* is likely to be applied, so as to prevent a citation to propound being issued.
[24] See para. 6–07 above.

lodged in the registry or satisfy the district judge that it is impracticable to do so.[25] A draft of the citation sought and an unsworn draft of the affidavit in support are lodged with the district judge for approval or amendment. The affidavit is then sworn and the citation is issued. The citation, unlike a modern writ, is still expressed as a command of the Sovereign. Personal ser/ice is required of a citation, unless the district judge authorises ano.her form of service.[26] There appears to be nothing in English law to prevent a citation being served out of the jurisdiction; but before serving a citation abroad it is prudent to ascertain the view taken of the propriety of such service under the law there.

7–08 Subsequent steps. After service[27] of a citation, the citee should enter appearance[28] to the citation.

A citee,[29] cited to accept or to refuse a grant, must either accept the grant, renounce the right to a grant, or be passed over in default of appearance.

A citee cited to *take* probate can be compelled to take probate or can be passed over.[30]

A citee cited to propound a will should enter appearance to the citation and issue a probate writ propounding it; otherwise a grant may be made on the uninvestigated assumption that the will is invalid.[31]

7–09 No citation after a grant in common form. The citation procedure is preliminary to a grant in common form; it is no longer available after a grant in common form has been made, when the right procedure to determine a dispute about the validity of a will is to bring a probate action.[32]

7–10 Citation and Legal Aid. Under the Legal Aid Act 1988, s.18 a successful unassisted party may obtain costs against the Legal Aid Fund, at the Court's discretion subject to the conditions in section 18. One of those conditions is that the proceedings were "instituted" by the party with legal aid ("the assisted party").

Where the assisted party has issued a Citation to Propound compelling the unassisted party to issue a writ, successfully establishing the will (see paragraph 7–04 above), it appears that the

---

[25] N.C.P.R. 1987, r. 46.
[26] N.C.P.R. 1987, r. 47(4).
[27] N.C.P.R. 1987, r. 46(4).
[28] N.C.P.R. 1987, r. 46(6).
[29] Under N.C.P.R. 1987, r. 47.
[30] See para. 7–04 above.
[31] See para. 7–05 above.
[32] *Re Jolley* [1964] P. 262.

proceedings are for this purpose "instituted" by the assisted party's Citation to Propound, not by the unassisted party's writ.[33]

---

[33] See para. 7–01 above for the history; *Crickett v. Crickett* [1902] P. 177, on a probate summons; distinguishing *Moran v. Place* [1896] P.214 and *Salter v. Salter* [1896] P. 291, as dealing only with a caveat; *Re Langton* [1964] P. 163, Willmer L.J. at p.174. See also on the word "instituted" (under the Married Women's Property Act 1893) *Hood Barrs v. Cathcart* [1895] 1 Q.B. 873; and *Nunn v. Tyson* [1901] 2 K.B. 487; and (under the Judicature Act 1925, s.51(1), since replaced by S.C.A. 1981, s.42) *Re Becker* [1975] 1 W.L.R. 842.

8. Informing the beneficiaries

8–01 No duty in theory. An executor has (in legal theory and subject to what is said in paragraph 8–05 below) no obligation to inform a beneficiary of the beneficiary's rights under a will.[1] This decision was reached in a case where it benefited the executor not to inform the beneficiary. In practice an executor almost always informs a beneficiary.

8–02 Reason for this rule. In a modern case where it was held on the other hand that a *trustee* has a duty to inform a beneficiary, it was said that:

> "there is a distinction between a will, which is a public document in the sense that anybody can go to Somerset House and see it, and a trust deed, which is a private document to which the cestui que trust [beneficiary] has no access."[2]

8–03 Exceptions. It appears to follow that this doctrine is confined to *wills*; and does not apply on an intestacy when there is no will to see at Somerset House, only a grant of letters of administration; nor does it apply to the will of a member of the Royal Family, sealed up on the grant of probate.[3]

---

[1] *Re Lewis* [1904] 2 Ch. 656, following *Chauncey v. Graydon* (1743) 2 Atk. 616. The same was assumed in Ireland: *Re Tighe* [1944] Ir. 171, decided on construction.
[2] *Hawkesley v. May* [1956] 1 Q.B. 304, at p. 322, Havers J. He added that the doctrine of *Re Lewis* had no attraction for him on the merits.
[3] See para. 9–02.

8–04 U.S.A. law on this point. In the U.S.A., although there are old cases either way, statutes commonly require the personal representatives to give notice to beneficiaries[4]; and

> "even in the absence of a statute, a personal representative who will profit by failure of a legatee to claim a legacy within a prescribed period must use all reasonable diligence to inform the legatee of such legacy. Failure to do so is tantamount to fraud."[5]

This might be held to be the modern law in England and Wales.

8–05 Future development. This principle is anomalous in the light of modern extensions in other fields of the duty of care[6]; the principle, such as it is, might nowadays be held inapplicable at first instance by being restrictively distinguished; and might be overruled in the House of Lords.

8–06 Present position. At present, it is unsafe to rely on this principle in any case. A deliberate decision not to tell a beneficiary might be found to be fraudulent; an inadvertent omission to tell a beneficiary might be found to be a breach on the facts of the case of the executor's duty, as understood nowadays.

8–07 Potential claimants under the Inheritance (Provision for Family and Dependants) Act 1975. There is no duty on personal representatives to inform a potential claimant under the Inheritance (Provision for Family and Dependants) Act 1975. Until an order has been made a claimant under that Act is not yet a beneficiary.[7]

---

[4] 31 Am. Jur. 2d, Executors and Administrators para. 404.

[5] *ibid.* para. 405, citing authorities.

[6] The overriding principle of equity is nowadays that no one may place himself in a position where his interest and his duty conflict: *Industrial Development Consultants Ltd* v. *Cooley* [1972] 1 W.L.R. 443; *Re Thompson* [1986] Ch. 99. Two previous cases, not cited in *Re Lewis*, might have supported, though they would not have required, a decision in *Re Lewis* that an executor must notify a beneficiary: *Burrows* v. *Walls* (1855) 5 de G.M. & G. 233 and *Brittlebank* v. *Goodwin* (1868) 5 Eq. 545, *obiter* at p. 550. Moreover the general duty of care in tort is nowadays wider than it was thought to be in 1904 when *Re Lewis* was decided.

[7] *Re Jennery* [1967] Ch. 280.

9. Public access to proved wills

9–01 Public right of inspection
9–02 Royal Family
9–03 Method of avoiding public access

9–01 Public right of inspection. Every will and codicil admitted to probate in England is open to public inspection and to a right to obtain a copy.[1] This is a valuable right for members of the public who are potential beneficiaries or claimants under the Inheritance (Provision for Family & Dependants) Act 1975. This right, however, is occasionally used, or misused, for the purposes of newspaper publicity.

9–02 Royal Family. There is an exception: under a practice introduced in recent decades, the wills of deceased members of the Royal Family are ordered to be sealed and are only open to inspection on obtaining an order for inspection.[2] There appears to be no other occasion for a special privilege for a member of the Royal Family in English law; apart from the monarch, they may be sued like any other subject.[3] Anyone with a potential interest in such an estate would readily obtain an order for access to the will as proved and for the cost of the application, if opposed. The will, if proved in Ireland, of a member of the Royal Family who dies holding land in the Republic of Ireland would, like anyone else's, be public.[4]

9–03 Method of avoiding public access. A testator may have, or think he has, a good reason to avoid public access to his testamentary dispositions after his death. It is easy to avoid it. Such access is

---

[1] S.C.A. 1981, ss.124 and 125. As regards personal property, this goes back to the Court of Probate Act 1857, s.69, representing the previous practice: Tristram & Coote (14th ed.), (1906) at p. 218. As regards real property, this was a consequence of the Land Transfer Act 1897, Pt I.

[2] Tristram & Coote (27th ed.), at p. 138. The first mention of such a practice is in the 18th ed. (1940) at p. 8, citing two unreported cases; *The Princess Royal* (1931) and *Prince Arthur of Connaught* (1939).

[3] *Supreme Court Practice 1995*, Vol. 2, para. 4652 at p. 1463.

[4] Wylie, *Irish Conveyancing Law* (1978) para. 13.78 at p. 637.

avoided by making a settlement, or several settlements, while alive, of a nominal sum on trusts declared in the settlement to operate after the settlor's death; the will then makes gifts to the trustees of such settlement or settlements on the trusts thereof: "Nothing is more common than to give legacies to be held on the trusts of a marriage settlement."[5] To avoid publicity, the will must not use language incorporating the settlement in the will (when it would be admitted to probate,[6] and consequent publicity). Incorporation can be avoided by an express declaration in the will against incorporation[7]; non-incorporation does no harm in the case of a duly executed settlement effective in itself.[8]

---

[5] *Quilhampton v. Going* (1876) 24 W.R. 917 at p. 918, Jessel M.R.
[6] *University College of North Wales v. Taylor* [1908] P. 140.
[7] *Re Louis* (1916) 32 T.L.R. 313.
[8] See para. 12–22.

10. Claim against the will or intestacy after probate or letters of administration

10–01 Introduction
10–02 Position before revocation of the grant
10–03 Revocation
10–04 Revocation by order of the district judge
10–05 Revocation action
10–06 Claim for revocation made by letter, but no other step taken

10–01 Introduction. Executors are often faced, after probate, with a claim that there was a later will, or that on some other ground the will admitted to probate is invalid; and similar claims may be made against administrators. The correct course is dependent upon the claimant's actions.

10–02 Position before revocation of the grant. The acts of the personal representatives carried out while the grant was in force remain valid, even though the grant is afterwards revoked.[1] The personal representatives are entitled to payment (out of the estate), of their expenses while acting.[2]

10–03 Revocation. A grant of probate or of letters of administration ranks as an order of the High Court.[3] Once made, an order is binding unless and until it is set aside.[4] Accordingly a grant remains in force, even if incorrectly made, until it is duly set aside. It is not possible to proceed by citation after a grant has been made.[5]

---

[1] A.E.A. 1925, s.27 and s.37; though afterwards avoided, a grant is never void: *Hewson v. Shelley* [1914] 2 Ch. 13; *McFarland v. Conlon* [1930] N.I. 138.
[2] Trustee Act 1925, s.30(2), applicable to personal representatives, s.68(17).
[3] *Re Bridgett & Hayes* [1928] Ch. 163; *Hewson v. Shelley* [1914] 2 Ch. 13.
[4] *Re South American & Mexican Company* [1895] 1 Ch. 37; *Livesey v. Jenkins* [1985] A.C. 424; and the *Ampthill Peerage* [1977] A.C. 547; and see n. 1 above and para. 6–01.
[5] *Re Jolley* [1964] P. 262.

10–04 Revocation by order of the district judge. The district judge has power to revoke or to amend a grant, calling it in if available.[6] Except on the application of the person to whom the grant was made or with that person's consent, this power may be exercised only in "exceptional circumstances." The power is exercised by a district judge on affidavit evidence. When the facts call for revocation and are not in dispute, there is likely to be such consent; or "exceptional circumstances" are likely to be found.

If the claim appears to the personal representatives to be likely to be correct, they should consent to the grant being revoked.[7]

10–05 Revocation action. A contested summons under the Non-Contentious Probate Rules 1987 is not a convenient method of determining a contested claim to revoke a grant, even in "exceptional circumstances."[8] A probate action, known as a revocation action, is usually brought for an order to revoke the grant.[9]

The executor, under a will that has been proved, is a necessary party to a revocation action.[10] An executor with no substantial beneficial interest may not wish to take an active part in such an action. In this situation the executor remains entitled to a grant of probate of any will established in the action[11]; and may plead in the defence that he adopts a position of neutrality.[12] If the executor positively alleges that the will is valid, the executor may incur a liability for costs.[13] There is no reason for someone interested only as executor to incur this risk; the law does not recognise a duty to litigate.[14]

10–06 Claim for revocation made by letter, but no other step taken. The tactic may be adopted of sending letters asserting that there is a later will, without taking positive steps about it. The executor cannot then distribute in reliance on the grant of probate, with notice of such a claim.[15] It is not for the executor to bring a probate action to establish the will that already has been admitted to probate. Unless a beneficiary under the will brings such an action, the

---

[6] N.C.P.R. 1987, r. 41, based on S.C.A. 1981, s.25(1)(b) and s.121.
[7] Under N.C.P.R. 1987, r. 41.
[8] See N.C.P.R. 1987, r. 41(2).
[9] See Chap. 41.
[10] Ord. 76, r. 3.
[11] *Bewsher v. Williams* (1861) 3 Sw. & T. 62.
[12] As was done by the executor in *Re Stott* [1980] 1 W.L.R. 246, see at p. 248C.
[13] *Rennie v. Massey* (1866) L.R. 1 P. & D. 118.
[14] *Lehmann v. McArthur* (1868) L.R. 1 Ch.App. 496; *Williams Torrey & Co. v. Knight* [1894] P. 342; *Pilkington v. Wood* [1953] Ch. 770; and *obiter Williams v. Glenton* (1866) L.R. 1 Ch.App. 200 at p. 208. Cases decided under the system in force before the Judicature Act 1873 are not a safe guide to the modern law on this point.
[15] *Guardian Trust and Executors Co. of New Zealand v. Public Trustee of New Zealand* [1942] A.C. 115.

right course is for the executor to apply for the directions of the court.[16] Such applications are heard in chambers. The directions usually given are that unless the claimant serves a probate writ before a specified day, the executor is to distribute the estate without regard to the claim that there was a later will.[17]

---

[16] Under Ord. 85, r. 2.

[17] Such an order is narrated in *Re Langton* [1966] 1 W.L.R. 1575 at p. 1578:
"On June 3, 1957 Danckwerts J. made an order that, in default of the respondent commencing an action before a certain date against the executors, the executors should be at liberty to ignore any claim made by the respondent."
(The proceedings resulting from that order are reported: *Re Langton* [1964] P. 163.)

11. System of law applicable to succession

11–01 Domicile
11–02 Applicable system
11–03 Practical consequences of the distinction between immovable and movable property and methods of avoiding those consequences
11–04 Ascertaining foreign law

11–01 Domicile. In England and Wales, the "domicile" of a person[1] is to be determined by ascertaining what, according to the law of England, was his/her permanent home, even when that results in a finding that someone was domiciled in a country that held he or she was not domiciled there.[2] According to the law of England, the deceased's last domicile is either his domicile of origin (where he was born) or a domicile of choice, on his abandonment of his domicile of origin and choice of another permanent home. In modern conditions of mobility, the ascertainment of someone's last domicile may give rise to difficulty.[3]

11–02 Applicable system. According to the law of England and Wales, *immovable* property devolves at death under the law of the place where it was situated; but *movable* property devolves under the law of the deceased's last domicile.[4] This principle applies whether land and buildings are freehold, leasehold[5] or otherwise,[6] and

---

[1] Including a married woman: Domicile & Matrimonial Proceedings Act 1973, s.1.
[2] *Re Annesley* [1926] Ch. 692. The continental concept of someone's "domicile" is in practice often somewhat different from that held in England.
[3] See *Re Fuld (No. 3)* [1968] P. 675, and *Re Flynn* [1968] 1 W.L.R. 103: reviewing numerous authorities; the decision tends to turn on the facts of the particular case.
[4] *Phillipston-Stow v. I.R.C.* [1961] A.C. 727; thus the acquisition of a domicile in England enlarged the deceased's capacity from that of making a will of one-fourth of her estate to that of making a will of her entire estate: *Re Groos* [1915] 1 Ch. 572.
[5] *Freke v. Carberry* (1873) 16 Eq. 461; *Duncan v. Lawson* (1889) 41 Ch.Div. 394; *Re Moses* [1908] 2 Ch. 235 (life-tenant entitled to the rights over a long leasehold conferred by the law of the site, being the Transvaal).
[6] *Re Berchtold* [1923] 1 Ch. 192. Investments held as land under the S.L.A. 1925 have even been held to devolve in England by statute as land: *Re Cutcliffe* [1940] Ch. 565;

—cont. on next page

whether they are in the United Kingdom or are elsewhere. Movable property means anything that is not classified as immovable.

Continental countries may however apply the law of the deceased's nationality to devolution on death, and may reserve portions of a deceased person's assets that are incapable of being given by will.

At first instance in England, the "law" of a foreign country means the law that would be applied there, to the actual case.[7]

11–03 Practical consequences of the distinction between immovable and movable property and methods of avoiding those consequences. This approach of English law can produce unexpected results.[8] English company law provides a simple means of avoiding, as far as the law of England is concerned, the application of the law of the site to the devolution of immovables at death. Someone domiciled in England, who wishes to avoid the compulsory devolution at death of immovables under the law of their site, therefore vests the immovable property (such as a holiday home on the Continent) in a limited company registered in England, or in a third country, of which he holds 99 per cent of the shares.[9] At his death, English law then treats the *shares* as devolving under the law of the domicile as movables, not under the law of the place where the company's own property is situated.[10]

—*cont. from previous page*

so have the rights of a mortgagee: *Re Hoyles* [1911] 1 Ch. 179, and a right to a rentcharge: *Chatfield v. Berchtoldt* (1872) 7 Ch.App. 192. The question whether for this purpose, an uncompleted contract of sale of land, or of an option over land, creates rights that are movable or that are immovable does not appear to have been decided; their effect for other purposes is stated in Jarman, *Wills* (8th ed.), at pp. 739–742.

[7] *Re Annesley* [1926] Ch. 692; where the French courts would apply French domestic law, and so that was applied in England; *Re Ross* [1930] 1 Ch. 377, where the Italian courts would apply the law of England, being that of the deceased's nationality, to the devolution of Italian immovable property and so the law of England was applicable here ("*renvoi*"). This is the reconciliation of those two cases: *Re Adam* [1967] Ir. 424, Budd J. at p. 456. To the same effect, *Re Wellington* [1947] Ch. 506 at pp. 513–514; there was no appeal on this point: [1948] Ch. 118. The doctrine of *renvoi* is open to review in the Court of Appeal: see Dicey & Morris, *The Conflict of Laws* (11th ed.), at pp. 74–91.

[8] Where there was a total intestacy, the widow of the intestate was held entitled to the statutory legacy under A.E.A. 1925 out of immovable property in England, without being put to her election, although she had taken $1m in the estate in Trinidad: *Re Collens* [1986] Ch. 505.

[9] Shares in a limited company are situated at the place where a company is incorporated: *New York Life Assurance Co. v. Public Trustees* [1924] 2 Ch. 101, approved *Kwok v. Estate Duty Commissioner* [1988] 1 W.L.R. 1035, P.C.; a shareholder in a company holds his shares, but not the company's assets: *Salomon v. Salomon & Co.* [1897] A.C. 22; and *Rayner v. Department of Trade* [1990] 2 A.C. 418 at p. 515.

[10] The effectiveness of this scheme in practice depends, however, on the view taken by the law of the place where the immovable property is situated. Even in England, the court will sometimes look through the shareholding to the ownership behind it; as in *Jones v. Lipman* [1962] 1 W.L.R. 832, where the company was (p. 836) "the creature of the first defendant, a device and a sham, a mask which he holds before

11–04 Ascertaining foreign law. Whenever a foreign element is involved, the personal representatives in England should obtain advice about the relevant foreign law before distributing the estate. Those who know the law of most continental countries, and of many other countries can generally be found in London; or if necessary in the relevant country. The directions of the court in England are often necessary to protect the personal representatives.

The law elsewhere is not always certain; thus (an extreme example), after the death of the sixth Duke of Wellington who was also a duke in Spain in circumstances in which the two dukedoms devolved on different persons, a judge in England said that he was faced with the task:

> "of expounding for the first time either in this country or in Spain the relevant law of Spain as it would be expounded by the Supreme Court of Spain, which up to the present time has made no pronouncement on the subject, and having to base that exposition on evidence which satisfies me that on this subject there exists a profound cleavage of legal opinion in Spain, and two conflicting decisions of courts of inferior jurisdiction."[11]

The problem is to some extent diminished in England by the admissibility of other decisions in English courts about what is the law of a foreign country.[12]

---

his face in an attempt to avoid recognition by the eye of equity." The extent of this exception to company law is not settled: see Palmer's *Company Law* (25th ed.), paras. 72·1519–1522.

[11] Wynn-Parry J. in *Re Wellington* [1947] Ch. 506 at p. 515; there was no appeal on this finding: [1948] Ch. 118.

[12] Civil Evidence Act 1972, s.4.

Part Two: Wills and Intestacies

12. Capacity to make a will; power to make a will

12–01 Capacity. A will can be made, or revoked, only by a testator who has capacity: that is to say when he is of sound mind, memory and understanding.[1] In the absence of capacity, a will may be entirely invalid; or only those parts affected by the testator's incapacity may be invalid.[2] In practice the outcome depends on the

---

[1] Mortimer, *Probate* (2nd ed.), pp. 40–65; Jarman, *Wills* (8th ed.), pp. 50–55; Tristram & Coote, pp. 643–645. A will made for a patient by the Court of Protection (see para. 12–19) is an exception.
[2] *Re Bohrmann* [1938] 1 All E.R. 271.

facts of each case, viewed in the light of current medical knowledge[3]; the numerous reported cases[4] turn on their own facts.

12–02 Standard of proof. The standard of proof in a court in England, on capacity and on the other requirements of a valid will, is that of English law, even when the deceased was domiciled elsewhere.[5]

12–03 Instructions to prepare a will given by a testator of full capacity followed by its execution when of diminished capacity. A testator who has given instructions for his will to a solicitor when of full capacity, may afterwards, with diminished capacity validly execute a will drawn in accordance with those instructions if aware he had given instructions for his will and that he is executing such a will.[6] This principle may need to be applied when making a will is postponed until the last illness. Where, however, instructions are transmitted to a solicitor through a lay intermediary, this principle should be applied "with the greatest caution and reserve" on account of "the opportunities for error in transmission and of misunderstanding and deception."[7]

POWER TO MAKE A WILL

12–04 Power of will-making as to property. The law of England and Wales authorises a person (a "testator") to dispose of all his property at death by will[8]; including property acquired after the date of the will[9]; and even property of which he is tenant-in-tail in possession.[10] The requirements of the law of England and Wales for a duly executed will in writing to be admitted to probate were summarised as follows[11]:

> " 1. An instrument cannot be a 'provable will' (by which expression I mean the type of instrument which will be admitted

---

[3] See *Re Bohrmann* at p. 279.

[4] Collected in the books cited in n. 1.

[5] *Re Fuld (No. 3)* [1968] P. 675.

[6] *Parker v. Parker* (1883) 8 P.D. 171; where it is reported that the deceased was roused from a coma to execute the will; *Perera v. Perera* [1901] A.C. 354.

[7] *Singh v. Amirchand* [1948] A.C. 161 at p. 169; where the Privy Council refused to apply the principle.

[8] Wills Act 1837, s.3. A blind person may make a will: *Fincham v. Edwards* (1842) 4 Moo.P.C. 198.

[9] s.24.

[10] L.P.A. 1925, s.176. Entails are infrequent, and are associated with landed estates and hereditary titles.

[11] Mustill L.J. in *Re Berger* [1990] Ch. 118 at pp. 129–130 referring to previous authorities. (The case concerned a *zavah*, that is to say a will of someone with a domicile in England executed with two witnesses under Jewish religious law; rather strangely, see p.126 at "I" no evidence was given about Jewish religious law).

to probate in the English courts) unless it contains a revocable ambulatory disposition of the maker's property which is to take effect on death.

2. An instrument cannot be a 'provable will' unless the maker had an *'animus testandi.'*

3. This expression does not mean that a document cannot be a 'provable will' unless the maker has addressed his mind to the question whether the instrument will be capable of admission to probate in the English court, and wishes that it shall be so. Rather, it conveys only that the maker must intend that his document shall effect the kind of disposition referred to under item 1, above.

4. Thus, it is possible to make a 'provable will', whatever its form or appearance or mode of expression and irrespective of the language in which it is written, so long as it combines the requirements above-mentioned, the necessary intention, and execution as required by the Act (if the circumstances are such as to require execution).

5. If the document has the necessary dispositive effect, and is duly executed, the necessary animus will be presumed. This presumption is however rebuttable, either by other terms of the document itself, such as the statement that the document is intended for guidance only, or be strong extrinsic evidence.

These propositions, if correct, will serve to illuminate the source of the present problem, for they distinguish between the (necessary) intention to make a revocable disposition which is to operate on death and the (unnecessary) intention to make a "provable will." At first they seem to disclose a contradiction. Imagine a document headed with the words, "This is not a will and is not intended to be admitted to probate." To hold that it could nevertheless be proved would seem to be not only absurd, and an unjustifiable thwarting of the testator's intentions, but would also contravene the rule that internal evidence can negative animus; and yet, the conclusion would seem to be justified by the distinction between animus testandi and the desire to make a "provable will." In my judgment there is no true contradiction here, for the heading would show that the maker did not intend the document to be enforced by the probate court; and in the absence of any other mode of enforcement he would thereby have demonstrated that he did not wish his dispositions to be enforced at all: and thus took away one of the essential characteristics of a will."

On this principle, a deed executed before two witnesses and intended to operate at death was admitted to probate.[12] This absolute right of

---

[12] *Re Slinn* (1890) 15 P.D. 156; and see *Milnes v. Foden, ibid.* 105.

testamentary disposition is restricted by the right, both when there is a will and when there is an intestacy, of dependants to apply after the death for an award of maintenance.[13] A successful application makes the applicant a beneficiary in the estate.[14] This situation is quite different from that in continental countries which restrict the power of disposition at death.[15] Practical difficulties, not discussed here, arise at the first death when two (or more) living persons have unwisely executed the same will: it is unusual.

12–05 Power of will making as to guardianship. A parent or a guardian, of a child aged under 18 years with parental responsibility[16] for that child, has power to appoint another individual to be that child's guardian in the event of the appointor's death.[17] The appointment must be in writing and dated and signed by the appointor, or be by will. This appointment may be revoked,[18] by another writing signed and dated, or by the destruction or revocation of the instrument or of the will that made the appointment. On a death on or after January 1, 1996, the appointment of the appointor's husband or wife as a guardian is revoked by a decree of dissolution or nullity (regardless of the date of the appointment or of the decree), unless the appointment shows a contrary intention.[19] The disclaimer of such an appointment by the guardian and the court's jurisdiction about guardianship are outside the scope of this book. The existence of this important power to provide for a child's future welfare should never be overlooked when a will is being made, by a widowed parent, or by two parents who might be involved together in one fatal accident.

12–06 Age. The minimum age to make a will is now 18 years.[20] The exception for military personnel[21] still applies to those aged 17 years.

12–07 Requirements for execution of a will. Whether a will was made before or after January 1, 1983, on a death on or after January 1, 1983, the formalities required for the due execution of a will or

---

[13] Under the Inheritance (Provision for Family and Dependants) Act 1975. Such applications are frequently made and often compromised; and are outside the scope of this book. See para. 17–06.

[14] *Re Jennery* [1967] Ch. 280.

[15] See Pugh, *The Administration of Foreign Estates. Passim.*

[16] Under the Children Act 1989, s.2, s.3 and s.4.

[17] Children Act 1989, s.5.

[18] s.6.

[19] Law Reform (Succession) Act 1995, s.4; for the recognition of overseas decrees, see para. 27–07 below.

[20] Wills Act 1837, s.7 as amended by the Family Law Reform Act 1969, s.2. A will made before January 1, 1970, when that Act came into force, by someone aged between 18 and 21 years remains invalid under s.7 as originally enacted; unless valid as a military will.

[21] See paras. 12–12 and 12–13.

codicil are governed by the Wills Act 1837, s.9 as substituted by the Administration of Justice Act 1982, s.17; as follows:

> **"Signing and attestation of wills**
>   **9.** No will shall be valid unless—
>   (a) it is in writing, and signed by the testator, or by some other person in his presence and by his direction; and
>   (b) it appears that the testator intended by his signature to give effect to the will; and
>   (c) the signature is made or acknowledged by the testator in the presence of two or more witnesses present at the same time; and
>   (d) each witness either—
>   (i) attests and signs the will; or
>   (ii) acknowledges his signature,
>   in the presence of the testator (but not necessarily in the presence of any other witness),
>   but no form of attestation shall be necessary."

Decisions on the previous version of section 9 are authority where the words are the same.

(a) "signed by the testator."

There is an effective signature when the testator's hand is guided[22]; and when too weak to write all his surname.[23] The testator may validly sign a will by making his mark[24]; or thumb print[25]; or using a stamp bearing his name or initials[26]; or by initialling it[27]; or writing some other words of identification, such as "your loving mother."[28]

The testator's name written by him at the top of a hand-written will does not necessarily satisfy section 9(b); but though it is not a normal signature, it is capable of satisfying section 9 when there is affirmative

---

[22] *Wilson v. Beddard* (1841) 12 Sim. 28; *Fulton v. Kee* [1961] N.I. 1.
[23] *Re Chalcraft* [1948] P. 222, where "E.Chal" was held a sufficient signature. As regards the signature of a witness, it was held that writing the words "servant to Mr Sperling" sufficed as attestation: *Re Sperling* (1863) 3 Sw. & T. 272; but writing "Saml," without the witness's surname, was an insufficient signature: *Re Maddock* (1874) 3 P. & D. 169; distinguished in *Re Chalcraft* at p. 223 on the basis that the surname is required. Another distinction might be that the testator's name is to be found in the will and so need not be written (see the cases in the next three notes); but it is essential to have witnesses properly identified by their surnames. There is no reported case, on the lines of *Re Maddock*, about a will attested by a member of the Royal Family, accustomed to sign without a surname.
[24] *Re Field* (1837) 3 Curt. 752; *Baker v. Dening* (1838) 8 Ad. & El. 94; *Re Holtam* (1913) 108 L.T. 732.
[25] *Re Finn* (1935) 154 L.T. 242.
[26] *Jenkins v. Gaisford* (1863) 3 Sw. & T. 93; *Re Bulloch* [1968] N.I. 96.
[27] *Re Blewitt* (1879) 5 P.D. 116.
[28] *Re Cook* [1960] 1 W.L.R. 353.

evidence to show that the testator intended to validate the will by writing his name at the outset before the dispositive parts of the will; that was shown by his writing his name at the outset in a single operation and his oral acknowledgment to the witnesses that it was his intended signature of his will; the will in question was however anyhow held invalid for lack of capacity.[29]

"or by some other person in his presence and by his direction."

This is an alternative method of validating a guided signature.[30] The person so directed may sign his own name[31]; or the testator's name. Some evidence is needed of such a direction being given.[32]

"(b) it appears that the testator intended by his signature to give effect to the will."

The signature to the will ordinarily demonstrates such an intention. This new sub-paragraph may avoid the difficulties[33] that arose under the 1837 version of section 9 about signature on an envelope.

"(c) the signature is made or acknowledged by the testator in the presence of two or more witnesses present at the same time."

The testator's pre-existing signature may be acknowledged expressly, or by implication from the circumstances[34]; but the testator's signature must be visible when it is acknowledged.[35] What amounts to actual "presence" is in each case a question of fact, both under this sub-paragraph and under sub-paragraph (d).[36]

"(d) each witness either (i) attests and signs the will or (ii) acknowledges his signature in the presence of the testator (but not necessarily in the presence of the other witness)".

---

[29] *Wood v. Smith* [1993] Ch. 90, reversing the decision at first instance also reported there; *Wetherall v. Pearce* [1995] 1 W.L.R. 592.

[30] See n. 2.

[31] *Re Clark* (1839) 2 Curt. 329; where Mr Fulton signed his own name, not that of the testator Mr. Clark.

[32] *Re Marshall* (1866) 13 L.T. 643.

[33] See *Re Beadle* [1974] 1 W.L.R. 417.

[34] *Daintree v. Butcher and Fasulo* (1888) 13 P.D. 102.

[35] *Blake v. Blake* (1882) 7 P.D. 102; *Re Groffman* [1969] 1 W.L.R. 733.

[36] There was no such "presence" in the following cases: attestation 20 minutes after the testator's signature, made in an adjoining room with the door open: *Jenner v. Ffinch* (1879) 5 P.D. 106; attestation by one witness in a shop out of sight: *Brown v. Skirrow* [1902] P. 3; a nurse who was a witness went to another part of a hospital ward to attend to a patient while the testator was writing his signature: *Re Colling* [1972] 1 W.L.R. 1440.

The same principles apply as to "presence." A witness may attest the execution of a will by making his mark[37]; or by signing with his hand being guided.[38] A witness may even attest a will by himself using a rubber stamp bearing his name[39]; but not by someone else, even his wife, using the rubber stamp for him in his presence.[40] The frailty of subsequent evidence makes the use of a rubber stamp instead of a manuscript signature hazardous.

12–08 Blindness. A blind person is not a competent witness to a will[41]; though a competent testator.[42]

12–09 A minor as an attesting witness to a will. Langton J. granted probate in solemn form of a will when one of the attesting witnesses was aged 16 years at the time, and was not available to be called as a witness at the trial[43]; but the reports of the case rather suggest that this point was not argued on behalf of the defendants; it was moreover "an unusual case in every way"[44] The Wills Act 1837, s.14 was not treated as relevant to this question; it probably refers to the common law disabilities to give evidence, no longer in force.

The attestation of a testamentary document by two minors, or by a minor and an adult, is however not a protection to those interested under an intestacy or under a previous will. The solemn act of validating another person's will by attesting its due execution is not at all the same juridically as the capacity of a minor to give evidence about events a minor has seen[45]; nor is it the same as the capacity to incur personal liability at common law.[46] As a minor has no capacity to make a will (paras. 12–06), a minor might also lack the legal capacity required to validate another person's will. The decision of Langton J. should, it is submitted, not be followed; it contrasts with the approach of Pearce J. to attestation by a blind witness.[47]

12–10 Attestation of a will by a witness with mental incapacity. There appears to be no satisfactory authority about a will attested by a witness or by witnesses with mental incapacity. It is submitted that if a will is attested by such a person, its validity should

---

[37] *Clarke v. Clarke* (1879) 5 L.R.Ir. 407.
[38] *Bell v. Hughes* (1880) 5 L.R.Ir. 407.
[39] *Re Bulloch* [1968] N.I. 96.
[40] *Re Bulloch.*
[41] *Re Gibson* [1949] P. 434.
[42] *Edwards v. Fincham* (1842) 4 Moo.P.C. 198.
[43] *Smith v. Thompson* (1931) 146 L.T. 14 and 47 T.L.R. 603; both reports of this case need to be read.
[44] *Lowthorpe-Lutwidge v. Lowthorpe-Lutwidge* [1935] P. 151 at p. 155, also Langton J.
[45] Phipson, *Evidence* (14th ed.), para. 9–09.
[46] Chitty, *Contracts* (27th ed.), para. 8–066.
[47] *Re Gibson*, above; where *Smith v. Thompson* was not cited. The lack of capacity caused by blindness and the lack of capacity caused by infancy are not the same; but perhaps they resemble each other.

be held to depend on whether or not the attesting witness could understand what he or she was doing.[48]

12–11 Surrounding circumstances. When determining the validity of the execution of a will, regard is had to all the surrounding circumstances[49]; including the presumption of due execution.

12–12 Presumption of due execution. Making a will is a solemn act. After the death, the court owes a duty not only to the litigants but also to the deceased to see his last wishes carried out.[50] Accordingly a document that on its face appears to be a duly executed will is presumed to be validly executed unless the contrary is proved.[51] This was presumed in cases where: what appeared to be a duly executed will was admitted to probate where the witnesses could not remember signing it[52]; where the witnesses deposed that the will was not duly attested, but were disbelieved[53]; where the witnesses were found to be unreliable.[54] The presumption has even been applied disregarding the affidavit evidence of at any rate one of the testamentary witnesses when neither was called to give oral evidence.[55]

A copy will with a regular attestation clause was admitted to probate when the original will had been destroyed by enemy action and the only surviving witness could not remember the occasion.[56] Due execution was even presumed when there was no attestation clause, but two signatures of persons who were dead[57]; and where there was no attestation clause but two signatures on the back of the will, due attestation was presumed.[58]

12–13 When the presumption is not applied. Looking at the surrounding circumstances as a whole, the presumption is not applied when the circumstances indicate that the will was not duly executed.[59]

---

[48] Compare the test for the validity of a contract made by a mentally disordered person: Chitty, *Contracts* (27th ed.), paras. 8–064 to 8–067.

[49] *Re Strong* [1915] P. 211.

[50] Tristram & Coote (14th ed.) (1906), the last in Dr Tristram's lifetime, at p. 443; (27th ed.), at p. 665.

[51] *Harris v. Knight* (1890) 15 P.D. 170; there does not appear to be a Commonwealth decision on this point.

[52] *Woodhouse v. Balfour* (1887) 13 P.D. 170.

[53] *Dayman v. Dayman* (1895) 71 L.T. 699.

[54] *Neal v. Denston* (1932) 147 L.T. 460; *Re McClean* [1950] Ir. 180.

[55] *Wetherall v. Pearce* [1995] 1 W.L.R. 592: *Neal v. Deanston* was cited in argument, but not in the judgment; *Dayman v. Dayman* and *Re McClean* were not cited. This decision takes the presumption in favour of due execution rather beyond what has previously been understood; and might not be followed.

[56] *Re Webb* [1964] 1 W.L.R. 509.

[57] *Re Peverett* [1902] P. 205.

[58] *Re Denning* [1958] 1 W.L.R. 462.

[59] *Re Strong* above.

For example, when it was not the relevant signature of the testator on the will, but another signature, that the witnesses attested.[60] The presumption of due execution is less readily applied to a will that is in form unusual or irregular.[61]

12–14 Inadmissible evidence about execution. The formalities for execution of a will are imposed by statute on the testator. Accordingly the testator's own subsequent declarations are not to be admitted in evidence to establish that he complied with the formalities.[62] The testator's own contemporary declaration, made in a letter, is admissible in support of the presumption of due execution.[63]

MILITARY WILLS

12–15 Formalities not required for military wills. A member of the armed forces of the Crown on actual military service and any mariner or seaman at sea may validly make a will without observing any formalities.[64] Such a will may be oral[65]; or in writing, as in an unattested letter.[66] It may validly be made while the testator is a minor[67]; when majority was at the age of 21, instead of 18 as now,[68] minors on military service often made wills. The capacity to make a will without formalities applies to each sex.[69]

12–16 Actual military service. The expression "actual military service" means *active* military service, and its existence is a question of fact in each case.[70] A member of the Home Guard may be on active military service.[71] The current situation in Northern Ireland may constitute actual military service.[72] The same principles apply to seamen; thus a minor who was a seaman on leave on shore was held not to be "at sea."[73]

---

[60] *Re Bercovitz* [1962] 1 W.L.R. 321.
[61] *Re Bercovitz* above.
[62] *Atkinson v. Morris* [1897] P. 40; *Barkwell v. Barkwell* [1928] P. 91.
[63] *Re Gilliard* [1940] N.I. 125.
[64] Wills Act 1837, s.11; The Wills (Soldiers and Sailors) Act 1918. This includes power to appoint a testamentary guardian: the 1918 Act, s.4.
[65] *Re Jones* [1981] Fam. 7.
[66] *Re Booth* [1926] P. 118; *Re Heywood* [1916] P. 47 where part of a testamentary letter was omitted from probate on the grounds of military security.
[67] Wills (Soldiers and Sailors) Act 1918, s.1.
[68] Until January 1, 1970, under the Family Law Reform Act 1969, s.3.
[69] *Re Rowson* [1944] 2 All E.R. 36, W.A.A.F.; *Re Wingham* [1949] P. 187.
[70] *Re Wingham* [1949] P. 187; restating the law under the Acts and overruling previous decisions; at p. 196 there is a useful summary by Denning L.J. of who is and who is not on actual military service.
[71] *Blyth v. L.A.* [1945] A.C. 32, on the same question as regards estate duty; *Re Wingham* above.
[72] *Re Jones* above.
[73] *Re Rapley* [1983] 1 W.L.R. 1069.

12–17 Limit on the power to make a military will. The result of the A.E.A. 1925, s.51(3) seems to be to deprive an unmarried infant of the power to make a military will of land to which he was entitled under a "settlement."[74]

12–18 Duration of a military will. Once made, a military will continues in force like any other will unless revoked.[75] Such a will can only be revoked (after the end of the military service) in the same way as any other will can be revoked, not informally. Thus a military will made on active service in Egypt in 1882 took effect at the testator's death aged 81 years in 1924.[76] The rule of Roman law restricting the operation of a soldier's will to one year after his discharge was held not to be part of the law of England; although the testator regarded himself as intestate.[77] Long-forgotten military wills, made in quite different circumstances, sometimes have to be admitted to probate; the adoption by statute of the rule of Roman law would improve the law of England.

12–19 Will of a mental patient. There is a statutory power, often exercised, for the Court of Protection to make a will for a mental patient.[78] This enables the court to make for a patient a will that he would have made if lucid. When exercising the power, "the patient is to be envisaged as taking a broad brush to the claims on his bounty, rather than an accountant's pen."[79]

12–20 Execution for the purposes of English law, under external law. A will of someone dying after January 1, 1964, may (whenever the will was made) in England be treated as duly executed if its execution conformed to the relevant external law. It is treated as properly executed under the Wills Act 1963, s.1:

> "A will shall be treated as properly executed if its execution conformed to the internal law in force in the territory where it was executed, or in the territory where, at the time of its execution or of the testator's death, he was domiciled or had his habitual residence, or in a state of which, at either of those times, he was a national."

---

[74] Defined in s.55(1)(xxiv); see Mortimer, *Probate* (2nd ed.), at p. 257; and Shebbeare on the A.E.A. 1925 at p. 40.
[75] *Re Booth* above; *Re Coleman* above.
[76] *Re Booth* above.
[77] See *Re Booth* at p. 121.
[78] Mental Health Act 1983, s.96(1)(e) and (4); and s.97.
[79] *Re D. (J.)* [1982] Ch. 237 at p. 244; the leading case on the principles to be followed when the power is exercised.

Under section 2, a will of immovable property is well executed if conforming to the internal law of the territory where the property was situated; similar provisions apply to revocation of wills. Provision is made for wills exercising a power of appointment, and for wills made on board ship or on an aircraft.

The 1963 Act may apply to a complete document, when evidence of the external law has to be provided for the district judge[80]; it may also apply when an unattested addition is made to an existing English will.

12–21 International wills. An international will may be made in England before a solicitor or a notary public, under statutory provisions.[81] An international will is well executed in every country that has adopted the uniform law on the form of an international will.[82] This provision seems likely to be useful for those with assets in other countries with similar provisions; or those who, while out of England, wish to make a will valid in England. It is difficult to ascertain from English law sources what other countries have adopted the convention.[83] Inquiry should be made of a lawyer familiar with the law of the relevant country; or of its consulate here.

12–22 Documents incorporated in a will. A testator may and sometimes does incorporate another document into his will. A document so incorporated into a will becomes part of the will and the document or a copy of it may be admitted to probate[84]; unless it is too bulky, when other arrangements are made for its safe preservation.[85] A document that is legally in force, such as an executed settlement, need not be admitted to Probate.[86] An incorporated document operates as if it had been written into the will as part of the will, operating at the death.[87]

The incorporation of a written document into a will is not to be confused with the imposition by a secret trust on a legatee or devisee of an obligation on the donee, whether or not mentioned in the will.[88]

A document can only be incorporated in the will, when it is in existence at the date of the will and is identified as existing in the

---

[80] N.C.P.R. 1987, r. 19.
[81] Under A.J.A. 1982, ss.27 and 28 and Sched. 2.
[82] A convention signed in Washington, U.S.A. on October 26, 1973; the text is printed as Sched. 2 to A.J.A. 1982. The Convention itself was published as 1975 Cmd. 5950; it was signed by nine countries (one not recognised by the U.K.); 42 other countries were represented, and eight others sent observers.
[83] There appears to be no available published list of them.
[84] *Re Mardon* [1944] P. 109, as to the Schedule, see rule 14(3).
[85] *Re Balme* [1897] P. 261, library catalogue.
[86] *Re Edwards* [1948] Ch. 440 at p. 446; *Bizzey v. Flight* (1876) 3 Ch.Div. 269.
[87] *Re Edwards* [1948] Ch. 440.
[88] See Snell, *Equity* at pp.108–113.

will, not merely by extraneous evidence.[89] This is part of the requirement that no one may reserve a power to make a future unattested testamentary document, not complying with the Wills Act 1837.[90]

Accordingly the effect of a codicil confirming a will that speaks of documents depends on the language of the will. When the will speaks of existing identifiable documents, a codicil confirming the will incorporates documents brought into existence between the date of the will and of the codicil.[91] When, however, the will speaks of future documents, a codicil confirming it cannot incorporate a document brought into existence between the date of the will and the date of the codicil.[92] A codicil may however be formulated so as itself to incorporate specified documents.[93]

A result of these rules was that where a codicil duly incorporated entries in the testator's accounts, those entries made before the date of the codicil were incorporated, and those made after its date were not.[94]

Incorporation is avoided by an express declaration in the will against incorporation.[95]

12–23 Power to make a conditional will. A will may validly be made to take effect only on a condition expressed in the will.[96] It has even been held that a will may validly be made subject to a condition not appearing on the face of the will, but established by extrinsic evidence.[97] This decision was based on *Halsbury*[98] and a *dictum* in 1830 cited there; it did not follow *Mortimer* (2nd ed., 1927), at page 248[99]; and did not refer to the statutory requirement under the Wills Act 1837 for a will to be in writing.[1] It was plainly fair on that case; but in other circumstances might open the way for a false claim. For a conditional revocation, to which different considerations apply, see para. 14–18.

---

[89] *Singleton v. Tomlinson* (1878) 3 A.C. 404; *Re Sutherland* (1866) L.R. 1 P. & D. 198; *University College of North Wales v. Taylor* [1908] P. 140; *Re Smart* [1902] P. 238. The decision *Re Saxton* [1939] 2 All E.R. 418 seems to have turned on its own facts and not to lay down a general principle; it is difficult to reconcile with the cases cited above.

[90] *Re Keen* [1937] Ch. 236; *Re Jones* [1942] Ch. 328.

[91] *Re Truro* (1866) L.R. 1 P. & D. 201; *Re Deprez* [1917] 1 Ch. 24.

[92] *Durham v. Northern* [1895] P. 66; *Re Smart* above.

[93] *Re Deprez* [1917] 1 Ch. 24.

[94] *Re Deprez* above.

[95] *Re Louis* (1916) 32 T.L.R. 313.

[96] Mortimer, *Probate* (2nd ed.), p.248.

[97] *Corbett v. Newey* [1994] Ch. 388.

[98] 4th ed., vol. 5, para. 250, citing *King's Proctor v. Daines* 3 Hag. Ecc. 218 at p. 219.

[99] See [1994] Ch. at p. 397.

[1] s.9.

13. Circumstances invalidating a will

13–01 Grounds to oppose a will or codicil: the influence of the 1862 Rules

13–02 Lack of knowledge and approval: suspicious circumstances

13–03 "Undue influence": coercion

13–04 Choice of claim of suspicious circumstances or of coercion

13–05 Forgery and fraud

13–06 Due execution and capacity

13–01 Grounds to oppose a will or codicil: the influence of the 1862 Rules. The question whether and to what extent a valid will had been made was largely governed by the Contentious Probate Rules 1862 amended in 1865 for a century, until those Rules were repealed from January 1, 1964. The Contentious Probate Rules 1862 continue to affect the way that a question about the validity of a will is formulated. Under Rule 40A there, only five pleas against a will or codicil were permitted, except by leave of a judge. Those five grounds remain the basis of probate practice and pleading; although it is convenient nowadays to consider those grounds in a different order.

The five grounds formulated in the 1862 Rules were (in summary) as follows:

(1) The will or codicil was not duly executed;

(2) The deceased was not of sound mind memory and understanding;

(3) The execution of the will or codicil was obtained by undue influence;

(4) The execution of the will or codicil was obtained by fraud;

(5) The deceased did not know and approve the contents of the will or codicil.

To these, there are to be added a plea that the will or codicil was revoked; or a plea that the document in question is a forgery.

13–02 Lack of knowledge and approval: suspicious circumstances. The existence of suspicious circumstances casts on whoever propounds a will, the burden of removing that suspicion:

> "It is not the law that in no circumstances can a solicitor or other person who has prepared a will for a testator take a benefit under it. But that fact creates a suspicion that must be removed by the person propounding the will. In all cases the court must be vigilant and jealous. The degree of suspicion will vary with the circumstances of the case. It may be slight and easily dispelled. It may, on the other hand, be so grave that it can hardly be removed."[1]

This is a rule of evidence; it "calls upon the court not to grant probate without full and entire satisfaction that the instrument did express the real intentions of the deceased."[2] The rule is not restricted to cases where the will was drawn by someone benefiting from it; the "court's vigilance is called for whenever circumstances reasonably excite suspicion."[3]

This principle is invoked under the formula that the deceased "did not know and approve" the document.

13–03 "Undue influence": coercion. A will made under coercion is invalid. Coercion is, in probate matters, alleged under the formula that the will was made under "undue influence," meaning coercion, and nothing short of coercion.[4] This formula is not to be confused with the somewhat different meaning of the phrase undue influence in connection with trusts,[5] or contracts.[6] The distinction makes it less difficult to set aside a gift between living persons for undue influence in equity than to impugn a will for undue influence. This distinction is fair. A gift may deprive the donor of property that the donor might

---

[1] *Wintle v. Nye* [1959] 1 W.L.R. 284 at p. 291; reversing, in the House of Lords, a verdict upheld in the Court of Appeal in favour of a will in the solicitor's own favour, drawn by that solicitor. It looks from the reports of *Wintle v. Nye* as if *Tyrell v. Painton* was not cited in *Wintle v. Nye*. The case in the House of Lords (Lincoln's Inn Library 1958 Volume 7) shows however that *Tyrell v. Painton* was mentioned in the summing up (page 189 there) as mentioned by the plaintiff's counsel (one of whom was Mr Scarman), and in the dissenting judgment in the Court of Appeal of Sellers L.J. (page 247 there). So the decision *Tyrell v. Painton* was before the House of Lords in *Wintle v. Nye*.
[2] *Re Fuld (No. 3)* [1968] P. 675 at pp. 698–699.
[3] *Tyrell v. Painton* [1894] P. 202; *Re Fuld (No. 3)* above at p. 712, citing an incorrect reference for *Tyrell v. Painton*. The decision *Re R.* [1951] P. 10 is on pleading, as is shown by it not being cited in *Wintle v. Nye* nor in *Re Fuld (No. 3)*: see *Re Stott* [1980] 1 W.L.R. 246.
[4] *Hall v. Hall* (1868) 1 P. & D. 481; *Wingrove v. Wingrove* (1895) 11 P.D. 81; this remains the law nowadays: *Re Stott* [1980] 1 W.L.R. 246.
[5] *Re Pauling* [1964] P. 303.
[6] *National Westminster Bank v. Morgan* [1985] A.C. 686.

have enjoyed; but a will can operate only on what the deceased can no longer enjoy.

13–04 Choice of claim of suspicious circumstances or of coercion. It is open to a litigant to allege suspicious circumstances ("lack of knowledge and approval") without also alleging coercion ("undue influence").[7] Coercion should never be alleged without proper grounds[8]; and it ought not to be alleged as frequently as it was in the past.[9] An unsuccessful allegation of undue influence may impose a liability for costs that would not have been imposed had the allegation on the same facts only been of lack of knowledge and approval.[10]

13–05 Forgery and fraud. A forgery is not a will and can be pronounced against. A testamentary document executed under fraud, for example a will executed under false representations to the testator,[11] can also be pronounced against.

13–06 Due execution and capacity. See Chapter 12.

---

[7] *Re Stott* above; construing R.S.C., Ord. 76, r. 9(3) and treating *Re R.* above as a decision to the same effect.

[8] *Re Stott* above at p. 251H; *Spiers v. English* [1907] P.122 at p.124.

[9] Now that *Wintle v. Nye* has been decided: *Re Fuld (No. 3)* above at p. 722F–G.

[10] *Re Cutcliffe's Estate* [1959] P. 6; *Re Fuld (No. 3)* above.

[11] *Riding v. Hawkins* (1889) 14 P.D. 56.

14. Revocation and variation of wills by the testator or by acts of the testator in his lifetime

14–01 No presumption[1] of revocation. A will is not revoked by presumed intention nor by a change of circumstances.[2] A will is not

---

[1] Except the presumption from the absence of the will itself: see para. 15–03 below.
[2] Wills Act 1837, s.19.

83

revoked either, by a conveyance, so that when part of property is conveyed away, or an interest is created out of property, the will remains effective in respect of what the testator has power to dispose of at his death.[3]

14–02 Revocation of a will by marriage: definition of "marriage." Most marriages present no problem; but three types of ceremony need to be considered: void marriages, voidable marriages, and polygamous marriages.

Void "marriages." For a marriage to revoke a will, there must be a valid marriage.[4] "Marriage" for this purpose means a marriage valid in the view of English law; a void marriage ceremony does not revoke a will.[5] A void marriage[6] is a nullity and only an idle ceremony that achieves no change in the status of the participants and achieves nothing of substance.[7]

Voidable marriages. A voidable marriage[8] however is a marriage and it operates as a marriage to revoke a will, whether the voidable marriage is afterwards avoided or not.[9]

Application of this distinction to overseas marriages. This distinction for the purposes of succession in England and Wales between a void marriage and a voidable marriage is likely to raise difficulty when there has been a decree of nullity recognised in England,[10] in a country that does not have this distinction between void and voidable marriages; or that has the distinction but draws a different line between the two classes.[11]

Polygamous marriages. For the purposes of succession, English law recognises a polygamous marriage solemnised abroad, if it is valid according to English law[12]; it follows that such a second valid polygamous marriage can revoke a will under the law of England.[13]

---

[3] s.23.
[4] Wills Act 1837, s.18, as originally enacted and as amended.
[5] *Mette v. Mette* (1859) 1 Sw. & T. 416: where a marriage abroad to the testator's half-sister was held to be no marriage for the purposes of English law; and so did not revoke his will, even though celebrated at a place where it was lawful. *Warter v. Warter* (1890) 15 P.D. 152; where a remarriage within six months after a divorce in India, in breach of the Indian Divorce Act prohibiting remarriage within that period, was not a marriage; and a subsequent marriage between the same two persons was valid and therefore revoked the testator's will, made in the intervening period.
[6] Defined in the Matrimonial Causes Act 1973, s.11.
[7] *Re Spence* [1990] Ch. 652 at p. 661.
[8] Matrimonial Causes Act 1973, s.12.
[9] *Re Roberts* [1978] 1 W.L.R. 653.
[10] Family Law Act 1986, Pt II.
[11] See Dicey & Morris, *The Conflict of Laws* at pp. 721 and 762; and Cheshire & North, *Private International Law* at pp. 652—654.
[12] See paras. 27–19 and 27–20 below.
[13] For example: a will validly made in English form, disposing of land in England by someone having one wife, who is domiciled in a country where polygamy is permitted; who then validly takes a second wife there.

14–03 Intention not relevant. The original version of the Wills Act 1837, s.18 was superseded by a new version enacted by the Administration of Justice Act 1982. The revocation, or not, of a will by marriage is a question of construction of the version of the Act in force at the relevant time, in the light of the facts; evidence is not admissible of the deceased's intentions whether or not the marriage should revoke the will.[14]

14–04 Revocation by marriage of wills made on or after January 1, 1983. In respect of a will made on or after January 1, 1983, A.J.A. 1982, s.18 has substituted for the original Wills Act 1837, s.18:

"**Wills to be revoked by marriage, except in certain cases**

  18.—(1) Subject to subsections (2) to (4) below, a will shall be revoked by the testator's marriage.

  (2) A disposition in a will in exercise of a power of appointment shall take effect notwithstanding the testator's subsequent marriage unless the property so appointed would in default of appointment pass to his personal representatives.

  (3) Where it appears from a will that at the time it was made the testator was expecting to be married to a particular person and that he intended that the will should not be revoked by the marriage, the will shall not be revoked by his marriage to that person.

  (4) Where it appears from a will that at the time it was made the testator was expecting to be married to a particular person and that he intended that a disposition in the will should not be revoked by his marriage to that person,—

  (a) that disposition shall take effect notwithstanding the marriage;
       and

  (b) any other disposition in the will shall take effect also, unless it appears from the will that the testator intended the disposition to be revoked by the marriage."

This section seems unlikely to cause difficulty. The *expectation* of marriage must under the section appear "from the will"; it is not enough for it to appear from some other source.

14–05 Revocation by marriage of wills made on or before December 31, 1982. A will made on or before December 31, 1982, is revoked by marriage[15]; unless being made on or after January 1, 1926, the will

---

[14] *Re Coleman* [1976] Ch. 1 at p. 11 citing Commonwealth cases; also *Marston v. Roe d. Fox* (1838) 8 Ad. & E. 14 not cited in *Re Coleman*.
[15] Under the originally enacted s.18.

is "expressed to be made in contemplation of marriage."[16] This section gave rise to narrow distinctions for pre-1983 wills. The section requires the expression to be in the will. It was not satisfied by the will merely declaring it was made in contemplation of marriage. To avoid statutory revocation by a subsequent marriage, the will must specify the particular marriage contemplated and be followed by the solemnisation of that marriage.[17] The requirement is met by a reference in a will to the testator's fiancee as his "wife"[18]; but a pre-1983 will speaking of the testator's "fiancee" is revoked by his subsequent marriage to her.[19]

14–06 Partial revocation of a will by a decree of divorce or of nullity. On a death between January 1, 1983 and January 1, 1996, the Wills Act 1837, s.18A inserted by A.J.A. 1982, s.18(2) provides as follows:

"Wills to be revoked by marriage, except in certain cases
18.—(1) Subject to subsections (2) to (4) below, a will shall be revoked by the testator's marriage.

(2) A disposition in a will in exercise of a power of appointment shall take effect notwithstanding the testator's subsequent marriage unless the property so appointed would in default of appointment pass to his personal representatives.

(3) Where it appears from a will that at the time it was made the testator was expecting to be married to a particular person and that he intended that the will should not be revoked by the marriage, the will shall not be revoked by his marriage to that person.

(4) Where it appears from a will that at the time it was made the testator was expecting to be married to a particular person and that he intended that a disposition in the will should not be revoked by his marriage to that person,—

(a) that disposition shall take effect notwithstanding the marriage; and

(b) any other disposition in the will shall take effect also, unless it appears from the will that the testator intended the disposition to be revoked by the marriage".

In subsection (1) the word "lapse" only means "fail"; so that when applying other provisions of the will, the former spouse is not treated

---

[16] L.P.A. 1925, s.177, operating from January 1, 1926. Few wills of living testators, even military wills, can be extant now if made before January 1, 1926.

[17] *Sallis v. Jones* [1936] P. 43.

[18] *Pilot v. Gainfort* [1931] P. 103.

[19] *Re Coleman* above; not following *Re Langston* [1953] P. 100, "my future wife."

as if dead; and a gift conditional on her predeceasing the testator is a gift on a condition that was not satisfied and it fails.[20] It is unwise after a marriage has been dissolved or annulled to rely on section 18A: "the truth of the matter is, that both marriage and divorce are events of such moment as to require the parties at least to reconsider their testamentary dispositions."[21] On a death on or after January 1, 1996, such a gift takes effect as if the former spouse had died on the date that the marriage was dissolved or annulled (regardless of the date of the will and of the date of the dissolution or annulment).[22]

The recognition in England and Wales of divorce and nullity decrees made abroad is stated in paragraph 27–07 below.

The question cannot arise on *intestacy*, since a decree absolute, but only a decree absolute, puts asunder the state of marriage.[23]

14–07 Distinction between the effect of marriage on a will and the effect of a decree of dissolution or of nullity on the form of the grant of representation. When a will is revoked by marriage, it is not admitted to probate. When a will is partially revoked by a decree of dissolution or of nullity, it is however admitted as it stands to probate without, unfortunately, any note on the grant of probate to draw attention to the decree,[24] even when the deceased's status (as a divorced person) appears in the papers lodged for probate.

14–08 Practical steps to be taken by personal representatives on the death of someone who lived apart from his or her spouse. On the death of someone living apart from his wife or from her husband, the personal representatives should ascertain whether there has been a decree of divorce or of nullity. Members of the family or friends or the deceased's solicitor or bank are usually able and willing (or indeed in the case of relatives, very willing) to give information. There is a public right to obtain from the court a copy of any decree of divorce or of nullity made in England and Wales.[25] Decrees made in the United Kingdom are numerous and not always easy to trace. It may be difficult or impossible to trace judicial decrees made abroad, and valid divorces in countries where divorce does not require a judicial process. Before administering an estate, personal

---

[20] *Re Sinclair* [1985] Ch. 446.

[21] *Re Sinclair* at first instance: [1984] 1 W.L.R. p. 1246D.

[22] Law Reform (Succession) Act 1995, s.3.

[23] *Re Seaford* [1968] P. 53 (where the death occurred a few hours before the decree was ineffectively expressed to be made absolute: so that the marriage remained in force for the benefit of the deceased's widow, formerly his wife).

[24] There was no such note on the grant in *Re Sinclair* above: the rules make no provision for compulsory notification of any known decree of divorce or nullity and noting it on the grant.

[25] Matrimonial Causes Rules 1977, r. 58(2) and r. 130(3).

representatives should ask members of the family whether there has been a divorce or a declaration of nullity, whenever the personal representatives have any reason to suppose that there might have been.

There is so far no reported authority on the obligation of personal representatives to trace such a decree. Personal representatives suspecting that there might have been an undisclosed divorce or nullity decree should protect themselves if necessary by applying to the court for directions. Personal representatives with no knowledge of and no reason to suspect such a decree who consequently distribute an estate incorrectly in disregard of the effect of such a decree, would be likely to be excused liability having acted honestly and reasonably and ought fairly to be excused.[26]

14–09 Revocation of a will by another will or writing. The testator may revoke a will at any time by another duly executed will or writing.[27] Someone entitled, for the time being, to *make* a military will without formality, is likewise entitled during the military privilege to revoke a will without formality.[28] A later will or duly executed testamentary writing may revoke an earlier will expressly, as is usual. A later will may revoke an earlier will by implication, disposing of the property in a way inconsistent with the earlier will; then only the later will is admitted to probate.[29] A later writing that revokes previous wills and makes no positive disposition is not itself admitted to probate. Under the modern practice, a grant of letters of administration is made with an explanatory note, but without the later writing being annexed to the grant.[30] In a remarkable recent instance of conditional revocation, three successive wills gave 75 per cent of residue to a named beneficiary and each will contained a clause revoking previous wills; the beneficiary's husband attested the two last wills, so that under the Wills Act 1837, s.15 the gift to her in the last two wills of a share of residue was void. It was held, after a review of 28 authorities, that the revocation clause should be read distributively; and that the revocation, in the second will and in the third will, of the 75 per cent residuary gift in the first will was conditional on its renewal in each subsequent will taking effect; and so the beneficiary took her 75 per cent of residue under the still unrevoked gift thereof in the first will.[31]

---

[26] Trustee Act 1925, s.61 with s.68(17).

[27] Wills Act 1837, s.20.

[28] *Re Gossage* [1921] P. 194.

[29] *Dempsey v. Lawson* (1887) 2 P.D. 98; *Re Bryan* [1907] P. 125; *Jones v. Treasury Solicitor* (1932) 147 L.T. 340.

[30] *Toomer v. Sobinska* [1907] P. 106; for the distinction between a will and a duly executed writing under s.20, see *Re Fraser* (1869) 2 P. & D. 40.

[31] *Re Finnemore* [1991] 1 W.L.R. 793.

14–10 Variation of a will by codicil; simultaneous wills. A will may be varied by another testamentary document, duly executed,[32] known as a codicil. The deceased's duly executed testamentary documents are then all admitted to probate together, as constituting in the aggregate the deceased's *will*.[33] The principle is to reconcile the deceased's dispositions if possible, especially when they were executed simultaneously. Where there are simultaneous wills and the matter is left in doubt, neither can be admitted to probate.[34] This is a position that the court will seek to avoid. The grant of probate may omit words in an earlier will subsequently duly revoked by a testamentary writing not itself required to be admitted to probate.[35] When the court is satisfied[36] that as a matter of fact the words of revocation of an earlier will contained in the later will were not intended by the testator, the words of revocation may be omitted from probate.[37] This goes to the verge of the law; and is less likely to be claimed now that rectification of a will is available.[38]

14–11 Alterations and interlineations. Alterations and interlineations are valid if proved to have been made before the will is executed; or if made afterwards and the alterations are themselves executed.[39] For this purpose alterations made after the execution of the will itself are sufficiently executed by being initialled in the margin by the testator and the witnesses.[40]

14–12 Revocation by destruction. A will is revoked:

"by the burning, tearing, or otherwise destroying the same by the testator or by some other person in his presence and by his direction with the intention of revoking the same."[41]

A will may thus validly be revoked by a testator without anyone else being aware of it; provided that the testator has capacity, for without capacity a testator cannot have the necessary intention.[42] To

---

[32] Wills Act 1837, s.21, including duly executed interlineations.
[33] *Re Pechell* (1874) 3 P. & D. 153; *Townsend v. Moore* [1905] P. 66; *Simpson* v. *Foxon* [1907] P. 54.
[34] *Townsend v. Moore* above; and *Re Kennaghen* [1938] N.I. 130. The grant made in *Re Griffith* (1872) 2 P. & D. 457 was by consent of all parties.
[35] *Re Hodgkinson* [1893] P. 339.
[36] On which oral evidence may be admitted: *Jenner v. Ffinch* (1879) 5 P.D. 106; *Re Bryan* [1907] P. 125.
[37] *Lowthorpe-Lutwidge v. Lowthorpe-Lutwidge* [1935] P. 151; earlier examples are *Re Moore* [1892] P. 378, and the other way *Collins v. Elstone* [1893] P. 1.
[38] See para. 17–04.
[39] Wills Act 1837, s. 21.
[40] *Re Blewitt* (1880) 5 P.D. 116.
[41] Wills Act 1837, s.20.
[42] *Brunt v. Brunt* (1873) 3 P. & D. 37; *Re Brassington* [1902] P. 1.

be an effective revocation, the will must be burnt, torn or destroyed. It is not revoked by an unexecuted writing on it that the will is revoked, even accompanied by the will being treated as abandoned.[43] To effect the revocation of the will, the destruction of the will must be done deliberately: a will accidentally destroyed is not revoked even when the testator acquiesces in the accidental destruction.[44]

14–13 Physical acts sufficient to revoke by destruction. The testator's destruction or obliteration of the testator's signature, or of the testator's and the witnesses' signatures, amounts to a revocation of the will. The destruction with a knife of the testator's and the witnesses' signatures amounts to a revocation of the will[45]; but not a destruction of the testator's signature that fails to render it illegible.[46] A testator who pasted unexecuted paper with different figures for legacies over words in the will was held not to have varied the original legacies; but as the original legacies were no longer "apparent" within the Wills Act 1837, s.21, they too failed; even though x-ray photography revealed what lay below.[47]

14–14 Revocation of one duplicate will. When a will has been executed in duplicate, the destruction of one original revokes the other.[48]

14–15 Partial revocation by destruction. The testator's destruction of part only of a will, with the inferred intention of revoking that part, revokes that part of the will only.[49]

14–16 No contracting out of the right to revoke or to vary a will: contracts to make a will. The statutory right to revoke, or to vary, a will is effective at law. Therefore, when a will is revoked in breach of a binding contract not to revoke it, probate is nevertheless granted on the basis that the revocation was effective at law[50]; and the contractual obligation may be enforceable by way of trust.[51] The same reasoning applies to varying a will by codicil, in breach of a

---

[43] *Cheese v. Lovejoy* (1877) 2 P.D. 251.
[44] *Re Booth* [1926] P. 118, a military will.
[45] *Re Morton* (1887) 12 P.D. 141; or the signatures of only the witnesses: *Re Dallow* (1862) 31 L.J.P.M. & A. 128; *Re Adams* [1990] Ch. 601.
[46] *Re Godfrey* (1893) 69 L.T. 22, where the order was made by consent.
[47] *Re Itter* [1950] P. 130; *Ffinch v. Coombe* [1894] P. 191.
[48] *Atkinson v. Morris* [1897] P. 40.
[49] *Re Nunn* [1936] 1 All E.R. 555; *Re Everest* [1975] Fam. 44 (where *Re Nunn* was not cited): both cases followed *Re Woodward* (1871) 2 P. & D. 206, a similar case on the appointment of executors. In one remarkable case, the testator's "meddling" with his duly executed will by substituting other pages was held to have produced an intestacy: *Leonard v. Leonard* [1902] P. 243.
[50] *Re Heys* [1914] P. 192.
[51] Snell, *Equity*, pp. 190–192.

binding contract. This question may arise after a death when spouses or others make "mutual wills": that is to say, wills that each contracts not to revoke, after the death of the first to die.[52]

14–17 No automatic revival. The revocation of a will does not automatically revive a previous will. To be revived, a previous will must be revived by a duly executed testamentary disposition.[53] This is often misunderstood, especially by those accustomed to the law of Scotland.

14–18 Conditional revocation. When a testator revokes his will,[54] or part[55] of his will, and it is proved by evidence that the revocation was made subject to a *condition*, the revocation is ineffective if the condition is not satisfied; this principle is also called "dependent relative revocation". Examples of the application of this principle are the revocation of a will on the basis, found on the evidence to be a *condition* of its revocation, that: a previous will would be reinstated;[56] that an unexecuted memorandum would take effect;[57] that (by a testator who died in 1921) his widow would take his estate on intestacy[58]; that he would validly make a subsequent will.[59] For the principle to operate, the revocation must be proved to have been conditional; it is not enough that there was an incorrect assumption not amounting to a condition;[60] or an unfulfilled intention not amounting to a condition.[61]

The principle is not in doubt; the numerous reported cases run to fine distinctions.[62] Although reported, they amount largely to decisions on the facts of each particular case. Now that rectification of a will is possible[63] similar evidence might be found not to establish the necessary requirement that the revocation was *conditional*.

---

[52] If a binding contract is proved to have been made in fact; the making of such a contract is not inferred. Proof of making such a contract is often lacking: as in *Re Oldham* [1925] Ch. 75, and *Gray v. Perpetual Trustee Co.* [1928] A.C. 391; but it was found in *Re Cleaver* [1981] 1 W.L.R. 939. For further authorities on this foolish and rare form of agreement, see the judgments in those cases and Snell, *Equity*, at pp. 189–190; and paras. 22–09, 22–10 below.

[53] Wills Act 1837, s.22.

[54] See the cases cited below.

[55] *Dancer v. Crabb and Thompson* (1873) 3 P. & D. 98; *Re Cockle* [1960] 2 All E.R. 289 and [1960] 1 W.L.R. 491, where the revocation clause in the second will was omitted from probate under this principle. Both reports of *Re Cockle* need to be read; the All E.R. reports the judgment, but not the arguments of counsel; the W.L.R. reports the arguments but not the judgment.

[56] *Powell v. Powell* (1866) 1 P. & D. 209.

[57] *Dancer v. Crabb* (1873) 3 P. & D. 98.

[58] *Re Southerden* [1925] P. 177.

[59] *Re Botting* [1951] W.N. 571; *Re Bromham, ibid.* 1149, where there was an interval of five years; *Re Davies* [1951] 1 All E.R. 920.

[60] *Re Feis* [1964] Ch 106.

[61] *Re Jones* [1976] Ch. 200.

[62] See Theobald, *Wills*, at pp. 80–84.

[63] See para. 17–04.

15. Missing wills

15–01 Probate of copy will. A duly executed will remains in effect, unless duly revoked.[1] A missing will is therefore admitted to probate in the form of a copy or a reconstruction[2]; unless it is presumed or proved to have been revoked.

15–02 Missing will not revoked. There is no revocation when there is an explanation of the will's absence. A will cannot have been revoked when it is shown to have been destroyed by accident. It is not treated as revoked, for example:

(1) when the will was probably destroyed in a fire[3];
(2) where the will had been fraudulently destroyed[4];
(3) where others than the testator had had access to the place where the will was kept, although fraud was not suggested[5];
(4) where the testator had had possession of the will when he had lost capacity, so that he had no capacity to revoke it[6]; and

---

[1] See Chap. 14.
[2] On an application to the district judge under r. 54.
[3] *Re Phibbs* [1917] P. 93; *Re Webb* [1964] 1 W.L.R. 509, enemy action. The principle goes back as far as *Etheringham v. Etheringham* (1670) Aleyn 2 where after the death the will had been "gnawed all to pieces with rats."
[4] *Podmore v. Whatton* (1864) 3 Sw. & T. 449.
[5] *Sugden v. St. Leonards* (Lord) (1876) 1 P.D. 154.
[6] *Harris v. Berrall* (1858) 1 Sw. & T. 153.

(5) where he was subject to habitual drunkenness sufficient to negative capacity to revoke it.[7] The same would apply to drug addiction sufficient to negative capacity.

15–03 Presumption of revocation in certain circumstances. When the will was traced into the testator's possession, and was not still in existence at the death,[8] its absence raises a presumption that the testator duly revoked it by destruction.[9] This is a question of fact in each case.[10] The modern view is:

> "Those presumptions were not intended to be regarded as rigid statutory rules, when they would produce absurd results, but as an indication of the inferences which would be drawn by the court from a given state of evidence. The court would approach the question by considering what was the most probable explanation of the absence of the will on the testator's death."[11]

When resisting the application of the presumption of revocation, there is no need for those who claim that the will remained valid to say what has become of the original[12]; they are unlikely to know.

15–04 Torn will. The same principles apply to a will found torn, as to one that is missing.[13]

15–05 Duplicate will torn or missing. When a will is executed in duplicate, if the facts lead to the conclusion that one original was revoked, then such revocation revokes the other original too.[14]

15–06 Codicil, torn or missing. For this purpose a codicil is treated in the same way as a will.[15]

15–07 Will or codicil with a pin mark or staple mark. It is important not to pin or staple any paper to a will or codicil. When a testamentary document lodged at the Registry bears an indication

---

[7] *Re Brassington* [1902] P. 1, where the will was found torn.
[8] For if in existence at the death, it cannot have been revoked: *Finch v. Finch* (1867) 1 P.D. 371.
[9] *Allan v. Morrison* [1900] A.C. 604.
[10] *Allan v. Morrison* above at p. 609.
[11] *Re Yule* (1965) 109 S.J. 317, Wrangham J. This is close to Lord Upjohn's view of the presumption of advancement as "no more than a long stop to provide the answer when the relevant facts and circumstances fail to yield a solution": *Vandervell* v. *I.R.C.* [1967] 2 A.C. 291 at p. 313.
[12] *Patten v. Patten* (1858) 1 Sw. & T. 55.
[13] *North v. North* (1909) 25 T.L.R. 322; and two cases where on applying these principles a torn will was admitted to probate: *Harris v. Berrall* above, and *Re Brassington* above. The decision, by consent, *Re Mackenzie* [1909] P. 305 was made without a full citation of the authorities and does not lay down a general rule.
[14] *Atkinson v. Morris* [1897] P. 40.
[15] *Re Donnisthorpe* [1947] W.N. 226.

that anything was one fastened to it, the position has to be fully explained[16] before a grant is issued. This can cause considerable trouble after a death.

15–08 No solicitor's lien over a will. A will is not subject to the lien that, when unpaid, a solicitor may obtain over other documents[17]; and it must be lodged with the court having probate jurisdiction after the testator's death[18]. This exception from a solicitor's lien has not been questioned in modern times; "the exception is far too thoroughly established to be dependent upon logic for its existence."[19]

[16] By an Affidavit of Plight and Condition, made by the attesting witnesses or other: rules 14, 15 and 16.
[17] *Georges v. Georges* (1811) 18 Ves. 294; *Lord v. Wormleighton* (1822) Jac. 581; *Balch v. Symes* (1823) Turn. & R. 87 at p. 92.
[18] *Ex p. Law* (1834) 2 A. & E. 45; decided when Probate procedure was different.
[19] Atkinson, *Solicitors' Liens and Charging Orders* (1905) at p. 84.

16. Variation of the beneficial devolution after the death[1] without applying to the court

DISCLAIMER

16–01 Disclaimer. There is no obligation to accept a gift. A testamentary donee may disclaim the gift in writing[2] or by deed[3]; or by conduct[4]; but only before accepting it.[5] One of the *joint* donees cannot disclaim the rights of the other or others.[6] If one joint donee purports to do so, there is a severance of the joint beneficial interest into a beneficial interest in common, and the interest of the joint beneficiary purporting to disclaim devolves on the other testamentary joint beneficiary.[7]

---

[1] For variation before the death see Chap. 14.
[2] *Re Schar* [1951] Ch. 280.
[3] *Townson v. Tickle* (1819) 3 B. & Ald. 31.
[4] *Re Clout & Frewer's Contract* [1924] 2 Ch. 230, a vendor and purchaser case; *Re Parsons* [1943] Ch. 12 at p. 17, an estate duty case.
[5] *Re Wimperis* [1914] 1 Ch. 502. After acceptance, the donee can assign the subject-matter but can no longer disclaim it; the authorities on disclaimer are collected in *Re Stratton* [1958] Ch. 42, a case on estate duty.
[6] *Bence v. Gilpin* (1868) L.R. 3 Ex. 76; *Re Schar* above.
[7] *Re Schar*, where *Bence v. Gilpin* was not cited. But for *Re Schar*, the share of the "disclaiming" joint tenant might fall into residue: see nn. 9 and 10 below.

16–02 Destination of disclaimed property. A disclaimer is a refusal to accept the gift[8]; accordingly (with the exception, mentioned above, of a gift to joint donees) what was left to the disclaiming beneficiary falls into residue,[9] or (if a residuary gift is disclaimed) into a partial intestacy.[10] The same principle applies on an intestacy. Therefore, when every member of the statutory class taking on intestacy disclaims, the interest falls into the next class.[11]

16–03 Withdrawal of disclaimer. A disclaimer duly made by deed[12] binds the person making it, like any other deed.[13] An effective disclaimer not made by deed but duly acted upon, cannot afterwards be withdrawn.[14] It has, however, been held that as regards testamentary gifts, a disclaimer not by deed on which no one has changed their position may be withdrawn[15]; and that a refusal to accept the trust income under a will may be withdrawn for the future.[16] On the other hand, a refusal of a gift made between living persons cannot afterwards be withdrawn.[17] The law about the withdrawal of a refusal to accept a testamentary gift is not yet settled. When a refusal to accept a testamentary gift is withdrawn, or is expressed to be withdrawn, legal advice is necessary.

16–04 Partial disclaimer under a will. The principle applicable to a partial disclaimer of a testamentary gift is:

> "Where there are two distinct gifts to the same person, one being onerous and the other beneficial, the donee may disclaim the onerous gift and take the other. If however the onerous and beneficial property are included in the same gift, *prima facie* the donee cannot disclaim the onerous and accept the beneficial property, but must take the whole or none."[18]

---

[8] *Re Wimperis* [1914] 1 Ch. 502; *Re Stratton* [1958] Ch. 42.
[9] As in *Re Parsons* above.
[10] *Re Sullivan* [1930] 1 Ch. 84, where a partial intestacy was more favourable to the composer's widow; *Re Backhouse* [1931] W.N. 168.
[11] *Re Scott* [1975] 1 W.L.R. 1260; that is however not quite what the Administration of Estates Act 1925, s.46 says.
[12] See the Law of Property (Miscellaneous Provisions) Act 1989, s.1 for new rules about executing deeds.
[13] *Townson v. Tickell*, above.
[14] *Att.-Gen. v. Christ's Hospital* (1831) Taml. 393; 1 Russ. & M. 626; *Att.Gen. v. Munby* (1858) 3 H. & N. 826.
[15] *Doe d. Smyth v. Smyth* (1826) 6 B. & C. 1121; *Re Cranstoun's Will Trusts* [1949] Ch. 523.
[16] *Re Young* [1913] 1 Ch. 272.
[17] *Re Paradise Motor Co.* [1968] 1 W.L.R. 1125; doubting the decisions or dicta that a disclaimer of a testamentary gift may be withdrawn; but without *Doe v. Smyth* being cited.
[18] *Re Kensington* [1902] 1 Ch. 203 at p. 207; *Re Joel* [1943] Ch. 311.

The testator's intention as disclosed in the will governs the application of this test[19]; that is the "pole star."[20] A gift of residue or a general gift of land is a single gift for this purpose[21]; other gifts by will are likely to be separate gifts[22]; gifts of burdensome shares with other property may be distinct gifts for this purpose.[23]

16–05 Partial disclaimer under an intestacy. On the death of someone intestate, there is no will and so there is no opportunity to ascertain from the will what was the deceased's intention about a partial disclaimer. Accordingly a disclaimer of part of the benefit is permissible on an intestacy.[24]

16–06 Partial disclaimer of benefits on a partial intestacy. There is no reported case about a disclaimer of part of the benefit on a partial intestacy. On a partial intestacy, (i) the principle as to a will is likely to apply to a partial disclaimer of what the will disposes of; and (ii) the principle as to intestacy to apply to what devolves on a partial intestacy.

DEED OF VARIATION

16–07 Deeds or other binding documents. In an estate that is solvent, those with beneficial interests under the will or under the intestacy are the persons concerned with the beneficial devolution of the estate; they may be relatives or friends of the deceased, or charities. When those concerned are all ascertained persons of full capacity or charities, they have power together to vary the provisions of the will or intestacy.[25]

A variation is known as a "family arrangement," even when made between those who are not related to each other or to the deceased. A variation should be by deed,[26] so as to avoid the technical rules about when a deed is required to make an agreement effective; but a signed memorandum intended to have legal effect varies the will, even though it contemplates the parties making a subsequent deed,

---

[19] *Warren v. Ruddall* (1860) 1 J. & H. 1 at p. 12; *Re Hotchkys* (1886) 32 Ch.Div. 408 (where some of the dicta are inaccurate: *Re Joel* at p. 325).

[20] *Re Pearce* [1926] N.Z.L.R. 696, where the Court of Appeal, New Zealand, reviewed the authorities; it was not cited in *Re Joel*.

[21] *Green v. Britten* (1872) 27 L.T. 811 (land with an ornamental park); *Re Hotchkys* (general gift of land); *Re Kensington* (the same); *Re Joel* (house and contents).

[22] *Warren v. Ruddall* above (two distinct gifts of land).

[23] *Long v. Kent*; *Ashton v. Wood* (1874) 31 L.T. 293.

[24] *Re Holt* (1916) 115 L.T. 73.

[25] *Re Chrimes* [1917] 1 Ch. 30; *Re Wale* [1956] 1 W.L.R. 1346; *Crowden v. Aldridge* [1993] 1 W.L.R. 433.

[26] See L.P.A. 1989, s.1 for the modern provisions about making a deed.

and such a deed is not made.[27]. A charity with a beneficial interest in an estate ordinarily has power to agree to a variation, or can acquire the power.[28]

16–08 Separate advice. Those with different beneficial interests usually obtain separate advice. On questions of law or of construction and questions about what rearrangement might save tax, the parties need not instruct separate solicitors. The solicitors acting for the personal representatives may instruct counsel (other than the barrister advising the personal representatives) on behalf of the various respective beneficiaries. A discussion between counsel is the usual way to clear up any question. The usual provision is that the costs of the deed are to fall on the estate.

Where young adults are concerned, separate advice is needed, from separate solicitors as well as separate counsel. A transaction between parent/s and a child which benefits the parent/s, is presumed (that is to say is assumed without proof) to have been achieved by undue influence. This is one instance of a relationship of trust which is not permitted to be abused.[29] The presumption of undue influence is not excluded by showing that there was no actual domination.[30] The importance of the doctrine to personal representatives, assenting to and acting on a variation of beneficial interests, is that where the person in a fiduciary position has notice of the facts raising a presumption of undue influence, such personal representatives may be held liable for acting on the transaction, even though it did not benefit those personal representatives.[31] Personal representatives must not take that risk.

There are two ways for personal representatives to avoid that risk. One way is to make sure that the variation benefits the persons (such

---

[27] *Crowden v. Aldridge* [1993] 1 W.L.R. 433.
[28] A charity will be likely either to be a trust, when its trustees have the powers conferred by the Trustee Act 1925, s.15; or to be incorporated, when it will have the powers of a corporation: Companies Act 1989, s.108, amending (from the commencement of the 1989 Act: s.215 there) Companies Act 1989, s.35. In addition a charity may acquire a power to compromise by being advised by the Charity Commissioners under the Charities Act 1993, s.29, replacing the Charities Act 1960, s.24 that it is entitled to effect the compromise; or by being authorised by the Commissioners to effect it under the Charities Act 1993, s.26, replacing the Charities Act 1960, s.23.
[29] *Re Pauling* [1964] Ch. 303 where advancements of trust money nominally to a child were to be transferred by the child to the parent:
    "it is assumed that so unnatural a transaction would have been brought about by undue use of the natural influence which a parent has over a child, and of the filial obedience which a child owes to his parent."
    Goldsworthy v. Brickell [1987] Ch. 378 at p. 401, listing other relationships raising the presumption; such as superior and member of a sisterhood, doctor and patient, solicitor and client. However, "there are many and various other relationships lacking a recognisable status to which the presumption has been held to apply."
[30] *Goldsworthy v. Brickell* above.
[31] *Re Pauling* above at p. 338.

as a child) in a position to be influenced; this is because a transaction can only be set aside, as made under *presumed* undue influence, when it is to the manifest disadvantage of the person presumed to have been influenced.[32] The other way is for the child or other person liable to be influenced to act under separate advice, after "full free and informed thought about it."[33] It is usual to recite in a deed the fact that the relevant parties had separate advice. It is not an objection to such independent advice that it is to be paid for out of the estate.[34]

In addition to the presumption of undue influence, a transaction may be set aside when there is *actual* undue influence (that is to say victimisation).[35] Personal representatives with any ground to suspect that this has occurred, must refuse to carry the transaction into effect; and may need the protection of acting under the directions of the court.

16–09 Rule against self-dealing. When formulating a deed, it is necessary to keep in mind the rule against self-dealing, which prevents anyone with conflicting interests or duties from binding others.[36] This is an overriding rule of equity.[37] When this question arises, the difficulty can be overcome by applying to the court to approve the variation under the Variation of Trusts Act 1958.[38]

16–10 Accumulation and maintenance trust. When making a variation of a will or of an intestacy, it is an advantage to constitute an "accumulation and maintenance trust" (as narrowly defined) for the benefit of one or more persons aged under 25 years. An accumulation and maintenance trust is exempt from the so-called "exit charge" to inheritance tax when the property is distributed; and is exempt from the periodic charge to inheritance tax on discretionary settlements.[39] These benefits are worth acquiring even when there might otherwise be reasons for formulating the trust in terms outside the statutory definition of an "accumulation and maintenance trust": for example by making the property vest at an age over 25 years.

---

[32] *C.I.B.C. Mortgages v. Pitt* [1994] 1 A.C. 200, explaining *National Westminster Bank v. Morgan* [1985] A.C. 686.

[33] *Zamet v. Hyman* [1961] 1 W.L.R. 1442 (fiancee) at p. 1446; *Goldsworthy v. Brickell* above at p. 408F–H.

[34] This follows from *Bank of Credit and Commerce v. Aboody* [1990] 1 Q.B. 923; not over-ruled on that point in *C.I.B.C. Mortgages v. Pitt.*

[35] *Re Craig* [1971] Ch. 95; *Goldsworthy v. Brickell* above, p. 400.

[36] See Chap. 34.

[37] *Industrial Developments Consultants Ltd v. Cooley* [1972] 1 W.L.R. 443.

[38] See para. 17–02 below.

[39] Inheritance Tax Act 1984, s. 71: see McCutcheon, *Inheritance Tax* (3rd ed.), at pp. 582–597.

17. Variation of the beneficial devolution after the death on application to the court

17–01 Compromise of a probate action. A probate action may be brought to dispose of a dispute. A probate action may also be brought as a convenient and speedy way to vary the devolution of the estate, by an order obtained by consent. Parties, all of whom are of full capacity, may readily obtain an order.[1] When there are beneficiaries without full capacity, the court can approve the order on behalf of those beneficiaries if the order is beneficial to them.[2] The decision of a probate action results in an order creating rights in favour of testamentary beneficiaries who are not parties; and so it is, in a sense, an action *in rem*.[3] A compromise, as distinct from a decision, of a probate action does not, however, bind those who are not parties to the compromise.[4] Such a compromise should, therefore, provide for anyone not a party, the maximum that on any view such a person can claim.

17–02 The Variation of Trusts Act 1958. The consent of minors and of unborn or unascertained persons may be obtained to a variation of trusts by an order of the court under V.T.A. 1958. Such

---

[1] A.J.A. 1985, s.49; R.S.C., Ord. 76, r. 12; for the form of order see *Supreme Court Practice 1995*, Vol. 2, para. 539 at p. 155.
[2] See para. 41–09.
[3] *Re Langton* [1964] P. 163, Danckwerts L.J. at p. 175.
[4] *Wytcherley v. Andrews* (1871) 2 P. & D. 327; *Re Langton* above.

an order can be made when the variation is for the benefit of the persons on whose behalf the consent is sought (or in the case of those who are only objects of the discretion, to arise on the failure of a protected life interest, without it being necessarily for their benefit). Personal representatives (like trustees) usually, but not always, leave it to those beneficially interested, or their parents, to apply under the Act.[5] Such applications are frequently made in the High Court; the jurisdiction of the county court[6] is little used.

17–03 Trustee Act 1925, s. 57. When the variation proposed only concerns administrative powers or powers of investment, there is an alternative jurisdiction under the Trustee Act 1925, s.57. An order made under section 57 similarly binds all person interested; that is to say, an order made under section 57 (unlike an order under V.T.A. 1958) is effective without the consent of every adult beneficiary.

An application under section 57 is usually made by the personal representatives or the trustees and may be less costly. It has recently been held that an application concerning administrative powers or powers of investment is better made under section 57.[7]

17–04 Rectification of a will. On a death on or after January 1, 1983, there is, under A.J.A. 1982, s.20, power to rectify a will:

> "**20.**—(1) If a court is satisfied that a will is so expressed that it fails to carry out the testator's intentions, in consequence—
>
> > (a) of a clerical error; or
> >
> > (b) of a failure to understand his instructions,
>
> it may order that the will shall be rectified so as to carry out his intentions.
>
> (2) An application for an order under this section shall not, except with the permission of the court, be made after the end of the period of six months from the date on which representation with respect to the estate of the deceased is first taken out.
>
> (3) The provisions of this section shall not render the personal representatives of a deceased person liable for having distributed any part of the estate of the deceased, after the end of the period of six months from the date on which representation with respect to the estate of the deceased is first taken out, on the ground that they ought to have taken into account the possibility that the court might permit the making of an application for an order under this section after the end of that period; but this subsection shall not prejudice any power to recover, by reason of

---

[5] *Re Druce's Settlement Trusts* [1962] 1 W.L.R. 363.
[6] Under the County Courts Act 1984, s.23(b)(ii) and s.24(3).
[7] *Anker-Petersen v. Anker-Petersen* Ch. 1990 A 2903, unreported, December 6, 1990, Judge Paul Baker Q.C. sitting as a Judge of the High Court, Chancery Division.

the making of an order under this section, any part of the estate so distributed.

(4) In considering for the purposes of this section when representation with respect to the estate of a deceased person was first taken out, a grant limited to settled land or to trust property shall be left out of account, and a grant limited to real estate or to personal estate shall be left out of account unless a grant limited to the remainder of the estate has previously been made or is made at the same time."

The rectification jurisdiction may be exercised in the Family Division when no probate action has been begun[8]; or in the course of a probate action in the Chancery Division.[9] The reference to a "mistake" in section 20 may confer jurisdiction to rectify a will on the county court.[10]

Rectification was ordered by inserting in a will words exercising a power of appointment; where those words had been included in a previous will and omitted by error from a subsequent will replacing it.[11] It was held[12] that:

"The words 'clerical error' used in section 20(1)(a) of the Act of 1982 are to be construed as meaning an error made in the process or recording the intended will of the testator in the drafting or transcription of his will. That meaning is to be contrasted with an error made in carrying his intentions into effect by the drafter's choice of words and with a mistaken choice of words because of a failure to understand the testator's intentions, a circumstance covered by subsection (b)."

17–05 Standard of proof on a rectification claim. On claims to rectify documents other than wills, it was held before the Judicature Act 1873, when the courts of Law and of Equity were separate courts, that there was a specially heavy standard of proof on a rectification claim.[13] Similar statements have been made in judgments in modern times,[14] but without the result depending on this point.

---

[8] N.C.P.R. 1987, r. 55.

[9] R.S.C., Ord. 76, r. 16.

[10] C.C.A. 1984, s.23(g); or s.32.

[11] *Wordingham v. Royal Exchange Trust* [1992] 1 W.L.R. 496.

[12] p. 502.

[13] *Shelburne v. Inchiquin* (1784) 1 B.C.C. 338 at p. 341; *Townshend v. Stangroom* (1801) 6 Ves. 328 at p. 334; *Fowler v. Fowler* (1859) 4 de G. & J. 250 at p. 265: see Snell, *Equity,* at p. 632.

[14] *Crane v. Hegman-Harris* [1939] 4 All E.R. 68 at p. 664; and on appeal [1939] 4 All E.R. 68 at p. 71; *Joscelyne v. Nissen* [1970] 2 Q.B. 86 at p. 98; *Lloyd v. Stanbury* [1971] 1 W.L.R. 535 at p. 543; *Thomas Bates and Son v. Wyndhams (Lingerie)* [1981] 1 W.L.R. 505 at p. 543; also cited in Snell at p. 616. There are also *The Nai Genova* [1984] 1 Lloyd's Rep. 353 at p. 359; and *Industrial Life Assurance v. Dublin Land Securities* [1986] Ir. 332 at p. 351.

Notwithstanding the bulk of authority cited, it is doubtful whether there is a standard of proof recognised by modern law other than the civil standard (balance of probability, taking the gravity of the allegation into account) and the criminal standard (being completely satisfied).[15] In a suitable case the doctrine that a rectification claim requires a higher standard of evidence than other claims might be overruled in the House of Lords.

17–06 The Inheritance (Provision for Family and Dependants) Act 1975. The freedom of testamentary disposition allowed by English law is modified by the right of five categories of persons to apply to the court for financial provision after the death; whether the deceased left a will or died intestate. Those entitled to apply are:

(a) a husband or wife of the deceased;

(b) a former husband or wife of the deceased;

(c) a child of the deceased, even if adult;

(d) anyone (not the deceased's own child) treated by the deceased as a child of the deceased's family;

(e) any other person maintained by the deceased until his death.

(f) a further class had been added by the Law Reform (Succession) Act 1995, s.2. Where the death is on or after January 1, 1996, then (in effect) a lover or mistress of two years duration may also apply under the 1975 Act.

Except by leave, an application under the Act must be made within six months of the date of probate.[16] Once that six-month period is over, personal representatives may distribute without regard to a potential claim under the Act,[17] unless they have notice of a claim under the Act, pending or impending.[18]

The right to make an application is not a right to receive an award. A claim for an award depends on the applicant showing that the disposition of the estate is "not such as to make reasonable provision for the applicant."[19] An order made, or agreed to, under the Act renders the applicant a beneficiary in the estate[20]; and is noted on the grant.[21] Applications under the Act may be made in the Family

---

[15] *Hornal v. Neuberger* [1957] 1 Q.B. 247; *Re Dellow* [1964] 1 W.L.R. 451; *R. v. Home Secretary, ex p. Khawaja* [1984] A.C. 74 at p. 113; and *Bhandari v. Advocates Committee* [1956] 1 W.L.R. 1442 at p. 1452.

[16] s.4.

[17] s.20.

[18] *Re Ralphs* [1968] 1 W.L.R. 1522.

[19] s.1(1) of the Act; see *Re Coventry* [1980] Ch. 461; *Re Fullard* [1982] Fam. 42; and *Re Leach's Will Trusts* [1986] Ch. 226 for the need for the applicant to demonstrate this.

[20] *Re Jennery* [1967] Ch. 280.

[21] S.19(3).

Division or the Chancery Division of the High Court[22]; or in an estate within its jurisdiction in the county court.[23] Personal representatives with no beneficial interest in the estate (or no significant beneficial interest in the estate) should take an attitude of impartiality between those taking under the will or intestacy and a claimant under the 1975 Act. Personal representatives who themselves have a beneficial interest under the will or intestacy are entitled to oppose an application under the 1975 Act. The practice and procedure under the 1975 Act is outside the scope of this book.

---

[22] R.S.C., Ord. 99, r. 2.
[23] C.C.A. 1984, s.25.

18. Effect on inheritance tax of a variation; variation consequent on criminal killing

18–01 Disclaimers, deeds, and orders under the Variation of Trusts Act 1958. An instrument in writing,[1] varying any benefit or disclaiming any benefit, ranks (if those concerned so elect) for inheritance tax purposes as if it was the deceased's disposition[2]; this is so, unless the instrument is made in consideration of money or money's worth, other than that variation.[3] Compliance with a request by the deceased about what is to happen to property bequeathed by his will has the same effect.[4] There is a statutory time limit[5] of two years from the death for such an instrument; this time limit does not appear to be capable of being enlarged. There is a statutory time

---

[1] But not a subsequent instrument varying it: *Russell v. I.R.C.* [1988] 1 W.L.R. 834; several beneficiaries may however each make separate variations for this purpose.

[2] Inheritance Tax Act 1984, s.142. The election requirement does not apply to a *disclaimer*, made by someone unwilling to accept the gift: see Chap. 16.

[3] s.142(3).

[4] s.143; this section, unlike s.142, does not relate to an intestacy.

[5] s.142(1).

limit of six months from the date of the document (capable of being enlarged) for electing that the variation is to rank as if made by the deceased. The personal representatives need not so elect if the variation attracts further inheritance tax that they do not have assets in the estate to meet. The same applies to such a variation for the purposes of Capital Gains Tax: see paragraph 4–09.

18–02 Orders under the Inheritance (Provision for Family and Dependants) Act 1975. The two-year time limit from the death for an agreement does not apply to orders under the 1975 Act, which rank for inheritance tax purposes as if made by the deceased.[6] A consent order under the 1975 Act, if available, is therefore advantageous when the two-year period from the death has elapsed.

18–03 Order in a probate action or order to rectify a will. An order in a probate action, or an order to rectify a will, determines what was the true last will of the deceased.[7] Accordingly, however long ago the period of two years from the death elapsed, inheritance tax is levied on the footing that the true devolution of the estate has been so determined.

18–04 Orders under the Inheritance (Provision for Family and Dependants) Act 1975 or consent orders in a probate action and the *Ramsay* doctrine. The doctrine recently introduced, that a pre-ordained series of transactions may have no fiscal effect,[8] is not (as the law stands at present) applicable to an order under the 1975 Act, nor to an order in a probate action. Under the relevant sections, anything ordered under the 1975 Act ranks for fiscal purposes as if done by the deceased.[9] As regards a probate action, it is the court's decision that declares what constituted the true last will of the deceased.[10] An order for rectification establishes the true form of the document from the outset.[11]

Once an order of the court, giving effect to an agreement, is made and the agreement embodied in that order of the court, its legal effect is derived from the court order itself and does not depend any longer on the agreement between the parties.[12] The effect of a court

---

[6] 1975 Act, s.19(1); 1984 Act, s.146.
[7] See para. 17–01.
[8] *Ramsay v. I.R.C.* [1982] A.C. 300 and other cases down to *Craven v. White* [1989] A.C. 398.
[9] See para. 17–06.
[10] "The will is either good or bad against all the world"; *Birch v. Birch* [1902] P. 130, Cozens-Hardy L.J. at p. 138, with whose judgment Stirling L.J. had agreed at p. 137. "A probate action is, in a sense, an action *in rem*" Danckwerts L.J., *Re Langton* [1964] P. 163 at p. 179.
[11] *Craddock Brothers v. Hunt* [1923] 2 Ch. 136 at p. 151.
[12] *Jenkins v. Livesey* [1985] A.C. 424 at p. 435, following *de Lasala v. de Lasala* [1980] A.C. 546 at p. 560.

order applies equally to an order pronounced after a contest,[13] and to an order made by agreement on the compromise of a case, (as many orders are), even though the court is not concerned with the terms of a consent order.[14]

It follows that in any ordinary circumstances, the *Ramsay* doctrine of a pre-ordained series of transactions having no fiscal effect, ought not to apply to a consent order under the 1975 Act or under the probate jurisdiction. The doctrine also appears not to apply to orders made under the jurisdiction under the Matrimonial Causes Act 1973.[15] (There is no question about a consent order for rectification of a will; rectification is not ordered by consent.[16])

VARIATION CONSEQUENT ON CRIMINAL KILLING

18–05 Common law. It is, at common law, contrary to public policy for a person who has committed murder or manslaughter to benefit from the crime. Accordingly a sane person who has committed murder is excluded from benefiting under the deceased's will,[17] or intestacy.[18] Someone convicted of manslaughter, having killed the deceased with diminished responsibility while suffering from mental illness, is also excluded from benefit at common law.[19] (There was no forfeiture under the previous law when such persons were, in similar circumstances, treated under the criminal law as not guilty but insane[20]).

The Criminal Procedure (Insanity and Unfitness to Plead) Act 1991 makes from January 1, 1992 (appointed under section 9(2) there) new provisions for criminal trials where the question of insanity or of unfitness to plead arises; but does not affect the substantive common law or the Forfeiture Act 1982 (see paragraph 18–08 below), as regards the variation of succession in consequence of a criminal killing.

---

[13] Such as the order that was afterwards considered in *The Ampthill Peerage* [1977] A.C. 547.

[14] *Noel v. Becker* [1971] 1 W.L.R. 355, the ordinary position; the court is of course concerned to approve an order by consent on behalf of a minor or other party without capacity.

[15] *Sherdley v. Sherdley* [1988] A.C. 213 at p. 225.

[16] *Whiteside v. Whiteside* [1950] Ch. 65.

[17] *Re Pollock* [1941] Ch. 219.

[18] *Re Pitts* [1931] 1 Ch. 546; *Re Sigsworth* [1935] Ch. 89.

[19] *Re Giles* [1972] Ch. 544, where the deceased's wife had been sentenced to be detained at Broadmoor having been guilty of manslaughter with diminished responsibility under the Homicide Act 1957, s.2.

[20] *Re Houghton* [1915] 1 Ch. 173. The difference between the facts of *Re Giles* above and *Re Houghton* seems, however, rather to be in the nomenclature of the criminal law than in the material facts.

18–06 Death of the criminal too. When the criminal is also dead, the principle applies and excludes the estate of the killer from benefit, even though there has been no conviction under the criminal law.[21] The subject-matter then devolves as if the deceased had not survived or had not been a member of the relevant class.[22] The same principles apply to someone who has unlawfully aided, abetted, counselled or procured the death.[23]

18–07 Co-owners and criminal killing. Where the murderer and the victim are co-owners of a life policy payable on the first death, which was charged to a mortgagee and duly paid at the death, the murderer is excluded by public policy from benefiting; and the policy money is treated as having been entirely that of the victim's estate.[24]

18–08 Statutory modification of the common law. Under the Forfeiture Act 1982 there is a statutory power for the court to modify the rule, and its application to the Inheritance (Provision for Family and Dependants) Act 1975, at the court's discretion.[25]

The Act applies to every sort of succession on death[26]; it does not apply for the benefit of someone who "stands convicted" of murder,[27] as distinct from other forms of unlawful killing. There is an exceptionally short period of limitation of three months from the date of the conviction,[28] not of the determination of any appeal. If no grant of representation has been made by then, the applicant proceeds against the deceased's estate without there being a grant.[29] The application is made by originating summons in the Chancery Division,[30] and is likely to be determined in chambers.

---

[21] *Re Callaway* [1956] Ch. 559; *Re Dellow* [1964] 1 W.L.R. 451.
[22] *Re Callaway* above; *Re Peacock* [1957] Ch. 310.
[23] Forfeiture Act 1982, s.1(2).
[24] *Davitt v. Titcumb* [1990] Ch. 110.
[25] See for indications of the way the discretion may be exercised *Re Royce* [1985] Ch. 22 and *Re K.* [1985] 85, affirmed [1986] Ch. 180.
[26] s.2(4).
[27] s.5; someone convicted of murder at the trial, whose conviction is on appeal reduced to manslaughter could probably apply for a modification under the Forfeiture Act 1982 within three months from the determination of the appeal; although the Criminal Appeal Act 1968, s.3(2) suggested that in such a case the substituted conviction for manslaughter dates from the time of the original conviction for murder. The Criminal Procedure (Insanity and Unfitness to Plead) Act 1991, s.4(2) has conferred new powers on the Court of Appeal under a substituted s.14 of the Criminal Appeal Act 1968 to "make an order" in such a case. Under s.14 of the 1968 Act the power of the Court of Appeal had been to "substitute a verdict". The question discussed in the first edition para. 18–08, note 27 will not arise under the new s.14 on orders made after January 1, 1992: when the three month period should run from any order that the Court of Appeal decides to "make" under it.
[28] s.2(3).
[29] Under R.S.C., Ord. 15, r. 6A.
[30] Under Ord. 5, r. 4(2); as in *Re K.* above.

18–09 Foreign domicile and criminal killing. The movable property in England of a deceased person with a foreign domicile devolves here under the law of the deceased's domicile.[31] In such a case the court in England and Wales would be likely to apply to the devolution the analogous rule of the law of the domicile.[32] If, however, the law of the domicile turned out to permit the killer to succeed to the estate of the victim, that part of the law of the domicile might be rejected here on the basis that "an English court will refuse to apply a law which outrages its sense of justice or decency."[33] The result would be that English common law and the Forfeiture Act 1982 would be applied to the devolution of the movables in England of the murdered person, and of any immovables elsewhere devolving by *renvoi* under English law.[34]

---

[31] See Chap. 11.
[32] On the analogy of *Re Ross* [1930] 1 Ch. 377.
[33] Scarman J. in *Re Fuld (No. 3)* [1968] P. 675 at p. 698; there is ample authority in other fields for this residual power in an English court: *Re Meyer* [1971] P. 298; *Oppenheimer v. Cattermole* [1976] A.C. 249; *Winckworth v. Christies* [1980] Ch. 496, *obiter* at p. 514.
[34] See Chap. 11 above as to the system of law applicable to succession.

113

19. Power to pay without proof of title: powers of nomination

19–01 Subject-matter. This chapter concerns powers resembling in their effect the power to make a will, but with a different legal basis.

19–02 Statutory power to make payment on death without proof of title. Under the Administration of Estates (Small Payments) Act 1965, s.1, the institutions mentioned in Schedule One may, after a death, make small payments[1] to relatives and dependants of the deceased without the necessity for probate or other proof of title under the private Acts scheduled there. This is a statutory power to make payment of money that is in law vested in someone else.

19–03 Statutory power of nomination. There are a few statutory powers to make an unwitnessed nomination of the nominator's own property at death, instead of making an attested will. Under section 2 of the Administration of Estates (Small Payments) Act 1965, the statutory power to make a "nomination" operating on death, under the enactments listed in Schedule 2, was increased to a limit of a fund of £5,000; with power under section 6 to provide for further increases. There was a power to make a nomination up to £500 until April 30, 1979, in respect of the Trustee Savings Bank; and until April 30, 1980, in respect of National Savings or National Savings Certificates.

---

[1] The limit has been increased from £100 to £5,000.

A nomination can only be made, when at the date of the nomination, the sum to the nominator's credit is within the statutory limit.[2] The question whether any excess at death over the statutory limit devolves under the nomination or devolves on the personal representatives of the deceased appears to depend on the particular power of nomination.[3] A statutory nomination can be revoked in the manner specified in the regulations governing it; but not by will.[4] A statutory nomination fails when the nominee dies in the lifetime of the nominator[5]; but probably does not have the benefit of the Wills Act 1837 as amended by section 33.[6] A nomination that is invalid because it related to a sum in excess of the statutory limit, if executed before two witnesses, is, however, admitted to probate as a will[7]; and then section 33 should apply.

The due exercise of a power of nomination excludes the personal representatives from the nominated fund; its potential liability to meet the deceased's liabilities is discussed in paragraph 26–12.

19–04 Private power of nomination, under a pension scheme or a similar trust. Pension fund schemes, and trusts of a policy of insurance, frequently confer on members a power of nomination (by an informal instrument) of those to benefit at the nominator's death. Although the same word "nomination" is used, this private power is different from the statutory powers mentioned in paragraph 19–03. A pension fund nomination, conferred by a private document, may relate to non-assignable interests over which the nominator does not have a full power of disposition during his lifetime. In such a case, the exercise of the power of nomination depends on the terms of the document conferring the power, as in the case of any other power of appointment. The nomination, or any revocation of a nomination, does not need to be executed as a will, under the statutory provisions for the execution of wills.[8] On the other hand, where, during his lifetime, the member making the nomination has, under the scheme, full power of disposition of the amount standing to his credit, "a disposition of that interest upon his death would normally constitute a testamentary disposition requiring attestation in accordance with the statutory requirements for the execution of a will."[9]

---

[2] *Eccles, etc., Society v. Griffiths* [1912] A.C. 483.
[3] Same case at p. 491.
[4] *Bennett v. Slater* [1899] 1 Q.B. 45.
[5] *Re Barnes* [1940] Ch. 267.
[6] Preserving for issue gifts to a predeceased child or issue made by *will*. The point does not appear to have been decided in a reported case.
[7] *Re Baxter* [1903] P. 12; approved in *Baird v. Baird* [1990] 2 A.C. 548 at p. 557.
[8] *Re Danish Bacon* [1971] 1 W.L.R. 248; *Baird v. Baird* above, where the Judicial Committee of the Privy Council reviewed the authorities. It is even more so (*a fortiori*) when the nomination or its revocation needs the consent of the trustees of the fund: *Baird v. Baird*.
[9] *Baird v. Baird* above at p. 561; see at pp. 558 to 560 discussing *Re MacInnes* [1935] 1 D.L.R. 401, *Re Shirley* (1965) 49 D.L.R. (2d) 474 and *Re Danish Bacon* above.

The liability of such nominated funds to the deceased's liabilities at death depends on whether the power of appointment is a general power of appointment (when the subject-matter is liable)[10]; or is not a general power (when it is not liable to meet the deceased's liabilities).[11]

19–05 Need for alteration of the law. The informality surrounding a statutory "nomination" facilitates improper pressure to sign one and obstructs any attack on the nomination after a death. The need to relieve the poorer members of a society from the expense of making a will[12] has ceased to be as important as the need to protect them and their true donees from improper pressure to make a nomination. This statutory power of nomination is of limited scope now; and ought to be abrogated by statute.

The protection of the formalities surrounding wills should, for the future, be extended to all privately conferred powers of nomination at death, under pension schemes or the trusts of policies of insurance. Substantial sums may devolve under these nominations. The nominator and his true donees need the protection of probate law relating to their exercise.[13]

---

[10] A.E.A. 1925, s.55(3); but at a late stage in the order of incidence of liabilities: and Sched. I, Pt. II, para. 7: see para. 26–12.

[11] *Ashby v. Costin* (1888) 21 Q.B. 401; *Re Davies* [1892] 3 Ch. 63.

[12] See *Eccles v. Griffiths* above, at p. 490.

[13] See paras. 41–12 and 41–13.

Part Three: Assets and Powers over Them

20. Getting in assets

20–01 Duty to get in assets. The personal representatives must get in the assets of the estate.[1] The assets must be safeguarded.[2] A will may give specific directions about converting assets or postponing their converting.[3] Apart from such directions, what should be done is a matter for the personal representatives' judgment. After collecting each asset, there are two courses that the personal representatives may properly take. They are (i) to get the asset in by realising it in cash; (ii) to decide[4] to postpone, during the administration of the estate, converting the asset into cash for the time being.[5] Personal representatives who on reasonable grounds decide to postpone converting an asset, are not liable if it afterwards falls in value, (showing that a decision to sell earlier would have been more beneficial)[6]; nor, for the same reasons, are they liable if they get in the asset and it afterwards rises in value.

Personal representatives are liable, however, for the ensuing loss (to the extent discussed in Chapter 45) if they behave with wilful default.[7] It is wilful default for the personal representatives not to consider whether or not to call in a debt.[8] In one case, personal representatives were held guilty of wilful default where they received interest regularly on a mortgage debt and did not inspect the property charged.[9] The property was in fact unoccupied and derelict; and when the principal money was called in, it was irrecoverable. Some cases, imposing a more severe liability,[10] decided before the test of

---

[1] A.E.A. 1925, s.25 as substituted by A.E.A. 1971, s.9.

[2] *Re Chapman* [1896] 2 Ch. 763; *Hiddingh Heirs v. de Villiers* (1887) 12 App.Cas. 624.

[3] As in *Re Rooke* [1953] Ch. 716 where a will was held to direct an immediate sale, excluding L.P.A. 1925, s.25. A.E.A. 1925, s.39 was not cited.

[4] Under A.E.A. 1925, s.39.

[5] *Re Chapman* above; *Marsden v. Kent* (1887) 5 Ch.Div. 598.

[6] For they acted under statutory powers; compare the position apart from those powers: *Marsden v. Kent* above, depreciating foreign shares; *Re Chapman*.

[7] *Hiddingh Heirs v. de Villiers* (1887) 12 App.Cas. 624 on appeal from the Cape of Good Hope: where it was found that in the circumstances there had been unreasonable delay and negligence in the sale of company shares with unlimited liability; *Re Chapman* above; *Grayburn v. Clarkson* (1868) 3 Ch.App. 605, where company shares with unlimited liability were retained for 15 years without explanation.

[8] *Re Greenwood* (1911) 105 L.T. 509. They had become trustees, but this did not affect the decision.

[9] *Re Brookes* [1914] 1 Ch. 558.

[10] Such as *Sculthorpe v. Tipper* (1871) 13 Eq. 232 which would be differently decided under modern law: see at p. 239 showing that the modern statutory requirements would be satisfied.

wilful default[11] was enacted, are not applicable now and are misleading.

One year from the death (not from the grant) is the standard time during which the personal representatives should either get in the assets,[12] or exercise their discretion to postpone conversion.[13] A longer period[14] or a shorter period[15] may be appropriate in special circumstances.

Personal representatives should, in all but the simplest cases, obtain advice about the estate's assets, and whether and how to realise them. They should also obtain advice as to how to exercise their power under A.E.A. 1925, s.39 to postpone sale during the administration in the light of current conditions. Modern rates of interest and modern stock exchange conditions are unlike those that underlie the authorities stating the general principle cited in the preceding footnotes.

20–02 Rights to be considered. An estate may be found to hold any rights known to the law. Some that need frequent consideration are mentioned below.

20–03 Land in England and Wales. Land to which title is not registered vests in the personal representatives.[16] They will also have the right to exercise an option over land.[17] Registered land does not automatically vest in personal representatives; they may be registered as proprietors,[18] or may deal with the land without being themselves registered.[19]

A house, whether freehold or leasehold, needs to be secured if vacant, and insured. The rent must be paid and other terms of a lease must be observed to avoid forfeiture of the lease. Chattels must be safeguarded and insured.

A house or other immovable property may be subject to charges, or to rights of occupation arising under a constructive trust or under

---

[11] Trustee Act 1925, s.30(1) and s.61 applying to personal representatives under s.68(17); replacing the Trustee Act 1893, s.24 and s.50 and the Judicial Trustees Act 1896, s.3.

[12] *Re Chapman* above.

[13] Under A.E.A. 1925, s.39 if applicable.

[14] In *Marsden v. Kent* above, 15 months was reasonable in the circumstances.

[15] *Hiddingh Heirs v. de Villiers* above, where the personal representatives should have sold shares with unlimited liability within six months.

[16] A.E.A. 1925, ss.1 and 2.

[17] *Re Adams & the Kensington Vestry* (1884) 27 Ch.Div. 394, where the right was annexed to a lease.

[18] The Land Registration Rules 1925, r. 168.

[19] The L.R.R. 1925, r. 170(1); although it seems that a purchaser may insist on the personal representatives being themselves registered as proprietors before completion: the Land Registration Act 1925, s.110(5). Any power of one of several personal representatives to deal with unregistered land (*Fountain Forestry v. Edwards* [1975] Ch. 1) is unlikely to be accepted as applicable to registered land; so that the question whether one of them may deal with land may become obsolete with the spread of registration of title.

an estoppel in equity entitling someone to reside there or to enjoy other rights.[20] The personal representatives can compromise or allow a claim to enjoy such rights under the Trustee Act 1925, s.15.[21]

20–04 Lost title documents. When the deceased's title documents cannot be found, there are several possibilities.

There may be a lien or equitable charge created (unknown to the deceased's personal representatives) by deposit of the land certificate,[22] or (in the case of land the title to which is not registered) of the title deeds.[23] The deceased may have held a land certificate that has been lost, where the registrar has power to issue a replacement.[24] An index map search under the Land Registration Rules 1925, r.286 shows whether title to the land is registered. When the title deeds to land in an area of compulsory registration of title[25] are lost, the registrar may grant first registration of title.[26] He may do so in the case of loss or destruction of the title deeds, by fire, flood, criminal acts, or in the custody of a solicitor, building society or bank or in the post to or from any of them.[27] Otherwise, the personal representatives face a difficult task in making title when the title deeds are missing. Before contracting to sell the deceased's property the personal representatives should instruct solicitors to apply for registration of the title, or formulate appropriate special conditions of sale[28]: this is important now that statute has withdrawn the protection justly given by the common law to a vendor whose title turns out to be bad.[29]

20–05 Registration of title on sale compulsory now. Registration of title on sale is compulsory throughout England and Wales now.[30] The opening of the Register of Titles to public inspection under L.R.A. 1988 is however of no practical help to personal representatives who do not know but wish to find out what land the deceased held; for the *public* right of inspection is only a right to inspect specified titles. A search against the *name* of a proprietor is needed to find out what land a deceased person held; but such a search is only allowed for official investigations.[31]

---

[20] See Snell, *Equity*, at pp. 568–579.
[21] See para. 23–08.
[22] L.R.A. 1925, s.66.
[23] Megarry & Wade, *Real Property* (5th ed.), at pp. 927–929.
[24] L.R.A. 1925, s.67(2); see Ruoff & Roper, *Registered Conveyancing* (5th ed.), at pp. 45–47.
[25] L.R.A. 1925, s.123.
[26] Ruoff & Roper, at pp. 234–238.
[27] Ruoff & Roper at pp. 234–238.
[28] See Williams, *Vendor & Purchaser*, (4th ed.) at p. 187; and Dart, *Vendors & Purchasers*, (8th ed.), at p. 310.
[29] L.P.A. 1989, s.3.
[30] Registration of Title Order 1989 (S.I. 1989 No. 1347).
[31] Land Registration (Open Register) Order 1990 (S.I. 1990 No. 1362).

20–06 Contracts to purchase land. *General rule.* Personal representatives may enforce by an Order for specific performance a contract to sell land to the deceased.[32]

Exception: "Right to buy". There is an exception. When a purchaser exercises his statutory right to buy[33] a freehold from the local authority but dies before the actual transfer, his personal representatives cannot obtain an Order for specific performance and are left to any remedy in damages.[34] This is a hard decision. On the facts, the local authority "had long overrun what anyone would deem a reasonable time for executing the conveyance ... and were in breach of their statutory duty and their claim for possession now [was] in fact based on their own dilatory conduct".[35] The Court of Appeal's reserved judgments are based on the words of the Act; but the decision contrasts with the doctrine that equity looks on that as done which ought to be done[36]; and with the way that earlier generations of judges dealt with the Statute of Frauds 1677, s.4 and L.P.A. 1925, s.40,[37] which required evidence in writing of a contract of sale of land; for unwritten agreements of sale of land were nevertheless enforced after part performance.[38] The decision cannot be supported on the ground that specific performance is a discretionary remedy[39]; because the discretion was that of the trial judge, who exercised it in favour of the personal representatives of the deceased purchaser. At present this is the law; but if the case is taken to the House of Lords, there may be a different result.

20–07 Land elsewhere. English law treats immovables (land and houses) outside England and Wales as governed by the law of the place where it is situated.[40] It is necessary to obtain legal advice about such property on the law of the place where it is situated. Problems may arise about obtaining title to it after a death; and about its devolution. It may devolve directly on those beneficially entitled, subject to provisions as to the deceased's liabilities; or it may be in a country that refers succession back (*renvoi*) to the law of the deceased's nationality.[41]

---

[32] Williams, *Vendor & Purchaser* (4th ed.), p. 566, citing numerous authorities in note (d). Their obligation to perform the deceased's contracts is however discussed below in para. 25–03.

[33] Housing Act 1985, s.118.

[34] *Bradford City v. McMahon* [1994] 1 W.L.R. 52, C.A., reversing the judgment at first instance in the County Court.

[35] *ibid.* at p. 59 B, quoting the judgment at first instance.

[36] Snell, *Equity* (29th ed.), at p. 40.

[37] Since repealed by the Law of Property (Miscellaneous Provisions) Act 1989, s.2.

[38] *Snell*, at pp. 600–601.

[39] *Snell* at p. 588.

[40] See para. 11–02 above and the cases cited there.

[41] See previous footnote.

20–08 United Kingdom shares. Shares or other securities in a publicly-quoted company registered in the United Kingdom are almost always transferable in writing[42] without restriction. Shares in a private limited company often have restrictions on transfer imposed in their articles of association; such restrictions bind the personal representatives of a deceased shareholder.[43] Personal representatives have a statutory right to transfer the deceased's shares, without themselves being registered[44]; and, subject to any relevant restrictions, they may themselves be registered as shareholders.[45] The personal representatives acquire the other rights that go along with the deceased's shares, such as a right to an allotment of new shares.[46] An attempt to deprive the personal representatives of such rights is treated strictly.[47]

20–09 Lost share certificates. From time to time the deceased appears not to hold certificates of shares registered in his name; which may have been lost or destroyed accidentally. The company is likely to require an indemnity for the issue of a new certificate.[48] There is no reason why the personal representatives should incur any personal liability, any more than trustees[49]; such an indemnity given by the personal representatives would endure after distribution of the estate. In such circumstances, the personal representatives should, at the cost of the estate, purchase from an insurance company an indemnity to the company in respect of the lost share certificate.[50]

20–10 Shares registered elsewhere. Shares or other securities in a company registered elsewhere can only validly be transferred or dealt with under the law of the place of the company's registration. Specialist advice is necessary about that. In some countries, one of which is France, bearer shares are found.[51] Caution is needed when dealing with them, and arranging for their custody.

20–11 Animals. The deceased's animals are part of his property, and vest in the personal representatives.[52] They often need costly

---

[42] Companies Act 1985, s.183.

[43] *Roberts v. Letter "T" Estates* [1961] A.C. 795.

[44] Companies Act 1985, s.183(3). All the personal representatives must execute the transfer: *Barton v. North Staffordshire Railway* (1888) 38 Ch.Div. 458; *Barton v. London & N.W. Railway* (1889) 24 Q.B.D. 77.

[45] *Scott v. Frank F. Scott (London) Ltd.* [1940] Ch. 794.

[46] *James v. Buena, etc., Syndicate* [1896] 1 Ch. 456; *Llewellyn v. Kastinoe Rubber Estates* [1914] 2 Ch. 670.

[47] *Ward v. Dublin North City Milling Co.* [1919] 1 Ir. 5 (company with notice of the death could not forfeit dividends by a notice sent to the deceased shareholder); the same principle underlies the cases cited in the previous note.

[48] As envisaged in Table A 1985, art. 7.

[49] Danckwerts J. in *Re Grimthorpe* [1958] Ch. 615 at p. 623.

[50] The absence of any reported cases on the point indicates that this has not been doubted.

[51] That is to say, shares, the ownership of which passes by delivery.

[52] *Re Ogilby* [1942] Ch. 288, cattle; *Re Hutchinson* [1955] Ch. 255, racehorses.

feeding and attention. Before accepting a grant, it is necessary to consider how any animals can be looked after, and insured. The R.S.P.C.A. can sometimes help personal representatives with practical problems about animals after the owner's death.

20–12 Other chattels. Other chattels may be valuable, perishable or in need of protection; and in need of insurance.

Personal representatives are not bound, though they are permitted, to procure the deceased's chattels which are situated in a foreign country.[53]

20–13 Blocked assets abroad. Various countries in the un-developed parts of the world block the remission of assets, under currency control regulations. If the deceased owned an asset of this kind at his death, the steps to be taken by the personal representatives depends upon what can be done to realise the asset in view of the local regulations. It may be practicable to sell the asset in England—to a bank or other institution with interests in that country. It may only be possible to make an assent of the asset, in favour of the beneficiaries or of trustees for them; and to await the time when the remission of funds is permitted.

PARTNERSHIP INTERESTS

20–14 Generally. On a partner dying, his personal representatives must get in his rights as a former partner. Those rights, if there are any, are governed by the partnership agreement. They may take many forms; but fall into three main classes.

20–15 The Partnership Act 1890 to apply. When there is no express provision, or there is an express provision that the Partnership Act 1890 shall apply, the partnership is dissolved at the death[54] and must then be wound up. The partnership assets must all be sold,[55] including the goodwill, if of saleable value.[56] After payment of partnership liabilities each partner is repaid rateably what is due to him for advances and in respect of capital. The ultimate residue, including the estate of the deceased partner, is divided among the former partners, in the proportion in which profits are

---

[53] *Re Scott* [1915] 1 Ch. 592 at pp. 606–607, and 610.
[54] Partnership Act 1890, s.33(1).
[55] s.39.
[56] *Hill v. Fearis* [1905] 1 Ch. 466; *Gifford v. Harris* [1961] N.Z.L.R. 622.

divided, unless otherwise agreed.[57] The winding-up is effected by the surviving partners,[58] unless otherwise ordered by the court in a partnership action, when a receiver is often appointed.[59]

This application of the Partnership Act 1890 is favourable to the estate of a deceased partner; for in this way the estate gets its share of the benefit of a rise in value of any assets after the death.[60] The estate also has a right to a share of profits or to interest between the death and the winding-up.[61]

20–16 Continuation on payment of the value at death. When the partnership agreement provides for the surviving partners or partner to take over the assets and to pay the estate of a deceased partner the *value* of the deceased's share in the assets, the personal representatives are entitled to receive the relevant proportion of the *actual* value of those assets at the death,[62] not merely the proportion of the book values. An arrangement for the estate to receive such payment is usually fair to the estate and to the surviving partners.

20–17 Continuation on payment of book values. A provision that the estate of a deceased partner is to receive the book value of the assets binds the estate[63]; it is likely to be unfavourable to the estate of the deceased partner.

20–18 Continuation "at par". An agreement that the estate of the deceased partner is to be paid "at par" entitles the estate only to the deceased partner's original capital contribution.[64]

20–19 Correction of a valuation. Personal representatives are entitled to have corrected a valuation made on an incorrect basis.[65] This is a valuable right. Personal representatives faced with an apparently inadequate variation should consider whether this right is available; an inadequate valuation is often increased by way of compromise, under the Trustee Act 1925, s.15.[66]

---

[57] s.44.
[58] s.38.
[59] R.S.C., Ord. 30, r. 1, and *The Supreme Court Practice* 1991, n. 30/1/15 at p. 534.
[60] *Chandroutie v. Gajadhar* [1987] A.C. 147, approving *Barclays Bank Trust Co. v. Bluff* [1982] Ch. 172.
[61] s.42.
[62] *Cruickshank v. Sutherland* (1922) 128 L.T. 449, H.L.; *Travis v. Milne* (1851) 9 Ha. 141 at p. 153; *Noble v. Noble* 1965 S.L.T. 415 (Scotland).
[63] *Coventry v. Barclay* (1878) 3 de G.J. & S. 320; *Lawes v. Lawes* (1878) 9 Ch.Div. 98; *Hunter v. Dowling* [1893] 3 Ch. 212.
[64] *Gifford v. Harris* [1961] N.Z.L.R. 622.
[65] *Smith v. Gale* [1974] 1 W.L.R. 9.
[66] See para. 23–08.

THE BUSINESS OF A DECEASED SOLE TRADER

20–20 Generally. A business carried on by a sole trader (including the last survivor of former partners) usually cannot be sold at once, and needs to be carried on meanwhile. This involves the personal representatives making new contracts and incurring personal liability[67] on such contracts; with a right of indemnity from the estate.[68] When the assets are sufficient to meet all liabilities, including those incurred after the death, the personal representatives need only consider their position as regards the beneficiaries; otherwise the rights of the creditors need to be considered, on any deficiency of assets. The rights of creditors involve difficult questions. The realisation of a business may be difficult in practice, especially for those not accustomed to business.

20–21 Authority of and indemnity to personal representatives to carry on the business. The personal representatives are, to the extent of the available assets, entitled to an indemnity for the liabilities incurred in carrying on the business after the death[69]; including liability for torts reasonably incurred in the course of the business.[70] This right of indemnity is subject to making good any financial default on their own part.[71]

A receiver administering the estate has the same right of indemnity.[72] Accordingly so has a judicial trustee, appointed under the Judicial Trustees Act 1896.

20–22 Postponement. The personal representatives are entitled by law to carry on the deceased's business "for such a reasonable time as was necessary to enable them to sell [the] business property as a going concern"[73]; how long that is, is a question of fact in each case. Whatever the will says, or the creditors or beneficiaries request, it is unwise for personal representatives to agree to carry on a business indefinitely.

20–23 No competition by personal representatives. A personal representative selling a business is not permitted to compete with it himself.[74]

---

[67] *Owen v. Delamere* (1872) 15 Eq. 134; *Farhall v. Farhall* (1871) 7 Ch.App. 123.
[68] See [1891] A.C. 190.
[69] *Dowse v. Gorton* [1891] A.C. 190; *Re Johnson* (1880) 15 Ch.Div. 548; *Re Kidd* (1894) 70 L.T. 648; *Re Frith*.
[70] *Re Raybould* [1900] 1 Ch. 199.
[71] *Re Johnson* above; as distinct from a default only in procedure, such as in lodging accounts: *Re Johnson*. See the analogous case *Jennings v. Mather* [1901] 1 K.B. 108, affirmed [1902] 1 K.B. 1 (where the assignee under a deed for the benefit of creditors incurred debts for which he was personally liable and then himself became bankrupt).
[72] *Re Brooke* [1894] 2 Ch. 600.
[73] *Dowse v. Gorton* above at p. 199.
[74] *Re Thomson* [1930] 1 Ch. 203; this is part of the overriding rule against a conflict of interest: exemplified in *Industrial Development Consultants Ltd v. Cooley* [1972] 1 W.L.R. 443.

20–24 Creditors of the business of a deceased sole trader. There are two classes of creditors: (i) creditors of the business at the death; (ii) subsequent creditors of the business to whom a liability is incurred while winding up the estate during a reasonable period or during any extended period to which they have agreed. Creditors at the date of the death do not take under the will or intestacy, and are not bound by the terms of any will.[75]

During the period necessary to sell the business, the right of the personal representatives to an indemnity from the estate for liabilities incurred to subsequent creditors in carrying on the business, has priority over the deceased's liabilities due at the death.[76] That continues as long as the creditors at the death assent to the continued postponement of a sale of the business.[77]

Once the reasonable time for winding up the business has elapsed, the claims against the estate of any creditors at the death, who have not assented to a continuance of the business, have priority over the personal representatives' right to indemnity for subsequently-incurred obligations.[78]

Creditors at the death must, in any application to the court, either treat the continued carrying on of the business as proper or (if entitled to do so) treat it as improper.[79] Making a claim based on the continuance of the business binds a creditor to treat the continuance as proper.[80] On the same principle, without litigation, the personal representatives are entitled to require the trade creditors to elect whether or not to accept the continued conduct of the business with a view to its realisation. It was held many years ago that merely standing by with knowledge of the business being carried on does not amount to such assent.[81] That was however before the modern expansion of the doctrine of equitable estoppel[82]; nowadays, standing by with such knowledge might amount to an assent that cannot be withdrawn.

20–25 Payment of interest to creditors. In an estate administered under the court's directions, at a time (1936) when it was widely thought that interest was not payable at common law on sums due,[83] trade creditors were held entitled (in priority to beneficiaries) to interest on sums due to them, at the rate of 4 per cent., as from the

---

[75] *Dowse v. Gorton* [1891] A.C. 190 at p. 199; *Re Salmen* (1912) 107 L.T. 108; *Re Oxley* [1914] 1 Ch. 604.
[76] *Dowse v. Gorton* above.
[77] *ibid.*
[78] *Re Oxley* above; *Re East* (1914) 111 L.T. 101, below.
[79] *Dowse v. Gorton* above at p. 203.
[80] *M'Ginley v. Gallagher* [1929] Ir. 307.
[81] *Re Oxley* [1914] 1 Ch. 604; *Re East* (1914) 111 L.T. 101.
[82] From *Inwards v. Baker* [1965] 2 Q.B. 29 onwards.
[83] *Chitty on Contracts* (25th ed.), para. 1744.

date when what was due had been ascertained.[84] The Supreme Court Act 1981, s.35A should enable trade creditors to claim interest now at a realistic rate.

20–26 Subrogation. Questions of priority arise when the estate turns out to be insufficient to pay, in full, both the creditors at the death and the subsequent trade creditors. Those subsequent trade creditors who have assented to the personal representatives continuing the business by subrogation, stand in the position of the personal representatives. They can assert for their own benefit the right of the personal representatives to an indemnity out of the estate.[85] This right is not available in so far as the personal representatives are in default of payment of money[86]; and it is not available to a trade creditor who has not assented to the business being carried on, but has merely stood by.[87]

20–27 Future development of the law. In or above the Court of Appeal it would be open to the court to disregard the narrow distinctions in the cases cited above; and to apply the "very much broader approach" nowadays adopted towards equitable claims.[88] The court could base the right of subrogation on what was the common intention of the parties at the time.[89]

20–28 Beneficiaries in the estate of a deceased sole trader. Beneficiaries take as donees, and so are bound by the terms of the will or intestacy. A will normally contains an express power to postpone sale of a business; or the power to postpone sale is implied by the L.P.A. 1925, s.25. On an intestacy, there is a trust for sale with power to postpone sale under the A.E.A. 1925, s.33. These powers authorise the personal representatives to carry on a business for a reasonable time[90]; what that is depends on the facts of each case.[91]

---

[84] *Re Bracey* [1936] Ch. 690.
[85] *Re Johnson* above; *Re Kidd* above; *Re Frith* above (although there had been a default in lodging accounts).
[86] *Re Johnson* above.
[87] *Re Oxley* [1914] 1 Ch. 605; similarly *Farhall v. Farhall* above.
[88] *Habib Bank v. Habib Bank* [1981] 1 W.L.R. 1265 at p. 1285, citing *Taylor Fashions v. Liverpool Victoria Trustees Co.* subsequently reported at [1982] Q.B. 133n. at pp. 151–152.
[89] See *Orakpo v. Manson Investments* [1978] A.C. 95, the second point; and in a company liquidation *Re Tramway Building & Construction Co.* [1988] Ch. 293.
[90] *Dowse v. Gorton* above.
[91] *Re Chancellor* (1884) 26 Ch.Div. 42; *Re Smith* [1896] 1 Ch. 171, where two years was found to be a reasonable time. The decision *Re Crowther* [1895] 2 Ch. 56, where 22 years was found not too long, may have gone too far: see *Re Smith* at pp. 174. Modern business conditions, and communications, are very different from what they were at that time.

20–29 Legatee of a business. The principles stated above about priority between creditors only apply to the creditors of those trading in a representative capacity; they do not apply to a legatee of a business who has taken possession of it.[92] Such a legatee is liable to his creditors under the ordinary law, not the subject of this book.

20–30 Practical position of personal representatives of a deceased sole trader. The administration of an estate of a deceased sole trader is difficult as a practical matter; and the state of the law, in the case of deficiency of assets, makes it hazardous. When realising a business, personal representatives are likely to require the protection of acting under the directions of the court.[93] This is so especially if there is a prospect of the assets being insufficient to pay all the creditors (both those owed money at the death and subsequently); or if realisation may take more than a few months. Beneficiaries are very ready to blame personal representatives for losses or expenses in the light of subsequent knowledge. The absence of modern reported litigation on these questions indicates that personal representatives rarely take the personal risks involved in winding up the business of a deceased sole trader when there is a possibility of a shortfall of assets to meet liabilities, or of delay in realisation.

THE DECEASED'S BENEFICIAL INTERESTS UNDER A TRUST

20–31 Co-ownership. Co-ownership of land can exist only under a trust.[94] Where the beneficial interest is as *joint* tenants, the beneficial interest at a death of one of them accrues by devolving automatically on the survivor/s. Where, however, the beneficial interests are as *tenants-in-common*, the share of any who die vests in his personal representatives, like any other asset.

This position may be confusing to those accustomed to a system of law that does not have these separate forms of co-ownership.

20–32 Other beneficial interests under a trust. Beneficial interests under a trust, or in the estate of someone who had died previously, vest in the deceased's personal representatives. They are got in by claiming them from the trustees or from the personal representatives holding the trust property. This applies to vested interests (that is to say unconditional interests, though still future interests).[95] It also applies to those contingent (that is to say, conditional) interests that

[92] *Re O'Kelly* [1920] 1 Ir. 205.
[93] See Chap. 42.
[94] L.P.A. 1925, s.34, s.35 and s.36.
[95] As *Re Cohn* [1974] 1 W.L.R. 1378 and similar cases: see Jarman, *Wills* (8th ed.), at p. 1393.

have not failed at the death, and are therefore transmissible to personal representatives.[96]

20–33 Entailed property. An entailed interest, rarely met nowadays, may be disentailed by will[97]; and if so disentailed it is likewise liable for the testator's debts.[98] If not disentailed, it devolves under the continuing entail, and forms no part of the deceased's estate; and is then not within the powers of the deceased's personal representatives.

PROPERTY SUBJECT TO A POWER OF APPOINTMENT

20–34 Powers of appointment. Under a will, or a trust, someone (the "appointor") may be given power to appoint by will or otherwise how the property of the original donor (whether a testator under a will, or a settlor under a trust) is to devolve. The right of a testator to create by his will a power of appointment is well-settled.[99] The right to create an intermediate power was recently challenged, as amounting to delegation; it was held that a testator may create an intermediate power.[1] There are three types of power, known as a general power, a special power and a hybrid power.

A *general* power is a power that authorises the appointor to appoint the property "in any manner he may think proper."[2] A power to appoint for any persons includes power to appoint on lawful trusts or for lawful purposes.[3] A power to appoint in any manner the appointer thinks proper is a general power, even though it has to be exercised with the consent of the *trustees* of the trust.[4] On the other hand, a power to appoint generally with the consent of someone else (not that of the *trustees*) is not a general power[5]; nor is a power of appointment held by two persons jointly.[6]

A *special* power, sometimes called a limited power, only authorises the appointor to appoint the property in favour of specified persons or classes.[7]

---

[96] Jarman, *Wills*, at pp. 1342–1343.
[97] L.P.A. 1925, s.176.
[98] A.E.A. 1925, s.55(3).
[99] See the cases cited in this paragraph and the next paragraph; and Sugden, *Powers* (8th ed.) (1861), for example at pp. 45 and 397.
[1] *Re Beatty* [1990] 1 W.L.R. 1503, where some of the cases were cited.
[2] Wills Act 1837, s.27.
[3] *Re Triffit* [1958] Ch. 852.
[4] *Re Phillips* [1931] 1 Ch. 347; *Commissioner of Estate and Succession Duties (Barbados) v. Bowring* [1962] A.C. 171 (on estate duty).
[5] *Re Watts* [1931] 2 Ch. 302; *Commissioner of Estate, etc. v. Bowring* above at p. 187.
[6] *Re Churston's Settled Estates* [1954] Ch. 334; approved in *Commissioner of Estate, etc. v. Bowring* above at p. 187.
[7] Farwell, *Powers* (3rd ed.), at p. 8.

A *hybrid* power (sometimes called an intermediate power) is a power that authorises an appointment to anyone except specified persons.[8] It is turned into a general power when the excluded persons cease to exist, or have never existed.[9]

The exercise by will of each type of power may produce different results, as below. Numerous questions[10] are capable of arising under powers: it is enough to say here that personal representatives normally need legal advice whenever the testator had a power of appointment.

20–35 Devolution of property subject to a general power of appointment. Personal representatives are not concerned with a power exercised by an instrument other than the deceased's will or codicil.

A residuary gift by will, or codicil,[11] operates as a gift of any property subject to a general power of appointment by the testator, unless a contrary intention is shown.[12] Such a contrary intention can only be shown from the words of the will; when the power was not even in the testator's mind, there is no such contrary intention.[13] The appointed property under a general power of appointment (whether exercised by a residuary gift or by an express appointment) becomes liable as assets to the testator's debts.[14] This happens even if the will does not give residue,[15] or gives residue in a way that fails or is revoked.[16]

It follows that whenever a testator has exercised a general power of appointment, the trustees of the fund over which the power was exercised ought to transfer the fund to the testator's personal representatives to be administered by them as part of the testator's own assets.[17] The testator's personal representatives should insist on a transfer of a generally appointed fund to themselves. If such a fund were left in the hands of the original trustees and then lost, the personal representatives would be liable for maladministration (*devastavit*) for having failed to get in that asset.

---

[8] Examples of a hybrid power are: a power to appoint to anyone except the appointor or a charity: *Re Park* [1932] 1 Ch. 580; and a power to appoint to anyone not related to the original testator's late wife: *Re Lawrence* [1972] Ch. 418, treating such a power as valid. A power to appoint to anyone living at the appointor's death is valid: *Re Jones* [1945] Ch. 105, treated as a hybrid power in *Re Lawrence* at p. 428.

[9] *Re Harvey* [1950] 1 All E.R. 491. a power to appoint to anyone except her husband when the appointor died a spinster.

[10] Summarised in Jarman, *Wills*, at pp. 787–861.

[11] A.E.A. 1925, s.57(1)(xxviii).

[12] Wills Act 1837, s.27.

[13] *Re Thirlwell* [1958] Ch. 146.

[14] A.E.A. 1925, s.55(3); but it is the last fund to be applied in a solvent estate: Sched. I, Pt II, para. 7.

[15] *Re Seabrook* [1911] 1 Ch. 151.

[16] *Re Jarrett* [1919] 1 Ch. 366.

[17] *Hayes v. Oatley* (1872) 14 Eq. 1; *Re Hoskin* (1877) 6 Ch.Div. 281, affirming 5 Ch.Div. 229; *Re Peacock* [1902] 1 Ch. 552; to the same effect, but turning on a question of estate duty, *O'Grady v. Wilmot* [1916] 2 A.C. 231.

If the general power is not exercised, or if it has been released,[18] then the subject-matter is not the concern of the testator's personal representatives.

20–36 Devolution of property subject to a special power of appointment. Property subject to a special power of appointment by the testator is not liable for the testator's debts. The trustees of the trust in which the appointment was made are entitled to administer the fund[19]; unless the power clearly authorises the appointor to appoint other trustees, and the appointor's will appoints as trustees his own personal representatives.[20]

20–37 Devolution of property subject to a hybrid power of appointment. A hybrid power[21] is not a general power.[22] Thus the exclusion, when the power is originally created, of a few unlikely persons as appointees prevents appointed property becoming liable for the appointor's debts at the death. The importance of hybrid powers is that this precaution is often adopted.[23]

The question, who should administer the trusts of property appointed by a hybrid power, has not been raised in a reported case. The conduct and duties of the trustees of a hybrid power are similar to those of the trustees of a special power[24]; and the subject-matter of a hybrid power is not liable for the appointor's debts. It follows that the original trustees should administer the property subject to a hybrid power: not the personal representatives of the appointor.

---

[18] A power of appointment may be released: L.P.A. 1925, s.155.

[19] *Busk v. Aldam* (1874) 19 Eq. 16; *Re Tyssen* [1894] 1 Ch. 56; *Re Mackenzie* [1916] 1 Ch. 125; *Re Mackenzie* [1917] 2 Ch. 58.

[20] *Re Adams' Trustees & Frost's Contract* [1907] 1 Ch. 695.

[21] See para. 20–32 above.

[22] *Re Byron's Settlement* [1891] 3 Ch. 474; unless the excepted person does not exist: *Re Harvey* [1950] 1 All E.R. 491 (exception of a spinster's husband).

[23] Thus the exclusion from the class of potential appointees of, say, any descendant of the Monarch is enough to make a power of appointment a hybrid power: so that the appointed property is then not liable at the death of the appointor for the appointor's debts. There is however a decision in Ireland, where property appointed by will under a hybrid power was held liable by statute for the appointor's debts at death: *Edie v. Babbington* (1854) 3 Ir. Ch. 568. This case is not consistent with the line of authority holding that a hybrid power is not a general power. If not a general power, a hybrid power does not fall within the words (A.E.A. 1925, s.32(1) "in pursuance of any general power". For a discussion of the case, see *Re Lawrence* [1972] Ch. at p. 428, Megarry J. *Edie v. Babbington* is not cited in *Wolstenholme & Cherry*, (12th ed.) (1932) or (13th ed.) (1972); nor in *Hood & Challis* (8th ed.) (1938). Although cited in other text books, *Edie v. Babbington* does not seem to represent the practice or the law in England: the test for the purposes of construing the words "any general power" in A.E.A. 1925, s.32(1) is whether the ambit of appointees is restricted, or not.

[24] *Re Manisty* [1974] Ch. 17.

APPORTIONMENT AT THE DEATH

20–38 The Apportionment Act 1870. Under the Apportionment Act 1870, income is considered to accrue from day to day and is apportionable accordingly. This means that income down to the death, apportioned on a day to day basis, forms part of the capital of the estate. The 1870 Act can usually be applied to the facts at each death. A dividend declared by what is now a private company[25] is within the 1870 Act.[26] A company dividend is within the Act when it is declared for a period during which the death occurs.[27] The 1870 Act is hardly ever excluded by will; the usual direction to treat as income the whole income of the testator's property does not exclude the Act;[28] nor do provisions in a company's Articles of Association, which can only operate between the company and the shareholder, not within the shareholder's estate.[29]

For the different question of apportionment under the 1870 Act between life-tenant and remainderman, see Gover, *Capital & Income* (3rd ed.) at pages 62–64.

---

[25] Companies Act 1985, s.1(3).
[26] *Re Jowitt* [1922] 2 Ch. 442.
[27] *Re White* [1913] 1 Ch. 231.
[28] *Re Edwards* [1918] 1 Ch. 142.
[29] *Re Oppenheimer* [1907] 1 Ch. 399.

21. Assets that need to be collected by litigation abroad

21–01 Litigation in England and Wales
21–02 Litigation in "convention countries"
21–03 Need for advice on the 1982 Act
21–04 The Civil Jurisdiction and Judgments Act 1991
21–05 Litigation in other parts of the United Kingdom
21–06 Litigation outside the United Kingdom

21–01 Litigation in England and Wales. The personal representatives of a deceased person may, in England and Wales, assert the rights of the deceased's estate in litigation[1] against any party liable to the estate (although as between the personal representatives and the beneficiaries the personal representatives need authority to cast litigation costs on the estate.[2] Assets requiring litigation may include claims for damages in tort and claims in contract (whether for damages or for specific performance or other relief).

21–02 Litigation in "convention countries." The intricate provisions of the Civil Jurisdiction and Judgments Act 1982 ("the 1982 Act") restrict the right to sue persons domiciled in one of the convention countries, or companies with a seat in one of the convention countries. Such persons or companies may normally be sued only in the country of the defendant's "domicile" (as defined for the purposes of the 1982 Act).[3] Exceptions likely to affect the collection of the assets of a deceased person relate to contract,[4] tort,[5]

---

[1] R.S.C., Ord. 15, r. 14; C.C.A. 1984, s.76.
[2] See para. 42–16.
[3] Domicile is defined for the purposes of the 1982 Act in s.41 and Sched. 1, art. 52 for individuals; and s.53 and art. 53 for companies; art. 2 provides for persons to be sued in the country of their domicile.
[4] Justiciable in the place for the performance of the contract: art. 5(1).
[5] Which may be made the subject-matter of a claim in the place where the harmful event occurred: art. 5(3).

insurance,[6] consumer contracts,[7] and agreed jurisdiction[8]; and to suing one of several necessary defendants.[9]

The convention countries are:

> Belgium
> Denmark
> Federal Republic of Germany
> France
> Republic of Ireland
> Italy
> Luxembourg
> Netherlands
> United Kingdom.

Greece, Spain and Portugal have been added to the Convention Countries.[10]

The 1982 Act does not apply to questions of wills and succession.[11]

A claim that someone is indebted or otherwise liable to the estate, as tortfeasor or by contract, should be characterised as a question of tort or contract rather than of succession.[12] A defence that the estate is not indebted to someone or is not liable to someone, should likewise not be characterised as a question of succession.

21–03 Need for advice on the 1982 Act. Before seeking to assert by litigation (either here or abroad) rights against any party within the 1982 Act, personal representatives need to obtain advice as to whether the Act applies. If the Act applies, they need advice on how they can and should, in the relevant convention country, assert their claim, as personal representatives, under the grant of representation in England; and the prospects and likely costs of success. The position of personal representatives under a grant may turn out to create difficulty in continental countries. Personal representatives also need due authority within the estate to engage in litigation.[13]

21–04 The Civil Jurisdiction and Judgments Act 1991. Under the Civil Jurisdiction and Judgments Act 1991 the Lugano Convention

---

[6] arts. 8 to 12A.
[7] arts. 13 to 15.
[8] arts. 17 and 18.
[9] art. 6(1).
[10] Civil Jurisdiction and Judgments Act 1982 (Amendment) Order 1989 (S.I. 1989 No. 1346; the Civil Jurisdiction and Judgments Act 1982 (Amendment) Order 1990 (S.I. 1990 No. 2591).
[11] Sched. 1, art. 1(1).
[12] According to Cheshire & North, *Private International Law* (12th ed.), at p. 288 "For English lawyers, there are no real problems in understanding what is meant by status, wills or succession."
[13] See para. 42–16.

took effect on May 1, 1992 (appointed by S.I. 1992 No. 745). The Lugano Convention, printed in English as a schedule to the Act, supplements and varies the Brussels Convention mentioned in paragraph 21–02. The Lugano Convention imposes provisions similar to the Brussels Convention in respect of "the Lugano Contracting States", being eighteen in number; they are:

Austria
Belgium
Denmark
Finland
France
Federal Republic of Germany
Hellenic Republic ("Greece")
Iceland
Republic of Ireland
Italy
Luxembourg
Netherlands
Norway
Portugal
Spain
Sweden
Switzerland
United Kingdom.

Under the Civil Jurisdiction and Judgments Act 1991 personal representatives need to obtain advice in relation to any of these Lugano Contracting States (as mentioned in paragraph 21–03).

21–05 Litigation in other parts of the United Kingdom. Schedule 4 to the 1982 Act provides for the allocation of jurisdiction within the United Kingdom. A defendant should normally be sued in the place of his domicile[14]; with exceptions:

(i) for contract,[15] and tort[16];
(ii) for provision for the enforcement of securities in the part of the United Kingdom where the charged property is[17];
(iii) for consumer contracts[18];
(iv) for provisions for suing one of several necessary defendants[19]; and

---

[14] art. 3.
[15] art. 5(1).
[16] art. 5(3).
[17] art. 5(8).
[18] arts. 13 and 14.
[19] art. 6.

(v) for agreements about which court shall have jurisdiction.[20]

Grants of representation made in England and Wales are recognised now in Northern Ireland and in Scotland.[21]

21–06 Litigation outside the United Kingdom. Specialist advice is needed before embarking, if necessary, on litigation elsewhere.

---

[20] arts. 14 and 15.
[21] A.E.A. 1971, ss.2 and 3.

22. Property not available as part of the estate

LIFETIME GIFTS AND ATTEMPTED GIFTS

22–01 Effect on the estate of gifts and imperfect gifts before the death. A gift validly made, however soon before the death, is effective when nothing more remained to be done by the donor.[1] When, however, anything more remained to be done by him to perfect the gift, there is no effective gift.[2] The rule is that the court will not perfect an imperfect gift.[3]

---

[1] *Re Stoneham* [1919] 1 Ch. 149 (chattels in the possession of the donee, given orally); *Re Westerton* [1919] 2 Ch. 104 (written assignment of bank credits handed to donee: the section cited is L.P.A. 1925, s.136 now); *Re Rose* [1949] Ch. 78; *Re Rose* [1952] Ch. 499 (another person of the same name): share transfers handed over with the necessary documents, but not registered before the death): *Letts v. I.R.C.* [1957] 1 W.L.R. 201, the 3rd point (a similar case).

[2] *Re Swinburne* [1926] Ch. 38 (the donor's own cheque not actually met before his death); *Re Hyslop* [1894] 3 Ch. 522 (letter cancelling a debt, not communicated to the debtor).

[3] *Milroy v. Lord* (1862) 4 de G.F. and J. 264; *Re Fry* [1946] Ch. 312 (where exchange control permission for the gift had not been obtained: a hard decision, since it was for the authorities not for the donor to decide whether or not to give such permission).

22–02 Exception: imperfect gifts, perfected in favour of an executor: *Strong* v. *Bird*. Under the anomalous rule in *Strong* v. *Bird*,[4] an imperfect gift to the person whom the deceased appointed as executor is perfected by that appointment. For the rule to operate there must be an intention continuing until the death to make a definite gift or a release of a definite debt.[5] Then the rule operates even though the donee is one of several executors[6]; or has not yet proved the will.[7] The effect of an executor renouncing probate in this connection has not been decided.[8]

The rule does not apply when any of its requirements are absent. It does not therefore apply when:

> (i) the sum to be paid remained indefinite[9]; (ii) an intention, continuing until the death, to make a gift was negatived by the deceased having taken security for the debt, vesting in her executor[10]; (iii) there was no intention to make an *immediate* gift, but only a gift at death[11]; (iv) there was no continuing intention, down to the death, to make the gift because the deceased forgot about it.[12]

To be within the rule in *Strong* v. *Bird*, the gift must be to the executor and for the benefit of the executor; not to the executor in trust for someone else.[13] It was even held that a gift of registrable land documents not registered before the death was not perfected by *Strong* v. *Bird*.[14]

22–03 Imperfect gifts in favour of an administrator. The rule in *Strong* v. *Bird* is based on the deceased's own appointment of the donee as his executor; but, in one case the rule was held to apply to an administrator.[15] This is open to doubt; the court selects an administrator indifferently, and so its extension to an administrator reduces the rule to "something in the nature of a lottery. I cannot

---

[4] (1874) 18 Eq. 315.

[5] *Re Stewart* [1908] 2 Ch. 251; *Re Pink* [1912] 2 Ch. 528; *Jenkins* v. *Jenkins* [1928] 2 K.B. 501; *Re James* [1935] Ch. 449.

[6] *Re Stewart* above.

[7] *Re Appelebee* [1891] 3 Ch. 422.

[8] The effect of A.E.A. 1925, s.5(iii) might be held to be that the renunciation is effective as at the date of the death; the section would probably prevent the executor from enjoying the benefit of the rule in *Strong* v. *Bird*, if renouncing probate.

[9] *Re Innes* [1910] 1 Ch. 188.

[10] *Re Eiser's Will Trusts* [1937] 1 All E.R. 244.

[11] *Re Freeland* [1952] Ch. 110.

[12] *Re Wale* [1956] 1 W.L.R. 1346; *Re Gonin* [1979] Ch. 16.

[13] *Re Halley* (1959) 43 M.P.R. 79, Winter J.; see at p. 83: this decision in Canada would probably be followed in England.

[14] *Cope* v. *Kelne* (1968) 118 C.L.R. 1. This decision in Australia might be distinguishable on L.R.A. 1925 in England.

[15] *Re James* [1935] Ch. 449.

think that equity is so undiscriminating."[16] An administrator should obtain the directions of the court, if minded to rely on the rule.

22–04 Conditional deathbed gifts (*donatio mortis causa*). English law recognises as valid a deathbed gift.[17] The subject-matter of such a gift does not devolve on the personal representatives.

To be valid, such a gift must be made in contemplation of death; it must be, or must be inferred from the circumstances to be, made conditionally on death; it must be made by delivery, of a chattel, or of a document evidencing the donor's rights to the investment or other asset given.[18] The delivery may be before or after the transaction[19]; and to one of two joint donees.[20] A *donatio* is only effective when the subject-matter is something capable of passing as a *donatio mortis causa*: the numerous cases on this run to narrow distinctions.[21] The test might, on the authorities, be that there may be a valid *donatio mortis causa* of chattels that anyhow pass by delivery,[22] or of rights that are represented by the document handed over.[23] This would not include rights that would not pass by the delivery effected, such as a cheque by the deceased not met (for whatever reason) in his lifetime,[24] even with the bank's passbook.[25] Land may be made the subject matter of a valid deathbed gift by handing over the title deeds.[26]

At first instance Mummery J. referred[27] to the need for judicial causation in extending the doctrine of *donatio mortis causa* beyond the limits previously decided and to the need for certainty in relation to land. The Court of Appeal[28] recognised that had the question arisen for decision in 1827 in *Duffield v. Elwes*,[29] the House of Lords would then have held that freehold land could not be made the subject matter of a *donatio mortis causa*; but, in the light of other

---

[16] Walton J. in *Re Gonin*, above at p. 35, *obiter*: where the application of the rule to an administrator was conceded. The decision in *Bailey's Case* (1682) 2 Mod. 315 is inconsistent with the rule being applied to an administrator; but *Bailey's Case* was not cited in *Re James* or in *Re Gonin*; and it might be distinguished as decided in an era when the law was rather different.

[17] In Latin: *donatio mortis causa*.

[18] *Re Craven* [1937] Ch. 423 at p. 426; *Birch v. Treasury Solicitor* [1951] Ch. 298 at pp. 300–301, and 303–306.

[19] *Re Craven* [1937] Ch. 423.

[20] *Birch v. Treasury Solicitor* [1951] Ch. 298.

[21] See Snell at pp. 383–384.

[22] As of a bag and its contents: *Delgoff v. Fader* [1939] Ch. 922.

[23] Deeds: *Duffield v. Elwes* (1827) 1 Bli. N.S. 497; *Wilkes v. Allington* [1931] 2 Ch. 104; savings bank books: *Birch v. Treasury Solicitor*, above.

[24] *Re Swinburne* [1926] Ch. 38; and the previous cases cited there.

[25] *Re Beak* (1872) 13 Eq. 489.

[26] *Sen v. Headley* [1991] Ch. 425.

[27] [1990] Ch. 728 at p. 741; compare *Cope v. Kelne* (1968) 118 C.L.R. 1 (cited in the first edition of this book, but not cited in *Sen v. Headley*).

[28] At p. 440.

[29] (1827) 1 Bli. N.S. 497.

subsequent developments in the law, the Court of Appeal extended the doctrine of *donatio mortis causa* to a gift of unregistered freehold land by delivery of the title deeds. The decision is formulated in language that, applied to other cases, might justify further extensions of this anomalous and dangerous form of deathbed disposition.

The Appeal Committee of the House of Lords gave leave to appeal[30]; a petition of appeal was lodged, but the appeal was compromised.[31]

Every claim to enjoy a deathbed gift needs in the present state of the law to be examined in the light of all the relevant reported authorities (which are not fully deployed here). The principle is:

"Because of these peculiar characteristics, the courts will examine any case of alleged *donatio mortis causa* and reject it if in truth what is alleged as a donatio is an attempt to make a nuncupative will, or a will in other respects not complying with the forms required by the Wills Act."[32]

22–05 Need for alteration of the law. The danger is that there is in every case of a *donatio mortis causa* a risk of fabricated claims appearing to be good on the evidence before the court. This risk and the infirmity of oral evidence are sound reasons to limit or to abolish the doctrine of *donatio mortis causa*. With the increased use of wills, the right to make such gifts is not needed nowadays. Those who would otherwise take the subject-matter often suppose that a claim to enjoy such a gift, made in the absence of anyone other than the deceased and the donee/s is fabricated; no doubt such a claim sometimes is. However, that cannot be alleged in the inevitable absence of *evidence* of the fraud. This right is "in many respects anomalous."[33] In 1827, Lord Eldon said[34] "and if, among those things called improvements, this *donatio mortis causa* was struck out of our law altogether, it would be quite as well."

22–06 Resorting to the subject-matter of a valid *donatio mortis causa* to meet liabilities. There is some authority that the subject-matter of a *donatio mortis causa* may be resorted to, to meet liabilities, apart from any statutory provision.[35] It has however been convincingly argued that this is not the law.[36] If there is, in law, no power to resort to the subject-matter of a *donatio mortis causa* to

---

[30] p. 441.
[31] Communication to the author.
[32] *Birch v. Treasury Solicitor*, above at pp. 307–308.
[33] *Birch v. Treasury Solicitor* at p. 307.
[34] *Duffield v. Elwes*, above at p. 533.
[35] *Re Korvine* [1921] 1 Ch. 343 at p. 348; and the cases cited in the article cited in the next note.
[36] Warnock-Smith in 1978, *The Conveyancer*, 130.

meet liabilities, a person on his death-bed has in some circumstances a convenient way to benefit his family and leave his creditors unpaid after his death. Judges might not wish to be driven to that result. Meanwhile, the point is uncertain; if it arises, the personal representatives should apply to the court for directions.

22–07 Joint property. The distinction between a *joint* interest and an interest *in common* affects what is comprised in an estate.

Land held by more than one person must be held by trustees[37]; the beneficial interests in land may either be held in trust for them as joint tenants beneficially or as tenants in common beneficially. The present question concerns beneficial interests.

On the death of one of joint owners, the property accrues by operation of law to the survivor/s[38]; and it then ceases at the death and is not an asset of the estate.[39] While the beneficial joint owners are alive, their joint beneficial ownership can readily be severed into a tenancy-in-common, so that an equal beneficial share passes to the estate of any one of them on death; severance can be effected by alienation, voluntary or involuntary, or by notice[40]; a Bankruptcy Order effects a severance at the first moment of the day on which it is made.[41] A joint owner cannot, however, sever the joint tenancy into a tenancy-in-common by will.[42] This distinction often perplexes those familiar with a continental system of law that does not have two systems of co-ownership.

22–08 Partnership interests not available to the estate. The estate of a deceased partner has no greater interest in the partnership assets than the partnership agreement or, if applicable, than is conferred by the Partnership Act 1890.[43]

PROPERTY SUBJECT TO "MUTUAL WILLS"

22–09 Agreements for "mutual wills." Wills, that two persons have made a binding agreement not to revoke, are called "mutual wills." An agreement not to exercise the legal right to revoke a will comes into force when the first death occurs. The principle underlying the

---

[37] L.P.A. 1925, s.34.
[38] Snell, *Equity*, at p. 36.
[39] A.E.A. 1925, s.3(4).
[40] See Megarry & Wade, *The Law of Real Property* (5th ed.) at pp. 419–433; and Snell, *Equity*, at pp. 37–39.
[41] Insolvency Act 1986, ss.278–283; *Re Palmer* [1994] Ch. 316, reviewing the authorities.
[42] *Gould v. Kemp* (1834) 2 My. & K. 304 at the foot of p. 309; not doubted since.
[43] See paras. 20–14 to 20–19 above.

doctrine of mutual wills is to prevent fraud on the first testator to die; and so the doctrine is not confined to cases where the survivor benefits under the will of the first to die; but includes cases where both leave their property to beneficiaries other than themselves, and make such an agreement.[44] The agreement is contrary to the legal power, under the Wills Act 1837, to revoke a will; and so if the agreement is broken at the second death a grant of representation is made in accordance with the duly executed will of the second party to die, not in accordance with the agreement[45]; this leaves the agreement to take effect by way of trust.

The agreement is effective to impose a trust when it is proved to the satisfaction of the court.[46] The personal representatives must therefore perform the trust with the subject-matter of the agreement vested in them under the grant of representation to themselves, in accordance with the terms of the agreement.[47] The rights of the third parties, beneficiaries under the agreement, vest at the first death; and so do not fail by lapse if such beneficiary dies in the interval between the deaths of the two parties to the agreement, but devolve on the personal representatives of that beneficiary.[48]

To establish mutual wills, it is not enough that people, usually spouses, have made identical wills; a positive agreement not to revoke them has to be proved; such proof is often lacking.[49] It is a "heavy burden of proof."[50] Mutual wills may be binding, when the will of the first to die does not confer a benefit on the survivor.[51]

22–10 Lawfulness of an agreement for mutual wills. The cases cited in paragraph 22–09 above establish that an agreement for mutual wills is lawful, although marriage revokes a will under the Wills Act 1837, s.18. A condition in a gift made by will for a married person not to remarry is valid.[52] If, however, an agreement for mutual wills was made by an unmarried person and then broken by that person's marriage, the agreement should be held void as contrary to public policy: a provision in total restraint of marriage is contrary to public policy and void.[53]

---

[44] *Re Dale* [1994] Ch. 31; the judgment contains a review of the authorities on mutual wills.
[45] *Stone v. Hoskins* [1905] P. 194; *Re Heys* [1914] P. 192.
[46] *Re Hagger* [1930] 2 Ch. 190; *Re Green* [1951] Ch. 148.
[47] See the previous footnote; and *Re Fox* [1951] O.R. 378, where the agreement provided for alterations.
[48] *Re Hagger*, above.
[49] *Re Oldham* [1925] Ch. 75; *Gray v. Perpetual Trustee Co.* [1928] A.C. 391; and *Re Cleaver* [1981] 1 W.L.R. 939, containing a useful review of the authorities.
[50] *Birmingham v. Renfrew* (1936) 57 C.L.R. 666 at p. 674, Latham C.J.; the case was followed in *Re Cleaver*, above.
[51] *Re Dale* [1994] Ch. 31.
[52] Jarman, *Wills*, at p. 1530.
[53] Jarman at pp. 1528–1530; and see *Chitty on Contracts* (27th ed.), para. 16–063.

22–11 Severance of a joint tenancy by agreement for mutual wills. A valid agreement to make mutual wills severs a beneficial joint tenancy into a tenancy in common as soon as it is made.[54]

22–12 Appointed property under a special power or under a hybrid power, entailed property, and settled land under a continuing settlement. Property devolving under a special power of appointment, under a hybrid power of appointment, or under an unexecuted general power of appointment, does not belong to the estate;[55] nor does entailed property left to devolve at the death under the entail. The same applies to other beneficial interests under a continuing trust. Sometimes when land continues to be settled land under the S.L.A. 1925 at the life-tenant's death, a general grant of representation is made, including therefore the settled land,[56] which vests in the personal representatives under the grant.[57] That only relates to the legal estate; such a grant does not render the settled land, where the settlement continues, assets of the estate of the deceased life tenant; accordingly the personal representatives must assent to the land vesting in whoever, under the continuing settlement, is entitled to it. It is more convenient for the general grant to except settled land, and for a distinct grant to be made as to settled land.

On the other hand property subject to a general power of appointment which the deceased executed is part of the assets of the estate.[58]

[54] *Re Wilford* (1879) 11 Ch.Div. 267; *Re Heys* [1914] P. 192.
[55] See paras. 20–35 to 20–37.
[56] Notwithstanding S.L.A. 1925, s.22.
[57] *Re Bridgett & Hayes* [1928] Ch. 163.
[58] See para. 20–35 above.

23. The personal representatives' powers of sale or of other disposition and power to allow or to compromise claims

23–01 General considerations about the powers of personal representatives. The exercise of a power is only useful when its exercise is clearly valid. This must be kept in mind whenever a power is exercised or is about to be exercised. In any case of doubt about the power of personal representatives to effect a proposal, they should obtain: the opinion of counsel; the approval (if available) of every beneficiary; or if necessary, the approval of the court. It is much better to obtain an order than to make an arrangement that might afterwards be open to question.

There is sometimes more than one way of effecting a transaction. *Trustees* should consider the tax consequences of the proposed exercise of their powers[1]; and so, it follows, should personal representatives. There appears to be no reported case in which that duty has been neglected.

23–02 Chattels. Personal representatives have a power to sell the deceased's chattels.[2] On intestacy, personal chattels should not be sold unless required for the purpose of administration owing to want of other assets[3]; under a will the same restriction is usually directed or implied.

23–03 Shares. The personal representatives have a power to sell United Kingdom shares.[4] The power to sell shares devolving on beneficiaries absolutely should only be exercised when the sale is necessary for the purposes of administration.[5]

23–04 Retention of land in England and Wales. When land is to be retained for the present time, the personal representatives may retain it as personal representatives; and (if the title is registered) may themselves be registered as proprietors of the deceased's registered land, as "personal representatives."[6] It is however not really convenient for them to retain land (whether the title is registered or not) as personal representatives; doing so necessitates making title after the death of the last surviving personal representative either through the "chain of representation"[7] or through a further grant *de bonis non*.[8]

The personal representatives are likely themselves to be trustees-for-sale of the deceased's land.[9] When land is not intended to be sold for the present time, a better course than retaining it as personal representatives is, therefore, for the personal representatives to make a written assent[10] in their own favour. After making an assent, they hold the land as trustees-for-sale. If title is registered, they may then

---

[1] *Re Collard's Will Trusts* [1961] Ch. 293 at p. 302; *Re Pilkington* [1964] A.C. 612 at p. 622; *Re Strafford* [1980] Ch. 28 at p. 48; *Nestle v. National Westminster Bank* [1993] 1 W.L.R. 1260 (investment in gilt edged stock exempt from tax and inheritance tax, when the beneficiaries are not resident or domiciled in the U.K.)

[2] *Attenborough v. Solomon* [1913] A.C. 76 at common law; and the A.E.A. 1925, s.33(1) on intestacy.

[3] s.33(1).

[4] See para. 20–08 above.

[5] See para. 33–13 discussing decided cases that entitled a beneficiary to a transfer of shares to himself. *Re Marshall* [1914] 1 Ch. 192; *Re Sandeman* [1937] 1 All E.R. 368; *Re Weiner* [1956] 1 W.L.R. 579; and on the other side *Lacoste v. Duchesnay* [1924] A.C. 166 (Quebec) and *Lloyds Bank v. Duker* [1987] 1 W.L.R. 1324.

[6] r. 168. The subsistence of this entry on the register draws attention to the fact that the title is held as personal representatives: with the consequences stated in the text.

[7] See paras. 2–02 and 5–08.

[8] See para. 2–11.

[9] Under the will or under the A.E.A. 1925, s.33.

[10] See para. 2–11.

be registered as proprietors,[11] without the qualification on the register that they are personal representatives. The advantage of holding land as trustees-for-sale, rather than as personal representatives, is that title may be dealt with by the appointment by deed of new trustees.[12] It is only an assent in writing that changes the title of those holding land as personal representatives to the title of those holding the land as trustees-for-sale.[13]

23–05 Sale of land in England and Wales. *Power of sale.* Personal representatives may intend to sell the deceased's land. They have power to convey freehold or leasehold land in England and Wales,[14] for the purposes of administration, during a minority or the subsistence of a life interest, with all the powers of sale, mortgaging and raising money by charge of trustees-for-sale of land[15]; in the case of intestacy there is also an express statutory trust-for-sale.[16] When more than one personal representative holds a grant of representation, it is necessary for all of them to convey the land,[17] unless the court otherwise orders.[18] The title to most land is registered: personal representatives may transfer registered land without themselves being registered as proprietors.[19] When land is to be sold promptly, it is simplest for the personal representatives to make the sale as personal representatives, whether the title is registered or not.

Covenants for title on sale. Until the commencement on July 1, 1995[20] of the Law of Property (Miscellaneous Provisions) Act 1994, the only covenant for title that personal representatives normally gave on a sale of land was that they had not themselves encumbered the title,[21] as they still do.[21a] They knew and could safely make that covenant. Now however they are likely to have to make a "limited

---

[11] L.R.R. 1925, r. 170(4).

[12] Trustee Act 1925, s.36. Trustees-for-sale do not need to meet the requirements for making title as personal representatives: under the "chain of representation" or under a new grant *de bonis non.* After the death of the last surviving trustee-for-sale, the personal representatives of the last survivor may appoint new trustees by deed: Trustee Act 1925, s.36(1)(b). This gets in the title to the land.

[13] *Re King* [1964] Ch. 542. At the time this was a questionable decision: see para. 33–10 n. 25; but it is unlikely to be overruled now.

[14] Land elsewhere is governed by the law of the place where it is: see para. 11–02 above.

[15] A.E.A. 1925, s.2(1) and s.39(1).

[16] s.33(1).

[17] s.2(2). The position when one only of several personal representatives contracts to sell the deceased's land is considered in para. 23–08 below.

[18] s.2(2).

[19] L.R.R. 1925, r. 170.

[20] S.I. 1995 No. 1317.

[21] L.P.A. 1925, Second Schedule Part VI.

[21a] L.P.A. 1994, s.3(3).

title guarantee"[22] covenanting that they have the right to dispose of the property and will at their own cost do all they reasonably can to give title to the covenantee. This is another extension of personal representatives' liabilities.[23] When freehold title absolute[24] is registered, this new covenant by way of limited title guarantee[25] should only create a risk in the event of it turning out that there was an over-riding interest.[26] When the deceased left an unregistered freehold title, the personal representatives should register the title before selling the land.

On making a contract to sell freehold land, whether or not the title is registered, personal representatives should seek to exclude this liability. There is nothing in the L.P.A. 1994 to prohibit contracting out of its provisions. Otherwise the personal representatives might remain liable under this covenant in unforeseen circumstances after having fully distributed the estate.

Covenants for title on sale of the deceased's leasehold title. If the deceased had a registered good leasehold title, or had an unregistered leasehold title, L.P.A. 1994 lays a trap for personal representatives on sale. The registration of a good leasehold title does not guarantee the validity of the lease[27]; personal representatives who contract to sell such a leasehold title normally give a limited title guarantee now[28]; that covenant is to the effect that the lease is subsisting without a breach of condition.[29] Personal representatives may not know whether the lease is subsisting or not.

On making a contract to sell a leasehold title, personal representatives should therefore similarly seek to contract out of this liability. Otherwise they may remain personably liable on their covenant that the leaser was subsisting, after fully distributing the estate.

23–06 Position of a purchaser. As regards a purchaser it is no objection to a sale by personal representatives that the deceased's debts, liabilities, funeral and testamentary expenses, appear to have been paid.[30] Until they have made an assent,[31] they are treated as holding the property as personal representatives.

---

[22] L.P.A. 1994, s.2 and s.12(3).
[23] The other one is the withdrawal of the common law protection against contractual liability when the vendor turns out to have a bad title: see the end of para. 20–04.
[24] L.R.A. 1925, s.5.
[25] For its exact extent, see L.P.A. 1994, s.2.
[26] L.R.A. 1925, s.70; L.R.R. 1925, rule 77(1)(c).
[27] L.R.A. 1925, s.10.
[28] L.P.A. 1994, s.12(3)(b).
[29] L.P.A. 1994, s.4.
[30] s.36(8).
[31] See Chap. 33.

23–07 Power of a sole personal representative. When there is a grant of representation to only one individual[32] as personal representative, he has all the powers of personal representatives[33] until the conclusion of the administration. This means that he can transfer or convey land (unlike a sole trustee, unless the sole trustee is a trust corporation.[34]) Only an assent in writing[35] puts an end to this power of sale of land as sole personal representative.[36] Where there is a sole personal representative, it is therefore convenient for a sale to be made as personal representative.[37] A note of an assent ought to be made on the grant of representation.[38]

23–08 Powers of one only of several personal representatives. It is unwise for one only of several personal representatives to seek to exercise the powers of *all* the personal representatives in the present state of the law.

Chattels. The common law power of one only of several personal representatives to sell chattels[39] probably survives today.[40]

Contract to sell land. The Law of Property (Miscellaneous Provisions) Act 1994, s.16 avoids the difficulties[41] that formerly arose about a contract to sell land made by one only of the personal representatives; the concurrence of all the personal representatives is required in a contract of sale from the commencement on July 1, 1995[42] of the Act.

Conveyance or transfer of land. All the personal representatives must convey or transfer land, not one only of them.[43]

POWER TO MAKE AGREEMENTS OR COMPROMISES ON EXTERNAL QUESTIONS.

23–09 The Trustee Act 1925, s.15. A wide statutory power is conferred by the Trustee Act 1925, s.15 for personal representatives to make compromises as follows:

---

[32] A trust corporation, within A.E.A. 1925, s.55(1)(xxvi) is anyhow not affected by the restrictions imposed on a sole individual *trustee*.
[33] s.2(2).
[34] L.P.A. 1925, s.27(2); the Trustee Act 1925, s.14(2).
[35] A.E.A. 1925, s.36(4); *Re King* [1964] Ch. 542.
[36] *Wise v. Whitburn* [1924] 1 Ch. 460; *Re King* [1964] Ch. 542.
[37] As in *Re Spencer & Hauser's Contract* [1928] Ch. 598.
[38] A.E.A. 1925, s.36(5).
[39] *Attenborough v. Solomon*, above.
[40] *Fountain Forestry v. Edwards* [1975] Ch. 1 at p. 11.
[41] See para. 23–07 of the previous edition of this book.
[42] S.I. 1995 No. 1317.
[43] A.E.A. 1925, s.2(2); the L.R.R. 1925, r. 170.

"**15.** A personal representative, or two or more trustees acting together, or, subject to the restrictions imposed in regard to receipts by a sole trustee not being a trust corporation, a sole acting trustee where by the instrument, if any, creating the trust, or by statute, a sole trustee is authorised to execute the trusts and powers reposed in him, may, if and as he or they think fit—

(a) accept any property, real or personal, before the time at which it is made transferable or payable; or

(b) sever and apportion any blended trust funds or property; or

(c) pay or allow any debt or claim on any evidence that he or they think sufficient; or

(d) accept any composition or any security, real or personal, for any debt or for any property, real or personal, claimed; or

(e) allow any time of payment of any debt; or

(f) compromise, compound, abandon, submit to arbitration, or otherwise settle any debt, account, claim, or thing whatever relating to the testator's or intestate's estate or to the trust;

and for any of those purposes may enter into, give, execute, and do such agreements, instruments of composition or arrangement, releases, and other things as to him or them seem expedient, without being responsible for any loss occasioned by any act or thing so done by him or them in good faith."

This section relates to questions between the estate as a whole and those claiming or claimed against outside the estate. It does not relate to internal questions, within the estate, about beneficial interests.[44] The principle is clear but (as the case cited shows) it is not always clear whether a question is external or internal.

23–10 Duty of personal representatives exercising the powers under section 15. The duty, in addition of course to that of good faith, of personal representatives exercising the power is to consider the interest of the estate as a whole,[45] after paying due attention to the

---

[44] *Re Strafford* [1980] Ch. 28 at pp. 32–33, and on appeal at p. 46E.

[45] *Re Hayes* [1971] 1 W.L.R. 758, applying *Re Charteris* [1917] 1 Ch. 379; in this respect the duty of personal representatives is not the same as the duty of trustees under this section. Trustees have a duty to consider the several individual interests of the beneficiaries and to hold the scale fairly between them: *Re Strafford* [1980] Ch. 28 at p. 45A. The reason for this distinction is that until the estate is fully administered, a testamentary beneficiary does not have an interest in any particular asset of the estate: *C.S.D. (Queensland) v. Livingston* [1965] A.C. 694, applying *Sudeley v. Att.Gen.* [1897] A.C. 11 and *Dr Barnardo's Homes v. Income Tax Special Commissioners* [1921] 2 A.C. 1. These revenue cases have settled the general law: *Re Leigh* [1970] Ch. 277; *Re K.* [1986] Ch. 180; *Marshall v. Kerr* [1995] 1 A.C. 148.

views of the beneficiaries. The exercise of the power does not however require the consent of the beneficiaries.[46] The discretion is wide; it is no objection to a proposed compromise that it involves a surrender of a beneficial interest under the relevant will.[47]

23–11 Restrictions on the power. This is a fiduciary power; it may not therefore be exercised in a manner that infringes the rule against self-dealing[48]; fiduciary power may not be delegated[49]; but it may be exercised at the discretion of the personal representatives consistently with legal advice. As the section makes clear, the only relevant requirement is good faith on the part of the personal representatives; a compromise made by them without good faith is set aside.[50] From time to time section 15 is used, or misused, by personal representatives making, supposedly in good faith, what is little more than an *ex gratia* payment to someone who has rendered voluntary services to the estate for which payment might be hard to exact at common law.[51]

23–12 Paragraphs (a), (b), (c), (d) and (e). These five paragraphs do not usually cause difficulty. Before exercising them, personal representatives often obtain legal advice, especially if the sum in question is significant, or the question is open to doubt. A principle often in point under paragraph (c) of the section is that when a claim is first made against the estate of a deceased person after the death, the claim is to be approached with suspicion[52]; but does not require corroboration.[53]

23–13 Paragraph (f): compromise. The power under paragraph (f) to make a compromise is frequently used. The same principles apply to it. The object of exercising the power is to bind others concerned in the estate, by its lawful exercise. Its lawful exercise binds all concerned, including creditors, beneficiaries and the Inland Revenue. A convenient and frequent compromise on a question of construction is to agree to obtain, by way of arbitration, the opinion of a named barrister; and that his opinion shall bind the estate and the other party. The cost of that is far less than the cost of legal proceedings on the question.

---

[46] *Re Ezekiel* [1942] Ch. 230.
[47] *Re Strafford*, above.
[48] See Chap. 34.
[49] Farwell, *Powers* (3rd ed.), at p. 499.
[50] *De Cordova v. De Cordova* (1879) 4 App.Cas. 692.
[51] See Goff & Jones, *Restitution* (3rd ed.), at pp. 137–149.
[52] *Thomas v. Times Book Club* [1966] 1 W.L.R. 911 at pp. 915–916, where a strange claim about the manuscript of *Under Milk Wood* succeeded when so approached; following *Re Garnett* (1885) 31 Ch.Div. 1 at p. 8, where a claim failed.
[53] *Re Cummins* [1972] Ch. 62, where *Thomas v. Times Book Club* was not cited.

This power to bind others without their consent cannot however be exercised in the circumstances where it is not applicable or not certainly applicable. The authorities[54] as regards a compromise with another personal representative are in a confusing state.

23–14 Purported extension of the power of compromise by will. A will is often expressed to confer wide powers on executors to act on the advice of counsel or at their own discretion. Such powers should not be relied upon. A power for the executors to decide the identity of charitable donees was held to be invalid, as ousting the jurisdiction of the court.[55] A power for the executors to decide questions of doubt was also held to be invalid.[56] These cases lay down a general rule and are not undermined by the decision of the Court of Appeal on a trust deed, conferring a power of decision of an internal matter on an expert not a trustee.[57]

23–15 Internal questions. The powers of compromise mentioned above relate only to questions arising between the estate and others; they have no application to internal questions as to the devolution within the estate.[58]

The statutory power to act on counsel's opinion with judicial approval[59] applies however to both internal and external questions; and so does the power to obtain the court's directions.

---

[54] Stated in paras. 34–04 to 34–09.

[55] *Re Raven* [1915] 1 Ch. 673. It is quite different from a gift by will to such charity as the executors nominate: as formulated in (1960) 24 *The Conveyancer*, 669.

[56] *Re Wynn* [1952] Ch. 271; see also *Re Davis* [1953] V.L.R. 639 (capital and income).

[57] *Re Tuck* [1978] Ch. 49 (the Chief Rabbi to decide on someone's Judaism).

[58] The distinction between external questions affecting the estate as such and internal questions within the estate is well-recognised: *Re Bowen-Buscarlet's Will Trusts* [1972] Ch. 463; *Re Strafford* above at pp. 32–33, and p. 48.

[59] See para. 42–01.

Part Four: Debts and Liabilities

24. Advertisement for claimants

24–01 Need for protection. It is the duty of personal representatives to pay creditors[1] and to distribute the estate to the correct beneficiaries. Personal representatives therefore need protection, before distributing the estate, against the possibility of there being other creditors or other beneficiaries not known to the personal representatives. There is greater need for protection in respect of unknown beneficiaries now that relationships on succession at death are to be ascertained without regard to whether a person's parents (that is to say physical parents) were married to each other.[2] A beneficiary may exist whose relationship to the deceased has been concealed by the deceased from his family in his lifetime.

24–02 The Trustee Act 1925, s.27. Before distribution personal representatives may give notice of their intention to distribute by advertisement in (i) the London Gazette, (ii) a newspaper circulating where there is any land and (iii) other notices that in any special case the court would have directed: to require claimants to notify their claims within not less than two months.

Afterwards the personal representatives may distribute having regard only to the claims of which they then had notice; without being liable in respect of claims of which the personal representatives did not have notice *at the time of distribution*, so that a claimant's notice given before actual distribution may be effective after the expiry of the period fixed in the advertisement.

---

[1] See para. 25–01 below.
[2] Family Law Reform Act 1987, ss.1, 18 and 19; with an exception about artificial insemination: s.27.

Section 27 does not prejudice the right to follow property into the hands of anyone (other than a purchaser); and does not exempt personal representatives from the obligation to make the searches a *purchaser* should make: such as searches under L.R.A. 1925 or under L.C.A. 1972.

Section 27 can never be excluded: s.27(3).

24–03 Effect of the advertisement. An advertisement under section 27 is no protection in respect of a claim of which the personal representatives have notice.[3]

The advertisement authorises distribution of the estate and protects the personal representatives against claims, after distribution, of which they had no notice whether such claims are by creditors or by beneficiaries.[4] It "was intended to embrace all classes of claims."[5]

The terms of the section must be complied with; thus an advertisement fixing a time shorter than the statutory two months would not protect the personal representatives against unknown claims.[6] Notice to a personal representative in an estate or a trust does not constitute notice in another trust "in the absence of fraud"[7]; which appears to mean in the absence of conscious knowledge on the part of the personal representatives in the other estate.

24–04 Court's directions about advertisement. On rare occasions when there is a difficulty or doubt about what advertisements should be made, the personal representatives can be protected by an order usually made by the Master, directing or approving an advertisement[8]; for example where there may be creditors or claimants overseas.[9] An order directing or approving advertisements only approves the advertisement. When there are future or contingent (that is to say conditional) liabilities actually known to the personal representatives, the question to be brought before the court is not advertisement but distribution.[10]

24–05 Distribution for the purposes of section 27. Distribution for the purpose of section 27 includes, in addition to outright transfers to

---

[3] *Guardian Trust, etc. Co. of New Zealand v. Public Trustee of New Zealand* [1942] A.C. 115, where counsel for the respondents were not called upon; *Re Beatty* (1892) 29 L.R. Ir. 290.

[4] *Re Aldhous* [1955] 1 W.L.R. 459 applying *Newton v. Sherry* (1876) 1 C.P.D. 246.

[5] *Newton v. Sherry* above at p. 257, Archibald J. on the previous Act.

[6] *Stuart v. Babbington* (1891) L.R. Ir. 551, on the practice of the court; *Re Bracken* (1889) 43 Ch. Div. 1 is not an authority to the contrary.

[7] A.E.A. 1925, s.28.

[8] *Re Letherbrow* [1935] W.N. 34 and 48.

[9] *Re Holden* [1935] W.N. 52.

[10] *Re Holden* above.

persons absolutely entitled, the appropriation of settled property by the personal representatives to themselves as trustees to be held on the trusts of the will.[11]

---

[11] *Clegg v. Rowland* (1866) 3 Eq. 368.

25. Payment of debts and provision for future debts

25–01 Debts, other than funeral expenses.[1] The personal representatives have power and have a duty to pay the deceased's debts,[2] including tax due from the deceased.[3] The personal representatives should ascertain as far as practicable what the debts are; and should advertise for debts under the Trustee Act 1925, section 27.[4] They should pay the debts presently due,[5] with due diligence, whatever that is in all the circumstances.[6] There is nothing to prevent debts and

---

[1] For funeral expenses see para. 1–05.
[2] A.E.A. 1925, ss.25(a), 32(1) and 39(1); in the case of intestacy, also s.33(1), which does not add much to s.39(1), applicable in every case. The former right of retainer and power of preference among creditors has been abolished: A.E.A. 1971, s.10(1).
[3] T.M.A. 1970, s.74.
[4] See para. 24–02.
[5] As to future debts, see paras. 25–10 and 25–11 below.
[6] *Re Tankard* [1942] Ch. 69.

liabilities being met by the personal representatives out of the first assets coming to their hands, with the ultimate burden being afterwards adjusted, as is proper, between the beneficiaries.[7]

Creditors have a legal right to be paid (unless statute-barred). The duty to pay debts with due diligence is also owed to the beneficiaries (subject to any relevant provision in the will); for it is in the interest of the beneficiaries to have the debts paid and the estate distributed. If damaged by delay in the payment of debts on the part of the personal representatives, the beneficiaries may make the personal representatives liable for any loss arising from the delay (such as extra legal costs incurred).[8]

A personal representative must pay, by allowing against himself in account, a debt due that at the death he owed the deceased[9]; unless the executor is released under the rule in *Strong v. Bird*.[10] Because the debt is treated in account as an asset in the hands of the personal representative, a delay of its payment beyond the limitation period under the Limitation Act 1980 does not destroy his liability to account for the debt, even when the grant is only obtained after the expiry of the limitation period.[11]

25–02 Foreign creditors. In an administration in England, foreign creditors are entitled to be paid equally with those here.[12] Under the Civil Jurisdiction and Judgments Acts 1982–1991, or its equivalent legislation in Convention countries, creditors in Convention countries may only be able to assert claims against the estate in England.[13]

Debts in foreign currency are, in an administration here, converted into United Kingdom currency at the rate of exchange prevailing at the date of the death.[14]

25–03 Pending obligations. The personal representatives owe a duty to the beneficiaries, or in case of insolvency to the other creditors, to raise the technical objection that a contract is unenforceable as not complying with the Statute of Frauds[15]; now

---

[7] *Re Tong* [1931] 1 Ch. 202, Romer L.J. at p. 212; *Re Cohen* [1960] Ch. 179.

[8] *Re Tankard* above.

[9] *Re Bourne* [1906] 1 Ch. 697, where the position was explained in the Court of Appeal on an application for committal of a defaulting executor; *C.S.D. v. Bone* [1977] A.C. 511, executors. A.E.A. 1925, s.21A, executor by representation or administrator. The technicalities of the common law are therefore not of practical importance.

[10] See para. 22–02.

[11] *Ingle v. Richards (No. 2)* (1860) 28 Beav. 366.

[12] *Re Kloebe* (1884) 37 Ch.Div. 175; evidently still the law, applied to company law in *Re Azoff-Don Commercial Bank* [1954] Ch. 315 at p. 333.

[13] See para. 21–02.

[14] *Re Hawkins* [1972] Ch. 714.

[15] *Re Rownson* (1885) 29 Ch.Div. 358.

L.P.A. 1989, s.2, replacing L.P.A. 1925, s.40. The personal representatives ought however to perform contractually valid and enforceable obligations of the deceased, even if it would be profitable to break an onerous contract and to pay damages.[16]

25–04 Debts barred by limitation. Personal representatives must not pay a debt that has been declared by the court to be statute-barred.[17] If the matter comes before the court for directions, the personal representatives will be directed to take the objection that it is statute-barred.[18] There survive (largely from another era) authorities deciding that (in the absence of a court decision that the debt is statute-barred) an executor may retain his own debt though statute-barred[19]; or may pay a statute-barred debt[20]; and *obiter dicta* to that effect, when the point did not arise for decision.[21] It is doubtful, even so, whether one of several executors may pay a statute-barred debt against the wish of the others.[22]

The right of the personal representatives (if unanimous and if not otherwise directed by the court) to pay a statute-barred debt is established at present[23]; but it is in conflict with principle:

> "The general principle is, that it is the executor's duty to protect the estate against demands which by law cannot be enforced against it. That is his duty. That general principle is a wholesome principle, not to be cut away or narrowed. ... "[24]

A right for personal representatives to pay a statute-barred debt is also in conflict with the principle that there is no right for a liquidator to pay a statute-barred debt, in the analogous case of winding up a

---

[16] *Anguillia v. Estate and Trust Agencies* [1938] A.C. 624, where the Privy Council examined the earlier authorities. Accordingly a devisee of a house is entitled to have a pending contract to repair it performed: *Cooper v. Jarman* (1866) 3 Eq. 510; *Re Day* [1898] 2 Ch. 510; *Re Rushbrook* [1948] Ch. 421. It is otherwise when the deceased had, without consideration from a freeholder, contracted to have work done on that freeholder's property: *Re Day*; on this point doubted in *Anguillia v. Estate and Trust Agencies* above at p. 636.

[17] *Midgley v. Midgley* [1893] 3 Ch. 282.

[18] *Re Wenham* [1892] 3 Ch. 59; also *Sherwin v. Vanderholt* (1831) 1 Russ. & M. 347, and *Moodie v. Bannister* (1859) 4 Dr. 432, where beneficiaries were allowed to raise the statute although the executors did not.

[19] *Stahlschmidt v. Lett* (1853) 1 Sm. & G. 415; *Hill v. Walker* (1858) 4 K. & J. 166; even when the beneficiaries take the point on the statute: *Sharman v. Rudd* (1858) 31 L.T.O.S. 325; *Clinton v. Brophy* (1847) 10 Ir.Eq. 139. This was based on the right of retainer, abolished by the A.E.A. 1971, s.10(1); A.E.A. 1925, s.21A.

[20] *Lowis v. Rumney* (1867) 4 Eq. 451; *Re Green* [1932] 3 D.L.R. 48.

[21] *Norton v. Frecker* (1737) 1 Atk. 524 at p. 526; *Re Wenham* above at p. 62; *Re Rownson* above at pp. 362, 363 and 364; *Anguillia v. Estate and Trust Agencies* above at p. 635. This right was assumed, but only assumed, in *Midgley v. Midgley*.

[22] *Midgley v. Midgley* above.

[23] See Snell, *Equity* at p. 330.

[24] *Midgley v. Midgley* above at p. 299, Lindley L.J. approving *Re Rownson* above.

company.[25] Moreover, the court will direct the personal representatives to plead the defence of limitation.[26]

Any right to pay a statute-barred debt might not survive nowadays in an appellate court (especially after the abolition of the right of retainer, on which it was in part based). It is unsafe for personal representatives to act out of court on the basis that a right still exists to pay a statute-barred debt.

The point, though at one time important, may become less frequent now that the time for limitation purposes for repayment of a loan no longer runs from the date of the loan but from the relevant time for repayment.[27]

25–05 Liabilities not asserted, and not yet statute-barred. Personal representatives are in a difficult position when they have notice of a liability, in tort or in contract, incurred by the deceased that the creditor has not yet asserted, where the limitation period is still running, without the claim having been asserted by the issue of proceedings. The difficulty is that, if the personal representatives distribute without regard to the potential claim, they may be liable to the creditor as having been taken thereby to have admitted assets[28]; but if the personal representatives voluntarily communicate with the potential creditor, inviting the claim, beneficiaries might say that was maladministration (*"devastavit"*). The personal representatives' duty to pay debts[29] would, however, be likely to be an answer to such a claim by beneficiaries; especially as personal representatives may, as the law seems to stand at the moment,[30] even pay statute-barred debts. That does not demonstrate what the personal representatives should do in such circumstances, when the time for distribution[31] to beneficiaries has arrived. The beneficiaries ought to authorise the postponement of distribution until the relevant limitation period has elapsed. If not, the personal representatives should protect themselves by applying for the court's directions. On such an application, the court would be likely to direct notice to be given to the potential claimant to come in to establish his claim.[32]

---

[25] *Re Fleetwood, etc. Syndicate* [1915] 1 Ch. 486; *Re Art Reproduction* [1952] Ch. 89.
[26] *Re Wenham* above.
[27] Under the Limitation Act 1980, s.6.
[28] *Taylor v. Taylor* (1870) 10 Eq. 477.
[29] See para. 25–01 above.
[30] See para. 25–04 above.
[31] See Chap. 33.
[32] One of the inquiries under an order for general administration is an inquiry as to debts: Chancery Masters' Practice forms no. 10, *Supreme Court Practice 1995*, Vol. 2, para. 511; and Seton, *Judgments & Orders* (7th ed.), at p. 1411. This direction could be given under Ord. 85, r. 2(1) and Ord. 44, r. 2; see *Finers v. Miro* [1991] 1 W.L.R. 35, *obiter* at p. 40B–C; at p. 45F to p. 46D, the point was dealt with on a different basis.

25–06 Doubtful debts. When it is often open to doubt whether or not a claim against an estate is valid, the personal representatives must either at their discretion compromise or agree the position with the claimant;[33] or submit the question to the court for determination.[34]

25–07 Financial penalties on a deceased offender. It was held in the House of Lords that the personal representatives of a deceased offender who had been sentenced to a financial penalty have no right to continue his appeal (or, it must follow, to lodge an appeal themselves) on the ground that the penalty was too high.[35] This harsh decision was reached on the basis of cases decided in the criminal courts, without referring to the analogous cases in civil courts where an estate is protected against payments that might be open to question.[36] It has been reversed by statute[37] in England and Wales; and might not be followed in the Commonwealth where House of Lords' decisions are not binding precedents.

FUTURE LIABILITIES

25–08 Landlords: The Trustee Act 1925, s.26. On making distribution of a leasehold to beneficiaries, the personal representatives can protect themselves against future liability by complying with the Trustee Act 1925, s.26 (as amended by the Landlord and Tenant (Covenants) Act 1995, Schedule 1).

25–09 Liabilities of personal representatives under leases. The Landlord & Tenant (Covenants) Act 1995 ("the 1995 Act"),[38] in force from January 1, 1996, radically alters the relationship of landlord and tenant that has operated for some centuries; it may give rise to questions that are not yet apparent. The potential effect of the 1995 Act on personal representatives is briefly summarised here; questions under the 1995 Act will normally require recourse to books on landlord and tenant.

An agreement restricting the operation of the 1995 Act is void[39]; except that covenants may be released.[40]

The effect of the 1995 Act on a sale of a leasehold interest or of a reversion to a leasehold interest depends on the relevant date; falling into three categories.

---

[33] See paras. 23–09 to 23–13.
[34] See para. 42–02.
[35] *R. v. Kearley* [1994] 2 A.C. 414, affirming [1993] 1 W.L.R. 555.
[36] See the author's article; (1994) 138 *Sol. Jo.* 157.
[37] Criminal Appeal Act 1995, s.7.
[38] The sections are cited in this paragraph without repeating the name of the Act.
[39] s.25.
[40] s.26.

Sale before the commencement of the 1995 Act. The former law applies.[41]

Sale after the commencement of the 1995 Act of a previously existing leasehold or reversion. On a sale of a leasehold that was created before the commencement of the 1995 Act,[42] the liability of a vendor tenant, and so of his personal representatives, ceases on the sale[43]; but not in respect of any previous breach.[44] There is an exception: within six months of a "fixed charge" becoming due the landlord may serve a notice to claim such a "fixed charge" from the tenant: a "fixed charge" is a liability for rent, service charges and any liquidated sum payable in respect of failure to perform a covenant.[45] Personal representatives who sell a leasehold in this category should therefore wait six months before distributing the estate. This category of a previously existing leasehold includes a lease made after the commencement of the 1995 Act but under an agreement made before its commencement, or under an order of the court made before its commencement.[46]

There is no similar provision in the 1995 Act about the sale of a reversion; the Trustee Act 1925, s. 26[47] will continue to apply to such a sale.

Sale after the commencement of the 1995 Act of a lease or a reversion created after its commencement. The sale of a leasehold interest that was created after[48] the commencement of the 1995 Act releases the vendor tenant and therefore his personal representatives from the covenants of the lease[49]; but not in respect of any previous breach.[50] On the sale of a reversion the landlord, and therefore his personal representatives, may obtain by consent or by an order of the county court a release from the landlord's covenants in the lease[51]; but not in respect of any previous breach.[52]

Other provisions. There are provisions for the cases of apportionment on a sale of part only of a leasehold interest or reversion[53]; and guarantees[54] and for the release of other persons liable on a released covenant.[55] There are also provisions about

---

[41] See para. 25–07 of the first edition of this book; and *City of London v. Fell* [1993] Q.B. 589.
[42] s.1(2).
[43] s.17.
[44] s.24.
[45] s.17.
[46] s.1(3).
[47] Amended in respect of a guarantee by Schedule One to the 1995 Act.
[48] s.1(1).
[49] s.5.
[50] s.24.
[51] ss.6, 7 and 8.
[52] s.24.
[53] ss.9 and 10 and s.21, as to forfeiture.
[54] s.12, s.17(3), s.18(1)(a).
[55] s.24.

assignments made in breach of covenant or made by operation of law[56]; and provisions for the creation of "overriding leases" on a tenant or guarantor making a payment under a lease.[57]

These provisions are unlikely to affect personal representatives.

25–10 Leasehold cases outside the 1995 Act. Personal representatives who go into possession of the demised premises or of the rent of the demised premises appear to continue to become liable, up to the value of the leasehold property, to the landlord in respect of the period of such occupation.[58] During such occupation by personal representatives the Trustee Act 1925, s.26 does not apply nor any provision of the 1995 Act. Accordingly personal representatives are at liberty to retain out of the estate a fund sufficient to indemnify themselves against any such liability,[59] for the period ending with their assent, whereby the privity of estate is ended.[60] That retained fund becomes distributable to the beneficiaries when the landlord's claims become statute-barred[61]; or, it follows, when such claims are satisfied. When personal representatives are made personally liable to a landlord in this way, the personal representatives are entitled by way of indemnity to compel the beneficiaries to refund the property[62]; even though the personal representatives had, when distributing, notice of the possibility of the liability that had not yet become a debt.[63]

On selling that leasehold interest personal representatives will have the benefit of the 1995 Act (see the previous paragraph).

25–11 Known future liabilities of the estate; potential personal liability of the personal representatives. Personal representatives are protected by advertisement in respect of claims not known to them.[64] Personal representatives need protection in respect of future or potential liabilities (otherwise than in respect of a lease, as above) known to them and not yet due to be met. Personal representatives who distribute any part of the estate with notice of such a liability are personally liable to the creditor when the debt becomes payable, to

---

[56] s.11.
[57] ss.19–20.
[58] *Hopwood v. Whaley* (1848) 6 C.B. 744; *Rendall v. Andreae* (1892) 61 L.J.Q.B. 630; *Re Bowes* (1887) 37 Ch.Div. 128; *Whitehead v. Palmer* [1908] 1 K.B. 151; *Minford v. Carse* [1912] 1 Ir. 245.
[59] *Re Owers* [1941] Ch. 389.
[60] *Re Bennett* [1943] 1 All E.R. 467.
[61] *Re Lewis* [1939] Ch. 232.
[62] *Jervis v. Wolferstan* (1874) 18 Eq. 18; *Whittaker v. Kershaw* (1890) 45 Ch.Div. 320; *Matthews v. Ruggles-Brise* [1911] 1 Ch. 194. The principle is the same as in cases, cited here, not concerning landlord and tenant. It is thought that this was not affected by *Ministry of Health v. Simpson* [1951] A.C. 251.
[63] *Whittaker v. Kershaw* above.
[64] See para. 24–02.

the extent of the sums distributed.[65] Such a personal liability was imposed on personal representatives after distribution, when the deceased's land turned out to be insufficient in value to meet a known mortgage over it[66]; or calls were made on partly-paid shares.[67] The personal representatives are however not personally liable when the claimant would have been no better off had the asset been retained and not distributed.[68]

The risk of such personal liability should not be undertaken. In the absence of a statutory provision, similar to section 26, personal representatives with notice of a future liability must act under the court's directions,[69] thereby obtaining full protection.

25–12 Practice of the court. The practice of the court is not to direct the retention of a fund in respect of a contingent, (conditional), liability[70]; but to direct the retention of a sufficient fund in the case of a vested, (definite), liability.[71] This is only a *practice*, not a rule of law; and may be departed from when it is held to be appropriate in the circumstances.[72]

PROPERTY SUBJECT TO A CHARGE OR TO OTHER RIGHTS

25–13 A.E.A. 1925, s.35. As between those interested beneficially, property that was at the death subject to a charge bears the liability, or its proportionate part, unless the deceased has otherwise directed. The law is enacted in A.E.A. 1925, s.35:

> "**35.**—(1) Where a person dies possessed of, or entitled to, or, under a general power of appointment (including the statutory power to dispose of entailed interests) by his will disposes of, an interest in property, which at the time of his death is charged with the payment of money, whether by way of legal mortgage, equitable charge or otherwise (including a lien for unpaid

---

[65] *Guardian Trust and Executors Co. of New Zealand v. Public Trustee of New Zealand* [1942] A.C. 115 (where counsel for the respondent were not called on); *Taylor* v. *Taylor* (1870) 10 Eq. 477; the payment of a legacy is an admission by the personal representatives of assets in favour of a creditor: *Savage v. Lane* (1847) 6 Ha. 32.

[66] *Re Beatty* (1892) 29 L.R. Ir. 290.

[67] *Taylor v. Taylor* above.

[68] *Standard Insurance v. Sidey* [1967] N.Z.L.R. 86: an important decision on this part of the law: partly-paid shares in an apparently prosperous company distributed. It was held that there was no liability on the personal representatives since the plaintiff company would have been no better off had those shares been retained.

[69] See Chap. 42.

[70] *Re King* [1907] 1 Ch. 72; as in the pre-1926 practice as regards landlords: *Re Nixon* [1904] 1 Ch. 638.

[71] *Re Arnold* [1942] Ch. 272 (covenanted life annuity, the only uncertainty being the length of the annuitant's life).

[72] *Re Johnson* [1940] W.N. 195 may have been such a case: see *Re Arnold* above.

purchase money), and the deceased has not by will deed or other document signified a contrary or other intention, the interest so charged shall, as between the different persons claiming through the deceased, be primarily liable for the payment of the charge; and every part of the said interest, according to its value, shall bear a proportionate part of the charge on the whole thereof.

(2) Such contrary or other intention shall not be deemed to be signified—

(a)   by a general direction for the payment of debts or of all the debts of the testator out of his personal estate, or his residuary real and personal estate, or his residuary real estate; or

(b)   by a charge of debts upon any such estate;

unless such intention is further signified by words expressly or by necessary implication referring to all or some part of the charge.

(3) Nothing in this section affects the right of a person entitled to the charge to obtain payment or satisfaction thereof either out of the other assets of the deceased or otherwise."

25–14 Scope of section 35.   The section relates to charges imposed otherwise than by the deceased himself; not to the testator's own testamentary directions to cast liabilities on specified assets.[73–74] Such a direction may, however, exclude the operation of the section.

The operation of section 35 is usually clear in any particular case, on its words. The section applies to a lien on shares held by the company that issued the shares[75]; to a solicitor's lien over title deeds[76]; and to a vendor's lien over the purchaser's rights under an uncompleted contract[77]; but not to the solicitor's charges for work on the contract, not protected by a lien[78]; to a charge to a bank for the testator's debts[79]; or as surety[80]; to a sum charged on a leasehold interest and due to the landlord at the death[81]; to a charging order, under the Charging Orders Act 1979, operating at the death on the testator's land[82]; and to sums charged on the testator's interest in an insolvent partnership and due at the death.[83] On the other hand, section 35 does not apply to: a solicitor's fees for work done not protected by a lien[84]; to a charge on company shares for sums due,

---

[73–74] See the A.E.A. 1925, Sched. 1, Pt. II, para. 4.
[75] *Re Turner* [1938] Ch. 593.
[76] *Re Riddell* [1936] 2 All E.R. 1600 (a point omitted from the other reports of the case).
[77] *Re Birmingham* [1959] Ch. 523, where *Re Riddell* above was not cited.
[78] *Re Birmingham* above.
[79] *Leonino v. Leonino* (1879) 10 Ch.Div. 460.
[80] *Re Hawkes* [1912] 2 Ch. 251.
[81] *Re Kidd* [1894] 3 Ch. 558.
[82] *Re Anthony* [1892] 1 Ch. 450 under the previous law.
[83] *Farquhar v. Hadden* (1871) 1 Ch.App. 1.
[84] *Re Birmingham* [1959] Ch. 523.

when at the death no sum was due[85]; to a charge by the testator over his interest in a solvent partnership.[86]

When section 35 applies, a bequest of several charged properties to one person throws the charges over on all those properties on to them all[87]; a bequest of several properties, subject to the same charge, to various people results in the properties bearing their respective charges proportionately.[88] Section 35 does not impose any personal liability.[89] Section 35 applies as between specifically given property and residue.[90] Detailed calculations are needed when property charged together is given to various beneficiaries.[91]

25–15 Contrary intention. Unusually, an unexecuted document may under section 35 exclude its operation. To exclude section 35, clear words are necessary[92]; a provision in a will directing liabilities to be met out of a specified fund is, for this purpose, enough to exclude section 35 in respect of liabilities charged on specified properties.[93] A letter telling a solicitor to pay a purchase price out of an enclosed cheque does not exclude section 35 in respect of the vendor's lien, on the testator dying before completion.[94] Section 35 may be excluded in part.[95]

25–16 Constructive trust or estoppel in equity. The Land Certificate or the title deeds do not necessarily show who is entitled to land in England. An occupier, along with the freeholder or leaseholder or apart form him, may have rights of occupation arising under a constructive trust or by way of estoppel in equity.[96] These rights may be held by spouses, lovers, or others[97]; or, by statute,[98] by those who

---

[85] *Re Dunlop* (1882) 21 Ch.Div. 583.

[86] *Re Ritson* [1899] 1 Ch. 128; *Re Holland* [1907] 2 Ch. 88.

[87] *Re Kensington* [1902] 1 Ch. 203.

[88] *Trestrail v. Mason* (1878) 7 Ch.Div. 655; *Re Newmarch* (1878) 9 Ch.Div. 12; *Leonino v. Leonino* above.

[89] *Syer v. Gladstone* (1885) 30 Ch.D. 614 (gift of the use of furniture and of a house that was charged for more than the house was worth; the legatees were entitled to enjoy the use of the furniture without contributing to the mortgage interest on the house).

[90] *Re Neeld* [1962] Ch. 643 the fifth point.

[91] As in *Leonino v. Leonino* above; and *Re Major* [1914] 1 Ch. 278.

[92] *Re Neeld* above at pp. 693–695, settling the law.

[93] *Re Fegan* [1928] Ch. 45, approved in the Privy Council, *Allie v. Katah* [1963] 1 W.L.R. 202.

[94] *Re Wakefield* [1943] 2 All E.R. 29.

[95] *Re Birch* [1909] 1 Ch. 787 (debt charged on one property cast on another property).

[96] See Megarry & Wade, *The Law of Real Property* (5th ed.), at pp. 473–475; and Snell, *Equity*, at pp. 639–711. A recent case elucidating this subject is *Grant v. Edwards* [1986] Ch. 638. The basis of the jurisdiction was explained in *Lloyds Bank v. Rosset* [1991] 1 A.C. 107.

[97] See the previous note.

[98] Law Reform (Miscellaneous Provisions) Act 1970, s.2.

have been engaged to marry. The jurisdiction is based on the court's view of what is unconscionable; and requires a broad approach.[99]

Personal representatives faced with such a claim need to obtain advice; and either to admit or compromise it, or to submit it to the court.[1]

25–17 Statutory charge. The statutory charge by way of right of occupation of a matrimonial home, which a spouse may obtain under the Matrimonial Homes Act 1983 ends at the death unless the court has made an order to the contrary.[2]

---

[99] *Habib Bank v. Habib Bank* [1981] 1 W.L.R. 1265 at p. 1285: see the passage in full.
[1] See Chap. 42.
[2] s.2(4).

26. Incidence of liabilities and of legacies, in a solvent estate

26–01 A.E.A. 1925, First Schedule. A.E.A. 1925, First Schedule, Part Two (quoted below) and section 34(3) govern the incidence of expenses and of legacies (subject to the effect of section 35).[1]

26–02 State of the authorities. The Schedule affects the incidence both of liabilities and of legacies. The rules applicable in ordinary cases ought to be clear and simple; but they are not. The judicial interpretation of these rules has given rise to confusing authorities. The root cause of the difficulty is the line of authority (cited below), holding that paragraph 1 of the Schedule covers a lapsed share of residue; although perhaps paragraph 1 might originally have been construed to refer to property not *purported* to be disposed of by the will. The secondary cause of the difficulty is the line of judicial decisions (also cited below), no doubt fair in each particular case, treating small indications in a will as enough to exclude the statutory order as regards expenses, debts and liabilities. The reported distinctions as regards expenses are "difficult to distinguish between"[2]; the provisions about legacies have been called "tortuous"[3]; and "notoriously obscure" and needing the attention of the Law Commission and the legislature.[4] That attention has not been provided, either as regards the incidence of liabilities or of legacies.

The present state of the law about the incidence of expenses and of legacies is a curious outcome of one of the 1925 Acts. "The main objects of the 1925 amendments are to assimilate the law of real and personal property wherever practicable, and to simplify and improve the practice of conveyancing, without interfering, more than is essential, with beneficial interests."[5] A.E.A. 1925 "is intended to simplify the administration of the estates of deceased persons. With that object, it assimilates the administration of real and personal estate, and provides a new system of devolution applicable to both realty and personalty."[6]

26–03 Practical solution. Personal representatives need to obtain advice and, if available, the consent of those beneficially interested before determining the incidence of expenses or of legacies; except in a clear case. Such advice is certainly needed when there is a partial intestacy, or a lapsed or a revoked gift of residue, or of its income. It is normally possible for legal advisers to give advice that avoids the cost of applying to the court, and of citing all the authorities. It is usually in the interest of adults to concede any doubtful point in

---

[1] See Chap. 25.
[2] Simonds J. in *Re Sanger* [1939] Ch. 238 at p. 248.
[3] "A tortuous way of legislating," Harman J. in *Re Midgley* [1955] Ch. 576 at p. 583.
[4] Salt Q.C., Ch. in *Re Taylor* [1969] 2 Ch. 245 at pp. 249 and 253.
[5] Wolstenholme & Cherry's *Conveyancing Statutes* (12th ed.) (1932) Vol. 1 at p. clxiii.
[6] Hood & Challis, *Property Acts* (8th ed.), (1938) at p. 677.

favour of minors or of future beneficiaries rather than to have such a point decided.

The practical solution in a case of doubt, when consent is not available, is for the personal representatives to obtain counsel's opinion and to seek the leave of the judge to act on the opinion, under A.J.A. 1985, s.48; such leave is given without a hearing.[7]

26–04 Possible amendment of the law. The difficulties would be overcome by a short enactment that: on deaths after a stated date, paragraph 1 of the Schedule shall not apply to a lapsed share of residue, unless the will expressly says it shall; the order of application of assets shall only be varied by a will expressly mentioning the Act or expressly mentioning the statutory order; and paragraph 3 and paragraph 4 of the Schedule are abrogated as otiose.

26–05 Marshalling. When, either for convenience in administration, or perhaps by overlooking the true legal position, the personal representatives have in fact paid liabilities or legacies out of property not liable, the position is afterwards adjusted in the distribution; this process is known as "marshalling."[8]

INCIDENCE OF LIABILITIES AND EXPENSES[9]

26–06 8(a) The order of application may be varied by the will of the deceased. The statutory order of application of assets is not excluded by the direction (found in almost every will) to pay debts, etc., without specifying out of what assets.[10] The statutory order is excluded by a gift of a residuary fund only asceretained after payment of debts[11]; by a gift of residue "subject to and after" such payment[12]; or "subject to" such payment[13]; or "after" such payment.[14]

Testators normally expect their residuary beneficiaries to survive them. These differences which Simonds J. found "it difficult to distinguish between"[15] seem to depend on what precedent or form was used, rather than on a conscious wish on the part of the testator.

---

[7] See para. 42–01.

[8] *Re Gilletts Will Trusts* [1950] Ch. 102 at p. 113; *Re Cohen* [1960] Ch. 179; *Re Matthews* [1961] 1 W.L.R. 1415; *Re Wilson* [1967] Ch. 53; and *Re Tong* [1931] 1 Ch. 202 at p. 212.

[9] Debts, funeral and testamentary expenses and administration expenses are usually held as a matter of construction all to be met in the same way: *Re Berrey's Will Trusts* [1959] 1 W.L.R. 30; *Re Taylor* above; but they might be directed in a will to be met in different ways.

[10] *Re Lamb* [1929] 1 Ch. 722; *Re Tong* [1931] 1 Ch. 202; *Re Worthington* [1933] Ch. 771; *Re Sanger* [1939] Ch. 238.

[11] *Re Petty* [1929] Ch. 238.

[12] *Re Kempthorne* [1930] 1 Ch. 268.

[13] *Re Harland-Peck* [1941] Ch. 182.

[14] *Re Berrey's Will Trusts* [1959] 1 W.L.R. 30; *Re Taylor* above.

[15] *Re Sanger* above at p. 248.

When the statutory order is excluded, the liabilities fall on residue as a whole before the lapsed share is ascertained.[16]

Paragraph 8(b) no longer applies.[17]

26–07 1. Property of the deceased undisposed of by will, subject to the retention thereout of a fund sufficient to meet any pecuniary[18] legacies. Paragraph 1 includes property not purported to be disposed of by the will. Paragraph 1 also includes a share of the residue given on a trust that is void[19] and a lapsed gift of a share of residue (when the legatee dies in the testator's lifetime).[20] When a gift for life of 75 per cent of the income of residue failed because the donee had attested the will,[21] it was held that such income was the first fund for the payment of liabilities[22] under paragraph 1. This was evidently possible on the figures in that estate. On some facts, practical difficulties may arise in administering an estate on this basis, while it remained unknown what would be the duration of the lifetime of the donee, the gift to whom had failed, and how far such aggregate income would extend in the event.

Similar problems arise when residue is given (in words held not to exclude the Schedule) to W for life and then equally between A, B and C; and A predeceases the testator or attests the will. Such residuary interest is itself not an asset in the hands of the personal representatives; and so it might not be assets within paragraph 1[23]; but then, it is difficult to see why the life interest of an attesting witness was an asset to be so applied.

26–08 2. Property of the deceased not specifically devised or bequeathed but included (either by a specific or general description) in a residuary gift, subject to the retention out of such property of a fund sufficient to meet any pecuniary[24] legacies, so far as not provided for as aforesaid. This paragraph applies to a true residuary gift, and also to a general gift (as of all the testator's realty) even though there is nothing of which it is the residue.[25] It is generally considered that property subject to a general power of appointment

---

[16] See nn. 9, 10, 11 and 12.

[17] It was repealed by F.A. (No. 2) 1983.

[18] This phrase includes an annuity, a general legacy and a demonstrative legacy in so far as not discharged out of the designated property, and any other general direction by a testator for the payment of money including inheritance tax (formerly death duties): A.E.A. 1925, s.55(1)(ix).

[19] As would be a trust for a purpose outside the legally recognised ambit of charity: *Re Endacott* [1960] Ch. 232.

[20] *Re Lamb; Re Worthington*; and *Re Sanger* above.

[21] Wills Act 1837, s.15.

[22] *Re Tong* [1931] 1 Ch. 202.

[23] On the analogy of *Re Bowen-Buscarlet's Will Trusts* [1972] Ch. 463.

[24] See n. 18 above.

[25] *Re Wilson* [1967] Ch. 53, explaining *Re Ridley* [1950] Ch. 415.

devolving by statute as part of the testator's residuary estate[26] is within paragraph 2[27]; and that paragraph 7 only applies to property *expressly* appointed in the exercise of a general power.

26–09 3. Property of the deceased specifically appropriated or devised or bequeathed (either by a specific or general description) for the payment of debts.
4. Property of the deceased charged with, or devised or bequeathed (either by a specific or general description) subject to a charge for the payment of debts. These paragraphs are misleading and would be better abrogated by legislation. If either appears to apply, the authorities cited in the next two notes need to be considered.

Notwithstanding these two paragraphs, undisposed-of property (paragraph 1) or residue (paragraph 2) must bear liabilities first, even though, on the face of the will, paragraph 3 or paragraph 4 of the Schedule looks applicable for debts and liabilities[28]; and so neither of these paragraphs applies. When, however, the appropriation or charge of debts amounts to an exoneration of residue, the statutory order is altered, throwing the liabilities on the property so appropriated or charged[29]; and so neither of these paragraphs applies.

26–10 5. The fund, if any, retained to meet pecuniary legacies.[30]
6. Property specifically devised or bequeathed rateably according to value. The result of these paragraphs is that, if this stage is reached, all pecuniary legacies fail before anything is taken from specific gifts. It is unlikely that this would have been the desire of the deceased, who would be more likely to prefer them to abate together rateably.[31]

The "value" mentioned in paragraph 6 is the value to the deceased: so that any mortgage is first deducted in account.[32] The value to be taken is the probate value,[33] when there is one; a probate valuation is not always needed nowadays.

26–11 7. Property appointed by will under a general power, including the statutory power to dispose of entailed interests, rateably according to value. This paragraph of the Schedule only applies to property *expressly* so appointed; not to property devolving as part of

---

[26] Under Wills Act 1837, s.27: see para. 20–34 above.
[27] Jarman, *Wills*, at p. 1897; Snell, *Equity* at p. 333.
[28] *Re Gordon* [1940] Ch. 769.
[29] *Re Littlewood* [1931] 1 Ch. 443; *Re James* [1947] Ch. 256; *Re Meldrum* [1952] Ch. 208.
[30] See n. 18.
[31] For the distinction between pecuniary or general legacies and specific legacies and the status of demonstrative legacies, see Chap. 29.
[32] *Re John* [1933] Ch. 370.
[33] *Re Cohen* [1960] Ch. 179.

residue, within paragraph 2 of the Schedule.[34] (This is another narrow and perplexing distinction.)

26–12 Other property.

Property appointed by deed or nomination. Property appointed by deed, as distinct from property appointed by will, is not mentioned in the Schedule; and so property so appointed under a general power meets liabilities only after those so mentioned.[35] The same logic applies to property of the deceased appointed at the death under a statutory power of nomination.

Testamentary option. When a will confers an option to purchase property below its value, the purchase price so payable is brought in as an asset to meet liabilities, but the property itself is the last to be resorted to.[36]

Donatio mortis causa. The question whether there is power finally to resort for the purpose of meeting liabilities to the subject-matter of a valid conditional deathbed gift (*donatio mortis causa*) is discussed in paragraphs. 22–04 and 22–06 above. The point is uncertain; if it arises, the personal representatives should apply to the court for directions.

INCIDENCE OF LEGACIES

26–13 Generally. The correct way to meet pecuniary legacies in the administration of estates ought also to be clear. It is not. The reported cases on the incidence of legacies are neither consistent nor logical; but they seem to fall into categories, as mentioned below. It is submitted, without much confidence, that the list which follows summarises the present state of the authorities.[37]

26–14 Express direction as to incidence. The court readily finds an express direction as to the incidence of legacies; then that direction is followed.[38] The consequence of that is usually to preserve the pre-1926 priority of personalty over realty for payment of legacies[39]

---

[34] See para. 26–08 above.

[35] *Re Phillips* [1931] 1 Ch. 347.

[36] *Re Eve* [1956] Ch. 479.

[37] See, for a full discussion, the article citing all the cases down to its date by Professor Ryder in 1956 *Cambridge Law Journal* 80; to which can be added the only subsequent reported case, *Re Taylor* [1969] 2 Ch. 245; and the article criticising *Re Taylor*, by Alberry Q.C. (1969) 85 L.Q.R. 464. See also the succinct summary of the authorities and of their reasoning in Theobald, *Wills*, (14th ed.) at pp. 791–796.

[38] *Re Ridley* [1950] Ch. 415; *Re Wilson* [1967] Ch. 53; *Re Feiss* [1964] Ch. 106.

[39] *Re Ridley* above; *Re Thompson* [1936] Ch. 676; *Re Anstead* [1943] Ch. 161; *Re Wilson* [1967] Ch. 53.

unless on construction that priority is held to be excluded by a will treating the estate as a single entity.[40]

26–15 No express direction as to incidence and partial intestacy. The cases where there is no express direction as to incidence and a partial intestacy fall into the following classes.

(a) *No trust for sale.* There is no trust for sale in the will and so the statutory trust for sale[41] applies; legacies are payable out of property undisposed of, including realty,[42] or out of residue, or (what is the same as residue) a general gift.[43]

(b) *Express trust for sale and part undisposed.* There is an express trust for sale in the will, and part of the estate is undisposed of; legacies are payable out of property undisposed of,[44] including realty.[45]

(c) *Express trust for sale and failure of a share of a fund.* There is an express trust for sale in the will, but what fails is not a gift of an item of property, but of a *share* of a fund; then, according to two reported cases, the pre-1926 law still applies[46]: so that legacies are payable out of a mixed residuary fund, before it is divided. This distinction between the correct way to pay legacies when there is a failure of a gift of an item of property and the correct way to pay legacies when there is a failure of a gift of a *share* of a fund is not apparent on the words of the Act, and might not be followed[47]; it is not safe to apply these two cases: personal representatives should obtain the directions of the court or the consent of all concerned.

26–16 No partial intestacy. This is the usual case, and usually there is, on the language of the will, no doubt about the application of assets in meeting legacies. When, however, a doubt arises, it has been held in three cases at first istance that the pre-1926 law applies.[48] If those cases are correct, the enactment of the relevant parts of A.E.A. 1925 seems hardly necessary.

---

[40] As *Re Timson* [1953] 1 W.L.R. 1361.
[41] Under A.E.A. 1925, s.33.
[42] *Re Worthington* [1933] Ch. 771; *Re Sanger* [1939] Ch. 238; *Re Berrey* above; also *Re Martin* [1955] Ch. 698, where the testamentary trust for sale did not apply to undisposed-of realty, and the realty was held liable to meet legacies.
[43] *Re Wilson* [1967] Ch. 53.
[44] *Re Gillett's Will Trusts* [1950] Ch. 102; *Re Midgley* [1955] Ch. 576; *Re Martin* [1955] Ch. 698.
[45] *Re Martin* above.
[46] *Re Beaumont* [1950] Ch. 462, Danckwerts J. (as explained by the same judge in *Re Beaumont* above at p. 705; and, it seems, doubted by him in *Re Berrey* above at p. 40); *Re Taylor* above. Harman J. appears to have disapproved *Re Beaumont*; see *Re Midgley* above.
[47] See previous footnote; the distinction was not taken in *Re Tong* above, on expenses, where a gift of income failed: see the article by Alberry Q.C. (1969) 85 L.Q.R. 464.
[48] *Re Thompson* above; *Re Rowe* below; *Re Anstead* [1943] Ch. 161.

26–17 Realty specifically given. Legacies do not fall on realty specifically given,[49] which is within paragraph 6 of the Schedule.

26–18 A different view as to incidence of liabilities and of legacies, only open on appeal. A view of the incidence of legacies that, on the reported cases, is wrong, would be clear and free of difficulty. That view is, that it does not matter in the administration of the estate when paying legacies whether there is a trust-for-sale under the will, a statutory trust-for-sale under A.E.A. 1925, s.33, or no trust for sale but only a power of sale under A.E.A. 1925, s.39. It also does not matter by which section Part Two of the Schedule[50] is enacted and applied. In any case, unless expressly directed otherwise in the will, legacies under paragraph 1 of the Schedule are in the first place payable out of a fund retained from undisposed-of property, and in the second place, under paragraph 2 of the Schedule, out of a fund retained from residue,[51] treating realty and personalty alike.[52] As the authorities cited above show, this cannot be supported at first instance, and probably only with difficulty in the Court of Appeal. It is open in the House of Lords, which has never heard an appeal on the Schedule.

---

[49] *Re Rowe* [1941] Ch. 343.

[50] Printed above.

[51] "What then is to be done with the fund which has been retained thereout? The answer, it seems to me, is that it must be used to meet the pecuniary legacies, because it has been retained for that purpose": Harman J. in *Re Midgley* [1955] Ch. 576 at p. 583. To the same effect, Danckwerts J. in *Re Berrey's Will Trusts* [1959] 1 W.L.R. 30 at p. 40.

[52] A.E.A. 1925, s.32. The desirability of protecting realty for the benefit of the *heir* ceased with the abolition of heirship on January 1, 1926 (except as to entailed interests): A.E.A. 1925, s.45.

Part Five: Distribution

27. Status of beneficiaries; accumulation of income; perpetuity

27–01 Relevance of status. The status of those beneficially interested in an estate may determine their rights, and the distribution of the estate; this applies to individuals, to companies and trusts. Status must therefore be considered by personal representatives.

MARRIAGE AND ITS TERMINATION

27–02 Marriage. Most ceremonies of monogamous marriage between persons free to marry are valid. The requirements for such a ceremony to be recognised under the law of England and Wales as a valid marriage are set out in Dicey & Morris, *The Conflict of Laws*[1]; and need to be considered in a case of doubt.

Points that may arise in the administration of an estate here in connection with a monogamous marriage are stated below, as are the problems faced in administering an estate where there was a polygamous marriage. At the death, the surviving husband or wife becomes the deceased's widow or widower, and retains the status of the deceased's widow or widower until, but not after, a valid remarriage.[2] A purported remarriage that is annulled does not end the status of widow or of widower[3]; but transactions completed before annulment on the basis that there had been a valid marriage are not set aside.[4]

27–03 Common law wife. The status of a wife at common law is well recognised; it is created by a marriage ceremony intended to constitute the relationship of husband and wife solemnised when and

---

[1] 12th ed. at pp. 639–711.
[2] *Re Hammond* [1911] 2 Ch. 342; *Hamar v. Cunard White Star* [1952] P. 148.
[3] *Re Dewhirst* [1948] Ch. 198; *Re D'Altroy* [1968] 1 W.L.R. 120.
[4] *Re Eaves* [1940] Ch. 109.

where, for some reason, the local form of marriage is not available.[5] The parties thereby become husband and wife for all purposes.

The expression "common law wife" or husband, does not apply to an unmarried couple permanently living together.[6]

27–04 Void and voidable marriages. When a marriage is *voidable* (liable to be avoided),[7] it is only the parties to it who can avoid it or affirm it; and so it ranks as an effective marriage after the death of one of the parties.[8] A *void* marriage[9] (wholly invalid) is, however, ineffective for any purpose; and so on the death of a party to a void marriage (under the current view of what constitutes a void marriage), those concerned succeed on the basis that there was no marriage.[10]

27–05 Decree in England and Wales of dissolution or annulment; position of former spouse. See paragraph 14–06.

---

[5] *Wolfenden v. Wolfenden* [1946] P. 61 (religious marriage celebrated in China by an unordained and unauthorised missionary); *Taczanowska v. Taczanowski* [1957] P. 301; *Preston v. Preston* [1963] P. 141 (marriages solemnised on the continent by Polish Army chaplains); and, on appeal from Singapore, *Penhas v. Eng* [1953] A.C. 304.

[6] But see para. 17–06 at (f): Law Reform (Succession) Act 1995, s.2 confers rights on such persons under Inheritance (Provision for Family and Dependants) Act 1975, on deaths on or after January 1, 1996.

[7] Matrimonial Causes Act 1973, s.12, and s.13 (replacing and extending M.C.A. 1965, s.9): for non-consummation, lack of valid consent in consequence of duress, mistake, unsoundness of mind or otherwise, mental disorder of either party at the time of the marriage of such a kind or to such an extent as to be unfitted for marriage, the respondent suffering at the time of the marriage from venereal disease in a communicable form, or at the time of the marriage the respondent was pregnant by some person other than the petitioner; see the sections in full for their terms.

[8] *Re Roberts* [1978] 1 W.L.R. 653.

[9] Currently defined by M.C.A. 1973, s.11 as amended (replacing the common law) as follows:

"**11.** A marriage celebrated after 31st July 1971 shall be void on the following grounds only, that is to say—
  (a) that is not a valid marriage under the provisions of the Marriages Act 1949 to 1970 (that is to say where—
      (i) the parties are within the prohibited degrees of relationship;
      (ii) either party is under the age of sixteen; or
      (iii) the parties have intermarried in disregard of certain requirements as to the formation of marriage);
  (b) that at the time of the marriage either party was already lawfully married;
  (c) that the parties are not respectively male and female;
  (d) in the case of a polygamous marriage entered into outside England and Wales, that either party was at the time of the marriage domiciled in England and Wales.

For the purposes of paragraph (d) of this subsection a marriage may be polygamous although at its inception neither party has any spouse additional to the other: *but see Addendum.*

Note: The reference in subsection (a) to "1970" has been amended by Marriage Act 1983, and now reads "1949 to 1986." "

[10] *Mette v. Mette* (1859) 1 Sw. & T. 416; *Warter v. Warter* (1890) 15 P.D. 152.

27–06 Decree in England and Wales of judicial separation; position of spouse. A decree of judicial separation (if made) only affects succession on intestacy, not succession by will; while a decree of judicial separation is in force, the other spouse does not succeed on intestacy.[11]

27–07 Recognition in England and Wales of foreign decrees ending a marriage. The Family Law Act 1986 governs what decrees or other process of divorce, nullity or separation made outside England and Wales are recognised here; and governs when an overseas process affects the parties' status here and accordingly the administration of an estate.

Doubts may arise whether a foreign determination should be characterised as a divorce or as a separation, in the view of the law of England[12]; the boundaries between a void marriage and a voidable marriage[13] may be different in other countries or may not exist; and personal representatives need to obtain advice in both countries before distributing.

CHILDREN AND ISSUE

27–08 Minors. A minor[14] cannot give personal representatives a good receipt under the general law. A provision in a will that a minor may give a good receipt entitles the personal representatives to pay to the minor on the minor's receipt, but does not compel them to do so.[15]

27–09 Steps to administer a minor's legacy or share of residue. The personal representative may, and almost always should, appoint two or more trustees (including any of themselves or not, as they think right), or perhaps a trust corporation, to be trustees of the minor's legacy or residuary interest under A.E.A. 1925, s.42; the personal representatives then obtain a good receipt from the trustees. Where the minor beneficiary is domiciled abroad, in a country that recognises trusts, section 42 authorises the appointment of trustees resident there[16]; and the court would, if asked, make an order approving such an appointment.

---

[11] Matrimonial Causes Act 1973, s.18(2).
[12] See *Tursi v. Tursi* [1958] P. 54.
[13] Matrimonial Causes Act 1973, ss.11 and 12.
[14] That is to say, someone under the age of 18 years: Family Law Reform Act 1969, s.1.
[15] *Re Somech* [1957] Ch. 165; where the discretion was surrendered to the court.
[16] On the analogy of *Re Windeatt* [1969] 1 W.L.R. 692 and *Re Whitehead* [1971] 1 W.L.R. 833 and the cases cited there.

27–10 Minors with a foreign domicile. In the era when the age of majority in England was 21, it was held that payment may be made to a minor with a foreign domicile on the minor attaining majority (at 18) under the law of the minor's domicile,[17] or on attaining majority under the law of England, whichever occurred first.[18] It is doubtful if these authorities would justify payment nowadays direct to a person domiciled in a country where majority is attained at an age regarded in England and Wales as too young, that is to say below 18 years.

A provision in the law of the minor's domicile, that the minor's father can give a good receipt, is not operative in England unless authorised by the court here to be acted upon.[19] In a proper case there is, however, power for the court here (not the personal representatives) to authorise payment to a parent overseas of the minor's property pursuant to a court order obtained in the country where the minor is domiciled.[20]

27–11 Children born in wedlock. A child born in wedlock in England and Wales is certainly legitimate; and so is a child born in wedlock elsewhere.[21] Questions of legitimacy no longer control succession to property in the manner that they did at one time.

27–12 Children conceived by artificial insemination. The status of children conceived by artificial insemination is regulated now by the Human Fertilisation and Embryology Act 1990, ss.27–35.

The Act constitutes an authority (section 5); enacts who in the case of artificial insemination is to rank (section 27) as a child's mother and (section 28) as a child's father[22]; this applies for all purposes

---

[17] *Re Hellman* (1866) 2 Eq. 363; *Re Schnapper* [1928] Ch. 420.
[18] *Re Hellmann* above.
[19] *Re Chatard* [1899] 1 Ch. 712, where there was no satisfactory evidence that the money would be applied for the infant's benefit and payment to the father was not allowed.
[20] *Re Duddy* [1925] 1 Ir. 198; *Dharamal v. Holmpatrick* [1935] Ir. 760.
[21] *Bamgbose v. Daniel* [1955] A.C. 107: polygamous marriages in Nigeria.
[22] Sections 27 and 28 enact as follows:

"**Meaning of "mother"**
27.—(1) The woman who is carrying or has carried a child as a result of the placing in her of an embryo or of sperm and eggs, and no other woman, is to be treated as the mother of the child.
(2) Subsection (1) above does not apply to any child to the extent that the child is treated by virtue of adoption as not being the child of any person other than the adopter or adopters.
(3) Subsection (1) above applies whether the woman was in the United Kingdom or elsewhere at the time of the placing in her of the embryo or the sperm and eggs.
Meaning of "father"
28.—(1) This section applies in the case of a child who is being or has been carried by a woman as the result of the placing in her of an embryo or of sperm and eggs or her artificial insemination.
(2) If—
(a) at the time of the placing in her of the embryo or the sperm and eggs or of her insemination, the woman was a party to a marriage, and
—cont. on next page

(section 29(1) and (2)) and documents (section 29(3)); except property devolving along with a title of honour, a hereditary peerage or a baronetcy (section 29(4)). An order about parentage may be made within six months after a birth, or within six months after the Act comes into force, declaring a child's parentage (section 30). There are provisions about information on parentage (sections 31 to 35); varied retrospectively by the Human Fertilisation and Embryology (Disclosure of Information) Act 1992. After a death the personal representatives may need to ascertain in what court any such order was made and to seek a copy of it, under R.S.C. Ord. 63, r. 4(1) or C.C.R., Ord. 22, r. 8. In most cases, there is unlikely to have been an order. In general information about the parentage of a

---

—cont. from previous page
    (b) the creation of the embryo carried by her was not brought about with the sperm of the other party to the marriage,
then, subject to subsection (5) below, the other party to the marriage shall be treated as the father of the child unless it is shown that he did not consent to the placing in her of the embryo or the sperm and eggs or to her insemination (as the case may be).
    (3) If no man is treated, by virtue of subsection (2) above, as the father of the child but—
    (a) the embryo or the sperm and eggs were placed in the woman, or she was artificially inseminated, in the course of treatment services provided for her and a man together by a person to whom a licence applies, and
    (b) the creation of the embryo carried by her was not brought about with the sperm of that man,
then, subject to subsection (5) below, that man shall be treated as the father of the child.
    (4) Where a person is treated as the father of the child by virtue of subsection (2) or (3) above, no other person is to be treated as the father of the child.
    (5) Subsections (2) and (3) above do not apply—
    (a) in relation to England and Wales and Northern Ireland, to any child who, by virtue of the rules of common law, is treated as the legitimate child of the parties to a marriage,
    (b) in relation to Scotland, to any child who, by virtue of any enactment or other rule of law, is treated as the child of the parties to a marriage, or
    (c) to any child to the extent that the child is treated by virtue of adoption as not being the child of any person other than the adopter or adopters.
    (6) Where—
    (a) the sperm of a man who had given such consent as is required by paragraph 5 of Schedule 3 to this Act was used for a purpose for which such consent was required, or
    (b) the sperm of a man, or any embryo the creation of which was brought about with his sperm, was used after his death,
he is not to be treated as the father of the child.
    (7) The references in subsection (2) above to the parties to a marriage at the time there referred to—
    (a) are to the parties to a marriage subsisting at that time, unless a judicial separation was then in force, but
    (b) include the parties to a void marriage if either or both of them reasonably believed at that time that the marriage was valid; and for the purposes of this subsection it shall be presumed, unless the contrary is shown, that one of them reasonably believed at that time that the marriage was valid.
    (8) This section applies whether the woman was in the United Kingdom or elsewhere at the time of the placing in her of the embryo or the sperm and eggs or her artificial insemination.
    (9) In subsection (7)(a) above, "judicial separation" includes a legal separation obtained in a country outside the British Islands and recognised in the United Kingdom."

child artificially conceived is not to be disclosed (section 33); except when ordered to be disclosed in court proceedings (section 34); or for purposes preliminary to or in connection with court proceedings (sections 33(6) and (6A), as extended by the 1992 Act, s.1).

When therefore personal representatives have reason to suppose that a child was artifically conceived, they may have to apply to the court under section 34 to obtain the necessary information. Otherwise the personal representatives will not know whether a particular child should be included in a distribution, or be excluded.

27–13 Adopted children. Under an Adoption Order made in the United Kingdom for purposes of succession and for all other legal purposes, being a lifelong commitment,[23] on death the adopted child is treated as the legitimate child of the adopters and not of any other person[24]; even when that is a disadvantage in some way to an adopted child.[25]

The same applies to overseas adoptions recognised in England and Wales by statute[26]; or at common law. When a question arises about an overseas adoption, personal representatives must obtain advice about the position, and may need to apply to the court.

27–14 Future children. Personal representatives often need to consider whether they can act on the basis that no child, or no further child, of a particular description can be born. The question does not arise on intestacy; for on intestacy those who take are ascertained at the death, with the addition of any child *en ventre* at the death.[27] A question about future children may arise under a will: either under a gift to someone's child or children or grandchild or grandchildren, with a gift over in default; or under a gift to a class of children, to a class of grandchildren or to some other class.[28]

---

[23] *Re B.* [1995] 3 W.L.R. 40, C.A.; where Adoption Order had been regularly made in England in July 1959 about a child then aged a few months; at the age of 36 years he was unable to have the Adoption Order set aside, on discovering that his natural parents had had a religious and ethnic background entirely different from that of his adopting parents (who had died meanwhile); although had the facts been known in 1959 the Adoption Order would have been unlikely to be made.

[24] Adoption Act 1976, s.38 and s.39; except in relation to an adoption by one only (usually the mother) of the child's natural parents: s.39(3); thus destroying the child's rights in relation to the child's rights in relation to the child's other natural parent: *Re Collins* [1990] Fam. 56 above. The same result occurred on a claim for damages for the death of the mother of a child, afterwards adopted. *Watson v. Willmott* [1991] 1 Q.B. 140, where *Re Collins* was not cited. *Watson v. Willmott* was decided on the wording of Children Act 1975; and see Adoption Act 1976, Sched. 4 and s.73(3).

[25] *Re Collins* [1990] Fam. 56: the first point refusing an adopted child the status to apply under the Inheritance (Provision for Family and Dependants) Act 1975; the reasoning is consistent with the Court of Appeal's decision in *Re Jennery* [1967] Ch. 280 not cited in *Re Collins*.

[26] Adoption Act 1976, s.17 (Convention countries), or s.38(1)(d) and s.71(2) (regulations).

[27] A.E.A. 1925, s.46, s.47 and s.54(3).

[28] Judicial decisions have laid down rules that determine when the class under a gift by will "closes": that is to say the time when the persons who take under a gift by will
—cont. on next page

Personal representatives are not at liberty to act on the footing that a male will have no future child[29]; nor in the absence of exceptional medical evidence will the court.

Until 1993 there was an age when (depending on the circumstances of each case) personal representatives might act on the assumption that a female aged 59 years would have no child or no further child[30]; and the position depended on the facts of each case, rather than on the reported cases from 1866 to 1901.[31]

Until 1993 personal representatives could act without judicial approval on an unconditional medical certificate that a lady could not have a child; or when her age made the fact obvious; or with the leave of the court to act on the footing that no further child would be born.[32] The court sometimes gave leave to act on that footing on the estate purchasing an issue risk policy; it was not normally satisfactory for personal representatives to obtain such a policy without judicial approval, on account of the difficulty of foreseeing the right figure for any future liability.

On December 27, 1993, it was widely reported in the press that a female domiciled in England had born twins in consequence of surgical procedures on the Continent[33]; she is their lawful mother.[34] This event raises in a new form the practical question whether a distribution may be made now on the assumption that a woman will not have a child. The safe course is to refuse to make such an assumption. If such an assumption is to be made, the personal representatives should seek the approval of the court in every case: rather than rely on relief from liability to any potential subsequent child or children being granted under the Trustee Act 1925, s.61.[35]

An Act of Parliament is desirable to authorise personal representatives and trustees to disregard the possibility of a female giving birth over a specified age.[36]

27–15 Legitimacy, succession on intestacy on death after April 4, 1988 or under a will made after that date. On an intestacy[37] on a death after April 4, 1988 or under a will or codicil made on or after

---

—cont. from previous page

to a class are finally ascertained, to the exclusion of any who come into existence afterwards. These rules are set out in Jarman (8th ed.), at pp. 1659–1702; and in a few subsequent decisions.

[29] Re Townsend (1886) 34 Ch. Div. 357; Re Scott [1975] 1 W.L.R. 1260 at p. 1262G.
[30] Re Westminster Bank's Declaration of Trust [1963] 1 W.L.R. 820.
[31] Collected in Re White [1901] 1 Ch. 570: Re Westminster Bank's Declaration of Trust, above. The question has been extensively considered in the U.S.A.: see Scott, Trusts (4th ed.), para. 340.1.
[32] Re Westminster Bank's Declaration of Trust, above. Such leave is given in chambers, that is to say in private, under Ord. 85, r. 2; not under the V.T.A. 1958: Re Pettifor [1966] Ch. 267.
[33] The Times, December 27, 1993, p. 1.
[34] Human Fertilisation and Embryology Act 1990, s.27.
[35] See para. 45–04 below.
[36] Compare Perpetuities and Accumulations Act 1964, s.2(1)(a).
[37] Family Law Reform Act 1987, s.18.

that date,[38] there is now no discrimination between those born within marriage and those born outside marriage. The Family Law Reform Act 1987, s.1(1) enacts:

> "**1.**—(1) In this Act and enactments passed and instruments made after the coming into force of this section, references (however expressed) to any relationship between two persons shall, unless the contrary intention appears, be construed without regard to whether or not the father and mother of either of them, or the father and mother of any person through whom the relationship is deduced, have or had been married to each other at any time."

Under section 1(2) and (3) this principle applies to references after April 4, 1988 to marriage or to not being married, to legitimacy and legitimation under the Legitimacy Act 1976 and to any person otherwise treated in law as legitimate.

27–16 Legitimacy: succession on intestacy on a death before April 4, 1988 or under a will made before that date. Wills or intestacies to which the 1987 Act does not apply (that is to say, intestacies on deaths before April 4, 1988 and after January 1, 1970; and wills made between those two dates) are governed by the Family Law Reform Act 1969, Part Two, to which reference should be made. On an intestacy, illegitimate children succeed to their parents, but not to anyone else.[39] Under a will made after January 1, 1970 a reference to a child, children or other relative of any person is taken as including such a person's illegitimate child or children unless the contrary intention appears.[40]

27–17 Legitimacy: children born outside England and Wales, out of wedlock. When a child is born out of England and Wales, and not in wedlock under a system of law that nevertheless treats such a child as legitimate, the question whether that child's legitimacy is recognised in England and Wales is doubtful.[41] If it arises in an estate, personal representatives need the protection of obtaining the court's directions.

27–18 Legitimation. Legitimation is quite different from legitimacy: the expression "legitimation" refers to rendering legitimate a child who had been born illegitimate, usually by the subsequent marriage of the child's parents.

---

[38] s.19.
[39] F.L.R.A. 1969, s.14.
[40] s.15.
[41] See Dicey & Morris, *The Conflict of Laws*, at pp. 854–859.

The parents' lawful marriage after the birth of a child legitimises that child[42]; and so may the legitimation of such a child by extraneous law.[43] When, however, the marriage ceremony, though reasonably believed by one or both of the parties to it to be valid, turns out to have been void,[44] it is only those children born after the void ceremony who are thereby legitimated, not any born before it.[45]

POLYGAMOUS MARRIAGES

27–19 Polygamous marriages abroad: position of children and wives in England and Wales. The children of lawful polygamous marriages, contracted elsewhere, rank in England and Wales as lawful children.[46] Recognition is likewise given to the status of polygamous wives under a marriage lawfully contracted elsewhere.[47] The same reasoning would apply to a polyandrous marriage lawfully contracted elsewhere, although the question does not appear to have arisen for decision: *but see Addendum.*

27–20 Rights of several polygamous widows. Under the system of law overseas, there may be differences in status between a man's polygamous wives; but the law of England and Wales disregards those differences in status and treats the principal wife and the secondary wives equally as wives.[48] The recognition of the status of a polygamous wife as a widow does not necessarily confer on her all the rights of a widow. The question occurs from time to time, but has not arisen for decision in any reported case in England and Wales.

In the absence of a reported case, the question depends on the construction of the A.E.A. 1925, as amended. The right[49] of the surviving spouse of an intestate to "*a* fixed net sum" (emphasis added) demonstrates a "contrary intention,"[50] so that the singular

---

[42] Legitimacy Act 1976 replacing Legitimacy Act 1926, as amended by Legitimacy Act 1959.

[43] s.3 of the 1976 Act.

[44] Matrimonial Causes Act 1973, s.11; as distinct from voidable: s.12.

[45] 1976 Act, s.1, re-enacting 1959 Act, s.2: *Re Spence* [1990] Ch. 652. This is rather hard on the older child/ren.

[46] *Bamgbose v. Daniel* [1955] A.C. 107, where a statute of Henry VIII applied in Nigeria.

[47] *Coleman v. Shang* [1961] A.C. 481; *Chaudry v. Chaudry* [1976] Fam. 148; *Re Sehota* [1978] 1 W.L.R. 1506. A convincing judgment refused U.K. tax relief to a man who had a polygamous wife: *Nabi v. Heaton* [1981] 1 W.L.R. 1052; but it was reversed by consent in the Court of Appeal: [1983] 1 W.L.R. 626. The Matrimonial Homes Act 1983 applies to polygamous marriages: s.10(2).

[48] *Cheang v. Tan* [1920] A.C. 369; *Khoo v. Khoo* [1926] A.C. 529; *Coleman v. Quartey* [1961] A.C. 481; see Wolff, *Private International Law* (2nd ed.), at p. 318.

[49] Under A.E.A. 1925, s.46(1).

[50] Within Interpretation Act 1978, s.6(c). At first sight, the view in the text is supported by the majority judgments in *Choo v. Neo* (1908) 12 Straits Settlements Reports 120 in the Court of Appeal there: see at pp. 192–193 by Hyndman-Jones C.J. and at pp. 214 and 222 by Braddell J. In that case there was however no claim

does not include the plural and only one such sum is payable between the polygamous widows of a deceased intestate. Likewise, only one life interest in half the estate is payable among them, under the provision that there shall be held "one-half upon trust for the surviving husband or wife during his or her life," etc. Similarly, where, on an intestacy, an estate is to be held "in trust for *the* surviving husband or wife absolutely,"[51] (emphasis added) it is likely that the estate would be held in trust for them both.[52] There are no words of severance,[53] and so two (or more) lawful polygamous widows would take jointly[54]; and the interest would then accrue to the other widow on the subsequent death of one of them without effecting a severance in equity.

The right of a surviving wife to have appropriated to her share under an intestacy a matrimonial home in which she was residing at the death,[55] is applicable when one of several lawful polygamous wives resided there with the deceased. If more than one resided there, the personal representatives would need to act under the directions of the court: it might be held that the reference to "*the* surviving husband or wife" (emphasis added) constitutes[56] a contrary intention: so that in such a case neither widow has a right to have the matrimonial home appropriated to her.

In the absence of a reported case on these points, personal representatives need to apply to the court for directions; unless those beneficially concerned are adults who all agree, and allow the maximum (on any view) to any minors.

BANKRUPTCY AND ITS EQUIVALENT

27–21 Bankruptcy in the United Kingdom of a beneficiary before the death. Personal representatives with notice of a beneficiary's bankruptcy in England and Wales or elsewhere in the United Kingdom, commencing[57] before the death, have notice that the bankrupt's rights in the estate are thereby vested in the trustee[58]; and must account to and pay the trustee not the bankrupt. A Bankruptcy Order effects a severance of a beneficial joint interest into an interest

---

to more than one widow's share: the question was whether or not the widows (as they were all found to be) took any share at all. It was held that they took one share among them.

[51] A.E.A. 1925, s.46(1).
[52] Interpretation Act 1978, s.6(c).
[53] Such as "equally": Jarman, *Wills*, at pp. 1793–1794.
[54] Compare in the case of spouses, *Re Cohen* [1953] Ch. 88 at p. 95; for the distinction between joint ownership and ownership in common, see para. 22–07.
[55] Under Intestates Estates Act 1952, Sched. 2.
[56] Under Interpretation Act 1978, s.6(c).
[57] Insolvency Act 1986, s.278 and s.426.
[58] s.306.

in common.[59] If they pay the bankrupt without notice of the bankruptcy, they are not liable.[60]

27–22 Bankruptcy in the United Kingdom of a beneficiary after the death. When a beneficiary's bankruptcy in England and Wales or elsewhere in the United Kingdom commences after the death, the beneficiary's rights under the will or the intestacy are, for bankruptcy purposes, "after-acquired property," only payable to the trustee on being claimed.[61] Once claimed, payment must be made to the trustee.

27–23 Bankruptcy (or its equivalent) of a beneficiary outside the United Kingdom. The law of England and Wales recognises as effective the assignment of assets in a bankruptcy outside England of someone domiciled at the place where the bankruptcy is proceeding, or of someone who has submitted to the jurisdiction of the courts there.[62] Payment should, in such a case, normally be made to the foreign trustee or other assignee in bankruptcy.[63]

27–24 Exceptions to the recognition of a bankruptcy outside the United Kingdom. There are, however, exceptions to this recognition of an overseas bankruptcy. It might be wrong for personal representatives in England to treat a foreign bankruptcy as effective where the foreign bankruptcy is to their knowledge based on a liability that the English courts will not enforce directly or indirectly: such as a liability to foreign revenue,[64] or a liability that would not be recognised in England on other grounds,[65] for example, a fine imposed abroad, especially if imposed, as in some countries, for conduct that in England is permissible; or a personal restraining order.[66]

27–25 Position of personal representatives as to a bankruptcy not in the United Kingdom. Before acting on the basis that a foreign bankruptcy is to be treated as operative here, personal

---

[59] See para. 22–07 above.
[60] *Re Bennett* [1907] 1 K.B. 149.
[61] s.307. It is not necessary to consider the previous law now: *Hunt v. Fripp* [1898] 1 Ch. 675 and *Re Ball* [1899] 2 Ir. 313.
[62] Dicey & Morris, *The Conflict of Laws* (12th ed.), at pp. 1175–1183.
[63] There is therefore no need for provisions in the Insolvency Act 1986 for mutual recognition of United Kingdom bankruptcies, although they are all under the same Act: see ss.265, 440, 441 and 442. The position may be complicated within the European Community when the proposed Bankruptcy Convention is in force.
[64] *Government of India v. Taylor* [1955] A.C. 491; *State of Norway's Application* [1990] A.C. 723.
[65] *Re Lorillard* [1922] 2 Ch. 638 (liability statute-barred in England).
[66] *Felixstowe Dock v. U.S. Lines* [1989] Q.B. 360.

representatives should obtain advice and consider applying for the court's directions.

27–26 Mental disorder of a beneficiary. When a beneficiary here suffers mental disorder, the personal representatives or the receiver should obtain the authority of the Court of Protection[67] for the payment of what is due. A receiver may be appointed in England for property of a person overseas suffering from mental disorder.[68] It is not safe or effective to make payment to a person with mental disorder.

27–27 Other disabilities imposed outside the United Kingdom. The court has a discretion to disregard a disability imposed outside the U.K. that is viewed as wrong.[69] Examples are the status of *prodigal* under the law of France[70]; a disability imposed by reason of physical infirmity (as distinct from mental infirmity) in California[71]; and the disabilities imposed by National Socialism in Germany.[72] There are other examples, such as slavery.[73] Before acting on the basis that someone has a status not known to the law of England and Wales, personal representatives should consider obtaining the directions of the court.[74] Otherwise they may be at risk of being held to have committed maladministration (*devastavit*).[75]

OTHER DONEES

27–28 Companies. A company, whether incorporated under the Companies Acts or by Royal Charter, is a legal entity or distinct from its members; a company may be a beneficiary under a will. Wills frequently make gifts to a company incorporated for charitable or similar purposes without the word "limited."[76] A company may even be the legatee of its own shares through a nominee.[77] An overseas

---

[67] Under Mental Health Act 1983.

[68] *Re Soltykoff* [1898] W.N. 77. This is the quickest and least costly course: there are doubts about payment in England to a foreign curator: Dicey & Morris, *Conflict of Laws* (11th ed.), at p. 893.

[69] *Worms v. de Valdor* (1880) 41 L.T. 791; *Re Selot* [1902] 1 Ch. 488; *Re Langley* [1962] Ch. 541; *Oppenheimer v. Cattermole* [1976] A.C. 249.

[70] *Worms v. de Valdor* above; *Re Selot* above.

[71] *Re Langley* above.

[72] *Oppenheimer v. Cattermole* above: the courts of this country are not "obliged to shut their eyes to the shocking nature of such legislation" (Lord Hodson at p. 265); it should not be recognised on the grounds of public policy (Lord Salmon at p. 282); likewise the other Law Lords in the majority on this question.

[73] See Dicey & Morris, *The Conflict of Laws* (11th ed.), at p. 96; and the passage from Story, *Conflict of Laws* quoted in *Worms v. de Valdor* above.

[74] See Chap. 42.

[75] See Chap. 45.

[76] Under Companies Act 1985, s.30.

[77] *Re Castiglione's Will Trusts* [1958] Ch. 549.

corporation recognised in England and Wales[78] may also be a beneficiary under a will.

27–29 Charities. A gift by will may validly be made to a charity (as "charity" is narrowly defined for legal purposes): a body not incorporated that is registered by the Charity Commissioners as a charity, or held by the Commissioners to be a charity exempt from such registration,[79] may give a good receipt to personal representatives.

27–30 Trust for purposes. Personal representatives need advice when a will does not make a gift to an established charity, but in trust for purposes, or makes a gift to an *unincorporated* body. When those purposes are within the legal definition of "charity,"[80] the gift is valid[81]; and a "*scheme*" is settled by the Charity Commissioners (or the court) to direct the details of the application of the gift.[82] On the other hand, a gift in trust for a purpose that is outside the legal definition of "charity" is void, although those purposes are beneficial or admirable[83]; so is a gift for a non-charitable body.[84] In such cases, the subject-matter devolves as if the will had not made the gift (into residue if it was a specific gift; or as on a partial intestacy if the gift was residuary).

A gift in trust for non-charitable purposes is valid when the words of the will are construed as benefiting ascertainable persons who have, under the documents governing their association and the will, power to apply the subject-matter, even though the gift is made to them for a specified purpose.[85] A gift to the deceased's club will be valid, when the club rules and the terms of the gift in the will enable the members to spend the subject-matter.

---

[78] Dicey & Morris, *The Conflict of Laws* (12th ed.), at pp. 1107–1116.

[79] Under the Charities Act 1993 s.3.

[80] This is not the place to formulate what amounts to a charity within the Act of 1601 and numerous subsequent cases, summarised in Tudor, *Charities* (8th ed.), at pp. 1 to 120. The starting point is that "charity" for legal purposes consists of four classes:
    (1)   trusts for the relief of poverty;
    (2)   trusts for the advancement of education;
    (3)   trusts for the advancement of [any] religion;
    (4)   trusts for other purposes beneficial to the community: *Commissioners for the Special Purposes of Income Tax v. Pemsel* [1891] A.C. 531 at p. 583.
These categories are subject to numerous qualifications and restrictions; see Tudor above.

[81] Jarman, *Wills* at pp. 230–233.

[82] Charities Act 1993 s.16.

[83] *Chichester Diocesan Fund v. Simpson* [1944] A.C. 341 (charitable or benevolent purposes); *Re Astor* [1952] Ch. 534 (newspaper standards, etc.); *Re Endacott* [1960] Ch. 232 (a useful memorial to the testator); *Re Grant's Will Trusts* [1980] 1 W.L.R. 360 (political party, on terms outside the line of cases in n. 85).

[84] *Re Macauley* [1943] Ch. 435 n., H.L. (Folkestone Lodge of the Theosophical Society); *Re Lipinski's Will Trusts* [1976] Ch. 235 at p. 245.

[85] *Re Clarke* [1901] 2 Ch. 110 (Corps of Commissionaires); *Re Drummond* [1914] 2 Ch. 90, the second point (Old Bradfordians); *Re Price* [1943] Ch. 422 (Anthroposophical Society of Great Britain); *Re Lipinski* above (Hull Judaeans).

The distinctions turn on the words of each will in all the circumstances. Personal representatives faced with a gift for purposes or with a gift to an unincorporated body must obtain legal advice and usually the directions of the court.

27–31 Accumulation of income. The L.P.A. 1925, s.164 and the Perpetuities & Accumulations Act 1964, s.13[86] impose restrictions on

---

[86] The sections read as follows:

"164. General restrictions on accumulation of income
  (1) No person may by any instrument or otherwise settle or dispose of any property in such manner that the income thereof shall, save as hereinafter mentioned, be wholly or partially accumulated for any longer period than one of the following, namely:—
    (a) the life of the grantor or settlor; or
    (b) a term of twenty-one years from the death of the grantor, settlor or testator; or
    (c) the duration of the minority or respective minorities of any person or persons living or en ventre sa mere at the death of the grantor, settlor or testator; or
    (d) the duration of the minority or respective minorities only of any person or persons who under the limitations of the instrument directing the accumulations would, for the time being, if of full age, be entitled to the income directed to be accumulated.
  In every case where any accumulation is directed otherwise than as aforesaid, the direction shall (save as hereinafter mentioned) be void; and the income of the property directed to be accumulated shall, so long as the same is directed to be accumulated contrary to this section, go to and be received by the person or persons who would have been entitled thereto if such accumulation had not been directed.
  (2) This section does not extend to any provision—
    (i) for payment of the debts of any grantor, settlor, testator or other person;
    (ii) for raising portions for—
      (a) any child, children or remoter issue of any grantor, settlor or testator; or
      (b) any child, children or remoter issue of a person taking any interest under any settlement or other disposition directing the accumulations or to whom any interest is thereby limited;
    (iii) respecting the accumulation of the produce of timber or wood;
  and accordingly such provisions may be made as if no statutory restrictions on accumulation of income had been imposed.
  (3) The restrictions imposed by this section apply to instruments made on or after the twenty-eighth day of July, eighteen hundred, but in the case of wills only where the testator was living and of testamentary capacity after the end of one year from that date.
13 Amendment of s.164 of Law of Property Act 1925
  (1) The periods for which accumulations of income under a settlement or other disposition are permitted by section 164 of the Law of Property Act 1925 shall include—
    (a) a term of twenty-one years from the date of the making of the disposition, and
    (b) the duration of the minority or respective minorities of any person or persons in being at that date
  (2) It is hereby declared that the restrictions imposed by the said section 164 apply in relation to a power to accumulate income whether or not there is a duty to exercise that power, and that they apply whether or not the power to accumulate extends to income produced by the investment of income previously accumulated."

the period during which a will may lawfully require or lawfully authorise income to be accumulated. One of the periods is a period 21 years from the testator's death.[87]

Under the Trustee Act 1925, s.31 there is an independent statutory power for trustees to accumulate unapplied income held in trust for minors, if within the words of section.[88] Its exercise does not form part of the administration of the estate and is dealt with in the books on trusts.

27–32 The rules against perpetuity. Until July 16, 1964, complicated common law rules invalidated an interest given in such a way that it might possibly (even if very improbably) vest absolutely in someone outside a period of lives in being when the gift was made (which for a gift by will was at the testator's death) plus 21 years thereafter. Those rules only apply now to wills of those who died before July 16, 1964.[89]

For the wills of those dying on or after July 16, 1964, the common law has been replaced by the Perpetuities and Accumulations Act 1964; allowing[90] a period for vesting up to 80 years to be specified in a will; and treating[91] a disposition as valid until (if ever) it turns out to vest outside the relevant period. When no perpetuity period is specified in the will, a period of 21 years from the death is allowed.[92] The Perpetuities and Accumulations Act 1964 is an example of clear drafting; and rarely gives rise to difficulty. A professionally drawn will should specify 80 years as the perpetuity period. A will drawn without professional help sometimes raises a question under the 1964 Act.

---

[87] For the inheritance tax benefits of an accumulation and maintenance trust, see para. 16–10 above.
[88] On this, see *Wolstenhome & Cherry* (13th ed.) Vol. 4, pp. 39–45 and *Re Vestey* [1951] Ch. 209.
[89] See Morris & Leach, *Perpetuities* (2nd ed.).
[90] s.1.
[91] s.3.
[92] *Re Hooper* [1932] 1 Ch. 38, as before the 1964 Act.

28. Lapse by prior death; uncertainty about survivorship; gifts to attesting witnesses

28–01 Lapse. A beneficiary must survive the testator to take under the will; otherwise the gift fails by lapse[1]: unless the will directs the gift to take effect if necessary in favour of the donee's personal representatives.

This does not mean that the gift must be immediate; a future but vested gift (for example a gift postponed to a life interest) takes effect at the death and vests in the donee, and passes to the donee's own personal representatives on the donee's death during the period of postponement.[2] Where the future interest is not contingent on the donee surviving the period of postponement, but is conditional on some other requirement which is satisfied, the donee takes a transmissible contingent interest which likewise passes to his or her own personal representatives.[3]

The lapse of a gift by the beneficiary dying before the testator, applies to every form of gift; including a gift by will made by cancelling a charge.[4] There is an exception, not clearly defined, that a gift made not by way of pure bounty but in satisfaction of a moral obligation may take effect in favour of the personal representatives of the donee if the donee dies first.[5] Personal representatives should

---

[1] Jarman, *Wills*, at p. 438.
[2] *Re Cohn* [1974] 1 W.L.R. 1378 see at p. 1381, Stamp L.J.
[3] Jarman, *Wills*, at pp. 1342–1343.
[4] *Re MacDonnell* [1927] Ir. 213.
[5] *Stevens v. King* [1904] 2 Ch. 30, citing previous authorities; *Re Leach* [1948] Ch. 232.

apply this anomalous doctrine only under the directions of the court, unless all concerned are of full capacity and authorise it.

28–02 Exception for gifts to issue. The Wills Act 1837, s.33 (as amended)[6] enacts as follows:

> **"Gifts to children or other issue who leave issue living at the testator's death shall not lapse**
> **33.**—(1) Where—
>> (a) a will contains a devise or bequest to a child or remoter descendant of the testator; and
>> (b) the intended beneficiary dies before the testator, leaving issue; and
>> (c) issue of the intended beneficiary are living at the testator's death,
>
> then, unless a contrary intention appears by the will, the devise or bequest shall take effect as a devise or bequest to the issue living at the testator's death.
>
> (2) Where—
>> (a) a will contains a devise or bequest to a class of persons consisting of children or remoter descendants of the testator; and
>> (b) a member of the class dies before the testator, leaving issue; and
>> (c) issue of that member are living at the testator's death,
>
> then, unless a contrary intention appears by the will, the devise or bequest shall take effect as if the class included the issue of its deceased member living at the testator's death.
>
> (3) Issue shall take under this section through all degrees, according to their stock, in equal shares if more than one, any gift or share which their parent would have taken and so that no issue shall take whose parent is living at the testator's death and so capable of taking.
>
> (4) For the purposes of this section—
>> (a) the illegitimacy of any person is to be disregarded; and
>> (b) a person conceived before the testator's death and born living thereafter is to be taken to have been living at the testator's death."

The substituted section seems likely to avoid the difficulties that arose under the previous version. To exclude section 33 the "contrary intention" must be shown "in the will." Under the previous version, a recital in a codicil that a gift of residue by the will to a predeceased

---

[6] As regards deaths from January 1, 1983: A.J.A. 1982, s.19 and s.76(11).

son had lapsed (when it would not have lapsed but been preserved by section 33 as then in force), followed by legacies to his children, was held to amount to a contrary intention.[7]

28–03 Uncertainty about survivorship. Under L.P.A. 1925, s.184, when two or more persons die in circumstances "rendering it uncertain which of them survived the other or others" they are presumed to have died in order of seniority and accordingly the younger shall be presumed to have survived the elder. The statutory presumption applies to deaths in a common disaster, such as an air raid[8]; or in a ship lost at sea, when it is not known who survived longer[9]; and to deaths in entirely unconnected disasters.[10] To exclude the presumption, the burden of proof rests on whoever asserts that the younger died first.[11] Words in a will are capable of excluding section 184 altogether; but there is only one reported case,[12] where as a matter of construction section 184 was excluded. For the purposes of inheritance tax, when it cannot be known which of two or more persons survived each other, they are treated as dying at the same instant[13]; thereby reducing such tax.

L.P.A. 1925, s.184 has been held to be a matter of substantive law, not of evidence; so that it does not apply when the succession to movables is in England governed by another system of law, being that of the deceased's domicile.[14]

28–04 The words in section 184, "subject to any order of the court". These puzzling words were inconclusively discussed in English authorities.[15] It is probable that these words have no significant meaning.[16]

28–05 Failure of gifts to attesting witnesses or their spouses. Gifts by will to an attesting witness or to his or her spouse are void,[17] unless the will was duly attested without that person's signature.[18]

---

[7] *Re Meredith* [1924] 2 Ch. 552.
[8] *Hickman v. Peacey* [1945] A.C. 304, by a majority, refusing to treat the deaths as simultaneous; see the illuminating discussion by Lord Simmonds at pp. 344–346.
[9] *Re Rowland* [1963] Ch. 1 by a majority; decided on the words of a will.
[10] *Re Watkinson* [1952] V.L.R. 123 on a similar Act.
[11] *Re Bate* [1947] 2 All E.R. 418; *Adair v. Fairplay* [1956] 2 D.L.R. (2) 67.
[12] *Re Pringle* [1946] Ch. 124.
[13] Inheritance Tax Act 1984, s.4(2).
[14] *Re Cohn* [1945] 1 Ch. 5; which could well have been decided the other way, but it has stood as the law for a long time now and would not be overruled.
[15] *Hickman v. Peacey* above; and the previous case *Re Lindop* [1942] Ch. 377.
[16] *Re Brush, Re Baird* [1962] V.R. 596 where there is a full discussion of these words, in a similar statute, by Adam J.
[17] Wills Act 1837, s.15.
[18] Wills Act 1968, s.1; it is not necessary to consider whether the 1968 Act applies to a military will as the Wills Act 1837, s.15 did not apply to a military will: *Re Limond* [1915] 2 Ch. 240.

They are not avoided by a marriage to a witness after the date of attesting the will or codicil.[19] For this purpose section 15 applies separately to each testamentary document; so that where there is a will and a codicil, an attesting witness to one of them is entitled to gifts given to him, or his or her spouse by the other document.[20]

The disqualification of an attesting witness from benefitting, applies to a provision (ranking in law as a gift), entitling a professional person to charge a solvent estate for his services.[21] It does not however apply to a trustee who, after the death, is appointed a new trustee of the trusts of the will.[22] A gift by will attested by someone who is a trustee of a charitable trust, benefitting under the will, is outside the disqualification of section 15.[23] Also outside the disqualification of section 15, was a gift to the person who should at the death of the testator be a certain abbess, when the attesting witness became the abbess after the date of the will.[24] The same would apply to someone appointed to any other position. It was held by Danckwerts J. that a beneficiary under a secret trust who attested the will did not thereby lose his legacy.[25]

---

[19] *Thorpe v. Bestwick* (1881) 6 Q.B.D. 311; approved in the Court of Appeal in *Re Royce* [1959] Ch. 626.

[20] *Anderson v. Anderson* (1872) 13 Eq. 381; *Re Trotter* [1899] 1 Ch. 764; *Re Tredgold* [1943] Ch. 69.

[21] *Re Pooley* (1888) 40 Ch.Div. 1.

[22] *Re Royce* above.

[23] *Cresswell v. Cresswell* (1868) 6 Eq. 69.

[24] *Re Ray* [1936] Ch. 520.

[25] *Re Young* [1951] Ch. 344 at pp. 350–351, not following *Re Fleetwood* (1880) 15 Ch. Div. 594 and applying decisions in Ireland.

29. Legacies

29–01   Types of legacy. Gifts by will[1] that are not of residue are divided into three categories: general legacies, specific legacies and demonstrative legacies. This division is made because they are treated differently as regards abatement (giving way when the estate is not large enough), as regards ademption (failing when the subject-matter is not there at the death), and as regards income or interest after the

---

[1] Which are normally express, but may be inferred from a mere list of names: *Re Barrance* [1910] 2 Ch. 419; *Re Stevens* [1952] Ch. 323, applying the principle stated in *Re Harrison* (1885) 30 Ch.Div. 390 that it is wrong to construe a solemn will as a "solemn farce".

death. Anything that the testator owns at the death may be made the subject-matter of a legacy: money, investments, land, chattels (including animals); and a debt due from someone else to the testator.[2] It is necessary to distinguish between different types of legacy in the application of A.E.A. 1925, Schedule. 1, Part II,[3] which concerns the order of application of assets to meet liabilities; and also in the administration and distribution of an estate, between different types of legacy.

It is often clear which type of legacy a gift is; the reported cases tend to concern those that are "very near the line"[4] and are not easy to reconcile.

29–02 General legacy. A general legacy is a gift not expressly related to the testator's ownership; as of a sum of money; or of a specified amount of stock or of shares, even if exactly what the testator owned.[5] A pecuniary legacy is a gift of money.

29–03 Specific legacy. A specific legacy is a gift that *specifies* property owned by the testator "identifying it by a sufficient description and manifesting an intention that it should be enjoyed or taken in the state and condition indicated by that description."[6] A specific gift is usually given by the word "my"; but that word is not essential to make a gift specific, if the will indicates that the legacy is a specific legacy.[7] A specific legacy may be made of things not yet acquired at the date of the will.[8]

29–04 Demonstrative legacy. A demonstrative legacy is a general legacy directed to be paid out of a demonstrated source.[9] If it is to be paid only out of the source mentioned and not out of any other source, it is not a demonstrative legacy.[10] This type of legacy was defined by Gibson J. in Northern Ireland, as follows[11]:

> "A demonstrative legacy is in the nature of a pecuniary sum bequeathed in terms that it should be payable out of the

---

[2] For the gift of such a debt, see *Commissioner of Stamp Duties v. Bone* [1977] A.C. 511 at p. 519 to p. 520, citing previous authorities.

[3] See Chap. 26.

[4] As *Re Rose* [1949] Ch. 78, Jenkins J. at p. 86.

[5] *Re Gray* (1887) 36 Ch.Div. 205; *Re Willcocks* [1921] 2 Ch. 327; *Re Gage* [1934] Ch. 536; *Re Bourne* [1944] Ch. 190; *Re O'Connor* [1948] Ch. 628.

[6] *Robertson v. Broadbent* (1883) 8 App.Cas. 812, Lord Selbourne L.C. at p. 813.

[7] *Re Rose* [1949] Ch. 78, where indications in the will were held to make a gift of a specified number of shares a specific legacy.

[8] As of the testator's library at the date of his death: *Robertson v. Broadbent* above, Lord Blackburn at p. 819.

[9] As in *Re Webster* [1937] 1 All E.R. 602.

[10] *Re O'Connor* [1950] N.I. 159.

[11] *Re O'Connor* above at pp. 163–164.

designated fund, but it is not every legacy directed to be so paid that is demonstrative. The essential character of a demonstrative legacy is that it is a legacy capable of existence quite independently of the fund, and the direction as to the fund out of which it is payable must be properly regarded as a subordinate provision of the will. If the source of payment is an integral and inseparable part of the nature of a legacy it cannot be demonstrative, because one of the features of a demonstrative legacy is that it should appear that if the fund prove insufficient the amount of the legacy can be made up out of other assets given by the will. If a testator gives a legacy and directs that it is to be paid out of a particular account or out of the proceeds of sale of particular property, the courts have consistently treated the legacy as demonstrative by notionally importing the word 'primarily' into the reference to the fund for payment. But such a conclusion can only follow if a will does not make it clear that the fund in question is to be the sole source of payment. If a will stipulates or provides that a particular fund and it alone is to feed the legacy, that negatives its character as merely demonstrative."

29–05 Annuities. During the period (approximately 1814 to 1914), when the pound sterling was stable, testators used to bequeath annuities. A gift of annuities[12] (rarely given in modern inflationary conditions) gives rise to difficulty in administration and is likely to require counsel's opinion. A discussion of annuities here would occupy space disproportionate to their practical importance.

Problems on annuities may concern: the extent to which an annuity is charged on income or on capital of an annuity fund[13]; to what extent capital may be recouped out of future surplus income[14]; whether surplus income should be retained to meet a possible future deficiency[15]; the destination during the lifetime of the annuitant of surplus income of an annuity fund[16]; how and to what extent annuities abate in case of a deficiency to meet both the annuities and other pecuniary legacies,[17] and interest[18]; the extent to which a donee of a "tax free" annuity must account for his personal allowances[19];

---

[12] See Jarman, *Wills* at pp. 1113–1131 and pp. 1945–1952. There is an authoritative text book: Bowles, *Testamentary Annuities* (1931).
[13] *Re Chance's Will Trusts* [1962] Ch. 593, citing the previous cases.
[14] *Re Berkeley* [1968] Ch. 744.
[15] *Re Cameron* [1955] 1 W.L.R. 140, a matter normally requiring the directions of the court: *ibid.* at p. 145.
[16] *Re Wragg* [1959] 1 W.L.R. 922; *Re Geering* [1964] Ch. 136.
[17] *Re Cottrell* [1910] 1 Ch. 402; *Re Cox* [1938] Ch. 556; *Re Hill* [1944] Ch. 270; *Re Thomas* [1946] Ch. 36.
[18] *Re Wyles* [1938] Ch. 313.
[19] *Re Pettit* [1922] 2 Ch. 765; *Re Kingcome* [1936] Ch. 566; *Re Lyons* [1952] Ch. 129.

how on abatement a "tax free" annuity is to be valued[20]; whether a direction to purchase an annuity for a beneficiary may be intercepted by the beneficiary claiming the purchase money instead, as it usually may.[21]

29-06 Legacies to an executor. An immediate legacy to the person appointed executor is presumed to be conditional on his acting as executor[22]; unless the will describes the legatee in words that rebut the presumption[23] that the gift is not conditional on acting as executor. In one case, it was held that postponing the legacy to a life interest rebutted the presumption.[24] To entitle an executor, or after his death, his personal representatives, to take a legacy left to him *as executor*, the executor must prove the will[25]; or take steps to administer the estate.[26] Interest only runs on a legacy given to an executor for acting from the date when the executor undertakes the administration of the estate.[27] The presumption that the gift is conditional on acting as executor does not apply to a gift of residue to the executor.[28]

29-07 Ademption; failure by the absence of the subject-matter. A *general* legacy is not subject to ademption: when therefore, there is a general legacy of a stated number of shares or of stock, the legatee is entitled to its value, if ascertainable[29]; but the gift fails if the value cannot be ascertained.[30] A *demonstrative* legacy is likewise not liable to fail by ademption.[31]

Ademption means the failure of a *specific* legacy by the absence, at the death, of the subject-matter. Thus a gift of a mortgage debt failed, when the mortgage had been repaid even though the mortgage

---

[20] *Re Twiss* [1941] Ch. 141; *Re Rothermere* [1944] Ch. 72 (annuity by deed, to be paid out of the estate).

[21] *Re Mabbett* [1891] 1 Ch. 707.

[22] *Re Appleton* (1885) 29 Ch.Div. 893.

[23] By describing the executor as his cousin: *Dix v. Reed* (1823) 1 Sim. & St. 237; as his brother: *Compton v. Bloxham* (1845) 2 Coll. 201; as his friend: *Re Denby* (1861) 3 de G.F. & J. 350, and as his friend giving the legacy as a remembrance: *Bubb v. Yelverton* (1871) 13 Eq. 131.

[24] *Re Reeve* (1877) 4 Ch.Div. 841.

[25] *Hollingsworth v. Grassett* (1845) 15 Sim. 52; *Angermann v. Ford* (1861) 29 Beav. 349.

[26] *Lewis v. Matthews* (1869) 8 Eq. 277 (doubted in another point in *Re Appleton* above); *Harrison v. Rowley* (1798) 4 Ves. 212.

[27] *Angermann v. Ford* above, where that was the date of probate.

[28] *Griffiths v. Pruen* (1840) 11 Sim. 202, where the executor who was residuary legatee only survived the testator for one day; *Re Maxwell* [1906] 1 Ir. 386.

[29] *Re Gage* [1934] Ch. 536 (general legacy of war loan); *Re O'Connor* [1948] Ch. 628 (general legacy of shares); *Re Bourne* [1944] Ch. 190 (general legacy of overseas stock, compulsorily acquired under wartime regulations).

[30] *Re Gray* (1887) 36 Ch.Div. 205.

[31] See para. 29–04 above.

money was kept in a distinct account by the testator.[32] A gift in a will fails by ademption when, after the date of the will, the subject-matter is sold by the testator[33] or the process of compulsory acquisition is validly imposed[34] on the subject-matter; or an option is exercised over the subject-matter,[35] unless the option is created before the date of the will[36] or at the same time.[37] In the absence of ademption the legatee is entitled, notwithstanding a change of form, to what is in substance the same property as is given by the will[38]; but not to anything, such as further shares, acquired as compensation for a reduction in the rights attached to the original property.[39] Where some of the original shares (within the gift) and some bonus shares (outside it) have been sold they are treated as having been sold rateably.[40]

In each case it is to be ascertained whether what exists at the death is in *fact* the same property in a different form (passing under the gift) or is a different asset (not passing under the gift). The reported cases cited in the previous notes to this paragraph appear to have been capable of being decided either way. Care is required before proceeding in any case where there may have been ademption.

29–08 Abatement of general legacies in favour of specific legacies. When the testator has given general legacies and specific legacies which cannot all be paid in full out of the estate, the *general* legacies must abate (diminish) or if necessary be extinguished, so as to enable the specific legacies to take effect. This ancient rule[41] of administration applies unless the will contains words excluding it.[42] Between themselves the general legacies abate rateably.[43] Abatement is imposed: (i) on a legacy given and accepted in satisfaction of an ascertained debt[44]; or (ii) to the testator's wife for her immediate

---

[32] *Re Bridle* (1879) 4 C.P.D. 336.
[33] *Re Rose* [1949] Ch. 78 the second point.
[34] *Watts v. Watts* (1873) 17 Eq. 217; *Re Slater* [1907] 1 Ch. 665; (compulsory acquisition of shares in a utility).
[35] *Re Carrington* [1932] 1 Ch. 1, applying *Lawes v. Bennett* (1785) 1 Cox 167.
[36] *Re Calow* [1928] Ch. 710.
[37] *Re Pyle* [1895] 1 Ch. 724.
[38] *Re Clifford* [1912] 1 Ch. 29; *Re Leeming* [1912] 1 Ch. 828; *Re Kuypers* [1925] Ch. 244; *Re O'Brien* (1946) 62 T.L.R. 594, the 1st point *Re Dorman* [1994] 1 W.L.R. 282 (change of bank account at the same bank effected under an enduring power of attorney): decided "after considerable hesitation" (p. 287 C); following *Re Heilbroner* [1953] 1 W.L.R. 1254.
[39] *Re Kuypers* above (shares); *Re Galway's Will Trusts* [1950] Ch. 1 (compensation for compulsory acquisition of mining rights in land); *Re O'Brien* above (bonus shares).
[40] *Re O'Brien* above.
[41] See *Clifton v. Burt* (1720) 1 P.W. 678.
[42] The will in *Re Compton* [1914] 1 Ch. 119 was construed to exclude the rule by giving a specific gift "as a general and not a specific legacy."
[43] *Clifton v. Burt* above.
[44] *Re Wedmore* [1907] 2 Ch. 277 followed but doubted in *Re Whitehead* [1913] 2 Ch. 56.

requirements[45]; and (iii) to remuneration authorised by the will for personal representatives, which ranks as a gift.[46]

Demonstrative legacies are met out of the fund demonstrated; if it is insufficient, the balance of a demonstrative legacy abates rateably with the other general legacies.[47]

29–09 Abatement of specific legacies. Such authority as there is indicates that when there is only property given specifically, the subject-matter abates rateably.[48] Once abatement is necessary in respect of specific legacies there appears to be no distinction in principle from general legacies.

29–10 Expenses (other than overseas duties) as regards property specifically given in the absence of an express direction in the will. The specific legatee must meet the costs from the death of: preservation and upkeep of property given[49]; packing and delivering the subject-matter[50]; getting the subject-matter to the United Kingdom and insuring it.[51] On the other hand, where what is given is a right of *selection*, the specific legatee need only meet the expenses from the date of selection and the expenses before then fall on residue.[52]

Only one case cited in this paragraph is in the Court of Appeal[53]; the earlier authorities at first instance (cited in the judgments) are not easily reconciled; as is said in Jarman[54] that "the law is not very clear." In practice, when the question arises it should usually be disposed of by agreement.

29–11 Incidence of overseas duties. As between specific legatees and residue, foreign duty falls on the specifically given property, notwithstanding a direction to pay debts[55]; even though there is a

---

[45] *Cazenove v. Cazenove* (1889) 61 L.T. 115; *Re Schweder* [1891] 3 Ch. 44; the will in each case did not say that the legacy was to have priority; and *Blower v. Morret* (1752) 2 Ves.Sen. 420 was followed. It might have been inferred that there was to be priority. Previously Malins V.C. had refused to follow *Blower v. Morret* and had awarded priority over other general legacies to such a gift to the testator's wife: *Re Hardy* (1881) 17 Ch.Div. 798. A modern judge might find it possible to follow *Re Hardy* on construction; and a modern Court of Appeal might approve *Re Hardy* and overrule the cases to the contrary. Personal representatives meeting this question should seek the directions of the court.
[46] *Commissioner of Stamp Duties New South Wales v. Pearse* [1954] A.C. 91; *Re Pooley* (1888) 40 Ch.Div. 1.
[47] *Mullins v. Smith* (1860) 1 Dr. & Sm. 204 at p. 210.
[48] See Jarman, *Wills,* at p. 1940.
[49] *Re Rooke* [1933] Ch. 970, where Maugham J. cited the previous authorities.
[50] *Re Leach* [1923] 1 Ch. 161.
[51] *Re Fitzpatrick* [1952] Ch. 86.
[52] *Re Collins* [1971] 1 W.L.R. 37.
[53] *Re Scott* below.
[54] *Wills* (8th ed., 1951) at p. 1892; repeating the 7th ed. (1930) by Mr Sanger at p. 1967.
[55] *Re Brewster* [1908] 2 Ch. 365.

direction to pay legacy duty.[56] Such expressions as "free of duty" are treated as referring only to United Kingdom duties[57]; and so the expression "free of tax" only refers to United Kingdom tax.[58] The surrounding circumstances may however show that overseas duty or tax is comprised in the expression "free of duty,"[59] and a specific legacy free of duty of overseas assets may be rendered free of the overseas duty by the operation of a double taxation agreement.[60]

As between shares of residue, however, overseas duties and taxes are part of the cost of getting in the asset and fall on residue as a whole.[61]

29–12 Ademption of legacy or of a share of residue by the subsequent gift of a "portion." Notwithstanding the Wills Act 1837, sections 21, 22, 23 and 24, it is settled that, as between the children of a testator, his gift, *after* the date of his will, of a "portion" (that is to say a substantial provision for that child's permanent provision in life, not merely a small gift or a series of small gifts) is taken in satisfaction or in part satisfaction of the previously dated gift to that child by will, unless the facts suggest the contrary (rebutting the presumption).[62–63]

The doctrine of ademption is summarised in Jarman[64] as follows:

"The doctrine, then, which is fully established although some modern judges dislike it, depends upon two assumptions: (1) that a legacy to a child is intended to be a portion; (2) that a subsequent portion is intended to be in substitution for the legacy. It is not very easy to ascertain the precise import of the first of these propositions, for the word portion is not a term of art. But it seems to be something which is given by the parent to establish the child in life or to make what is called provision for him. The second proposition is merely a special case of the general rule of equity which presumes that a testator does not intend a child to have double portion. This presumption is not a rule of law and may be rebutted."

---

[56] *Re Scott* [1915] 1 Ch. 592.

[57] *Re Scott* above; *Re Norbury* [1939] Ch. 528; *Re Cunliffe-Owen* [1951] Ch. 964.

[58] *Re Frazer* [1940] Ch. 326.

[59] *Re Quirk* [1940] Ch. 46 (British subject resident in Turkey, giving land in France free of all death duties, and not liable to any U.K. duty).

[60] As in *Re Goetze* [1953] Ch. 96.

[61] *Re Sebba* [1959] Ch. 166; two cases cited in argument but not mentioned in the Court of Appeal's judgments in *Re Scott* above were *Peter v. Stirling* (1878) 10 Ch.Div. 279 and *Re Maurice* (1897) 75 L.T. 415; they are to be explained as cases between shares of residue, not between specific legatees and residuary legatees: see *Re Brewster* above at p. 368 during argument. In Ireland, the law seems to be different: *Re Blake* [1955] Ir. 98.

[62–63] Jarman, *Wills,* at pp. 1137–1144; Theobald, *Wills,* at pp. 752–757.

[64] 7th ed. by Mr C. P. Sanger at p. 1123; 8th ed. at p. 1138.

On wills, this doctrine rarely arises nowadays; and so it is not discussed here. When the doctrine might apply, personal representatives need to obtain legal advice about its applicability in all the circumstances of the case; and if it applies, how income should be adjusted pending final distribution. Similar questions arise when a will directs sums to be brought into account.

29–13 Interest in account on portions. The usual method of calculating interest is to add in account to the income of the estate interest on the portion at four per cent. a year, less tax, from the death; and to treat the beneficiary who had the portion as having received such income.[65] Then capital, less inheritance tax,[66] is divided accordingly, valued at the date of actual distribution.[67] The unusual method, only adopted when the will so requires,[68] is "that for the purpose of ascertaining the proportions of the settled shares of the testator's children, the value of his net residuary estate at the date of his death ought to be ascertained, that there should be added thereto the amount of the several advances made to his children, that the actual income received from the testator's death ought to be divided in the respective proportions so ascertained, and that any calculation of interest was accordingly unnecessary."[69]

INTEREST ON LEGACIES GIVEN BY WILL

29–14 Specific legacies and residue. A specific legacy carries the income and the accretions to the subject-matter[70]; residue does not carry interest; it is what remains after previous gifts are met. Under L.P.A. 1925, s. 175, three classes of testamentary gifts carry income (as distinct from interest), unless such income is "otherwise expressly disposed of". They are: contingent or future specific gifts of property, real or personal; contingent residuary devises of *freehold* land; and specific or residuary devises of *freehold* land to trustees in trust for persons whose interests are contingent or executory. Such gifts do not often occur in practice.

Section 175 is strictly construed; thus the section does not apply to a vested defeasible future gift of residue.[71] When section 175 applies

[65] *Re Poyser* [1908] 1 Ch. 828; *Re Wills* [1939] Ch. 705, an illuminating judgment of Simonds J.; and the other cases cited in Theobald at p. 763, n. 50.
[66] *Re Turner* [1968] 1 W.L.R. 227.
[67] *Re Slee* [1962] 1 W.L.R. 496.
[68] *Re Wills* above, at pp. 716 and 717–718.
[69] *ibid.* Simonds J. explaining *Re Hargreaves* (1903) 88 L.T. 100 and similar cases: see, for the same result, *Re Mansel* [1930] 1 Ch. 352.
[70] Jarman, *Wills*, at p. 1079; unless deferred: *Re McGeorge* [1963] Ch. 544.
[71] *Re Gillett* [1950] Ch. 102, followed in *Re Geering* [1964] Ch. 136; *Re McGeorge* above.

to a future specific devise not yet vested indefeasibly, the income is (for the permitted period)[72] to be accumulated until its destination becomes known.[73] Section 175 is excluded by any testamentary disposition of the income, even if it is disclaimed.[74] Section 175 and the omissions from it create difficulties that have not been resolved; partly caused by the section being drafted on an incorrect view of the previous law.[75] Detailed advice is needed where section 175 might apply.

29–15 Interest on general legacies. General pecuniary legacies carry interest. Interest is given by law to compensate legatees at the expense of residuary legatees (who are entitled to nothing until all the legacies have been paid), for delay in payment; but it is not itself a legacy nor the testator's bounty.[76]

A general legacy carries interest at the expense of residue; the rate of interest on a legacy is six per cent. a year[77] now. This interest runs from the time when there is a right to receive the legacy: "The right to the legacy and the right to receive it are quite different things. The right to a legacy ordinarily accrues on the death of the testator, but the right to receive it does not arise until 12 months after his death."[78]

The cases run to narrow distinctions. The modern tendency is for residuary legatees to be advised that it is less costly to allow interest on legacies, in case of doubt, than to incur the costs of determining the legatees' right to interest. Personal representatives who improperly delay payment would be likely to be charged personally with the difference between the 6 per cent. payable at the expense of residue, and the general judicial rate of interest[79] at 15 per cent. now.[80]

29–16 Interest from the end of one year on immediate legacies. Interest is payable at the expense of residue in the course of

---

[72] See para. 27–31 above.
[73] *Re McGeorge* above.
[74] *Re Hatfeild* [1958] Ch. 469.
[75] See the article by Judge (as he is now) P.V.Baker Q.C. in (1963) 79 L.Q.R. 184; and *Re McGeorge* above.
[76] *Re Wyles* [1938] Ch. 313 at pp. 315–316 (on abatement). When legacies have to be paid late in the course of administration, payments are attributed to interest first, unless there is a direction to the contrary: *Re Morley* [1937] Ch. 491.
[77] R.S.C., Ord. 44, r. 10; applicable on the footing that personal representatives should administer the estate as the court would; like the previous rate of 5 per cent it "has been wholly inappropriate for many years": *Re Amalgamated Property Co.* [1985] Ch. 349 at p. 393 (company law). For a similar decision, see *Bartlett v. Barclays Trust Co. (No. 2)* [1980] Ch. 515 at p. 547 (awarding in a case of breach of trust realistic interest to "compensate for the continual erosion of the value of money by reason of galloping inflation").
[78] *Earle v. Bellingham* (1857) 24 Beav. 448 at pp. 449–450.
[79] On the converse of *Re Campbell* [1893] 3 Ch. 468, where there was no finding of maladministration.
[80] *Supreme Court Practice 1995*, n. 42/1/12.

213

administration from the end of one year, on the legacy being paid subsequently.[81] Accordingly, where on the construction of a will, a gift of shares was construed to be a general legacy not a specific legacy, the legatees only received interest and not the larger dividends down to the date when the legacy was paid.[82]

29–17 Interest from the date of the death on immediate legacies. Interest runs from the death when the will directs immediate payment of a legacy[83]; when the legacy is for the deceased's minor child who is to be maintained out of such interest[84]; or its income is charged with a child's maintenance, so as to indicate that such maintenance is the primary object of the legacy[85]; and where a legacy is given in satisfaction of a debt.[86] There are authorities that a legacy charged on land carries interest from the date of the death[87]; but that does not apply to legacies to be met from a trust for sale of land.[88] This point is unlikely to arise nowadays, when land in England forming part of an estate will almost always be subject to an express testamentary trust for sale or to a statutory trust for sale.[89] It might arise when a testator domiciled in England gives a legacy charged on land elsewhere (validly according to the law of the place where the land is situated).

29–18 Interest on future pecuniary legacies. A vested legacy given at a later date, carries interest only from such later date.[90] A contingent legacy does not carry interest until the contingency is met[91]; but a contingent legacy may be construed to carry interest

---

[81] *Walford v. Walford* [1912] A.C. 658. Other cases are: *Gough v. Bult* (1848) 16 Sim. 323, *Turner v. Buck* (1874) 18 Eq. 301 (trust for sale of land); *Re Whiteley* (1909) 101 L.T. 508 (power to postpone sale); *Re Palfreeman* [1914] 1 Ch. 877 (where the legatees satisfied a condition in the testator's lifetime); *Re Pollock* [1943] Ch. 338 the second point (settled legacy).

[82] *Re Hall* [1951] 1 All E.R. 1073.

[83] *Re Pollock* above the first point (directing a legacy to be paid to a widow "immediately").

[84] *Re Moody* [1895] 1 Ch. 101; *Re Stokes* [1928] Ch. 716; the statutory power of maintenance is the Trustee Act 1925, s.31 now.

[85] *Re Ramsay* [1917] 2 Ch. 64; distinguishing *Re Crane* [1908] 1 Ch. 379, on the ground that in *Re Crane* the childrens' maintenance was not the primary object. In a doubtful case the decision in *Re Ramsay* is more likely to apply.

[86] *Re Rattenberry* [1906] 1 Ch. 667 citing the authorities at p. 671.

[87] *Re Waters* (1889) 42 Ch.Div. 517; Jarman, *Wills*, at p. 1085.

[88] *Gough v. Bult* (1848) 16 Sim. 323; *Turner v. Buck* (1874) 18 Eq. 301.

[89] A.E.A. 1925, s.33.

[90] *Earle v. Bellingham* above; *Lord v. Lord* (1867) 2 Ch.App. 782; recognised in *Walford v. Walford* above, where it was held that there was in that will no such postponement (see [1912] A.C. at p. 664).

[91] *Re Dickson* (1885) 29 Ch.Div. 331; *Re Abrahams* [1911] 1 Ch. 108 (legacy to child contingent on attaining the age of 30); *Re Raine* [1929] 1 Ch. 716 (contingent legacy to a child at 21, the deceased not *in loco parentis*).

from the date of the death.[92] A legacy to a child of the testator or to a child to whom he is *in loco parentis*, carries interest from the death, when the legacy is directed to be set aside, and under the will, maintenance is payable for the minor from its income,[93] but not when the testator makes other provision for the child's maintenance.[94] A contingent general legacy is outside L.P.A. 1925, s.175, and so section 175 does not confer a right to interest thereon pending the contingency.[95]

29–19 Delay affecting interest on legacies. A legatee remains entitled to interest on the legacy even though there has been a delay of many years in its payment.[96] When there has been acquiescence,[97] a legatee is restricted to six years' interest on the legacy, back from the date of commencement of proceedings, by analogy to the statute.[98]

LEGACIES TO THE DECEASED'S CREDITORS AND DEBTORS

29–20 Legacy to a creditor. An immediate and unconditional legacy to the testator's creditor of the amount or of more than the debt due at the date of the will was presumed only to be given to satisfy the debt.[99] When that principle applies, the donee-creditor is put to election which benefit to choose[1] and is not entitled to receive the legacy if the debt is paid after the date of the will.[2] The principle is readily excluded by slight indications in the will, or by slight variations between the debt and the legacy:

> "Long ago a false principle was established, *viz.* that if a man
> owes a debt, and then gives a legacy to his creditor, the legacy is

[92] As in *Re Jones* [1932] 1 Ch. 642, and *Re Pollock* above, the 2nd point.
[93] *Re Richards* (1869) 8 Eq. 119; *Re Bowlby* [1904] 2 Ch. 685; *Re Jones* [1932] 1 Ch. 642 (the reference to discretion in the headnote appears to be incorrect).
[94] *Re West* [1913] 1 Ch. 345.
[95] *Re Raine* [1929] 1 Ch. 716.
[96] *Re Blatchford* (1884) 27 Ch.Div. 676, where executors acted properly in not selling a reversion but waiting for it to fall in; *Re Morley* [1937] Ch. 491 where there was necessary delay in an administration by the court.
[97] *Thomson v. Eastwood* (1877) 2 App.Cas. 215. Under the law then in force there was no period of limitation applicable to the legacy itself: the modern law is enacted in the Limitation Act 1980, s.21.
[98] Limitation Act 1980, s.36(2).
[99] *Talbot v. Shrewsbury* (1714) Prec. Ch. 394; *Fowler v. Fowler* (1735) 3 P.W. 353; *Re Rattenbury* [1906] 1 Ch. 667; and numerous other cases applying or excluding the principle collected in Jarman, *Wills*, at pp. 1152–1155; and Theobald, *Wills*, at pp. 750–752.
[1] *Atkinson v. Littlewood* (1874) 18 Eq. 595.
[2] *Re Fletcher* (1888) 38 Ch.Div. 373; a strange decision, since the will speaks from death: Wills Act 1837, s.24.

a satisfaction of the debt; that the creditor cannot legally have both the debt and the legacy. That principle being established, successive judges have said they cannot alter it. But what they have done is to rely on the minutest shades of difference to escape from that false principle."[3]

The principle is excluded by a direction to pay debts, or to pay debts and legacies.[4] As that direction is found in almost every will and printed will form, the principle is "of small practical importance".[5] There is only one modern reported case where the principle was applied: it was a will in the testator's own handwriting which was "a very curious and imperfect document".[6]

The existence of the principle means however that when a testator has left to a creditor a legacy equal to or more than the amount of the debt due at the date of the will, the personal representatives need to obtain advice about the principle.

This principle is not to be confused with the somewhat different principle that a child may not receive from her or his father or the estate of her or his father both a substantial permanent provision, known as a "portion" outside the will or intestacy and also similar provision under the will or intestacy abrogated on intestacy from January 1, 1996.[7]

29–21 Gift by release of a debt; legacy to a debtor. A debt due to the deceased may have been released in the deceased's lifetime by conduct raising an estoppel against the deceased and his estate.[8] A debt remaining due at the death is an asset of his estate, to be got in by the personal representatives[9] and may be needed by the personal representatives to meet liabilities. A debt that remains due at the death and is not required by the personal representatives to meet liabilities, may be bequeathed to the debtor, when the bequest is a release of the debt;[10] or to anyone else, when the legatee will become entitled to enforce the debt.

A gift of a legacy to a debtor does not itself release the debt. There is no set formula required for the release or forgiveness of a

---

[3] Kindersley V.-C. in *Hassell v. Hawkins* (1859) 4 Dr. 468 at p. 470; holding that the principle does not apply to a gift of residue, ascertainable only after payment of all the debts.

[4] *Re Manners* [1949] Ch. 613 at p. 618, approving Hawkins, *Wills* (3rd ed.), at p. 618.

[5] Theobald, *Wills*, at p. 750.

[6] *Re Haves* [1951] 2 All E.R. 928.

[7] See paras. 29–12 (will), 31–13 and 31–19 (intestacy).

[8] *Yeomans v. Williams* (1863) 1 Eq. 184; *Cross v. Sprigg* (1849) 6 Ha. 552, where a mere voluntary declaration did not release the debt. See now the cases from *Inwards v. Baker* [1965] 2 Q.B. 29 onwards discussed in Snell, *Equity*, at pp. 569–579: it has become a "much broader approach" now: *Habib v. Habib* [1981] 1 W.L.R. 1265 at p. 1285.

[9] See Chap. 20.

[10] *C.S.D. v. Bone* [1977] A.C. 511 at pp. 519–520, citing authorities back to 1815.

debt in a will, all that is required is for the testator to make his intention clear.[11] It is a question of construction of each will. The personal representatives may set off against a pecuniary legacy or against a share of residue given absolutely a debt due from the legatee to the estate at the death; including a debt that had become statute barred. The principle is that someone who owes the estate money cannot claim in the estate without making good what he owes.[12] This principle applies when the deceased's estate had to pay sums under a suretyship undertaken by the deceased; for the legatee was bound to recoup those sums to the estate.[13] It applies where the legatee owed the estate sums ascertained under a composition with the legatee's creditors.[14] When the legatee is indebted to the estate at the death but the amount of the legatee's indebtedness remains to be judicially ascertained, it is likely that by analogy to company law the legacy should be held in a separate account and not paid pending such ascertainment.[15]

This right of recoupment or set-off does not however apply when the debtor-legatee became bankrupt before the testator's death.[16] It does not apply when the debt is not owed by the legatee himself but by a partnership of which the legatee is a member;[17] it does not apply to the future instalments of a debt payable by instalments;[18] nor does it apply to a fund devolving on the issue of the debtor, by a gift in the will substituting them.[19] The principle has been held not to apply to a specific gift of stocks, though readily realisable.[20]

Although the reported cases concern wills, the same principle would apply to the fixed net sum payable on intestacy to an intestate's surviving husband or wife,[21] if he or she was indebted to the estate; and to shares of residue vesting absolutely on intestacy.

In practice it is rare for there to be a gift to a creditor outside the family. This question tends to arise as part of a family dispute.

---

[11] *Re Horn* [1946] Ch. 254 at the foot of p. 257; where there was no release in the will; *Hyde v. Neate* (1847) 15 Sim. 554, where the gift of a legacy to a debtor was in terms that also realised the debt.
[12] *Re Akerman* [1891] 3 Ch. 212, explaining the rule in *Cherry v. Boultbee* (1839) 4 My. & Cr. 442.
[13] *Re Watson* [1986] 1 Ch. 295.
[14] *Re Orpen* (1880) 16 Ch.Div. 202.
[15] *Re Rhodesia Goldfields* [1910] 1 Ch. 239.
[16] *Cherry v. Boultbee* above; *Re Hodgson* (1878) 9 Ch.Div. 673.
[17] *Turner v. Turner* [1911] 1 Ch. 716.
[18] *Re Abrahams* [1908] 2 Ch. 69.
[19] *Re Binns* [1929] 1 Ch. 677.
[20] *Re Savage* [1918] 2 Ch. 146.
[21] See para. 31–06.

30. Residue given by will

30–01   Residuary gift. A gift of residue is made by words disclosing, as a matter of construction, an intention to give the testator's general estate.[1] General words are readily construed as a residuary gift nowadays. A gift of the deceased's "money" will be construed in the ordinary way as including his residuary property and not just what might legalistically be called "money";[2] unless there is a context to show that the word "money" does not mean residuary property, such as "money in the bank."[3] In a suitable context a gift of "worldly goods and chattels" may even include residuary real property.[4]

30–02   Operation of a residuary gift. A gift of residue, whether to one or to several, and whether outright or to persons in succession, is a gift of what remains after meeting all liabilities and all other gifts. A residuary gift (unless the will shows an intention to the contrary) includes everything owned by the testator at his death,[5] not effectively given in any other way.[6] A residuary gift also includes

---

[1] See Theobald, *Wills* (14th ed.), at pp. 301–304; and Jarman, *Wills* (8th ed.), at pp. 966–1015. The construction of wills is outside the scope of this book.

[2] *Perrin v. Morgan* [1943] A.C. 399; *Re Barnes* [1972] 1 W.L.R. 587.

[3] *Re Trundle* [1960] 1 W.L.R. 1388.

[4] *Re Young (No. 2)* [1950] 2 All E.R. 1245 (omitted from [1951] Ch. 344).

[5] Wills Act 1837, ss.24, 25 and 26.

[6] *Blight v. Hartnoll* (1883) 23 Ch.Div. 218 (gift of all the deceased's property except a wharf, given on trusts that failed; *Re Bagot* [1893] 3 Ch. 348; *Re Barnes' Will Trusts* [1972] 1 W.L.R. 587; *Re Sinclair* [1985] Ch. 446 (where a residuary gift to a former wife was subject to "lapse" under A.J.A. 1982, s.18 and the subject-matter devolved on intestacy); no longer the law on death on or after January 1, 1996: Law Reform (Succession) Act 1995 s.3; see para. 14–06 above.

219

property over which the testator had a general power of appointment.[7] Thus a residuary gift includes a disclaimed legacy,[8] or a lapsed legacy[9]; and interim income not effectively disposed of pending a condition being met.[10]

30–03 Failed or revoked share of residue. A will may, and usually should, direct that a failed share of residue is to accrue to the other shares[11]; and so should a codicil revoking a gift of a share of residue. Otherwise, a gift of a share of residue that fails or is revoked, does not accrue to the shares given effectively, but devolves as on a partial intestacy[12]; when it may be the first fund to bear liabilities or legacies. This usually defeats the actual wish of the testator. A partial intestacy does not however arise in this way under a class gift. In that case, those who are the members of the designated class take the subject-matter and there is no partial intestacy.[13] There is likewise no partial intestacy when there is a gift to a named group that is not technically a "class" and the gift to one of the group is revoked[14]; and so the members of the group take the gift between them. They do so, even when one member of the class is struck out on grounds of public policy, having killed the deceased.[15]

This is a question of construction of each will and the decision run to narrow distinctions. The cases cited might create an impression that as a matter of construction the court tends to lean against a partial intestacy; but there is no *presumption* against a partial intestacy, as distinct from the presumption against total intestacy.[16]

---

[7] s.27: see para. 20–32.

[8] *Re Backhouse* [1931] W.N. 168; the same applies when there is a disclaimer yielding a partial intestacy: *Re Sullivan* [1930] 1 Ch. 84; the same principle underlies *Re Scott* [1975] 1 W.L.R. 1260, the second point (disclaimer by all those in one class entitled on intestacy benefits the next class).

[9] Jarman, *Wills*, at p. 1022.

[10] This follows *a fortiori* (even more so) from cases where such income devolved on a partial intestacy, being outside any testamentary gift: *Re Wragg* [1959] 1 W.L.R. 922; *Re Geering* [1964] Ch. 136; *Re Lawrence* [1972] Ch. 418.

[11] As in *Re Wilkins* [1920] 2 Ch. 63.

[12] *Sykes v. Sykes* (1868) 3 Ch.App. 301 (where a gift of one-fifth of residue had been revoked by a codicil; and the one-fifth share devolved on a partial intestacy); *Re Barker* (1880) 15 Ch.Div. 635; *Harrison v. Harrison* [1901] 1 Ch. 136; *Re Forrest* [1931] 1 Ch. 162; *Re Midgley* [1955] Ch. 576; Jarman, *Wills*, at p. 1030.

[13] *Re Palmer* [1893] 3 Ch. 369; *Re Allan* [1903] 1 Ch. 276; *Re Wand* [1907] 1 Ch. 391; *Re Dunster* [1909] 1 Ch. 103; *Re Wilkins* [1920] 2 Ch. 63. There was held to be no partial intestacy on a gift to a number of persons, the gift to some of whom was revoked, *Re Whiting* [1913] 2 Ch. 1; but it is not likely to be followed: see *Re Wilkins, Re Forrest* and *Re Midgley* above.

[14] *Re Woods* [1931] 2 Ch. 138.

[15] *Re Peacock* [1957] Ch. 310; *Re Midgley* above was not cited.

[16] *Re Abbott* [1944] 2 All E.R. 457, at p. 459; *Re Wragg* [1959] 1 W.L.R. 922 at p. 929. The presumption is only against a total intestacy: Jarman, *Wills*, at p. 2030; but, like any other presumption, its application depends on the circumstances of each case. As a matter of construction, wills construed so as not to yield a total intestacy could have been so construed without a presumption against total intestacy: *Re Harrison* (1885) 30 Ch.Div. 390 ("when a testator has executed a will in solemn form

30–04 Settled residue; adjustment for liabilities between capital and income. The rule in *Allhusen v. Whittell*,[17] applies (unless excluded by the will) when a testator settles residue on persons in succession.[18] Under the rule, there should be an equitable adjustment so as to cast liabilities on so much capital as with its income, less income tax,[19] meets the liabilities[20] over the period down to the relevant payment; the calculation is made at the same average rate throughout the period,[21] usually but not necessarily one year. The rule does not apply where "the nature of the property concerned or the circumstances affecting it are such that the rule cannot be applied according to its terms."[22]

The case is founded on the broad equitable principle that when residue is given to persons in succession, their successive enjoyment should be an enjoyment of the same fund. For effecting that result, there should be a sort of equitable bookkeeping or adjustment[23]; and when the rule applies it need not be followed "slavishly"[24]; where Sargant J. said[25]:

"I do not by any means wish to lay down that this is the only method available, or that extremely elaborate and minute calculations must be gone through, in every case. If, for instance, a particular asset of a testator, such as part of a sum of Consols or an amount on deposit with a bank, were applied with the intermediate interest on it in the discharge of the whole or the bulk or some one large item of the liabilities of the estate at any time during the first year, as, say, three months or six months after the death, the executors might well, in my judgment, leave the matter there to that extent, ... The capital and interest of the asset would merely have disappeared in the course of ascertaining residue, without leaving any proper subject-matter for adjustment. Or in cases where the average income of the estate is quite low, there would be no appreciable ground for

---

you must assume that he did not intend to make it a solemn farce": Lord Esher M.R. at p. 393); *Re Messenger* [1937] 1 All E.R. 355; *Re Turner* [1949] 2 All E.R. 935; *Re Stevens* [1952] Ch. 323.

[17] (1867) 4 Eq. 295.

[18] But not when it is given absolutely, subject to a gift over: *Re Hanbury* (1909) 101 L.T. 32.

[19] *Re Oldham* [1927] W.N. 113.

[20] Including payments made to a landlord in consequence of liability under a lease: *Re Shee* [1934] Ch. 345; and payments that the testator covenanted to make by instalments, such as an annuity: *Re Perkins* [1907] 2 Ch. 596; *Re Poyser* [1910] 2 Ch. 444; *Re Berkeley* [1968] Ch. 744.

[21] *Re Wills* [1915] 1 Ch. 769.

[22] *Re Darby* [1939] Ch. 905 at p. 917 (outright gift of property to a daughter charged with payment of an annuity to her mother but with no personal liability to pay it).

[23] *Re McEuen* [1913] 2 Ch. 704 at p. 713.

[24] *Re McEuen* above at p. 715.

[25] At pp. 716–717.

complaint if the capital of the estate duty itself were charged against capital, and the interest on it were charged against income, instead of dividing the total sum paid between capital and income with reference to the exact rate of interest yielded by the estate as a whole, or by the particular asset used to pay the duty. There may also be other methods of carrying out the equitable bookkeeping referred to in *Allhusen* v. *Whittell* which will give their fair relative rights in the same residuary fund to both tenant for life and remainderman; and some methods may be more appropriate in some cases and other methods in other cases. The actual accountancy will not be difficult so long as the true object is borne in mind."

Such a practical modification is not a breach of trust, but an example of what Uthwatt J. called "practice which reflects common sense, or what is to my mind the same thing, reason tempered by convenience"[26]; or else it is a *"judicious* breach of trust," that ought to be committed.[27] The calculation is costly and usually out of proportion to its value in practice; personal representatives tend to make an approximate calculation, with the consent of the adult beneficiaries, tending in favour of any beneficiary who is not of full capacity.

Expense would be avoided by an enactment in England similar to the United States statute, the Revised Uniform Principal and Income Act, s.5.[28]

30–05 Settled residue; adjustment for hazardous, wasting or unauthorised investments and for property not producing income. The rule in *Howe* v. *Dartmouth*[29] applies (unless excluded by the will) to wasting, hazardous or unauthorised investments forming part of residuary personalty given to persons in succession. Under the rule it is to be sold; or (when the rule applies) the capital[30] must be treated in account as sold, and only producing income at the rate of authorised investments.[31] A branch of the rule (when applying) requires property not producing income, when realised, to be treated in account as having produced income at the rate of authorised investments.[32] The rate for this calculation was fixed in 1883 at the standard rate of four per cent. a year; as recently as 1961, the rate of

---

[26] *Re Bradberry* [1943] Ch. 35 at p. 40.
[27] *Perrins v. Bellamy* [1899] 1 Ch. 797 at p. 798; emphasis in the original.
[28] Printed in Scott, *Trusts* (4th ed.), para. 234.4.
[29] (1802) 7 Ves. 138.
[30] The rule relates to the testator's capital; salary payable by agreement to a deceased person for a fixed period after his death is not income, but capital of the estate: *Re Payne* [1943] 2 All E.R. 675.
[31] *Dimes v. Scott* (1827) 4 Russ. 195; *Brown v. Gellatly* (1867) 2 Ch.App. 751.
[32] *Re Chesterfield* (1883) 24 Ch.Div. 643; *Re Chance's Will Trusts* [1962] Ch. 593.

four per cent a year less income tax on the proceeds of sale was in two cases directed under the rule.[33] This rate is nowadays unrealistic; and might by now have been long since challenged and increased,[34] but for the rarity of modern cases within the rule.

The rule does not apply to freeholds[35]; to leaseholds with over 60 years to run[36]; nor to property given absolutely subject to an overriding discretion as to payment of income[37]; nor to authorised investments, or investments authorised to be retained and duly retained[38]; nor income that the will shows the testator intended the beneficiary for life to have,[39] thereby excluding the rule. When the rule applies, it may apply to property that should have been sold and was not sold[40]; and the branch of the rule relating to future interests requires a payment to the life beneficiary or his estate on the subject-matter being got in.[41]

In practice, the rule rarely applies nowadays: gifts in succession are less frequent than formerly, except in a professionally drawn will; a professionally drawn will is likely to exclude the rule.[42] The rule in *Howe v. Dartmouth* is therefore not fully discussed here. In most

---

[33] *Re Berry* [1962] Ch. 97; *Re Chance* [1962] Ch. 593, see at p. 616; directing the calculation to be the sums which put out at compound interest at four per cent per annum at the date of the testator's death and accumulating at compound interest calculated at that rate with yearly rests [the word "rents" is a printing error in the report] and deducting income tax would with the accumulation of interest have produced the sums when eventually received.

[34] See Chap. 29, n. 77.

[35] *Re Woodhouse* [1941] Ch. 332, reversionary interest.

[36] *Re Gough* [1957] Ch. 323; for they are authorised investments: A.E.A. 1925, s.39, L.P.A. 1925, s.28(1), S.L.A. 1925, s.73(1)(xi).

[37] *Re Holliday's Will Trusts* [1947] Ch. 402.

[38] *Re Bates* [1907] 1 Ch. 22; *Re Nicholson* [1909] 2 Ch. 111; but it may apply where the subject-matter ought to have been sold: *Rowlls v. Bebb* [1900] 2 Ch. 107 (reversionary interest).

[39] Each case turns on the words of the particular will: *Re Astke* (1918) 118 L.T. 433, decided on the words of that will. The decided cases on whether the rule applies or is excluded are not easy to reconcile. The rule was excluded in: *Re Chancellor* (1884) 26 Ch.Div. 42, C.A. (trust for sale, power to postpone; testator's business not mentioned in the will); *Re Sheldon* (1888) 39 Ch.Div. 50 (power to continue investments or to convert them); *Re Thomas* [1891] 3 Ch. 482 (express gift of the income to the life beneficiary); *Re Bates* [1907] 1 Ch. 22 (power to retain); *Re Wilson* [1907] 1 Ch. 394 (no trust for conversion in the will); *Re Nicholson* [1909] 2 Ch. 111 (a similar case); *Re Inman* [1915] 1 Ch. 187 (trust for conversion and wide power to retain); *Re Barratt* [1925] Ch. 550 (language in the will indicating that the life beneficiaries were to have the entire income). The rule applied in: *Macdonald v. Irvine* (1878) 8 Ch.Div. 101; and in the following cases to wills of a business, containing a trust for sale and a power to postpone: *Re Chaytor* [1905] 1 Ch. 233, *Re Berry* above, and *Re Rudd* [1952] 1 All E.R. 254 (explaining that the distinction turns on whether the power to postpone is "ancilliary": Upjohn J. at p. 260F).

[40] *Rowlls v. Bebb* [1900] 2 Ch. 107.

[41] *Re Chesterfield* above (outstanding personal estate); *Re Hubbuck* [1896] 1 Ch. 754 (debt got in at death of the debtor); *Re Chance* above (claims against the Central Land Board under the Town & Country Planning Act 1947 then in force).

[42] See Rose & Bowles, *Conveyancing Precedents* (4th ed.), at p. 435; and Hallett's *Conveyancing Precedents* at p. 1028.

cases it is enough for personal representatives to be aware that the rule exists; and, if necessary, to seek legal advice about its potential application in the light of the authorities.[43]

---

[43] See Jarman, *Wills*, at pp. 1222–1232; and Theobald, *Wills*, at pp. 548–560.

31. Residue on total intestacy; residue on partial intestacy

31–01 Definition of intestacy. An intestacy occurs when the deceased left no valid will; or left an ineffective will.[1] Intestacy may, for practical purposes, be divided into total intestacy (below "intestacy"), when there is no effective disposition of the deceased's property; and partial intestacy, when there is an effective disposition of part only of his property.[2]

---

[1] A will may turn out to be ineffective for various reasons: beneficiaries may have died before the testator, occasioning a lapse; or may have attested the will, or be married to a witness who attested the will, thereby being disqualified from taking; or may be a spouse whose marriage to the deceased has been dissolved or annulled: these disqualifications are dealt with elsewhere in this book. Another cause of intestacy is a gift to someone who turns out not to exist; or on trusts for a non-charitable purpose.
[2] A.E.A. 1925, s.55(1)(vi).

31–02 Definition and ascertainment of residuary estate. On a total intestacy, the distribution of the residuary estate of an intestate is specified in the A.E.A. 1925, s.33(4). The principle stated in *Allhusen v. Whittell*[3] for adjusting liabilities[4] between capital and the income interest of a surviving spouse is regarded as applicable to an intestacy.[5] On an intestacy, the arguments for not applying the principle of *Allhusen v. Whittell*, or for not applying it "slavishly", are stronger. Its application to a will is based on what is taken to have been the testator's intention when giving an interest for life; an intestate who left no will showed no intention. If the question arises, it would be open to the court to hold that *Allhusen v. Whittell* does not apply on a total intestacy.

Another principle applicable under a will is the adjustment for hazardous, wasting and unauthorised investments and for property not producing an income, known in its various branches as *Howe v. Dartmouth*.[6] On intestacy, this principle does not apply to reversionary interests[7]; nor to other interests within the rule that the personal representatives positively decide to postpone selling.[8]

On intestacy, there is however uncertainty about the application or the non-application of *Howe v. Dartmouth* to any hazardous, wasting or unauthorised property which the personal representatives have not actually decided to postpone selling. One authoritative view is that *Howe v. Dartmouth* does not apply on intestacy.[9] On the other hand, it has been held that *Howe v. Dartmouth* applies on intestacy to interests that the personal representatives have not determined to postpone selling.[10] It is prudent therefore to avoid this question: the way for personal representatives to avoid the question is expressly to decide to postpone conversion for the present time in an intestacy; and to avoid doubt by making a note of that decision. The practice of doing so explains the absence of further reported authority on the question.

31–03 Overseas rights not brought into account on intestacy. Rights on intestacy are held to be rights in the intestate's property in England and Wales; and so the surviving spouse is entitled to the fixed net sum out of English immovable property, without being put

---

[3] (1867) 4 Eq. 295.
[4] See para. 30–04 above.
[5] See *Wolstenholme & Cherry* (12th ed.) by Sir B. Cherry and others, Vol. 2, at p. 1455; (13th ed.) Vol. 5, at p. 53.
[6] (1802) 7 Ves. 138. See para. 30–05 above.
[7] A.E.A. 1925, s.33(1).
[8] *Re Fisher* [1943] Ch. 377, *obiter*.
[9] A.E.A. 1925, s.33(5); Wolstenholme & Cherry (12th ed.), Vol. 2 at p. 1455 (13th ed., Vol. 5 at p. 50 is different), and at p. 1458 (13th ed., Vol. 5 at p. 53); Snell, *Equity*, at p. 226.
[10] *Re Fisher* [1943] Ch. 377.

to election,[11] even when she (or he) has already received much more on the same intestacy under an overseas administration.

31–04 Personal chattels. Unless required for purposes of administration owing to want of other assets, personal chattels are not to be sold except for special reason.[12] A.E.A. 1925, s.55(1)(x) defines the phrase "personal chattels" as follows:

> " "Personal chattels" means carriages, horses, stable furniture and effects (not used for business purposes), motor cars and accessories (not used for business purposes), garden effects, domestic animals, plate, plated articles, linen, china, glass, books, pictures, prints, furniture, jewellery, articles of household or personal use or ornament, musical and scientific instruments and apparatus, wines, liquors and consumable stores, but do not include any chattels used at the death of the intestate for business purposes nor money or securities for money."

In applying this definition the value of the subject-matter is irrelevant; the only question is whether an article comes within the ordinary meaning of the word used; the source of the articles is also irrelevant.[13] Accordingly the definition includes, as of "personal use", a yacht used for pleasure,[14] a stamp collection,[15] and a collection of clocks and watches, although inherited by the deceased as a collection[16]; and includes as jewellery, cut but unmounted diamonds,[17] and as horses, racehorses kept for pleasure.[18]

The exclusion of business chattels occurs three times in the definition. Thus in the case about the racehorses, a stud farm and its horses were outside the definition of personal chattels[19]; and animals kept as part of a farm business not worked for profit are outside the definition.[20]

It is only in the third place where the definition excludes chattels used for business purposes that there occurs the phrase "at the death of the intestate." The phrase "at the death of the intestate" may be implied in all three places,[21] in an Act dealing with what happens at death, but this is not certain. The question would arise (unless

---

[11] *Re Collens* [1986] Ch. 505.
[12] A.E.A. 1925, s.33(1).
[13] *Re Crispin's Will Trusts* [1975] Ch. 245, C.A. at p. 251.
[14] *Re Chaplin* [1950] Ch. 507.
[15] *Re Reynolds's Will Trusts* [1966] 1 W.L.R. 19.
[16] *Re Crispin* above.
[17] *Re Whitby* [1944] Ch. 210.
[18] *Re Hutchinson* [1955] Ch. 255.
[19] *Re Hutchinson* above at pp. 258 and 259.
[20] *Re Ogilby* [1942] Ch. 289.
[21] See *Re Crispin* above at p. 251C, *obiter*.

agreed) if for example a motor car (with no reference to the death in the relevant part of the definition) and furniture (with such a reference) both owned by the intestate for business purposes had been taken home for personal use at his retirement.[22]

31–05 Death of both spouses together, or (after January 1, 1996) within 28 days of each other. Husbands and wives may die in circumstances (such as one disaster) leaving it uncertain who died first.

On *intestacy* neither estate takes an interest in the other's in that event.[23] On the death of an intestate on or after January 1, 1996, a spouse must survive for 28 days to take on intestacy.[24]

Under a *will* however when persons die in circumstances leaving it uncertain who died first, there is a presumption[25] that the older died first, so that the estate of the younger may benefit.

There is no juridical reason for this strange difference, imposed by statute.

31–06 Rights of a surviving spouse. A surviving spouse's rights on intestacy under A.E.A. 1925, s.46(1), as amended by A.J.A. 1977, s.28(1), depend on what other relatives the intestate left.

A surviving spouse takes the estate when the intestate leaves no issue, no parent, and no brother or sister of the whole blood and no issue of a brother or sister of the whole blood.

When the intestate leaves issue,[26] a surviving spouse takes the personal chattels absolutely, and the residuary estate is charged with a fixed net sum, at present £75,000, and interest thereon until payment at the rate at present of 6 per cent a year[27]; and a life interest in half the rest of the estate. The personal representatives have under section 48(2) express powers to raise these sums and any sums required to redeem the life interest of the surviving spouse.[28]

When the intestate leaves no issue, but leaves a parent, a brother or sister of the whole blood or issue of a brother or sister of the whole blood, then the surviving spouse takes instead a fixed net sum of, at present £125,000, and interest thereon until payment at the same rate; plus the same rights in other respects as when the intestate leaves issue.

---

[22] See the article in (1966) 82 L.Q.R. 18 signed R.E.M.
[23] A.E.A. 1925, s.46(3).
[24] Law Reform (Succession) Act 1995, s.1, inserting in A.E.A. 1925, s.46 subs. (2A).
[25] See para. 28–03 above.
[26] Even if *en ventre* at his death: A.E.A. 1925, s.55(2).
[27] Intestate Succession (Interest and Capitalisation) Orders 1977 (No. 1491) and 1983 (No. 1374).
[28] See para. 31–08 below.

31–07 Polygamy. A.E.A. 1925 refers to a surviving spouse in the singular. The position when an intestate lawfully leaves two wives from valid polygamous marriages is discussed in paragraph 27–20 above: and see Addendum.

31–08 Redemption of life interest. Under A.E.A. 1925, s.47A, as amended by A.J.A. 1977, the surviving spouse is entitled within 12 months from the date of the grant to elect to have his or her life interest in the assets in possession (not those in reversion) redeemed by the personal representatives at its capital value, with power on certain grounds for judicial extension of the time, under regulations specifying the method of valuation.[29] Reference should be made to the section and the regulations when this arises.

31–09 Appropriation of the matrimonial home on intestacy. On intestacy, a surviving spouse is entitled to have appropriated to his or her absolute interest in the estate, the deceased's beneficial interest in the matrimonial home[30] under the powers of the personal representatives under A.E.A. 1925, s.41. This must be done[31] within 12 months after the grant, and during the lifetime of the surviving spouse; the matrimonial home must not be sold meanwhile otherwise than owing to want of other assets.[32] The appropriation is at the value at the date of the appropriation.[33] There are provisions for a judicial extension of the period of 12 months.[34] The right is exercisable even though the surviving spouse is one of two or more personal representatives[35]; and is exercisable, on payment of the difference, even though the house is worth more than the surviving spouse's rights.[36]

31–10 Rights of issue on intestacy. Where there is a surviving spouse, issue[37] only take on intestacy where the estate, apart from personal chattels, is worth more than £75,000 after redeeming the surviving spouse's life interest in half the residue. This outcome is harsh where (as often happens in modern social conditions) the surviving spouse is not the parent of the intestate's issue. Then they take half the residue at the intestate's death; and an interest on the surviving spouse's death in the other half of the residue.

---

[29] Intestate Succession (Interest and Capitalisation) Orders 1977 (No. 1491) and 1983 (No. 1374).
[30] Intestates' Estates Act 1952, Sched. 2.
[31] para. 3 there.
[32] para. 3(3).
[33] *Re Collins* [1975] 1 W.L.R. 309.
[34] para. 3(3).
[35] para. 5(5).
[36] *Re Phelps* [1980] Ch. 275.
[37] Includes children and more remote descendants.

Where there is no surviving spouse, the issue take the residuary estate.

31–11 Statutory trusts for issue or others on intestacy. The interest of the issue is held on the statutory trusts set out in A.E.A. 1925, s. 47:

"**47.**—(1) Where under this Part of this Act the residuary estate of an intestate, or any part thereof, is directed to be held on the statutory trusts for the issue of the intestate, the same shall be held upon the following trusts, namely:

(i)   In trusts, in equal shares if more than one, for all or any the children or child of the intestate, living at the death of the intestate, who attain the age of [eighteen years] or marry under that age, and for all or any of the issue living at the death of the intestate who attains the age of [eighteen years] or marry under that age of any child of the intestate who predeceases the intestate, such issue to take through all degrees, according to their stocks, in equal shares if more than one, the share which their parent would have taken if living at the death of the intestate, and so that no issue shall take whose parent is living at the death of the intestate and so capable of taking;

(ii) The statutory power of advancement, and the statutory provisions which relate to maintenance and accumulation of surplus income, shall apply, but when an infant marries such infant shall be entitled to give valid receipts for the income of the infant's share or interest;

(iii) Where the property held on the statutory trusts for issue is divisible into shares, then any money or property which, by way of advancement or on the marriage of a child of the intestate, has been paid to such child by the intestate or settled by the intestate for the benefit of such child (including any life or less interest and including property covenanted to be paid or settled) shall, subject to any contrary intention expressed or appearing from the circumstances of the case, be taken as being so paid or settled in or towards satisfaction of the share of such child or the share which such child would have taken if living at the death of the intestate, and shall be brought into account, at a valuation (the value to be reckoned as at the death of the intestate), in accordance with the requirements of the personal representatives;

(iv) The personal representatives may permit any infant contingently interested to have the use and enjoyment of any personal chattels in such manner and subject to such conditions (if any) as the personal representatives may consider reasonable, and without being liable to account for any consequential loss.

(2) If the trusts in favour of the issue of the intestate fail by reason of no child or other issue attaining an absolutely vested interest—

(a) the residuary estate of the intestate and the income thereof and all statutory accumulations, if any, of the income thereof, or so much thereof as may not have been paid or applied under any power affecting the same, shall go, devolve and be held under the provisions of this Part of this Act as if the intestate had died without leaving issue living at the death of the intestate;

(b) references in this Part of this Act to the intestate "leaving no issue" shall be construed as "leaving no issue who attain an absolutely vested interest";

(c) references in this Part of this Act to the intestate "leaving issue" or "leaving a child or other issue" shall be construed as "leaving issue who attain an absolutely vested interest."

(3) Where under this Part of this Act the residuary estate of an intestate or any part thereof is directed to be held on the statutory trusts for any class of relatives of the intestate, other than issue of the intestate, the same shall be held on trusts corresponding to the statutory trusts for the issue of the intestate (other than the provision for bringing any money or property into account) as if such trusts (other than as aforesaid) were repeated with the substitution of references to the members or member of that class for references to the children or child of the intestate.

[(4) References in paragraph (i) of subsection (1) of the last foregoing section to the intestate leaving, or not leaving, a member of the class consisting of brothers or sisters of the whole blood of the intestate and issue of brothers or sisters of the whole blood of the intestate shall be construed as references to the intestate leaving, or not leaving, a member of that class who attains an absolutely vested interest."

31–12 After-born children. The trusts must be read with A.E.A. 1925, s.55(2):

(2) References to a child or issue living at the death of any person include a child or issue en ventre sa mere at the death.

31–13 Accounting under section 47 on a death before January 1, 1996. Under section 47(1)(iii) the entire fund is brought into account at its capital value, when an interest given absolutely or settled on one branch of the family for one person for life and then for the issue. Where however a lesser beneficial interest is given, that beneficial interest itself is valued actuarially under the section.[38]

In this context, the expression "advancement" means a permanent provision for the recipient[39]; not a sum that, however large in relation to the deceased's assets, is too small to make such a provision[40]; the age of the son or daughter is relevant on whether or not there has been an "advancement."[41] There is no reported authority on the alternative "or on the marriage of a child of the intestate," in paragraph (iii). Notwithstanding the preceding phrase "any money or property," paragraph (iii) would be likely to be held only to apply to a substantial provision on marriage; perhaps under the words "or appearing from the circumstances of the case." Paragraph (iii) frequently gave rise to family friction; as Danckwerts J. said, "it would have been far better to have left the whole thing out."[42]

31–14 Accounting under section 47 on a death after January 1, 1996. The requirement to account on intestacy has been struck out now in respect of death on or after January 1, 1996.[43]

31–15 Other persons taking on intestacy. In the absence of issue taking on intestacy and of a surviving spouse, those who take on the same statutory trusts are specified in paragraphs (ii), (iii), (iv), (v) and (vi) of section 46(1):

> "**46.**—(1) The residuary estate of an intestate shall be distributed in the manner or be held on the trusts mentioned in this section, namely:—
>
> [(i)   If the intestate leaves a husband or wife, then in accordance with the following Table:

TABLE

If the intestate—	
(1) leaves—	the residuary estate shall be held in
(a) no issue, and,	trust for the surviving husband or wife absolutely.

---

[38] *Re Grover* [1971] Ch. 168, explaining *Re Young* [1951] Ch. 185 and *Re Morton* [1956] Ch. 644.

[39] As was the provision in *Hardy v. Shaw* [1976] Ch. 82; a controlling interest in a business establishing the children in life.

[40] *Re Hayward* [1957] Ch. 528, reviewing the authorities (an estate in 1949 of £1,780; nominations of £507).

[41] *Re Hayward* above; unmarried son aged 43.

[42] *Re Morton* above at p. 647.

[43] Law Reform (Succession) Act 1995, s.1(2).

(b) no parent, or brother or sister of the whole blood, or issue of a brother or sister of the wholeblood

(2) leaves issue (whether or not persons mentioned in sub-paragraph (b) above also survive) the surviving husband or wife shall take the personal chattels absolutely and, in addition, the residuary estate of the intestate (other than the personal chattels) shall stand charged with the payment of a [fixed net sum], free of death duties and costs, to the surviving husband or wife interest thereon from the date of the death [at such rate as the Lord Chancellor may specify by order] until paid or appropriated, and, subject to providing for that sum and the interest thereon, the residuary estate (other than the personal chattels) shall be held—

(a) as to one half upon trust for the surviving husband or wife during his or her life, and, subject to such life interest, on the statutory trusts for the issue of the intestate, and

(b) as to the other half, on the statutory trusts for the issue of the intestate.

(3) leaves one or more of the following, that is to say, a parent, a brother or sister of the whole blood, or issue of a brother or sister of the whole blood, but leaves no issue the surviving husband or wife shall take the personal chattels absolutely and, in addition, the residuary estate of the intestate (other than the personal chattels) shall stand charged with the payment of a [fixed net sum], free of death duties and costs, to the surviving husband or wife with interest thereon from the date of the death [at such rate as the Lord Chancellor may specify by order] until paid or appropriated, and, subject to providing for that sum and the interest thereon, the residuary estate (other than the personal chattels) shall be held—

(a) as to one half in trust for the surviving husband or wife absolutely, and

(b) as to the other half—

(i) where the intestate leaves one parent or both parents (whether or not brothers or sisters of the intestate or their issue also survive) in trust for the parent absolutely or, as the case may be, for the two parents in equal shares absolutely.

(ii) where the intestate leaves no parent, on the statutory trusts for the brothers and sisters of the whole blood of the intestate.]

[the fixed net sums referred to in paragraphs (2) and (3) of this Table shall be of the amounts provided by or under section 1 of the Family Provision Act 1966.]

(ii) If the intestate leaves issue but no husband or wife, the residuary estate of the intestate shall be held on the statutory trusts for the issue of the estate;

(iii) If the intestate leaves [no husband or wife and] no issue but both parents, then [...] the residuary estate of the intestate shall be held in trust for the father and mother in equal shares absolutely;

(iv) If the intestate leaves [no husband or wife and] no issue but one parent, then [...] the residuary estate of the intestate shall be held in trust for the surviving father or mother absolutely;

(v) If the intestate leaves no [husband or wife and no issue and no] parent, then [...] the residuary estate of the intestate shall be held in trust for the following persons living at the death of the intestate, and in the following order and manner, namely:—

First, on the statutory trusts for the brothers and sisters of the whole blood of the intestate; but if no person takes an absolutely vested interest under such trusts; then

Secondly, on the statutory trusts for the brothers and sisters of the half blood of the intestate; but if no person takes an absolutely vested interest under such trusts; then

Thirdly, for the grandparents of the intestate, and if more than one survive the intestate, in equal shares; but if there is no member of this class; then

Fourthly, on the statutory trusts for the uncles and aunts of the intestate (being brothers or sisters of the whole blood of a parent of the intestate); but if no person takes an absolutely vested interest under such trusts; then

Fifthly, on the statutory trusts for the uncles and aunts of the intestate (being brothers or sisters of the half blood of a parent of the intestate); [...]

(vi) In default of any person taking an absolute interest under the foregoing provisions, the residuary estate of the intestate shall belong to the Crown or to the Duchy of Lancaster or to the Duke of Cornwall for the time being, as the case may be, as bona vacantia, and in lieu of any right to escheat.

The Crown or the said Duchy or the said Duke may (without prejudice to the powers reserved by section nine of the Civil List Act 1910 or any other powers), out of the whole or any part of the property devolving on them respectively, provide, in accordance with the existing practice, for dependants, whether kindred or not, of the intestate, and other persons for whom the intestate might reasonably have been expected to make provision.

[(1A) The power to make orders under subsection (1) above shall be exercisable by statutory instrument subject to annulment in pursuance of a resolution of either House of Parliament; and any such order may be varied or revoked by a subsequent order made under the power.]

(2) A husband and wife shall for all purposes of distribution or division under the foregoing provisions of this section be treated as two persons.

[(3) Where the intestate and the intestate's husband or wife have died in circumstances rendering it uncertain which of them survived the other and the intestate's husband or wife is by virtue of section one hundred and eighty-four of the Law of Property Act 1925 deemed to have survived the intestate, this section shall, nevertheless, have effect as respects the intestate as if the husband or wife had not survived the intestate.

(4) The interest payable on [the fixed net sum] payable to a surviving husband or wife shall be primarily payable out of income.]"

A spouse who is also a first cousin of the deceased takes both the rights of a surviving spouse and those of a cousin.[44]

---

[44] *Re Morrison* [1945] V.L.R. 123. *Re Morrison* is consistent with *Re Kendrew* [1953] Ch. 291, C.A.: a testatrix made gifts to a servant ("Mary") on condition that the servant remained in the service of her husband until the husband's death; after the death of the testatrix, the surviving husband married Mary; who agreed by deed to continue to serve him: the Court of Appeal held that a woman might be to her husband both a wife and a servant and that Mary was: so that the testatrix's gift to her took effect at the husband's subsequent death. *Re Morrison* was not cited in *Re Kendrew*; but by the same reasoning a woman may be both a wife and a cousin (*Re Morrison*) or both a wife and a servant (*Re Kendrew*).

A.E.A. 1925, s. 47(1)(iii) required issue of the intestate to bring advancements into account on intestacy[45]; it does not apply to others nor to a death on or after January 1, 1996.[47a]

31–16 Disclaimer or disqualification on intestacy. Despite the words "if the intestate leaves no ... ," a disclaimer by every person entitled under one heading results in the property going to those entitled under the next heading.[46] The property would also go to the next class in the event of every person entitled under one heading being disqualified from taking on account of the criminal killing of the intestate.[47]

PARTIAL INTESTACY

31–17 A.E.A. 1925, s.49 (as amended). The provisions of a will may fail in part on account of lapse; disclaimer; or disqualification; or because the will is so drawn that part of the testator's property is not given by the will. A.E.A. 1925, section 49 provides:

> "**49.**—(1) Where any person dies leaving a will effectively disposing of part of his property, this Part of this Act shall have effect as respects the part of his property not so disposed of subject to the provisions contained in the will and subject to the following modifications:
>
> [(aa) Where the deceased leaves a husband or wife who acquires any beneficial interests under the will of the deceased (other than personal chattels specifically bequeathed) the references in this Part of this Act to [the fixed net sum] payable to a surviving husband or wife, and to interest on that sum, shall be taken as references to the said sum diminished by the value at the date of death of the said beneficial interests, and to interest on that sum as so diminished, and, accordingly, where the said value exceeeds the said sum, this Part of this Act shall have effect as if references to the said sum, and interest thereon, were omitted]
>
> (a) The requirements [of section forty-seven of this Act] as to bringing property into account shall apply to any beneficial interests acquired by any issue of the deceased under the will of the deceased, but not to beneficial interests so acquired by any other persons;
>
> (b) The personal representative shall, subject to his rights and powers for the purposes of administration, be a

---

[45] See para. 31–13 and 31–14 above.
[46] *Re Scott* [1975] 1 W.L.R. 1260.
[47] *Re Callaway* [1956] Ch. 559, applied in *Re Scott* above.

trustee for the persons entitled under this Part of this Act in respect of the part of the estate not expressly disposed of unless it appears by the will that the personal representative is intended to take such part beneficially.

[(2) References in the foregoing provisions of this section to beneficial interests acquired under a will shall be construed as including a reference to a beneficial interest acquired by virtue of the exercise by the will of a general power of appointment (including the statutory power to dispose of entailed interests), but not of a special power of appointment.

(3) For the purpose of paragraph (aa) in the foregoing provisions of this section the personal representative shall employ a duly qualified valuer in any case where such employment may be necessary.

(4) The references in subsection (3) of section forty-seven A of this Act to property are references to property comprised in the residuary estate and, accordingly, where a will of the deceased creates a life interest in property in possession, and the remaining interest in that property forms part of the residuary interest (which, until the life interest determines, is property not in possession).]"

Sub-sections (1)(aa) and (a) no longer apply on a death on or after January 1, 1996.[47a]

There is a partial intestacy where there is undisposed of income[48]; a reversionary interest given by the will that fails to take effect[49]; or a lapsed share of residue.[50]

31–18 Surviving spouse on partial intestacy. There is no satisfactory authority on paragraph (aa).[51]

The right of the surviving spouse to have the matrimonial home appropriated to him or her under the Intestates' Estates Act 1952[52] applies on a *partial* intestacy. The 1952 Act is to be construed "as one with Part Four of" A.E.A. 1925[53]; where the word "intestate" includes someone who is partially intestate.[54]

A widow or widower with a life interest may merge the life interest in the fixed net sum in the right to that sum at the end of the life interest and so take it at once.[55]

[47a] See para. 31–14.
[48] *Re Tong* [1931] 1 Ch. 202.
[49] *Re McKee* [1931] 2 Ch. 145.
[50] *Re Worthington* [1933] Ch. 711; *Re Sanger* [1939] Ch. 238.
[51] *Re Osoba* [1979] 1 W.L.R. 247 was on appeal only a decision on the construction of the will in that case; the decision at first instance [1978] 1 W.L.R. 791 was overruled.
[52] See para. 31–09 above.
[53] para. 7(2) there.
[54] A.E.A. 1925, s.55(1)(vi).
[55] *Re Bowen-Buscarlet's Will Trusts* [1972] Ch. 463; explaining *Re Douglas* [1959] 1 W.L.R. 744; reported somewhat differently [1959] 2 All E.R. 620; and distinguishing *Re McKee* above on this point.

31–19 Accounting on partial intestacy. The requirements for bringing beneficial interests into account under section 49(1)(a) created practical difficulties in cases concerning present interests[56]; usually overcome by applying common sense. There are further potential problems not yet elucidated:

> "All sorts of difficulties arise in taking the date for the valuation where there is a partial intestacy and the various interests on intestacy do not fall into possession until a date long after the death of the testator. It may be that in certain circumstances it is necessary, in applying section 49, to depart from the words in brackets in section 47(1)(iii) "(the value to be reckoned as at the death of the intestate)."[57]

Personal representatives faced with a partial intestacy usually need legal advice. It no longer applies to a death on or after January 1, 1996: Law Reform (Succession) Act 1995, s.1.

---

[56] See *Re Grover* [1971] Ch. 168, explaining *Re Young* [1951] Ch. 185 and *Re Morton* [1956] Ch. 644.
[57] *Re Grover* above at p. 179.

32. Occupation of the deceased's home pending realisation or distribution

32–01 Introduction. Where a house or flat was the sole property of the deceased, questions arise about the occupation of the property pending realisation or distribution. This question does not of course arise when the occupier has a right of occupation as a tenant; or as a person entitled in equity to remain in occupation as licensee[1]; under the will; or otherwise. It only arises when, quite naturally, someone merely continues to live at the deceased's home after the death.

32–02 General rule about occupation of property. Apart from the administration of estates, there is a general rule about the occupation of property not held by a sole beneficial owner.

Living co-owners of property are necessarily trustees[2]; they are entitled to occupy their property together.[3] When, however, one co-owner does not occupy the property and the other does, the one in occupation has no liability to the other for an occupation rent[4]; with

---

[1] See Megarry & Wade, *The Law of Real Property* (5th ed.), at pp. 577–578; and Snell, *Equity* (29th ed.), at pp. 569–579.
[2] L.P.A. 1925, ss.34, 35 and 36.
[3] *Bull v. Bull* [1955] 1 Q.B. 234, unless the court orders a sale.
[4] *Jones v. Jones* [1977] 1 W.L.R. 438; *Dennis v. McDonald* [1982] Fam. 63. The previous decisions *Re Howlett* below and *Re Jennery* below are so clearly on different facts, that they were not cited in *Jones v. Jones* or in *Dennis v. McDonald*.

the exception that a co-owner who *wrongfully* excludes another co-owner is liable to pay the other an occupation rent,[5] or in any other case where imposing an occupation rent is held by the court to be necessary to do equity between the parties.[6]

Someone holding property in a fiduciary position, that is to say a trustee or a personal representative, who *unlawfully* occupies trust property is (like a co-owner who excludes the other co-owner) accountable to those beneficially entitled for an occupation rent, less the cost of repair. This liability arises only if the occupation was in breach of trust.[7] There is no such liability for occupation not in breach of trust,[8] unless so ordered by the court. Such an allowance does not appear to be within the powers of personal representatives.

32–03 Occupation of the deceased's property after the death, when not unlawful. Applying this general rule to the continued occupation of the deceased's house after the death, someone who was living there before the death and continues temporarily to occupy the deceased's home after the death is normally not liable for an occupation rent. This is so, whether it is the deceased's widow, widower, child or children or anyone else; and whether such an occupier is a personal representative of the deceased or not. Such occupation is unlikely to be a breach of trust.

32–04 When occupation becomes unlawful. Occupation (not by the personal representatives) becomes unlawful when the personal representatives duly determine the occupation by notice to quit,[9] or serve effective possession proceedings.[10] Occupation of the deceased's property for his own benefit (by the personal representatives or by one of them) is retrospectively treated as unlawful from the date when the property should have been sold on the open market. This is because not getting in that asset would, from that date, be maladministration (*devastavit*).[11]

32–05 Consequences of occupation becoming unlawful. The consequence of such occupation becoming unlawful is that the occupier becomes liable to give up possession and to pay to the estate an

---

[5] *Dennis v. McDonald* above, where the occupation rent was assessed on the basis of a fair rent under the Rent Act 1977, s.70(1) and (2).
[6] *Re Pavlou (a bankrupt)* [1993] 1 W.L.R. 1046; see the summary of the law by Millett J. at p. 1050D.
[7] *Re Howlett* [1949] Ch. 769 the 3rd point; where an administrator was held liable but an allowance was made for the defendant's maintenance of the plaintiff; *Re Jennery* [1967] Ch. 280 at p. 286, *obiter*.
[8] The decisions cited in the previous notes turned on the defendant's breach in each case.
[9] *Williams v. Holland* [1965] 1 W.L.R. 739.
[10] *Canas Property Co. v. K.L. Television Services* [1970] 2 Q.B. 433, the 2nd point (landlord and tenant, but on the same basis).
[11] See para. 45–01 below.

occupation rent from the date when the occupation became unlawful.[12]

The occupation rent, called "mesne profits" (that is to say, intermediate profits), is calculated at the property's market letting rent during the period of the wrongful occupation, even if not in fact let.[13]

This liability may be asserted either by any other personal representative, or by any beneficiary.

32–06 Effect of lawful occupation on the right to interest on a legacy. The person continuing in occupation after the death (often, but not necessarily, a widow or widower of the deceased) may also be a pecuniary legatee entitled to a legacy with interest on the legacy (under the general law; or on intestacy).[14] That occupier may afterwards have the house or flat appropriated to him or her in or towards satisfaction of the legacy.[15] In trusts of property, lawful occupation of the property is assumed to be equivalent to the enjoyment of its income.[16] It follows that, in respect of the period of such occupation, the legatee is not entitled to interest on the legacy (or on as much of the legacy as is represented by the value of the property); having enjoyed the equivalent of its income by occupation.

---

[12] *Re Howlett* above; *Williams v. Holland* above; *Re Jennery* above, *obiter*.

[13] *Swordheath Properties v. Tabet* [1979] 1 W.L.R. 285; *Inverguie Investments v. Hackett* [1995] 1 W.L.R. 713, P.C.

[14] A.E.A. 1925, s.46(1), the surviving spouse's fixed net sum.

[15] Under A.E.A. 1925, s.41 or Intestates' Estates Act 1952 Sched. 2.

[16] As appears from cases where this was not really in dispute: *Baylies v. Baylies* (1844) 1 Coll. 537, *Mannox v. Greener* (1872) 14 Eq. 456, before the S.L.A. 1882; *Re Bagot* [1894] 1 Ch. 177, *Re Newen* [1894] 2 Ch. 297, under the S.L.A. 1882. Since 1926, see S.L.A. 1925, s.19(1) and L.P.A. 1925, s.28 and s.29; and *Re Wellsted* [1949] Ch. 296 at p. 313. Treating lawful beneficial occupation of property as equivalent to the enjoyment of its income may be part of the doctrine that equity looks to the intent rather than to the form: Snell, *Equity* (29th ed.), at pp. 39–40. Likewise, by analogy, between vendor and purchaser occupation by the purchaser normally involves payment of interest: *Fluyder v. Cocker* (1806) 12 Ves. 25, at pp. 27–28; between vendor and purchaser, it is a question of contract: *Re Priestley's Contract* [1947] Ch. 469.

33. Distribution to those beneficially entitled

33–01   Time for distribution. Before distributing the estate, the personal representatives must ascertain and pay the liabilities of the estate, or make provision for their payment,[1] ensuring that creditors come before beneficiaries.

Two modern statutes impose an interval of six months from the date of the grant of representation, before distribution to beneficiaries. Under the Inheritance (Provision for Family and Dependants) Act 1975 an application may not be made more than six months after the date of the grant, except with leave; and personal representatives are not liable for distributing after six months.[2] It follows from this negative formulation that the personal representatives are or might be liable for distributing within six months from the date of the grant. When the personal representatives

---

[1] See para. 24–01 above: otherwise the personal representatives may be personally at risk, unless acting under the directions of the court.
[2] s.4 and s.20(1).

243

know that an application under the Act is pending or impending, they should only make an interim distribution to beneficiaries with the consent of those concerned or (if necessary) the leave of the court.[3]

Under A.J.A. 1982, s.20 an application may not be made to rectify a will more than six months after the date of the grant, except with leave; and personal representatives are not liable for distributing after such six months. Here too it appears to follow that they are or might be liable for distributing within six months from the date of the grant. As regards a pending or impending application for rectification, the same reasoning applies about an interim distribution.

33–02 Executor's year. A.E.A. 1925, s.44 provides:

> "**44.** Subject to the foregoing provisions of this Act, a personal representative is not bound to distribute the estate of the deceased before the expiration of one year from the death."

33–03 Distribution before a year from the death. Outright gifts by will vest at the death.[4] Personal representatives may distribute before the year from the death has elapsed.[5] Before the Judicature Act 1873, personal representatives were not compellable to distribute within a year of the death[6]; but the procedure was different then.[7] Personal representatives may nowadays be compellable to distribute before a year has elapsed from the death, if so directed in the will: a testator often directs an immediate payment of a legacy to (say) his wife. In an estate clearly sufficient for the purpose, the court would nowadays be likely to hold that there is jurisdiction to order a direction for immediate payment to be performed,[8] within the executors' year, if there was no risk to creditors.

APPROPRIATE AND ASSENT

33–04 Power of appropriation. There is a statutory power of appropriation under A.E.A. 1925, s.41 as follows:

> "**41.**—(1) The personal representative may appropriate any part of the real or personal estate, including things in action, of

---

[3] *Re Ralphs* [1968] 1 W.L.R. 1522, on the similar previous Act.
[4] Jarman, *Wills* (8th ed.), at p. 1346; unless there is anything in the will to prevent such vesting.
[5] *Wilson v. Spencer* (1732) 3 P.W. 172.
[6] *Benson v. Maude* (1821) 6 Madd. 15. There seems to be no modern case holding that personal representatives cannot be compelled to distribute before the year has expired: *Re Llangattock* (1918) 34 T.L.R. 341 did not decide this point, no reasons are reported for the decision and it seems to have turned on construction of the will in that case.
[7] See *Thomas v. Montgomery* (1829) 1 Russ. & M. 729 on anticipatory payments to pecuniary legatees.
[8] Under R.S.C., Ord. 85, r. 2(1); on the basis of *Re Riddell* [1936] 2 All E.R. 1600 (a point omitted from [1936] Ch. 747).

the deceased in the actual condition or state of investment thereof at the time of appropriation in or towards satisfaction of any legacy bequeathed by the deceased, or of any other interest or share in his property, whether settled or not, as to the personal representative may seem just and reasonable, according to the respective rights of the persons interested in the property of the deceased:

Provided that—

(i) an appropriation shall not be made under this section so as to affect prejudicially any specific devise or bequest;

(ii) an appropriation of property, whether or not being an investment authorised by law or by the will, if any, of the deceased for the investment of money subject to the trust, shall not (save as hereinafter mentioned) be made under this section except with the following consents:—

(a) when made for the benefit of a person absolutely and beneficially entitled in possession, the consent of that person;

(b) when made in respect of any settled legacy share or interest, the consent of either the trustee thereof, if any (not being also the personal representative), or the person who may for the time being be entitled to the income;

If the person whose consent is so required as aforesaid is an infant or [is incapable, by reason of mental disorder within the meaning of [the Mental Health Act 1983] of managing and administering his property and affairs], the consent shall be given on his behalf by his parents or parent, testamentary or other guardian [..] or receiver, or if, in the case of an infant, there is no such parent or guardian, by the court on the application of his next friend;

(iii) no consent (save of such trustee as aforesaid) shall be required on behalf of a person who may come into existence after the time of appropriation, or who cannot be found or ascertained at that time;

(iv) if no [receiver is acting for a person suffering from mental disorder], then, if the appropriation is of an investment authorised by law or by the will, if any, of the deceased for the investment of money subject to the trust, no consent shall be required on behalf of the [said person];

(v) if, independently of the personal representative, there is no trustee of a settled legacy share or interest, and no person of full age and capacity entitled to the income thereof, no consent shall be required to an appropriation

245

in respect of such legacy share or interest, provided that the appropriation is of an investment authorised as aforesaid.

[(1A) The county court has jurisdiction under proviso (ii) to subsection (1) of this section where the estate in respect of which the application is made does not exceed in amount or value the county court limit.]

(2) Any property duly appropriated under the powers conferred by this section shall thereafter be treated as an authorised investment, and may be retained or dealt with accordingly.

(3) For the purposes of such appropriation, the personal representative may ascertain and fix the value of the respective parts of the real and personal estate and the liabilities of the deceased as he may think fit, and shall for that purpose employ a duly qualified valuer in any case where such employment may be necessary; and may make any conveyance (including an assent) which may be requisite for giving effect to the appropriation.

(4) An appropriation made pursuant to this section shall bind all persons interested in the property of the deceased whose consent is not hereby made requisite.

(5) The personal representative shall, in making the appropriation, have regard to the rights of any person who may thereafter come into existence, or who cannot be found or ascertained at the time of appropriation, and of any other person whose consent is not required by this section.

(6) This section does not prejudice any other power of appropriation conferred by law or by the will (if any) of the deceased, and takes effect with any extended powers conferred by the will (if any) of the deceased; and where an appropriation is made under this section, in respect of a settled legacy, share or interest, the property appropriated shall remain subject to all trusts for sale and powers of leasing, disposition, and management or varying investments which would have been applicable thereto or to the legacy, share or interest in respect of which the appropriation is made, if no such appropriation had been made.

(7) If after any real estate has been appropriated in purported exercise of the powers conferred by this section, the person to whom it was conveyed disposes of it or any interest therein, then, in favour of a purchaser, the appropriation shall be deemed to have been made in accordance with the requirements of this section and after all requisite consents, if any, had been given.

(8) In this section, a settled legacy, share or interest includes any legacy, share or interest to which a person is not absolutely entitled in possession at the date of the appropriation, also an annuity, and "purchaser" means a purchaser for money or money's worth.

(9) This section applies whether the deceased died intestate or not, and whether before or after the commencement of this Act, and extends to property over which a testator exercises a general power of appointment, including the statutory power to dispose of entailed interests, and authorises the setting apart of a fund to answer an annuity by means of the income of that fund or otherwise."

In addition there was, and still is, a power of appropriation at common law[9]; which no longer needs to be used. A will may contain a power of appropriation wider than that in section 41: for example dispensing (usually unwisely) with consent on the part of the beneficiary. There may be tax consequences that the personal representatives should consider when making an appropriation.[10]

33–05 Effect of the exercise of the power of appropriation. An appropriation is made at the value at the date of the appropriation.[11] Thereupon the "property appropriated is taken by the legatee for better or worse"[12]; and so the appropriation separates the appropriated legacy or share of residue from the rest of the estate for all purposes.[13] On this principle, an appropriation to meet a fractional share satisfies the rights of those entitled to that share, even though the retained property afterwards increases, or decreases, in value.[14] When a fractional share is satisfied by appropriation, and then it turns out that the fraction was too small, the first appropriation is taken at its cash value at the time of the appropriation.[15]

33–06 Appropriation to the personal representatives themselves. The power of appropriation under section 41 is conferred by statute. It appears, therefore, not to be subject to the rule against self-dealing: although otherwise the rule against self-dealing is an over-riding rule[16]; that is to say, it is incorrect, under section 41, to speak of a "notional sale of the appropriated assets to the beneficiary."[17]

---

[9] *Re Lepine* [1892] 1 Ch. 210; the common law power is narrower than section 41 because it is restricted to authorised investments: *Re Beverly* [1901] 1 Ch. 681. The common law power gave rise to difficulties, not arising under section 41, in respect of a legacy not absolutely vested in an adult: *Re Hall* [1903] 2 Ch. 226, *Re Salamons* [1920] 1 Ch. 290.

[10] See para. 35–08 below.

[11] *Re Collins* [1975] 1 W.L.R. 309.

[12] Withers, *Reversions* (2nd ed.), at p. 26.

[13] *Ballard v. Marsden* (1880) 14 Ch. Div. 374; *Re Richardson* [1896] 1 Ch. 512; Withers above.

[14] *Re Abergavenny* [1981] 1 W.L.R. 843.

[15] *Re Gollin's Declaration of Trust* [1969] 1 W.L.R. 1858.

[16] See Chap. 34

[17] As was done in *Re Collins* above at p. 314C.

The common law power of appropriation was (unlike the statutory power under section 41) based on a notional sale; and anomalously the common law power of appropriation could be exercised in the personal representatives' own favour, personally or as trustees.[18] A *sole* personal representative might not appropriate to himself property of uncertain value at his own price.[19]

Personal representatives may if necessary ask the court to approve[20] an appropriation to themselves, either beneficially or in another fiduciary capacity.

33–07 Power to assent. The power to make an assent is conferred by the A.E.A. 1925, s.36:

"**36.**—(1) A personal representative may assent to the vesting, in any person who (whether by devise, bequest, devolution, appropriation or otherwise) may be entitled thereto, either beneficially or as a trustee or personal representative, of any estate or interest in real estate to which the testator or intestate was entitled or over which he exercised a general power of appointment by his will, including the statutory power to dispose of entailed interests, and which devolved upon the personal representative.

(2) The assent shall operate to vest in that person the estate or interest to which the assent relates, and, unless a contrary intention appears, the assent shall relate back to the death of the deceased.

(3) The statutory covenants implied by a person being expressed to convey as personal representative, may be implied in an assent in like manner as in a conveyance by deed.

(4) An assent to the vesting of a legal estate shall be in writing, signed by the personal representative, and shall name the person in whose favour it is given and shall operate to vest in that person the legal estate to which it relates; and an assent not in writing or not in favour of a named person shall not be effectual to pass a legal estate.

(5) Any person in whose favour an assent or conveyance of a legal estate is made by a personal representative may require

---

[18] *Barclay v. Owen* (1889) 60 L.T. 220; *Re Richardson* [1896] 1 Ch. 512; *Re Brooks* (1897) 76 L.T. 771; and, on appeal from Scotland, *Fraser v. Murdoch* (1881) 6 App.Cas. 855. These cases are at first sight inconsistent with the modern rule against self-dealing, which was clarified or expanded after they were decided. The explanation may be that at common law (though not in equity) the personal representatives owned the assets of the estate.

[19] *Re Bythway* (1911) 104 L.T. 411.

[20] On originating summons under R.S.C., Ord. 85, r. 2.

that notice of the assent or conveyance be written or endorsed on or permanently annexed to the probate or letters of administration, at the cost of the estate of the deceased, and that the probate or letters of administration be produced, at the like cost, to prove that the notice has been placed thereon or annexed thereto.

(6) A statement in writing by a personal representative that he has not given or made an assent or conveyance in respect of a legal estate, shall, in favour of a purchaser, but without prejudice to any previous disposition made in favour of another purchaser deriving title mediately or immediately under the personal representative, be sufficient evidence that an assent or conveyance has not been given or made in respect of the legal estate to which the statement relates, unless notice of a previous assent or conveyance affecting that estate has been placed on or annexed to the probate or administration.

A conveyance by a personal representative of a legal estate to a purchaser accepted on the faith of such a statement shall (without prejudice as aforesaid and unless notice of a previous assent or conveyance affecting that estate has been placed on or annexed to the probate or administration) operate to transfer or create the legal estate expressed to be conveyed in like manner as if no previous assent or conveyance had been made by the personal representative.

A personal representative making a false statement, in regard to any such matter, shall be liable in like manner as if the statement had been contained in a statutory declaration.

(7) An assent or conveyance by a personal representative in respect of a legal estate shall, in favour of a purchaser, unless notice of a previous assent or conveyance affecting that legal estate has been placed on or annexed to the probate or administration, be taken as sufficient evidence that the person in whose favour the assent or conveyance is given or made is the person entitled to have the legal estate conveyed to him, and upon the proper trusts, if any, but shall not otherwise prejudicially affect the claim of any person rightfully entitled to the estate vested or conveyed or any charge thereon.

(8) A conveyance of a legal estate by a personal representative to a purchaser shall not be invalidated by reason only that the purchaser may have notice that all the debts, liabilities, funeral, and testamentary or administration expenses, duties, and legacies of the deceased have been discharged or provided for.

(9) An assent or conveyance given or made by a personal representative shall not, except in favour of a purchaser of a legal estate, prejudice the right of the personal representative or any other person to recover the estate or interest to which the assent or conveyance relates, or to be indemnified out of such

estate or interest against any duties, debt, or liability to which such estate or interest would have been subject if there had not been any assent or conveyance.

(10) A personal representative may, as a condition of giving an assent or making a conveyance, require security for the discharge of any such duties, debt, or liability, but shall not be entitled to postpone the giving of an assent merely by reason of the subsistence of any such duties, debt or liability if reasonable arrangements have been made for discharging the same; and an assent may be given subject to any legal estate or charge by way of legal mortgage.

(11) This section shall not operate to impose any stamp duty in respect of an assent, and in this section "purchaser" means a purchaser for money or money's worth.

(12) This section applies to assents and conveyances made after the commencement of this Act, whether the testator or intestate died before or after such commencement."

33–08 Effect of an assent. An assent by personal representatives vests the property comprised in it in the person to whom the assent is made and is a recognition that the property is no longer held by them as personal representatives (see the next two paragraphs).

33–09 Form of assent. An assent need not be by deed. An assent can only be made under section 36 in respect of property to which the deceased was entitled, or over which he exercised by will a general power of appointment (but not over property subject to a special or a hybrid power of appointment,[21] nor over property appointed otherwise than by will). An assent made when a conveyance should have been made, will however be construed as a conveyance, provided that the assent was by deed[22] (because a conveyance must be under seal[23]). An assent may under section 36(10) be made subject to security for a remaining liability; but this is in practice rarely done.

Forms of assent are printed in the precedent books.

33–10 Assent of land. An assent of a legal estate in land must be in writing.[24] A note of the assent should be made on the grant of representation, under section 36(5).

---

[21] See para. 20–34 to 20–37 above for the forms of powers of appointment.

[22] *Re Stirrup* [1961] 1 W.L.R. 449.

[23] L.P.A. 1925, s.52.

[24] A.E.A. 1925, s.36(4) and s.55(1)(vii); this means a freehold or leasehold under the L.P.A. 1925, s.1(1); and the interests tabulated in s.1(2); a charge by way of legal mortgage is frequently found.

An assent in writing is required now even when the assent is by personal representatives in their own favour but in another capacity.[25] As a result, to make title to a legal estate the title to which is not registered, a grant of representation *de bonis non*[26] might be needed many years after a death when the estate was administered on the previous view. The spread of registration of title has reduced the inconvenience of this decision. As regards unregistered land in an area where registration of title is available,[27] the registrar may accept the title as a safe title to be registered under the L.R.A. 1925, section 13(c), disregarding the absence of an assent in writing[28]; and the same applies in respect of a title already registered.

Now that registration of title on sale has become compulsory throughout England and Wales,[29] voluntary regustration is available and L.R.A. 1966, section 1(2) cannot operate. Title may therefore be got in by voluntary registration of title, disregarding *Re King* (see note 28) and without needing to resort to a grant of representation *de bonis non*. This reduces the harm done by *Re King*.

An assent can be made to an individual to whom land devolves. Land that devolves beneficially on more than one person is subject to an express trust for sale or to a statutory trust for sale[30]; and an assent can be made on trust for sale to the personal representatives themselves or to other trustees.[31] The personal representatives have power to appoint new trustees under the Trustee Act 1925, s.36 when the estate has been fully administered.[32] Land devolving in trust for a beneficiary for life and then on others, is often subject to an express trust for sale. If not, it may be settled land under S.L.A. 1925. Personal representatives should not just make an assent of settled land; but a *vesting* assent: that is to say, an assent complying with the requirements of S.L.A. 1925, section 5 and section 6; or a vesting deed under section 5.

---

[25] *Re King* [1964] Ch. 542. Before that decision "it was fairly generally thought by conveyancers that, where the legal estate in land had become vested in a person beneficially entitled to that land but had become so vested in some capacity (e.g. as executor of the previous owner) other than the capacity of beneficial owner, no assent in writing was necessary to clothe that person with the legal estate in his capacity as beneficial owner": Buckley L.J. in *Re Edwards' Will Trusts* [1982] Ch. 30 at p. 33; the Court of Appeal assumed (at p. 40) that *Re King* was correctly decided. For the previous view of conveyancers, see Rose & Bowles, *Conveyancing Precedents* (4th ed.) (1951), at pp. 65–66, n. (2); and see now Megarry & Wade, *The Law of Real Property* (5th ed.), at p. 564, n. 87. It seems unlikely that *Re King* will be overruled now.
[26] See paras. 2–08 and 23–04 above.
[27] L.R.A. 1966, s.1.
[28] Ruoff & Roper, *Registered Conveyancing* (6th ed.), para. 12–47, citing *Re King* as within section 13(c).
[29] Registration of Title Order 1989 (S.I. 1989 No. 1347).
[30] Under L.P.A. 1925, s.35; or A.E.A. 1925, s.33.
[31] See the statutory form: L.P.A. 1925, Sched. 5, form 9.
[32] *Re Pitt* (1928) 44 T.L.R. 371.

33–11 Assent of property other than land. There is no need for a *written* assent in respect of assets other than legal estates, outside section 36,[33] for example, a beneficial interest arising under a trust in equity,[34] or chattels passing by delivery. In the absence of documentation, disputes or errors are apt to arise about an oral assent or an implied assent by personal representatives in favour of beneficiaries. An assent should be documented, by a receipt or by signing the personal representatives' accounts, or otherwise.

33–12 Transfer of United Kingdom company shares. Shares in a company registered in the U.K. are not transferred to a beneficiary by assent, but by a share transfer, subject to any restrictions on transfer in the articles of a private company.[35] The personal representatives of a deceased shareholder take the shares subject to all the restrictions applying to the shares under the company's memorandum and articles.[36]

33–13 Gifts of United Kingdom company shares. Gifts of shares in United Kingdom companies raise difficulty.

As regards shares in a *public* company, with the suffix "P.L.C."[37]: A beneficiary is entitled to insist on a transfer to himself of his number of quoted company shares in a public company, although the shares might be more influential if kept together by the trustees of the will.[38]

As regards shares in a *private* company, with the suffix "Limited"[39]: In two cases at first instance, the same right to demand transfer of shares was held to apply to a shareholding in a private limited company.[40] The cases were analysed and distinguished in a recent reserved judgment relating to shares in a private company, where a sale was ordered of all the shares and not a transfer.[41] At present the law appears to be that at first instance in a private company the beneficiary of part of the shares may call for a transfer even though it would break up a controlling interest, thus reducing the value of the shareholding as a whole. That right does not apply

---

[33] *Wise v. Whitburn* [1924] 1 Ch. 460 (leaseholds before the 1925 Acts: still the law as to assets other than land).

[34] L.P.A. 1925, s.1(3).

[35] See para. 20–08 above, on transfers of U.K. shares.

[36] *Roberts v. Letter "T" Estates* [1961] A.C. 795.

[37] Or its Welsh equivalent: Companies Act 1985, s.1(3) and s.25(1).

[38] *Re Marshall* [1914] 1 Ch. 192.

[39] Or an abbreviation or its Welsh equivalent: Companies Act 1985, s.1(3) and s.25(2).

[40] *Re Sandeman* [1937] 1 All E.R. 368; *Re Weiner* [1956] 1 W.L.R. 579; the decision in the Privy Council apparently to the contrary *Lacoste v. Duchesnay* [1924] A.C. 166 was not cited; it turns on the language of the Civil Code of Quebec. The law of Scotland on such points appears to be based on a different approach and not really to throw light on this question: see *MacCulloch v. Anderson* [1904] A.C. 55 and the cases cited there.

[41] *Lloyds Bank v. Duker* [1987] 1 W.L.R. 1324.

however when there is evidence[42] about the reduction in value of the other shares by such a transfer, on account of the principle that an even hand is to be held between the beneficiaries.

The two cases where such a transfer was ordered in a *private* company might be overruled in the Court of Appeal. When a transfer of shares is ordered, in disregard of a clause to the contrary in the will, it is a curious restriction on the general power of making a will[43] and of determining by will the ambit of the gifts made in the will.

The question arises when a controlling block of shares in a private company is settled by will; and some interests are vested absolutely and others are not. Personal representatives should obtain advice and, if necessary, the directions of the court before making a transfer of shares in a private company, especially if it might be disadvantageous to the remaining shares.

33–14 Property overseas. Assets outside England and Wales need to be transferred to beneficiaries in a manner complying with the law of the place where they are: whether land, shares in a company, debts or charges, or anything else. This will have been considered when recovering such assets.[44]

When a testator domiciled in England and Wales leaves a block of shares in a company incorporated elsewhere (for example on the continent) the power of transfer depends on the law of the place where the company is incorporated. The applicability in an administration here of the cases requiring a transfer of shares in a company here[45] has not been considered in a reported case; but the principle is the same, subject to any restriction imposed under the overseas law governing the company.

33–15 Remedies of a dissatisfied beneficiary. A beneficiary may be dissatisfied with the administration of the estate for a number of reasons: often lack of sufficient information or delay; sometimes neglect, loss or other faults real or suspected. Before applying to the court, a solicitor's letter mentioning an intended application to the court for one or more of these available remedies usually produces full information and a prompt and satisfactory administration; especially as personal representatives who have acted unreasonably can be disallowed their costs or even ordered to pay costs[46]. Those remedies, mentioned elsewhere in this book, are as follows.

---

[42] Tendered in the case cited in n. 41, but not in the two previous cases about private companies.

[43] Wills Act 1837, s.3.

[44] See Chap. 20 above.

[45] See nn. 38, 39 and 40.

[46] R.S.C. Ord. 62, r.6(2).

An application for an order for an account.   See paragraphs 36–04, 42–02 and 42–14.

An application to remove the personal representative/s or to appoint a Judicial Trustee.   See paragraphs 43–01 to 43–04.

An application to appoint a receiver.   See paragraph 2–12; but a receiver is rarely appointed in such a case.

An action for maladministration (in Latin, *devastavit*).   See paragraphs 45–01 to 45–07.

An order for the court to administer the estate.   See paragraph 42–11. This is however not a practicable remedy for a beneficiary.

Part Six: The Personal Representatives' Powers, Accounts, Expenses and Remuneration; Completion of the Administration

34. The rule against self-dealing

34–01   The rule against self-dealing.   An overriding rule of equity "repeated in innumerable cases of the highest authority"[1] prevents anyone acting for others, such as an executor an administrator or a trustee, from being a party to a binding contract with himself, even if others are parties to the transaction.[2] A transaction effected in breach of the rule is voidable (liable to be set aside), not void (wholly invalid).[3] It is imprudent to infringe the rule; a claim to avoid a transaction as having been in breach of the rule might be raised some years later, perhaps by someone who was a child when the original

---

[1] See *Industrial Developments Ltd v. Cooley* below at pp. 448–453; citing cases back to 1726.

[2] *Industrial Developments Ltd v. Cooley* [1972] 1 W.L.R. 443; *Re Thompson* [1986] Ch. 99, citing authorities back to 1802. Megarry V.-C. elucidated the rule in *Tito v. Waddell (No. 2)* [1977] Ch. 106 (the South Sea island case) at pp. 240–243. This rule of equity is not to be confused with the somewhat different and narrower rule at common law about contracting with oneself: *Rye v. Rye* [1962] A.C. 496, a leasehold case.

[3] *Holder v. Holder* [1968] Ch. 353; where the rule was held not to apply to an executor who had renounced probate ineffectually and taken no part in the administration.

transaction was effected. A subsequent court order avoiding the transaction can result in a complicated position.[4]

It is only a beneficiary who can have the transaction avoided. If a transaction infringes the rule but turns out to be advantageous to the estate, a personal representative is held to it.[5]

34–02 Express exclusion of the rule against self-dealing. The rule cannot be excluded so as to authorise personal representatives to engage in self-dealing as against creditors: for the rights of creditors are superior to provisions in a will. It is assumed by textbooks that the rule against self-dealing may be excluded or modified by will.[6] This is consistent with principle, for a beneficiary takes only as much as the testator gives that beneficiary. In practice it is however hazardous for a personal representative to rely on such a provision in a will without the approval of the beneficiaries or the directions of the court (see next below). The position is similar to that of the purported extension by will of the personal representatives' powers of compromise under the Trustee Act 1925, s. 15.[7] Self-dealing may be authorised by the court.[8]

34–03 Practical ways to obtain authority for a compromise when the rule against self-dealing applies, or might apply. There are two ways to effect such an arrangement.

Beneficiaries' approval. When every person beneficially interested in the estate is ascertained and of full age, they have power together to authorise the transaction. If there is any doubt about the position, the beneficiaries should have separate advice before agreeing to authorise the transaction; this is obtained at the expense of the estate.[9] Depending on the circumstances, the solicitors acting for the personal representatives may instruct counsel (other than the one advising the personal representatives) to advise the various beneficiaries, thereby reducing the costs; alternatively another firm of solicitors may advise the beneficiaries.

---

[4] See *Holder v. Holder* above at p. 377, setting out the order made at first instance; on appeal it was held that the rule did not apply to that transaction.

[5] *Holder v. Holder* above at first instance; the point did not arise in the Court of Appeal.

[6] *Underhill on Trusts* (8th ed.), by Sir A. Underhill (1926), at p. 324, citing authorities not precisely in point (14th ed. at p. 572 omits those authorities); *Scott on Trusts* (4th ed.), para. 170.9, citing U.S. authorities; Snell, *Equity*, at p. 250, not citing authority.

[7] See para. 23–14 above.

[8] *Re Drexel Burnham Lambeth Pension Fund* [1994] 1 W.L.R. 32; suggesting at page 43A that the question whether the rule can be overcome by express direction is difficult; but, as far as the report shows, without citation of the books cited in note 6 above.

[9] On the analogy of *Re Buckton* [1907] 2 Ch. 406 at p. 414; since the costs of all parties in an application to the court fall on the estate.

Judicial approval. Approval from the beneficiaries is not always available: as where minors or unborn or unascertained beneficiaries are concerned; or where one or more of the adult beneficiaries refuses to approve.[10]

34–04 Agreements with others without the authority of the beneficiaries or judicial approval. There are four classes of person with whom personal representatives may wish to make an agreement. They are, a personal representative's co-administrator, co-executor and spouse, and partner. Questions may arise too about small limited companies. Transactions with them are discussed in the next five paragraphs. It is not safe, or wise, for personal representatives to make an agreement with any of them.

34–05 Agreement with a co-administrator. An *administrator* has no power under the general law to make a compromise with his co-administrator.[11] This is consistent with the fact that administrators are chosen by the court, not by the deceased.

34–06 Agreement with a co-executor. There is authority that an *executor* has power to make a compromise with his co-executor[12]; it is, however, not consistent with other authorities in England,[13] and elsewhere.[14] It is unwise to act on the view that an executor has power to make a compromise with his co-executor.

In New Zealand, the law was stated by Richmond J. as follows:

> "The power recently conferred on an executor to compromise and submit to arbitration claims by and against the estate of their testator does not affect the question. It would be as easy to argue that a power of sale enables them to sell to one of themselves."[15]

---

[10] For the procedure to obtain judicial appoval under R.S.C., Ord. 85, see paras. 42–02 to 42–04.

[11] *Hudson v. Hudson* (1737) 1 Atk. 460.

[12] *Hudson v. Hudson* above; *Smith v. Everett* (1859) 27 Beav. 446; *Re Houghton* [1904] 1 Ch. 622. The point was left open in *de Cordova v. de Cordova* (1879) 4 App.Cas. 692, a case of bad faith.

[13] *Re Fish* [1893] 2 Ch. 413; expressed to deal with *trustees*; but it is not clear from the report why those concerned were not still executors. In *Re Houghton* above, only some 10 years later, *Re Fish* was not cited. In *Holder v. Holder* [1968] Ch. 353 at first instance Cross J. applied the rule against self-dealing to someone whom he held to be an executor; none of the cases cited here in nn. 12 and 13 was cited. (The question did not arise on the view taken in the Court of Appeal.) *Smith v. Everett* and *Re Houghton* cannot be relied on, in this state of the authorities.

[14] See below.

[15] *Stupples v. Dransfield* (1888) 6 N.Z.L.R. 584 at p. 589. It was not cited in any of the reported cases in England.

In Ireland, an executor has no power to make a compromise with a co-executor.[16]

34–07 Agreement with a spouse of a personal representative. There appears to be no reported example of an attempt to make a compromise with the wife or the husband of either an administrator or an executor. When such a transaction is effected with the wife of a *trustee*, it can, according to Commonwealth cases, be set aside[17]; unless, as in a case in Scotland, justified on the facts.[18] The explanation is that "there are wives and wives."[19] The position was explained in New Zealand as follows[20]:

> "I should have thought that the same considerations of public policy under which a trustee is absolutely prohibited from selling the trust property to himself applied with equal force to prohibit him from selling the property to his wife. I do not think that an essential rule of public policy established to secure the honest and diligent exercise of a trustee's duty with a single eye to the interests of his beneficiaries should be capable of evasion by the simple device of substituting the trustee's wife for himself as the purchaser of the property. If there are any purposes for which a husband and wife are still to be treated as one person, I think that this is an instance in which the rule should be applied. In the first place, a husband has so direct an interest in the pecuniary advantage of his wife that in the administration of his trust her interests should be regarded as equivalent to his own. In the second place, the special nature of the matrimonial relationship is such as to render all but impracticable any inquiry into the question whether a purchase by the wife of a trustee is not in reality a purchase by the trustee himself in his wife's name, or at all events a purchase in which the husband possesses some concealed pecuniary interest.
>
> It is true there is no direct English authority establishing the rule that a trustee cannot sell to his wife. This circumstance, however, is not conclusive, for the rule that a trustee cannot sell to himself is not an isolated rule standing by itself, but is merely an illustration and application of the wider principle that a trustee must not place himself in any position in which his interests conflict with his duty. The question is whether he does not violate this rule when he sells the trust property to his wife, no less than when he sells it to himself."

---

[16] *Re Boyle* [1947] Ir.R. 61.
[17] *Robertson v. Robertson* [1924] N.Z.L.R. 552.
[18] *Burrell v. Burrell's Trustees*, 1915 S.C. 333.
[19] *Tito v. Waddell (No. 2)* above at p. 240; the case did not concern wives.
[20] *Robertson v. Robertson* above at p. 555, Salmond J.

And at p. 557, after citing authorities:

"Having regard to these authorities, it may be regarded as still an open question awaiting final determination in an appropriate case whether a sale of trust property by a trustee to his own wife, without the precedent approval of the Court, is not absolutely prohibited as contrary to public policy, and as amounting to a violation of the rule that a trustee must not place himself in a position in which his interest conflicts with his duty to his beneficiaries. As I have already indicated, however, it is not necessary to answer this question in the present case, for even on the assumption that the matrimonial relationship is not a ground of invalidity, but is merely a ground of suspicion, I must hold that such suspicion has not been effectually dispelled in the present instance."

34–08 Agreement with a partner of a personal representative. A partner has an interest in the partnership income and capital[21]; it follows that a personal representative cannot make a valid agreement with his partner.[22]

34–09 Agreement with a company in which a personal representative has an interest. The law concerning a transaction with a company in which a personal representative has an interest has not been fully developed.[23] The position of a personal representative may vary between having an interest so inconsiderable that it is irrelevant, and being identified with the company.[24] The test of the validity of an agreement with a company in which a personal representative has an interest is probably whether the personal representative has a personal interest "of such a substantial nature that it might affect his judgment in making" the transaction.[25]

34–10 Purchase of a beneficial interest. The purchase by someone in a fiduciary position of a beneficial interest from a beneficiary is subject to slightly different rules, so that it is not necessarily liable to be set aside, unless there is an indication of undue influence.[26] Such a purchase is not a normal feature of the administration of an estate; and it is not discussed here.

---

[21] Partnership Act 1890, s.9 and s.24.

[22] As mentioned in *Re Thompson* above, at p. 115.

[23] See *Farrar v. Farrars Ltd* (1888) 40 Ch.Div. 395; and *Re Thompson* above, at p. 114.

[24] As in *Jones v. Lipman* [1962] 1 W.L.R. 832 (a vendor and purchaser case) where the company was "the creature of the first defendant, a device and a sham, a mask which he holds before his face in an attempt to avoid recognition by the eye of equity": p. 836.

[25] *Scott on Trusts* (4th ed.), para. 170.1; citing authorities.

[26] See Snell, *Equity*, at pp. 250–251.

35. The personal representatives' discretionary powers

35–01 General principle against judicial interference with fiduciary powers
35–02 Effect of an application to the court
35–03 Principle that in exercising powers, certainty is preferred
35–04 Management powers during the administration of a minority
35–05 Power of investment
35–06 Principles that personal representatives should observe when investing
35–07 Powers during a minority
35–08 Tax

35–01 General principle against judicial interference with fiduciary powers. The general principle is that when those in a fiduciary position (such as personal representatives) have fiduciary powers, the court will not interfere with their unanimous exercise of a power, in good faith.[1] It is therefore not enough, in the absence of bad faith,[2] for those who complain to show that it would have been better to make a different decision. The extent of the doctrine against interference with discretionary powers is illustrated (though in a case concerned a trust, not an estate) by a decision that where the trustees had failed to exercise a discretion that they were permitted but not bound to exercise, the court would give the trustees liberty to make good their omission to exercise the discretion.[3]

35–02 Effect of an application to the court. This right to exercise fiduciary powers is not affected by an application[4] for the court's directions. On an application, the plaintiffs (usually the personal

---

[1] *Gisborne v. Gisborne* (1877) 2 App.Cas. 300; *Re Bryant* [1894] 1 Ch. 324; *Re 90 Thornhill Road* [1970] Ch. 261.
[2] Where persons in a fiduciary position act in bad faith, the court interferes: *Klug* v. *Klug* [1918] 2 Ch. 67; *Re 90 Thornhill Road* above at p. 266; bad faith amounts to maladministration.
[3] *Re Locker* [1977] 1 W.L.R. 1323.
[4] Under Ord. 85, r. 2, see para. 42–02 below.

representatives) may ask whether a specified transaction is within the power of the personal representatives, with a view to it being exercised should the court hold it within their powers. Alternatively, the personal representatives may even surrender the discretion to be exercised by the court.[5] It is only an order for administration of the estate by the court that overrides the discretion of the personal representatives by making them subject to judicial control.[6]

35–03 Principle that in exercising powers, certainty is preferred. It may be necessary in adjusting accounts to value interests of unknown amount, such as a reversion, a life interest or annuity for life, or a contingent (conditional) interest. The court (if the question is before the court) or the personal representatives (if administering the estate without obtaining the directions of the court) may have to adopt an actuarial valuation of the unknown.

An actuarial valuation should not, however, be adopted if during the course of the administration, the actual value becomes known. The actual value may become known by the reversion falling in by the interest for life ending, or, the condition being satisfied or failing to be satisfied. The rule in the administration of estates, as elsewhere in the law is that "the court should never speculate where it knows."[7]

35–04 Management powers during the administration of a minority. A.E.A. 1925, s.39 confers on personal representatives for the purposes of administration or during the minority of any beneficiary, the powers of trustees-for-sale of land.

As regards land, trustees for sale have under L.P.A. 1925, s.28(1) all the power of a life tenant under S.L.A. 1925 of selling, leasing, mortgaging and otherwise dealing with land.[8] They also have powers of investment.

35–05 Power of investment. A will may and usually does specify the range of investments that the personal representatives are authorised to make. Otherwise, the power of investment depends on the Trustee Investments Act 1961. The Act requires those concerned to have regard to the need for diversification of investment as far as appropriate to the trust,[9] and the suitability of a proposed investment

---

[5] See para. 42–06.
[6] *Re Furness* [1943] Ch. 415.
[7] *Curwen v. James* [1963] 1 W.L.R. 748 at p. 753; applying to an action for damages at common law the decision *Re Bradberry* [1943] Ch. 35 at p. 42 on valuing an annuity after the annuitant had died and its exact value become known. (The reference to using coupons for the mantle of Elijah on p. 42 is a slip; secondhand clothes were not subject to clothing coupons.)
[8] See S.L.A. 1925, ss.38 to 72.
[9] s.6(1)(a); probably only stating the general law: see Scott, *Trusts* (4th ed.), para. 230.

to that trust.[10] The Act recognises two "ranges" of investment called "narrower range investments" and "wider range investments." Narrower range investments include gilt edged investments (that have in practice been depreciated by inflation inflicted by successive governments); wider range investments include what might be called "blue chip" shares,[11] (the lists are printed in Sweet & Maxwell's *Conveyancing Statutes* (5th ed.), at pp. 373 to 376). Some narrower range investments may be made without expert investment advice, others only with such advice. Wider range investments may only be made after the fund has originally been divided into two halves of equal value, one for each range; thereafter either part may grow (or shrink) in value without requiring an adjustment.[12] There are provisions for transfers, when made, between the two ranges[13]; and for reconciling the 1961 Act with other powers of investment conferred on those making the fiduciary investments. The text of the Act needs to be referred to when making a fiduciary investment.

35–06 Principles that personal representatives should observe when investing. The first duty of the personal representatives is to acquaint themselves with the true extent of their power of investment, if necessary with legal advice.[14] The fact that an investment is within the *words* of an investment clause is not conclusive that it was a proper investment, if those who complain of it can show it was imprudent,[15] as occasionally happens.[16] The dangers of investing money in mortgages have been recognised by the courts,[17] and by trustees and personal representatives. Although authority to *invest* in land does not authorise the purchase of a residence,[18] a power to *apply* (as distinct from a power to invest) money in the purchase of a residence may be available as one of the S.L.A. powers under section 73(1)(xi).[19] The duties facing those exercising a power of investment were reviewed generally in a case about a pension fund (held not to be in a special category); they are in brief:

---

[10] s.6(1)(b).

[11] Although the phrase "blue chip" has been held to be without a definite objective meaning and so void: *Re Kolb* [1962] Ch. 531.

[12] See *Nestle v. National Westminster Bank* [1993] 1 W.L.R. 1260 per Staughton L.J. at p. 1278D–E.

[13] s.2.

[14] *Nestle v. National Westminster Bank* [1993] 1 W.L.R. 1260.

[15] Underhill, *Trusts* (8th ed.) by Sir Arthur Underhill, at p. 289; (14th ed.), at p. 257.

[16] See *Bartlett v. Barclays Bank* [1980] Ch. 515, where a trustee was liable for an imprudent speculation with trust money, and was not protected by the absolute investment clause.

[17] *Re Wellsted* [1949] Ch. 296, Greene M.R. at pp. 312–313.

[18] *Re Power's Will Trusts* [1947] Ch. 572.

[19] *Re Wellsted* above.

(i)   to hold the scales impartially between the different classes of beneficiary;

(ii)   to put aside their own personal interest and views (such as their views on alcohol, tobacco, armaments or other things) unless;

(iii) every beneficiary is an adult who holds the same views (a position unlikely in administering an estate);

(iv) to take the ordinary care that a prudent man would take of other people's money and to obtain advice, which should be rejected only if it really is prudent to reject such advice; and

(v)   to consider diversification of investments.[20]

In practice, the selection of investments that will retain their real value and provide a reasonable income is difficult.

35–07 Powers during a minority. When a minor is beneficially interested in the estate, the personal representatives become trustees,[21] of the assets held for the minors. They then have under A.E.A. 1925, s.39 and under the Trustee Act 1925, s.68(17) the powers of trustees. These powers are extensive. Important powers are, the power to apply income for a minor's benefit or to accumulate income under the Trustee Act 1925, s.31[22]; and the power of advancement of capital under the Trustee Act 1925, s.32, that is to say, the power to apply capital for the permanent benefit of a minor beneficiary with a future interest with the consent of anyone with a prior interest.

These powers are discussed in the books on trusts.

35–08 Tax. It is often possible for personal representatives to achieve a similar result in more than one way, having different tax consequences in England and Wales. There are also tax considerations in relation to property outside the United Kingdom. In some continental countries, the rate of tax on local property passing after a death varies according to the relationship of the deceased to the successor. Those in a fiduciary position should give attention to the tax consequence of any proposed exercise of their powers[23]; one power to which this may be relevant is the power of appropriation in the distribution of the residuary estate.

---

[20] *Cowan v. Scargill* [1985] Ch. 270: the judgment deals with the general duty of persons investing in a fiduciary capacity.

[21] *Re Smith* (1889) 42 Ch.Div. 302; *Re Ponder* [1921] 2 Ch. 59; *Re Cockburn's Will Trusts* [1957] Ch. 438.

[22] See Snell, *Equity*, at pp. 276–279.

[23] *Re Collard* [1961] Ch. 293 at p. 302; *Re Pilkington* [1964] A.C. 612 at p. 632; *Nestle v. National Westminster Bank* [1993] 1 W.L.R. 1260 (investment in gilt edged stock exempt from tax and Inheritance Tax, when the beneficiaries are not resident or domiciled in the U.K.).

36. Inventory and accounts; duty to disclose advice

36–01 Duty to keep accounts. Personal representatives must keep accounts[1]; and must make them available for inspection by a beneficiary or a creditor. The right of inspection includes a right to take copies[2]; but those exercising the right must pay the costs of supplying the information.[3] As regards obtaining copies from the personal representatives, it was held, in 1845 an era when copies could only be made by hand, that the right to inspect accounts only carries a right to receive a copy on payment of the copying cost[4]; text books repeat this as the current law.[5] It is open to doubt whether (now that copies can be made speedily and cheaply) it is still the law that those who ask for a copy must pay the copying cost: the question seems unlikely to arise. In 1845, this point and other points constituted "wanton, unnecessary and improper litigation" that was "perfectly useless to every party concerned in it."[6] The modern practice of personal representatives is not to ask for the photocopying cost.

36–02 Alternative remedies. For historical reasons there are two remedies open against personal representatives for those seeking information that has not been supplied: an inventory or an account.

---

[1] A.E.A. 1925, s.25(b) substituted by A.E.A. 1971, re-stating the previous law.
[2] Withers, *Reversions* (2nd ed.), at p. 169, citing *Mutter v. Eastern and Midlands Railway Co.* (1888) 38 Ch.Div. 92 at p. 105, and other authorities.
[3] *Re Bosworth* (1889) 58 L.J.Ch. 432.
[4] *Ottley v. Gilby* (1845) 8 Beav. 602.
[5] Underhill, *Trusts* (8th ed.) by Sir Arthur Underhill (1926) at p. 338; (14th ed.), at p. 584; Lewin, *Trusts* (16th ed.) p. 628, n. 49.
[6] *Ottley v. Gilbey* above.

36–03 Inventory. A remedy available in the Family Division is an order for an inventory of the estate; sought on a summons to a district judge.[7] This is occasionally done[8]; but the absence of a convenient procedure for further judicial investigation makes it a less satisfactory remedy than an account.

36–04 Account. In the Chancery Division the remedy available is an order for an account, which may be made on originating summons and affidavit evidence,[9] even when the plaintiff alleges misconduct by the personal representatives.[10]

The court may, and usually does, adjourn such an application to enable the personal representatives to furnish proper accounts.[11] Alternatively, the court may make an order for an account to be taken, and reserve the costs until the account has been taken.[12] When an account is ordered to be taken, the account is taken before a Master.[13] Then the usual course is for the party objecting to any entry in the accounts provided, to specify the error complained of[14]; the validity of each objection is then determined.

36–05 Account on the basis of wilful default, and maladministration appearing on taking accounts. These matters are discussed in paragraph 45–02 under maladministration.

36–06 Duty to disclose advice. Personal representatives, like trustees, often obtain advice from counsel or solicitors about the administration. The personal representatives must on request disclose such advice to any beneficiary in the estate[15]; but not to a mere claimant.[16] They are, however, not bound to disclose their reasons for the exercise of a discretion, nor any record of such reasons.[17] Once an adverse claim is made against the personal representatives, they need not disclose advice given in relation to the claim[18]; but they must still disclose previous advice not relating to the claim.[19]

---

[7] N.C.P.R. 1987, r. 61(2).
[8] As in *Re Thomas* [1956] 1 W.L.R. 1516 where a former administrator had been ordered to make an inventory.
[9] R.S.C., Ord. 85, r. 2(3)(a); Ord. 36, r. 2(3).
[10] Ord. 85, r. 4.
[11] Ord. 85, r. 5(2)(a).
[12] *Att.-Gen. v. Cockle* [1988] Ch. 414 at pp. 420–421, applying *Re Richardson* [1919] 2 Ch. 50.
[13] Ord. 85, r. 2(1) and r. 4; Ord. 43.
[14] Ord. 43, rr. 4 and 5.
[15] *Wynne v. Humbertson* (1858) 27 Beav. 421; *Re Londonderry* [1965] Ch. 918. See para. 36–01 about the copying cost.
[16] *Wynne v. Humbertson* above.
[17] *Re Londonderry* above; the dicta that the appeal there was irregular are in conflict with the decision of the Court of Appeal in *Re Radnor* (1890) 45 Ch. Div. 402 at p. 423: not cited in *Re Londonderry* and not mentioned in the headnote to *Re Radnor*.
[18] *Brown v. Oakshott* (1849) 12 Beav. 252.
[19] *Devaynes v. Robinson* (1855) 20 Beav. 42.

37. Expenses of personal representatives and remuneration of personal representatives

37–01 Expenses. The Trustee Act 1925, applying to personal representatives,[1] provides:

> "**s.68(17)** "Trust" does not include the duties incident to an estate conveyed by way of mortgage, but with this exception the expressions "trust" and "trustee" extend to implied and constructive trusts, and to cases where the trustee has a beneficial interest in the trust property, and to the duties incident to the office of a personal representative, and "trustee" where the context admits, includes a personal representative, and "new trustee" includes an additional trustee;"

The principle settled before the 1925 Act remains the law, that those who act in a fiduciary capacity:

---

[1] s.68(17).

"Are not expected to do any of the work at their own expense; they are entitled to be indemnified against the cost and expenses which they incur in the course of their office; of course that necessarily means that such costs and expenses are properly incurred and not improperly incurred."[2]

For this purpose what is proper or improper is considered from the point of view of the estate; it may therefore extend to liability in tort incurred by the ordinary and reasonable management of the deceased's business.[3] The personal representatives' costs and expenses falling on the estate include those of their solicitor acting in non-contentious business (that is to say when there is no litigation. Litigation costs are discussed in Chapter 42 below).

37–02 Incidence of expenses in the estate. Personal representatives, like trustees, are entitled to the indemnity out of capital and income of the estate. As between income and capital, income bears all ordinary outgoings of a recurrent nature, such as annual taxes, and interest on charges and incumbrances; capital must bear all costs, charges and expenses incurred for the benefit of the whole estate.[4]

37–03 Interest on expenses. In the ordinary way, personal representatives in need of money not immediately realisable in the estate, borrow it at interest. The interest is then itself a proper expense. A trust corporation, acting as executor, may lend the money to itself, being authorised to enjoy interest by its standard terms applicable under the deceased's will, or by the authority of the beneficiaries. Unless expressly authorised to lend the estate money at interest, it is unwise for a personal representative to lend his own money to the estate, even though it is solvent. There is authority to the effect that such a personal representative is not then entitled to interest on the money,[5] unless all the personal representatives have discharged an interest bearing debt.[6] The judicial attitude to the award of interest nowadays (with high rates of interest and a currency whose value tends to diminish) is different from what it was in

---

[2] Danckwerts J. in *Re Grimthorpe* [1958] Ch. 615 at p. 623; the dictum is of general application. The case concerned fees paid to counsel by trustees which had been in part disallowed by the taxing master; the fees were allowed to the trustees, on the basis that the disallowance was on a wrong principle. A similar earlier case is *Re Robertson* [1949] W.N. 225 (where the taxing master had disallowed £2 of charge that trustees had paid for a shorthand note and transcript, and the £2 was allowed to the trustees).

[3] *Re Raybould* [1900] 1 Ch. 199. The position of personal representatives as regards the deceased's business is discussed in Chap. 20.

[4] *Carver v. Duncan* [1985] A.C. 1082 (a tax case) at p. 1120, citing authorities.

[5] *Lewis v. Lewis* (1850) 13 Beav. 82; and *Gordon v. Trail* (1820) 8 Price 416.

[6] *Finch v. Pescott* (1874) 17 Eq. 554, as explained in *Re Bracey* [1936] Ch. 690 at p. 694.

Victorian times. Notwithstanding the rule against self-dealing,[7] and
the inapplicable terms of S.C.A. 1981, s.35A: if the point arises, the
court might be able to award interest on advances made by personal
representatives. Meanwhile personal representatives should not
themselves lend money for the benefit of the estate, but should
borrow it elsewhere.

QUANTIFICATION OF SOLICITORS' REMUNERATION

37–04 Quantification of solicitors' remuneration. Most personal
representatives employ a solicitor, and may need to know the three
different ways in which the reasonableness of the amount of a
solicitor's bill for non-contentious work may, if doubted, be
ascertained.[8]

37–05 Law Society's certificate. The personal representatives have
a right to require the Law Society to certify what sum is fair and
reasonable for the work done. That sum, if less than the amount of
the solicitor's bill, is what is then payable.[9] A solicitor must inform
the client in writing of this right and that the right may only be
exercised within one month after receiving such information. It may
not be exercised after the bill has been paid, nor after the court has
ordered the bill to be "taxed."[10]

This summary procedure does not involve costs and in practice it is
not found useful in reducing fees.

37–06 Taxation on the client's application. Another course open to
a client (here the personal representatives) is to apply to the court to
have the bill "taxed"[11] (that is to say judicially determined: the word
has in this context nothing to do with compulsory payments to the
government). Within one month of receiving the bill, there is right to
a taxation; and up to one year after receiving the bill, there is a
discretionary power for the court to order a taxation; after a year
there is no power to order a taxation.[12] The subject is dealt with in
the notes to the section in *The Supreme Court Practice 1995*, Vol. 2,
pp. 1173 to 1176. The papers are then lodged with the High Court's
Taxing Office; and the propriety of the bill is considered at a hearing
by one of the Taxing Masters[13] of the High Court (appointed to

---

[7] Chap. 34.
[8] See paras. 37–05, 37–06 and 37–07 below.
[9] Solicitors Remuneration Order 1972 (1972 S.I. No. 1139), art. 3.
[10] See para. 37–06 below.
[11] Under the Solicitors Act 1974, s.70.
[12] *Harrison v. Tew* [1990] 2 A.C. 523.
[13] R.S.C., Ord. 62, r. 1(2).

conduct taxations). The basis of such a taxation is the indemnity basis, defined[14] as follows:

> "r. 12(2) On a taxation on the indemnity basis all costs shall be allowed except insofar as they are of an unreasonable amount or have been unreasonably incurred and any doubts which the taxing officer may have as to whether the costs were reasonably incurred or were reasonable in amount shall be resolved in favour of the receiving party; and in these rules the term "the indemnity basis" in relation to the taxation of costs shall be construed accordingly."

and on the following presumption[15]:

> "r. 15(2) On a taxation to which this rule applies costs shall be taxed on the indemnity basis but shall be presumed—
> (a) to have been reasonably incurred if they were incurred with the express or implied approval of the client, and
> (b) to have been reasonable in amount if their amount was expressly or impliedly approved by the client, and
> (c) to have been unreasonably incurred if in the circumstances of the case they are of an unusual natureunless the solicitor satisfies the taxing officer that prior to their being incurred he informed his client that they might not be allowed on a taxation of costs inter partes."

The solicitor is normally entitled to require the client to pay the solicitor's own costs of the taxation, unless, as occasionally happens, the Taxing Master thinks it right in the circumstances of the case to make some other order.[16] For a convenient and accessible description of what actually happens on a taxation see the case cited in the footnote.[17] The outcome is hard to predict; for as was rightly said in argument there,[18] "Taxation is necessarily not a very precise art."

There is a right, rarely exercised, to have the Taxing Master's decision reviewed by a judge.[19]

37-07 Taxation on a beneficiary's application. It is not only the personal representatives who may have their solicitor's bill taxed. There is a discretionary power for the court to order the bill to be

---

[14] Ord. 62, r. 12(2).
[15] r. 15(2).
[16] Ord. 62, r. 27.
[17] *Re Eastwood* [1975] Ch. 112, the fees of an employed solicitor on taxation.
[18] *ibid.* at p. 129A.
[19] Ord. 62, r. 35.

taxed in the same way on the application of a beneficiary in the estate.[20]

REMUNERATION OF PERSONAL REPRESENTATIVES

37–08 General position. Personal representatives are only entitled to remuneration for their services when it is duly authorised.[21] Modern wills often confer such authority, which binds beneficiaries, who take only what the will gives them. Such a provision ranks as a gift by the deceased and so it is inoperative in favour of a witness who has attested the will.[22] It does take effect however in favour of an attesting witness to the will who is appointed a trustee after the death.[23]

When the will does not authorise remuneration, the personal representatives must either act without remuneration (which those in a professional position such as solicitors and accountants might be unwilling to do; and so might a corporate trustee), or they must obtain authority to charge remuneration.

37–09 Authority from beneficiaries for remuneration. When every beneficiary affected is an ascertained adult or corporation, they can together confer authority for the personal representatives to receive remuneration in a solvent estate. Those affected will usually be the residuary beneficiaries, and if one or more of them are without legal capacity, for example minors, the adult beneficiaries may wish to authorise remuneration out of their own beneficial shares only.

37–10 Authority from the court for remuneration. There is jurisdiction for the court to authorise remuneration of personal representatives[24]; either by an order made in the Family Division when the grant is sought, or at a later stage in the Chancery Division. The question should be considered at the outset. There is a dictum

---

[20] Solicitors Act 1974, s.71.

[21] *Re Duke of Norfolk's Settlement Trusts* [1982] Ch. 61; citing cases from *Robinson* v. *Pett* (1734) 3 P.W. 249, when the principle that such persons must act without charge was already an "established rule."

[22] *Re Pooley* (1888) 40 Ch.Div. 1.

[23] *Re Royce's Will Trusts* [1959] Ch. 626. The same reasoning applies to an attesting witness appointed a personal representative afterwards, either on a grant being made or under A.J.A. 1985, s.50.

[24] Under the statutory power when a trust corporation is *appointed* by the court to act: Trustee Act 1925, s.42 read with s.68(17); under the inherent jurisdiction in other cases: *Re Norfolk* above. This inherent jurisdiction goes back to *Brocksopp* v. *Barnes* (1820) 5 Madd. 90, and is not now open to doubt: *Re Norfolk* above at pp. 76 and 80. It includes power to authorise the retention by trustees of directors' fees paid by companies in which the trust has a controlling interest: *Re Keeler's Settlement Trusts* [1981] Ch. 156; the decision is applicable to personal representatives.

that after a grant, remuneration should only be allowed sparingly and in exceptional cases.[25] In practice, the power is exercised more readily than that; but the acceptance of a grant of representation without such a provision is an argument against authorising it later.

37–11 Greater effect of the court's authority. In an estate that turns out to be insolvent, authority conferred by a will or by the beneficiaries is ineffective; for it cannot bind creditors.[26] An order of the court, however, will bind creditors.

37–12 Subsequent court authority in special circumstances. There is a discretionary jurisdiction for the court to allow remuneration for exceptional services,[27] and this applies to personal representatives. In any ordinary state of affairs, however, such an application is in practice unlikely to succeed.

---

[25] *Re Worthington* [1954] 1 W.L.R. 526 Upjohn J. at p. 530; cited without comment in *Re Norfolk* above at p. 74. Remuneration is frequently authorised now, and no longer regarded with the suspicion it incurred at one time: *Ayliffe v. Murray* (1740) 2 Atk. 58; *Barrett v. Hartley* (1866) 2 Eq. 789: both decided on their own facts.

[26] *Re White* [1898] 2 Ch. 217; *Re Salmen* (1912) 107 L.T. 108.

[27] *Re Macadam* [1945] 2 All E.R. 664 at p. 669 (omitted from [1945] Ch. 73); *Phipps v. Boardman* [1964] 1 W.L.R. 993 at p. 1018 (where it was to be "on a liberal scale"); affirmed [1965] Ch. 992, and [1967] 2 A.C. 46; *Re Keeler* above. The jurisdiction was again recognised, but not applied on the facts, in *Guinness v. Saunders* [1990] 2 A.C. 663.

38. Completion of the administration

38–01 Completion of the administration and right to a release
38–02 Payment into court instead of distributing out of court, or applying for the court's directions: the last resort
38–03 Change of duty on becoming a trustee
38–04 Other results of personal representatives becoming trustees
38–05 Following assets

38–01 Completion of the administration and right to a release. When the personal representatives have paid the debts and legacies and distributed all the estate the administration is at an end.

On paying a legacy, the personal representatives are entitled to a receipt.[1] On distributing residue, they are entitled to have the accounts settled (that is to say agreed)[2]; that is normally done by the beneficiaries signing the accounts. There is normally no right to require a release to be by deed.[3] Nowadays the effectiveness of a release is unlikely to be affected by whether it is signed, or is by deed.

When the estate is not all immediately distributable, the personal representatives acquire the additional character of trustees; being either trustees of the trusts of the will, or trustees for the purposes of the intestacy (under the A.E.A. 1925, s.46 and s.47) or partial intestacy (section 49).

It is sometimes open to doubt whether that time has arrived or not on the facts of a particular case; as appears from the cases cited in paragraph 38–03 below.

38–02 Payment into court instead of distributing out of court, or applying for the court's directions: the last resort. Personal representatives who cannot otherwise get a good discharge for a

---

[1] *Re Roberts* (1868) 38 L.J.Ch. 708.
[2] *Chadwick v. Heatley* (1845) 2 Coll. 671.
[3] *King v. Mullins* (1852) 1 Drew 308; *Tiger v. Barclays Bank* [1951] 2 K.B. 556, affirmed on other points [1952] 1 All E.R. 85.

legacy or for residue may, as a last resort, pay the money into court.[4] It is hardly ever the right course to take; personal representatives should only pay money into court when advised that no other course is possible. In particular, it is almost always better to apply for the court's directions.[5] Payment into court incurs a risk depending on all the circumstances, of the personal representatives being deprived of their costs or of being ordered to pay costs. Thus, "I can find no excuse for their having paid the money into court except a restless anxiety to get rid of it, and I cannot relieve them from the payment of costs."[6]

38–03 Change of duty on becoming a trustee. As long as the administration is continuing, a beneficiary does not have an interest in any specified asset of the estate but only a right to have the estate duly administered.[7] This means that in dealing with the estate, personal representatives must consider the position of the estate as a whole; rather than hold a balance between the beneficiaries.[8] This is different from the duty of trustees to hold a balance evenly between the beneficiaries.[9] The point does not often make a practical difference; but it is important in theory, illustrating the continuing difference between the common law governing the administration of estates (though adjudicated in the Chancery Division) and equity governing trusts.[10]

38–04 Other results of personal representatives becoming trustees. Property other than land may be dealt with by one only of the personal representatives[11]; but a majority of trustees cannot bind the minority,[12] unless authorised to do so by the trust instrument or under the directions of the court. New trustees can only be appointed under the Trustee Act 1925 when those holding the property are trustees.[13] Land in England continues to be held by personal representatives in the character of personal representatives until an assent in writing is made.[14] Until that time, they may make title as

---

[4] Trustee Act 1925, s.63, read with s.68(17).
[5] See Chap. 42.
[6] Re Elliott (1873) 15 Eq. 194, Mallins V.-C. at p. 199.
[7] Sudeley v. Att.-Gen. [1897] A.C. 11; Dr. Barnardo's Homes v. Income Tax Special Commissioners [1921] 2 A.C. 1; Commissioner of Stamp Duties v. Livingston [1965] A.C. 694; Re Cunliffe-Owen (No. 2) [1953] Ch. 545; Marshall v. Kerr [1995] 1 A.C. 148.
[8] Re Hayes [1971] 1 W.L.R. 758.
[9] Re Hayes.
[10] See para. 2–10.
[11] Attenborough v. Solomon [1913] A.C. 76; and see Wise v. Whitburn [1924] 1 Ch. 460; no longer law as to leaseholds: A.E.A. 1925, s.2(2).
[12] Luke v. South Kensington Hotel (1879) 11 Ch.Div. 121; except that a majority of trustees of a charitable trust can bind the minority: Re Whiteley [1910] 1 Ch. 600.
[13] Re Ponder [1921] 2 Ch. 59; Re Cockburn [1957] Ch. 438.
[14] Re King [1964] Ch. 542.

personal representatives; and until then a sole personal representative may convey land and give a good receipt.[15] A sole *trustee* (unless a trust corporation) cannot convey land.[16]

The question whether personal representatives have become trustees may arise in an action concerning trust property, or the deceased's property. When time runs under the Limitation Act 1980,[17] an action to recover *trust* property is barred by limitation in six years[18]; but an action by a beneficiary to recover the *personal estate of a deceased person*[19] is barred only after 12 years.[20] This difference means that in the rare cases where an action is brought after the expiry of six years and before 12 years, it is necessary to determine whether the defendant has become a trustee.[21]

38–05 Following assets. The remedy of a claimant, whether as creditor or beneficiary, who finds the estate of a deceased person has been lawfully distributed, is to follow the assets into the hands of the recipient, who may be liable to recoup such assets, unless a purchaser for value without notice.[22] Such a claim is not part of the administration of the estate; and the personal representatives need not be made a party to such a claim.[23] An unlawful distribution is maladministration: see Chapter 45.

---

[15] L.P.A. 1925, s.28(1); A.E.A. 1925, s.2(1).

[16] L.P.A. 1925, s.27(2) applying "notwithstanding anything to the contrary in the instrument (if any) creating a trust for sale of land or in the settlement of the net proceeds"; Trustee Act 1925, s.14(2).

[17] Time does not run at all in respect of property wrongfully held or retained (section 21(1) of the Act) nor against those whose rights are future rights (section 21(3) there), nor in respect of those whose time limit to sue is extended under Part II of the Act.

[18] Limitation Act 1980, s.21.

[19] With the same exception.

[20] s.22; the section does not apply to a creditor: *Re Blow* [1914] 1 Ch. 233.

[21] *Re Swain* [1891] 3 Ch. 233; *Re Timmis* [1902] 1 Ch. 176; *Re Richardson* [1920] 1 Ch. 423. When this question arises, see the commentaries on the Limitation Act 1980.

[22] *Ministry of Health v. Simpson* [1951] A.C. 251, affirming *Re Diplock* [1948] Ch. 465; *Chase-Manhattan Bank N.A. v. Israel-British* [1981] Ch. 105; *Agip (Africa) v. Jackson* [1990] Ch. 265; Snell, *Equity*, at pp. 299–305.

[23] *Clegg v. Rowland* (1866) L.R. 3 Eq. 368; *Hunter v. Young* (1879) 4 Ex.Div. 256.

Part Seven: Insolvent Estates; Acting as Personal Representative without Authority

39. Insolvent estates

39–01 Insolvency. An estate is insolvent "if when realised it will be insufficient to meet in full all the debts and liabilities to which it is subject"[1]; including future payments during an annuitant's lifetime of an annuity for which the deceased was liable.[2] There is no benefit in taking out a grant of representation to an estate known at the outset to be insolvent, except to a creditor[3] who wishes to get the estate duly administered. The insolvency may emerge during the course of administration after a grant of representation has been made. The question of the estate's solvency or insolvency is not often in doubt; the personal representatives may obtain[4] an order for an inquiry whether or not the estate is solvent.[5] Under the modern practice, the point might be determined on the hearing of the application without ordering a formal inquiry.[6]

The personal representatives have to consider what to do when the estate turns out to be insolvent. There are three possibilities: to administer the estate themselves; to obtain the administration of the estate in bankruptcy; or to seek its administration by the court; the Chancery Division or the county court.

39–02 Administration of an insolvent estate without applying to the court. If administering the estate themselves, the personal representatives are bound to administer it in the same way as in

---

[1] Insolvency Act 1986, s.421(4).
[2] *Re Pink* [1927] 1 Ch. 237.
[3] Under N.C.P.R. 1987, r. 22(3), on clearing off those with a prior claim by citation.
[4] Under R.S.C., Ord. 85, r. 2. See Chap. 42.
[5] As in *Re Smith* (1883) 22 Ch.Div. 586 at p. 592.
[6] Ord. 85, r. 2.

bankruptcy.[7] This is a thankless task, even in a simple case. If the deceased's will had authorised remuneration for the executors, that provision will fail, for such remuneration, however well earned, is considered to be a testamentary gift[8]; unlike an Order of the court[9] authorising such remuneration, which (if made) would continue to operate.[10]

39–03 Application to the court under the Insolvency Act 1986, s.421. The simplest course is for the personal representatives to apply under the Insolvency Act 1986, s.421 to have the estate administered in bankruptcy, or to procure a creditor to apply for that. Then the personal representatives obtain complete protection[11]; and are rid of a troublesome and sometimes complicated task. It appears no longer to be the law that such administration can be ordered only when there is a subsisting grant.[12] Such an order does not require the estate to be administered by an insolvency practitioner.[13]

39–04 Administration by the court. The remaining course is administration of the estate by the court; that is to say, in practice under the directions of a Chancery Master or of a county court district judge. Where the estate is plainly insolvent, this procedure does not offer any practical advantage over administration in bankruptcy (except that relatives of the deceased may feel it is more respectful to the memory of the deceased). Administration by the court is appropriate when it is not certain whether the estate is solvent or is insolvent.

Administration by the court is sought on originating summons.[14] It may be ordered when sought by a creditor; it may probably be ordered when sought by the personal representatives against a creditor who is willing to be made a defendant for that purpose.[15] It has been held, however, that such an order will not be made for the

---

[7] Insolvency Act 1986, s.421 and Administration of Estates of Deceased Persons Order 1986 (S.I. No. 1999); replacing the repealed A.E.A. 1925, s.34(1) and First Schedule, Pt I. Moreover, the personal representatives have no protection from personal liability to a creditor of a higher degree if paying a debt of a lower degree once the personal representatives have reason to believe that the estate is insolvent: A.E.A. 1971, s.10(2); this is a deterrent to the administration of an insolvent estate without applying to the court.

[8] *Re Barber* (1886) 31 Ch.Div. 665; *Re Pooley* (1888) 40 Ch.Div. 1; *Re Brown* [1918] W.N. 118.

[9] See para. 37–11 above.

[10] S.C.A. 1981, s.19.

[11] *Re Bradley* [1956] Ch. 615 Upjohn J. at p. 622, on the previous Act.

[12] *Re a Debtor* [1939] Ch. 594 decided on the words of the repealed Act, see at p. 600.

[13] The 1986 Order (above), Art. 4(1).

[14] Under R.S.C., Ord. 85, r. 2.

[15] *Re Bradley* [1956] Ch. 615, Upjohn J. *obiter* at p. 621.

protection of the personal representatives against a creditor who is not willing to be a defendant[16]; they must procure a friendly creditor to claim administration by the court.[17]

---

[16] *Re Bradley* above, not following *Buccle v. Atleo* (1687) 2 Vern. 37, but applying *Mandeville v. Mandeville* (1888) 23 L.R.Ir. 339.

[17] *Re Bradley* would be followed now; an alteration in the rules to enable such relief to be given to personal representatives seems desirable. For further information on the law of insolvency—see Fletcher, *Law of Insolvency*.

40. Acting as personal representative without authority— executor *de son tort*

40–01 Executor *de son tort*. Someone, who without lawful authority acts as a personal representative of a deceased person, is known at common law as an executor *de son tort*. The statutory provision, in the Administration of Estates Act 1925, s.28, is:

> "**28.** If any person, to the defrauding of creditors or without full valuable consideration, obtains, receives or holds any real or personal estate of a deceased person or effects the release of any debt or liability due to the estate of the deceased, he shall be charged as executor in his own wrong to the extent of the real and personal estate received or coming to his hands, or the debt or liability released, after deducting—
>
> (a) any debt for valuable consideration and without fraud due to him from the deceased person at the time of his death; and
>
> (b) any payment made by him which might properly be made by a personal representative."

There are authorities going back some time[1] on the subject; but it is nowadays a question of fact in each case whether or not section 28

---

[1] From *Stokes v. Porter* (1558) 2 Dyer 166b.

applies. The requirements in the section of either defrauding creditors or getting property without full and valuable consideration protect those who after a death do acts of kindness, such as safeguarding the deceased's property or seeing to the burial. To incur liability under section 28, there must in fact be a positive meddling in the administration.

The following are examples of acts by an individual or a company being held to make such person an executor *de son tort*: (i) taking possession of the rents and profits of the deceased's land[2]; (ii) administering the estate as personal representative in England under an overseas grant, not effective in England[3]; (iii) a nominee company registered overseas causing money due to the deceased to be transmitted abroad[4]; and (iv) acting as administrator (though entitled to obtain a grant) before the date of the grant of letters of administration.[5]

A minor cannot be liable as an executor *de son tort*.[6]

40–02 Liability. An executor *de son tort* is liable under section 28 to account to the true personal representatives, or to the deceased's creditors or beneficiaries for the assets he has received. The liability is asserted by a claim for an account of the estate coming to his hands,[7] and for consequential relief.

An executor *de son tort* is allowed, in addition to what is mentioned in section 28, what he has paid to the lawful personal representative; and is discharged by settlement with such personal representative.[8] An executor *de son tort* may be made liable for inheritance tax[9]; and so care should be taken not to deal with the estate of a deceased person that might be liable to inheritance tax without a valid U.K. grant.

An executor *de son tort* of a deceased sole executor who died without completing the administration of the first testator's estate, is himself liable in addition as executor *de son tort* of the first testator.[10]

40–03 No authority. The position of an executor *de son tort* involves liability to the relevant extent, but it does not confer authority. When therefore an executor, *de son tort* made an agreement on behalf of the estate which afterwards turned out to be

---

[2] *Williams v. Heales* (1874) L.R. 9 C.P. 177, approved in *Stratford-upon-Avon v. Parker* [1914] 2 K.B. 562.
[3] *Re Lovett* (1876) 3 Ch.Div. 198; *New York Breweries v. Att.-Gen.* [1899] A.C. 62.
[4] *I.R.C. v. Stype Investments* [1982] Ch. 456.
[5] *Mills v. Anderson* [1984] Q.B. 704.
[6] *Stott v. Meanock* (1862) 6 L.T. 592, not affected by the Minors Contracts Act 1987.
[7] *Coote v. Whittington* (1873) 16 Eq. 534.
[8] *Hill v. Curtis* (1865) 1 Eq. 90.
[9] Inheritance Tax Act 1984 as amended s.199(4)(a); and A.E.A. 1925, s.55(1)(xi).
[10] *Meyrick v. Anderson* (1850) 14 Q.B. 719; this appears to be applicable to s.28.

unwise, it was held not to bind him as administrator on behalf of the estate when she afterwards became the lawful administratrix.[11]

40–04   No estate.   An executor *de son tort* is not liable personally to a lessor on the covenants of the lease by privity of estate; for an executor *de son tort* has no estate[12]; but may be liable to the lessor by estoppel.[13] The liability as executor *de son tort* is limited to the assets received.

40–05   Limitation.   The limitation period (unless extended by dis-ability) for a claim for an account against an executor *de son tort* is 12 years from the date when the right accrued.[14] In the present state of the authorities about accrual,[15] any such claim should be brought within 12 years of the date of the death.

40–06   Procedure.   When there is a lawfully constituted personal representative, a claim against an executor *de son tort* can be made by originating summons under R.S.C., Ord. 85. If not, Order 85 is not applicable; for it requires the lawful personal representatives to be a party[16]; and so, in the absence of any lawful personal representative, a claim against an executor *de son tort* must either be brought by writ, or by originating summons under the different provisions of Order 5, rule 4.

---

[11] *Mills v. Anderson* above; s.28 was treated as so clearly inapplicable that it was not mentioned according to the report; nor was the definition of "personal representative" in A.E.A. 1925, s.55(1)(xi); where the reference to a person who takes possession of or intermeddles with the property of a deceased person might have provided an argument, probably unsuccessful, in favour of the defendant.

[12] *Stratford-upon-Avon v. Parker* [1914] 2 K.B. 562.

[13] *Williams v. Heales* (1874) L.R. 9 C.P. 177 as explained in *Stratford-upon-Avon v. Parker* above.

[14] Limitation Act 1980, ss.22, 23 and 18.

[15] See Franks on *Limitation of Actions*, at pp. 50–51; and *Doyle v. Foley* [1903] 2 Ir. 95.

[16] Ord. 85, r. 3(1); as before the modern procedure, when general administration could not be ordered in the absence of the deceased's legal personal representative: *Rowsell v. Morris* (1873) 17 Eq. 20.

Part Eight: Proceedings in Court

41. Probate actions; actions to challenge a nomination

PROBATE ACTIONS

41–01 Definition. A probate action is defined[1] as:

"An action for the grant of probate of the will or letters of administration of the estate of a deceased person or for the revocation of such a grant or for a decree pronouncing for or against the validity of an alleged will, not being an action which is non-contentious or common form probate business."

In this connection, "will" includes codicil[2]; and "action" includes a counterclaim.[3] A probate action is brought by writ in the Chancery Division of the High Court.[4] It may be brought in the county court, when within the county court's jurisdiction.[5]

---

[1] R.S.C., Ord. 76, r. 1(2).
[2] r. 1(3).
[3] r. 8.
[4] r. 2(1).
[5] C.C.A. 1984, s.32.

41–02 Parties. A probate action is brought between those with an interest in the question,[6] including the executors under any will sought to be impugned.[7] The decision binds anyone with notice[8] of the action.[9] It is important to join (as defendants to the action or by a Court Notice under R.S.C., Ord. 15, r. 13A) all with an interest or a potential interest in the estate: so that they are bound by the result if the action is decided at a trial, or so that their consent to a compromise may be obtained. This is specially important in respect of anyone under a disability who can only agree to a compromise through the court's approval.[10] When an order is made in a probate action determining the question, the resulting grant is a grant in solemn form.[11] When the matter is agreed or is compromised after a probate action has been begun, this is more satisfactory than discontinuing the action and obtaining a grant in common form.[11a] The power to "pass over" (that is to say displace) an executor[12] is occasionally exercised at the trial of a probate action.[13]

41–03 Affidavit of scripts. Each party to a probate action (that is to say) the plaintiff and every defendant who has acknowledged service, (so as to take part in the action) must[14] at an early stage of a probate action lodge an affidavit of scripts specifying all "scripts"[15] known to that party and lodge with the court all scripts in that party's possession or under his control.[16] This must be done before knowing[17] the contents of any other party's affidavit of scripts. This salutary requirement[18] prevents the suppression of scripts, and preserves them. It facilitates the performance of the court's duty to the deceased to see his last wishes carried out.[19] It is distinct from *discovery on the pleadings*, which follows in the usual way under Order 24. The court takes custody of all scripts and of any subsisting grant impugned in the action.[20]

---

[6] r. 2(2).

[7] r. 3.

[8] Under Ord. 15, r. 13A, or otherwise.

[9] *Re Langton* [1964] P. 163, reviewing cases back to 1814.

[10] See para. 41–09 below.

[11] See para. 2–11

[11a] Ord. 76, r. 11.

[12] See para. 3–05.

[13] S.C.A. 1981, s.116 and Schedule One para. 1(h).

[14] Ord. 76, r. 5.

[15] Meaning a will or draft thereof, written instructions for a will made by or at the request or under the instructions of the testator and any document purporting to be evidence of the contents or to be a copy of a will which is alleged to be lost or destroyed.

[16] r. 5.

[17] r. 5(4), unless leave to the contrary is given; which is unlikely.

[18] Going back to the 1862 Rules: Pt 2, rr. 30 and 31, printed in Mortimer, *Probate* (2nd ed.), at p. 868.

[19] Tristram & Coote (14th ed.) (1905), the last in Dr Tristram's lifetime at p. 443; (27th ed.) at p. 665.

[20] r. 4.

41–04 Statements of the deceased person whose estate is the subject matter of the case; statements of witnesses to a script. A statement by the deceased does not rank as hearsay under the law of evidence[21]; but, according to Lord Eldon L.C.: "Few Declarations deserve less credit than those of Men as to what they have done by their Wills"; there must be taken into consideration "The Wish to silence importunity, to elude Questions from persons who take upon them to judge of their own Claims ... with a fair Regard to the prima facie import, and the possible Intention, connected with all the other circumstances"[22] Testators still have such wishes, and make misleading statements to those who hope to be testamentary beneficiaries.

On discovery, statements made by a witness to any will in so far as appertaining to attestation and execution must be disclosed. They are not subject to privilege, on the theory that witnesses to the will are the witnesses of the court, not of a party.[23]

41–05 Interlocutory relief. Interlocutory relief is often given, by appointment of an administrator pending the action, or (less often) a receiver.[24]

41–06 Position of *executors* with no beneficial interest or no significant beneficial interest. An *executor*, appointed or apparently appointed by the deceased, who is in this position is entitled to adopt a position of neutrality in the dispute[25] and afterwards to have probate of any will that is established.[26] Such an executor should do so, and thus be entitled to his costs on the indemnity basis in any event.[27] By taking part in the contest, an executor can render himself liable in costs, if unsuccessful.[28] An executor who proves a will is entitled to costs out of the estate without needing to ask the court to exercise its discretion to award costs, unless guilty of misconduct.[29] The reasoning of these cases has no application to *administrators* appointed afterwards by the court.

---

[21] R.S.C. Ord. 38, r. 21(3).
[22] *Pemberton v. Pemberton* (1807) 13 Ves. 290 at p. 301.
[23] *Re Fuld* [1965] P. 405.
[24] See para. 2–12 above.
[25] As was done by the executor in *Re Stott* [1980] 1 W.L.R. 246, see at p. 248C.
[26] *Bewsher v. Williams and Ball* (1861) 3 Sw. & Tr. 62: this is different from the position on a citation: see Chap. 7.
[27] Ord. 62, r. 6(2).
[28] *Rennie v. Massey* (1866) L.R. 1 P. & D. 118.
[29] *Re Plant* [1926] P. 139; *Re Fuld (No. 3)* [1968] P. 675 at p. 720; and Ord. 62, r. 6(2). The previous right of an executor to take costs out of the estate without an order of the court is not expressly abrogated by the words of Ord. 62, r. 3(2). In *Re Fuld (No. 3)* at the foot of p. 721, Scarman J. followed the practice that "there is no need to make any order in respect of their costs." The costs of an executor who is guilty of unreasonable conduct (even if he is in part successful) are in the judge's discretion: *Re Fuld (No. 3)* at pp. 723–724.

41–07 Compromise of a probate action. Judgment in a probate action not only affects the parties, it confers rights on non-parties who take under a will that is established[30]; and an order by consent in a probate action amounts to proof in solemn form.[31] Someone who has not taken part in the probate action is not bound by a compromise, as distinct from a decision, of the action.[32] When a person with an interest or a claim (either under a will or in the event of an intestacy or partial intestacy) receives the maximum that he or she would be entitled to on any view, the consent of that person is not needed. Otherwise the consent of every person with an interest is needed to a compromise. The court has power to make an order taking account of such consents, without the person consenting being a party to the action.[33] The Master may then make an order on affidavit evidence.[34]

The terms of compromise are set out in a Schedule to the order,[35] in what is known as a Tomlin Order.[36] The terms scheduled to the order then become part of the court's record, accessible to anyone who wishes to inspect it.[37] An order made by consent is enforceable like any other order of the High Court; and has the same effect as one made, in the exercise of judicial power, after a contest.[38] The consequence of expressing it as a Tomlin Order is that the order is enforceable by application in the action in which it was made, without having to bring other proceedings to enforce it.

41–08 Extraneous terms on a compromise. In a commercial matter, extraneous terms not mentioned in the Schedule to a Tomlin Order may apply between the parties.[39] If this decision is applied to a Tomlin Order made in a probate action in the Chancery Division now, when there are extraneous terms binding the parties, it will represent a change from the previous *probate* practice. Before the Judicature Act 1873 the practice in the Court of Probate was to make *all* the Terms of Compromise a Rule of Court[40]; and where there was a term not appropriate to be made a Rule of Court, the Court of

---

[30] "A probate action is in a sense an action *in rem*": Danckwerts L.J. in *Re Langton* above at p. 175.

[31] See para. 17–01 above.

[32] *Wytcherley v. Andrews* (1871) L.R. 2 P. & D. 327.

[33] A.J.A. 1985, s.49.

[34] Ord. 76, r. 12 and the notes to it in *The Supreme Court Practice 1995.*

[35] Chancery Masters' Practice Forms No. 36: *The Supreme Court Practice 1991*, Vol. 2, para. 539.

[36] Named after Tomlin J. who formulated it.

[37] Ord. 63, r. 4(1)(b).

[38] *Re South American and Mexican Co.* [1895] 1 Ch. 37; approved in the House of Lords in *Dinch v. Dinch* [1987] 1 W.L.R. 252 at p. 263.

[39] See *Horizon Technologies v. Lucky Wealth Consultants* [1992] 1 W.L.R. 24, P.C.

[40] *Harvey v. Allen* (1858) 1 Sw. & Tr. 151.

Probate refused to make the terms a Rule of that Court[41]. This practice was carried forward to the P.D.A. Division under the Judicature Act 1873; and is the practice in the Chancery Division when hearing probate actions. This commercial case[42] is not really applicable to a Tomlin Order in a probate action in the Chancery Division.

41–09 Compromise when a person concerned has a disability. Wills and intestacies may benefit those without capacity, being under the disability of being a minor or lack of mental capacity. Such persons with an interest or any potential interest in the deceased's estate should be made a party to a probate action; or, through their guardians, be served with notice of it.[43] The court may then, on their behalf, approve terms for their benefit.[44] Those without capacity should be represented by separate counsel from those with the same interest who have capacity[45]; and from those without capacity who have conflicting interests. In all but the simplest cases, the Master requires a written opinion of counsel with the instructions on which it is based, setting out the strengths and weaknesses of the case on behalf of those without capacity. It is exhibited to an affidavit of their guardian *ad litem* who ought himself or herself carefully to evaluate the position, and set out his or her view in an affidavit.[46] Approval of the proposed compromise is by no means a foregone conclusion; in case the intended compromise is not approved, care should be taken not to disclose this material to parties with an adverse interest. Occasionally those without capacity have interests that conflict with each other; then the court has to adopt the same procedure for each of their interests at one hearing.

On a compromise, unborn or unascertained beneficiaries under a will are not usually directed to be represented by a party; although there is power to make an order appointing a party to represent them.[47]

41–10 Probate actions generally. The progress of a probate action taken to trial is similar to that of other actions; and is not therefore stated here. There are, however, special practices about costs.

---

[41] *Hargreaves v. Wood* (1862) 2 Sw. & Tr. 602.

[42] See n.39 above.

[43] See para. 41–02 above.

[44] Ord. 80, r. 112, Ord. 76, r. 12; and the notes to those rules in *The Supreme Court Practice 1991*.

[45] *Re Whigham* [1971] 1 W.L.R. 831, under the analogous Variation of Trusts Act 1958.

[46] *Re Whittall* [1973] 1 W.L.R. 1027 at p. 1030, also under V.T.A. 1958.

[47] Under Ord. 15, r. 13. There is a general principle that *trustees* must represent before the court unascertained or absent: it might in a probate action be applied to executors whose executorship is not in dispute.

41–11 Costs in a probate action.

Normal rule. The normal rule (apart from the special position of executors[48]) is that costs follow the event, so that the losing party pays the costs of the winning party.[49] There are three exceptions to this in probate actions.

Exceptions to the normal rule. (i) **Deceased or those interested caused the litigation.** When the deceased or those interested in residue have been the cause of the litigation, the costs of those who unsuccessfully opposed probate may be ordered to be paid out of the estate.[50] This is in practice less likely when coercion ("undue influence") has been alleged unsuccessfully, instead of only suspicious circumstances ("lack of knowledge and approval").[51] Numerous reported cases illustrate this principle, but turn on their own facts.

(ii) **Investigation reasonably required.** When the facts reasonably required investigation, the unsuccessful party is left to bear his own costs but not ordered to pay another party's costs.[52] This exception is of limited importance, being included in the third exception (assuming it is invoked).

(iii) **Defendant's notice to cross-examine only.** A defendant may, with the defence in a probate action, give notice that he merely insists on the will being proved in solemn form and intends only to cross-examine the witnesses produced in support of the will. Then, no order for costs can be made against that defendant, unless "there was no reasonable ground for opposing the will."[53] This valuable protection for those faced with a will (or codicil) that ought only to be admitted to probate, if at all, after cross-examination, is of some antiquity[54]; it continued to operate under the Rules of 1862 and, after the Judicature Act 1873, under the Rules of 1883,[55] as under the current rules. The notice may be given when the defence is lack of due execution, lack of capacity or lack of knowledge and approval; because capacity, due execution and knowledge and approval are

---

[48] See para. 41–06 above.
[49] Ord. 62, r. 2(3).
[50] *Spiers v. English* [1907] P. 122; *Re Cutcliffe's Estate* [1959] P. 6.
[51] *Spiers v. English* above; *Re Cutcliffe's Estate* above; *Re Fuld (No. 3)* above. For the difference between these two allegations see para. 13–02 to 13–04 above. The costs of an unsuccessful litigant who had alleged undue influence were ordered to be paid out of the estate in *Orton v. Smith* (1873) L.R. 3 P. & D. 23; but the discretion would be differently exercised nowadays in such a case.
[52] *Spiers v. English* above.
[53] Ord. 62, r. 4(3).
[54] See Mortimer, *Probate* (2nd ed.), at p. 629.
[55] *ibid.* p. 630.

necessary ingredients of the burden of proof on propounding a will.[56] Such a notice is not effective when the defendant alleges coercion ("undue influence") or fraud.[57]

Under the current rules, as under the earlier practice, this point may not be *pleaded* in the defence; it must be the subject-matter of a separate notice on another piece of paper.

The operation of such a notice at the conclusion of the action depends on the facts of each case. "It does not at all follow that, because a defendant fails, there was no reasonable ground."[58]

ACTION TO CHALLENGE A "NOMINATION"

41–12 Procedure. A nomination is not a will,[59] and is, unfortunately, not within the definition of a will for the purposes of a probate action,[60] and so the special rules of procedure relating to probate actions do not apply to proceedings to challenge the validity of a nomination.

Proceedings to challenge the validity of a nomination after the death of the nominator are therefore brought under the court's general jurisdiction.[61] This is conveniently done by writ in the Chancery Division; issued by whoever challenges the validity of the nomination against those who benefit by it.

41–13 Substantive law on a nomination being challenged. The substantive law (as to capacity, knowledge and approval and so on) to be applied on a challenge to the validity of a nomination authorised by *statute* should be held to be the same as that applied on a challenge to a will. For a nomination "performs all the functions of a will"[62]; and a nomination is in its nature testamentary "because it has all the characteristics of a testamentary document."[63]

On the other hand a nomination authorised by a *private* pension fund is subject to the same rules as any other exercise of a power of appointment.[64]

---

[56] *Cleare and Forster v. Cleare* (1869) L.R. 1 P. & D. 655.
[57] *Ireland v. Rendell* (1866) L.R. 1 P. & D. 194; *Harrington v. Bowyer* (1871) L.R. 2 P. & D. 264.
[58] *Davies v. Jones* [1899] P. 161 at p. 164, making no order for costs against an unsuccessful defendant who had served such a notice.
[59] *Bennett v. Slater* [1899] 1 Q.B. 45; *Re Danish Bacon* [1971] 1 W.L.R. 248. See Chap. 19.
[60] R.S.C., Ord. 76, r. 1(3).
[61] As in *Bennett v. Slater* [1899] 1 Q.B. 45; *Griffiths v. Eccles Provident Industrial Co-operative Society* [1911] 2 K.B. 275, reversed [1912] A.C. 483; and *Re Barnes* [1940] Ch. 267.
[62] *Gill v. Gill*, 1938 S.C. 65 at p. 71; holding that a nominator did not die intestate for the purposes of the law of Scotland.
[63] *Re Barnes* above, at p. 273.
[64] *Baird v. Baird* [1990] 2 A.C. 548.

42. Applications to the court for directions within the estate

42–01 Authority to act on counsel's opinion. When a question of construction arises, an order may be obtained in a suitable case without a hearing[1] on an *ex parte* application,[2] authorising the personal representatives to act on the written opinion of counsel of at least 10 years' standing. This inexpensive and speedy procedure is effective; it is not available when a dispute exists that it is inappropriate to resolve without hearing argument.

Such an order only authorises the personal representatives so to act; it would not prevent a subsequent claim against those concerned, other than the personal representatives, that the advice and the order was incorrect.[3]

42–02 Application under Order 85. Other applications within the estate may be made to the court under R.S.C., Ord. 85, r. 2, reading as follows:

> **"Determination of questions, etc., without administration** (Ord. 85, r. 2)
>
> 2.—(1) An action may be brought for the determination of any question or for any relief which could be determined or granted, as the case may be, in an administration action and a claim need not be made in the action for the administration or execution under the direction of the Court of the estate or trust in connection with which the question arises or the relief is sought.
>
> (2) Without prejudice to the generality of paragraph (1), an action may be brought for the determination of any of the following questions:
>
> > (a) any question arising in the administration of the estate of a deceased person or in the execution of a trust;
> >
> > (b) any question as to the composition of any class of persons having a claim against the estate of a deceased person or a beneficial interest in the estate of such a person in any property subject to a trust;
> >
> > (c) any question as to the rights or interests of a person claiming to be a creditor of the estate of a deceased person or to be entitled under a will or on the intestacy of a deceased person or to be beneficially entitled under a trust.
>
> (3) Without prejudice to the generality of paragraph (1), an action may be brought for any of the following reliefs:

---

[1] Under A.J.A. 1985, s.48.
[2] Under R.S.C., Ord. 93, r. 21.
[3] Compare *Re Benjamin* [1902] 1 Ch. 723.

     (a)   an order requiring an executor, administrator or trustee to furnish and, if necessary, verify accounts;

     (b)   an order requiring the payment into court of money held by a person in his capacity as executor, administrator or trustee;

     (c)   an order directing a person to do or abstain from doing a particular act in his capacity as executor, administrator or trustee;

     (d)   an order approving any sale, purchase, compromise or other transaction by a person in his capacity as executor, administrator or trustee;

     (e)   an order directing any act to be done in the administration of the estate of a deceased person or in the execution of a trust which the Court could order to be done if the estate or trust were being administered or executed, as the case may be, under the direction of the Court."

These terms are wide. The rule is frequently used, both for non-contentious matters and for contentious matters. Most headings in Order 85, rule 2 do not require comment; some special forms of application under the rule are mentioned below. On an application under the rule, there is jurisdiction to make any certificate or order or to grant any relief, even on the basis of wilful default or of misconduct.[4]

42–03 Nature of non-contentious applications under Order 85. An application by personal representatives under Order 85 for the court's directions differs from hostile litigation, in that the defendants are entitled to assume that the personal representatives have placed all the relevant facts before the court. The result is that leave to adduce additional evidence may be available on appeal, when leave would not have been granted in hostile litigation[5]; and accordingly an order by a judge in chambers may be reviewed on appeal when it was made in the absence of relevant material.[6]

42–04 Procedure under Order 85. The application is made by originating summons in the Chancery Division, formulating the questions asked and the various potential answers, joining as defendants any personal representative who is not a plaintiff,[7] and

---

[4] r. 4. For court proceedings by or against the estate (that is to say outside the estate), see Chap. 44.

[5] *Re Herwin* [1953] Ch. 701. The test seems to be the same as the test for whether costs fall on the estate or follow the event: *Re Buckton* [1907] 2 Ch. 406 at pp. 414–415.

[6] *Re Herwin* above; *Re da Foras* (1958) 26 W.W.R. 131, Canada.

[7] Ord. 85, r. 3(1).

such of those with a beneficial interest as are thought appropriate[8]; others may be added as defendants afterwards.[9] Occasionally there is an interest that cannot be represented for some reason; it is then the duty of counsel for those in a fiduciary position to represent that interest in argument.[10] The application is supported by affidavit evidence (filed on each side).[11]

An appointment is taken before the Master[12]; who can sometimes determine the question[13]; subject to appeal to a judge.[14] Usually the Master refers the originating summons to a judge: to a judge in court when a question of law or of construction arises; to a judge in chambers when the question is how a discretion should be exercised or whether to approve a transaction. A reported example in Canada was an application to resolve a disagreement whether shares constituting almost all the estate should be sold or retained; their capital value had risen substantially but they yielded only a small income. It was held that the court could give the deciding vote, which was for a sale.[15] (There is a similar power in the county court[16] in small estates but it is little used, and in practice no quicker and no less costly.)

42–05 Application under Order 85, rule 2 in contentious matters: that is to say, when the facts are in dispute. When the facts are in dispute, the procedure on originating summons and affidavit evidence may turn out not to be suitable.[17] In such a case, the Master hearing the originating summons gives directions. The directions to be given in such a case may be: (i) to direct an issue to be tried[18]; (ii) to direct cross-examination on the affidavits[19]; or (iii) to direct the originating summons to be treated as a writ and give directions for pleadings (by statement of claim and defence) and consequential directions.[20]

42–06 Surrender of discretion. In the usual way, personal representatives ask whether a proposed course is within their powers with a view to exercising the power if it is held within their powers.

---

[8] Ord. 85, r. 3(2).

[9] Ord. 15, r. 6

[10] *The Supreme Court Practice 1995*, n. 15/14/5; argument was in one reported case presented by the executor's counsel on behalf of the unborn children of a bachelor: *Re Scott* [1975] 1 W.L.R. 1260 at p. 1265H.

[11] Under Ord. 38, r. 2(3), and Ord. 28, r. 1A.

[12] Under Ord. 28, r. 2—see Appendix 13, n. 21.

[13] See *The Supreme Court Practice 1995*, n. 32/14/2.

[14] Under Ord. 58, r. 1.

[15] *Re Billes* (1983) 148 D.L.R. (3) 512; cited by Megarry V.-C. in *Cowan v. Scargill* [1985] Ch. 270 at p. 297.

[16] C.C.R., Ord. 1, r. 6.

[17] R.S.C., Ord. 5, rr. 2 and 4; as in *Re Parkinson* [1965] 1 W.L.R. 372.

[18] Under Ord. 33, r. 3.

[19] Under R.S.C., Ord. 38, r. 2(2). The result of that is the costs of preparing affidavits being added to the costs of oral evidence; it is a procedure better avoided.

[20] Under Ord. 28, r. 8; as in *Re Parkinson* [1965] 1 W.L.R. 372.

Cases occur, however, usually before the judge in chambers, where the personal representatives actually surrender their discretion to the court in relation to a proposal[21] (for example, where there is personal embarrassment in exercising it, or there might be a suspicion of bias, or the personal representatives are unable to agree); then the judge makes the decision that ordinarily the personal representatives would have made.[22] This is not hostile litigation but a decision what ought to be done in the best interests of the estate; it is the duty of the personal representatives or the trustees to place the facts and any relevant expert advice fully and fairly before the court.[23]

42–07 Use of Order 85, rule 2 to protect the estate against numerous claims pending separately. An estate may be solvent, but be subject to a number of hostile claims, each proceeding separately. The estate can be protected against having to meet each claim separately by resort to Order 85, rule 2. On an application of the personal representatives, or of a beneficiary or of a creditor, the Master may make a formal order for general administration of the estate (that is to say administration by the court).[24] He may then transfer any pending action into the administration application[25]: "Orders transferring actions where an administration order has been made are commonly made *ex parte*, and for the very good reason that they normally go as of course."[26] Most practitioners know instances of such orders, although they are sometimes said to be unusual.

On the consequent inquiry in the administration as to creditors, the Master adjudicates, or gives directions for the adjudication of, the claim of each claimant to be a creditor and directs those held entitled to be paid.

42–08 Effect of such an order on the position of the personal representatives. After obtaining an order for general administration, the personal representatives' powers and discretions are thereby suspended, and may only be exercised with the approval of the court.[27]

42–09 Effect of an Administration Order on a solicitor's lien. A result of an order for general administration is that a solicitor holding documents over which the solicitor would normally have a lien is

---

[21] Reported examples are *Re Ezekiel* [1942] Ch. 230, see at the top of p. 233; and *Re Somech* [1957] Ch. 165.

[22] *Marley v. Mutual Security Merchant Bank & Trust Co.* [1991] 3 All E.R. 198, P.C.

[23] *Marley v. Mutual Security Merchant Bank & Trust Co.* above; also *Re Herwin* and *Re da Fores*, cited above in note 6, not mentioned in the report of *Marley v. Mutual Security*.

[24] Printed in *The Supreme Court Practice 1995*, para. 511.

[25] Under Ord. 85, r. 2(1) and, if it is not in the Chancery Division, Ord. 4, r. 4.

[26] Upjohn J. in *Re Capelovitch* [1957] 1 W.L.R. 102; holding that a plaintiff in such transferred action was entitled to apply to discharge the transfer.

[27] *Re Furness* [1943] Ch. 415.

bound to produce those documents, albeit formally subject to the lien.[28] This exception to the general rule about a solicitor's lien has practical advantages (except for the solicitor) on the rare occasions when an order for general administration is made.

42–10 Protection as regards proceedings out of England and Wales. If the personal representatives are being sued in a foreign court, it is not practicable to transfer such foreign proceedings into the administration action in England. There is, however, jurisdiction here to grant an injunction in a proper case against the continuation of foreign proceedings[29]; and although there is no reported example of such an injunction, it might be granted in England, when the place of the administration of the estate is in England.

42–11 Overriding the discretion of the personal representatives. There is power, rarely exercised, to override the discretions of the personal representatives (without displacing them under A.J.A. 1985, s.50 or under the Judicial Trustees Act 1896[30]) by making an order for administration of the estate by the court.[31] This is a matter of discretion, but is discouraged by the modern rules[32]; it is rarely done, except to protect the estate against numerous separate claims.[33]

42–12 Kin inquiries. At one time a Master would readily direct an inquiry as to kin, to ascertain missing beneficiaries and conduct it.[34] The result was sometimes to ascertain the persons or the estates of persons lawfully entitled; and sometimes to incur costs without much result. When (as often happens) there is a doubt about those entitled, or about some of them (likely to be more frequent as a result of the Family Law Reform Act 1987, ss.1, 18 and 19) personal representatives need the protection of acting under the court's directions; they have no special protection now about illegitimate relations.[35]

It may be suspected, but not known for certain, that the deceased left a child or children (legitimate or illegitimate). In such a situation

---

[28] *Re Hawkes* [1898] 2 Ch. 1, reviewing the authorities; this principle is well settled: *Belaney v. French* (1873) 8 Ch. App. 918, C.A.; *Re Boughton* (1883) 23 Ch. Div. 169; *Hutchinson v. Norwood* (1886) 54 L.T. 844.

[29] *Midland Bank v. Laker Airways* [1986] Q.B. 689.

[30] Discussed in para. 43–03.

[31] *Re Furness* [1943] Ch. 415.

[32] Ord. 85, rr. 2(1) and 4.

[33] See para. 42–07. See *Re Flynn* [1968] 1 W.L.R. at p. 105, narrating such an order there.

[34] For a reported example where a judge made such an order, see *Re Scott* [1975] 1 W.L.R. 1260 at p. 1272, setting out the order.

[35] s.20.

the Official Solicitor to the Supreme Court[36] usually agrees to be a party to the application to represent any unknown child or issue.

Recently a practice has grown up of directing insurance against claims rather than seeking the kin.[37] The absence of the unknown kin means that there is no party before the court concerned to assert that the court's function is to ascertain those truly entitled, rather than to direct insurance against their claims.

42–13 Leave to act on a specified footing: "Benjamin Order." When the relevant facts are unclear, an order may be made authorising the personal representatives to act on a specified footing, known as a "Benjamin Order."[38] A Benjamin Order may authorise the personal representatives acting on the footing that a missing person has died[39]; or that there are no claims abroad[40]; or that a missing document was in a specified form.[41] The order protects the personal representatives; but if the specified footing turns out to be wrong, such an order does not affect the rights of a claimant to follow the property against beneficiaries.

42–14 Failure to furnish accounts. When the application is made by a creditor or by a beneficiary against personal representatives who have not furnished accounts, Order 85, rule 5(2)(a) recognises the practice of adjourning the application for a specified time for the personal representatives to furnish proper accounts: see paragraph 36–04.

42–15 Applications based on maladministration. When the facts are not in dispute, a claim may be brought by originating summons under Order 85, rule 2 against the personal representatives alleging default or misconduct on their part.[42] That is often inappropriate procedure, resulting in the proceedings being treated as if begun by writ.[43]

APPLICATIONS FOR DIRECTIONS ABOUT LITIGATION

42–16 Authority to the personal representatives about hostile proceedings in England and Wales. The Trustee Act 1925, s.15 (like its predecessor, the Trustee Act 1893, s.21) does not authorise personal representatives, as a matter of administration of the estate,

---

[36] S.C.A. 1981, s.90; see the notes to the section in *The Supreme Court Practice 1995*, Vol. 2 for his functions and status.
[37] See *The Supreme Court Practice 1995*, n. 85/2/6.
[38] *Re Benjamin* [1902] 1 Ch. 723.
[39] *Re Benjamin* above; *Re Newsom Smith's Settlement* [1962] 1 W.L.R. 1748n.
[40] *Re Gess* [1942] Ch. 37, wartime Poland.
[41] *Hansell v. Spink* [1943] Ch. 396.
[42] Ord. 85, r. 4.
[43] See para. 42–05 and n. 19 above.

to incur costs for the estate by engaging as plaintiffs or as defendants in hostile litigation. The hostile litigant cannot take an objection to personal representatives doing so; but if personal representatives litigate without proper authority, they may be unable to obtain from the estate the costs incurred.[44] Authority in writing to litigate at the expense of the estate can be obtained when every beneficiary is an ascertained adult. A charity that is incorporated, under the Companies Act 1985 or by Royal Charter, has the powers of a corporation and can authorise litigation at the cost of the estate in which it is interested. The trustees of a charity constituted as a trust do not appear to have authority to authorise personal representatives to bring proceedings at the cost of the estate: in that being without that power themselves,[45] they would not appear to have power to authorise litigation by others. They can, however, obtain such authority from the Charity Commissioners.[46] The same applies to a charity constituted as a voluntary association.

When authority to litigate is not available out of court, the court's authority should be obtained by applying for the court's directions on the matter (if necessary, first issuing but not serving a writ to prevent a limitation period from expiring meanwhile). The affidavit evidence in support of the application should exhibit the relevant papers; with instructions to counsel and a written opinion. The evidence on the application should be formulated with care; for if obtained by another party to the action[47] it may be used in evidence in the action.[48] Directions are usually given on the judge's view of the position as it stands, down to a specified stage only in the litigation (such as discovery); and they then need to be renewed.[49] The application is usually heard in chambers.

The subsequent litigation is then listed before another judge and another Master.

These precautions are not taken in practice in plain cases, such as an unpaid debt;[50] or unpaid rent.

42–17 Principle to be applied about authorising litigation at the cost of the estate. The principle to be applied was stated as follows by Bowen L.J. in *Re Beddoe*[51]:

---

[44] *Re Beddoe* [1893] 1 Ch. 547; and see *Dagnall v. Freedman & Co.* [1993] 1 W.L.R. 388, H.L., at p. 396, saying that all *Re Beddoe* decides is that he "may be at risk in being entitled to such costs if he has acted imprudently, albeit on legal advice". (Although not mentioned there, this was the formulation in para. 42–15 of the first edition of this book, 1991.)

[45] *Re Beddoe* above.

[46] Charities Act 1993, s.26.

[47] Under Ord. 63, r. 4 or otherwise.

[48] *Midland Bank v. Green* [1980] Ch. 590 at pp. 608–610; the point was not raised on appeal there, or in the House of Lords [1981] A.C. 513.

[49] As in *Smith v. Croft* [1986] 1 W.L.R. 580, a similar case under company law.

[50] *Re Brogden* (1888) 38 Ch.Div. 546 is an example.

[51] Above, at p. 562.

"If there be one consideration again more than another which ought to be present to the mind of a trustee, especially the trustee of a small and easily dissipated fund, it is that all litigation should be avoided unless there is such a chance of success as to render it desirable in the interests of the estate that the necessary risk should be incurred."

The risk has been increased by V.A.T. on legal services at 17.5 per cent.

There is little reported authority on the outcome of these applications in chambers. In one reported case[52] where trustees were defendants they were authorised to defend the case with an indemnity from the trust fund. In another,[53] such authority was refused. The Court of Appeal, reversing the decision of the judge in chambers, held that the circumstances made such an authority inappropriate; one of those circumstances was that all the beneficiaries were adults, who could litigate the question themselves.

42–18 Position of defendants to an action being personal representatives. The personal representatives' need to protect themselves by obtaining judicial approval for their litigation is collateral to the main action; and so it does normally constitute a good reason for the personal representatives not serving proceedings within any applicable time limit.[54] Personal representatives may be unable to obtain a *Re Beddoe* Order within an applicable time limit; if in such circumstances, acting in accordance with the advice of competent counsel that they have a reasonable cause of action, they serve a writ "no judge will hold that the costs incurred by so doing are not payable out of the trust estate as being improperly incurred."[55]

42–19 Authority to personal representatives about litigation in England and Wales when an adverse litigant is also a beneficiary in the estate. The previous practice was not to join such a person on the application for directions; this is still permissible.[56] The present practice is however to join such a person as a defendant to the application for directions; and then to restrict his rights to see the evidence or to be present or represented when the application is heard.[57] The previous practice was preferable to the current practice

---

[52] *Re Dallaway* [1982] 1 W.L.R. 756.
[53] *Re Evans* [1986] 1 F.L.R. 319.
[54] *Dagnall v. Freedman & Co.* above.
[55] *Dagnall v. Freedman & Co.* above, at p. 396.
[56] Ord. 85, r. 3.
[57] *Re Moritz* [1960] Ch. 251; *Re Eaton* [1961] 1 W.L.R. 1269; where as a matter of concession counsels' opinions were made available to such parties.

of having second-class litigants; it could readily be reinstated by a Practice Direction.

An offer, on behalf of the personal representatives, to disclose material to counsel and solicitors on the basis that it is not to be disclosed to the lay client, if accepted, creates practical difficulty in giving subsequent advice to that lay client.

42–20 Position when a beneficiary wishes there to be litigation in England and the personal representatives are unwilling; or consider that the estate should not take the risk. The law does not recognise a duty to litigate.[58] When the personal representatives do not wish to litigate and one or more of the beneficiaries does, the right course is for the personal representatives to authorise the beneficiary to sue in the name of the personal representatives on an indemnity as to the costs.[59] Another solution is for the beneficiary to sue as plaintiff, joining the personal representatives as defendants.[60]

Beneficiaries (or alleged beneficiaries) were refused leave to be substituted for trustees as plaintiffs in a pending action, after (it was held) the expiry of the limitation period.[60a] The case is not (as Counsel in the case has kindly informed the author) under appeal; its result seems to be narrower than the law had previously been thought to be.

42–21 Litigation elsewhere than in England and Wales. The same principles apply to litigation outside England and Wales. The Civil Jurisdiction and Judgments Acts 1982–1991[61] may require claims to be asserted abroad by personal representatives now.

42–22 Costs on an application under Order 85. On an application under Order 85, the costs on the indemnity basis of all parties to the application fall on the estate, except when this convenient procedure is used to determine what is, in substance, hostile litigation.[62] Then

---

[58] In addition to *Re Beddoe* above, see in other parts of the law: *Lehmann v. McArthur* (1868) 3 Ch.App. 496; *Williams Torrey & Co. v. Knight* [1894] P. 342; *Pilkington v. Wood* [1953] Ch. 770; and *obiter, Williams v. Glenton* (1866) 1 Ch.App. 200 at the foot of p. 208. This was assumed, rather than decided, in *London & South of England Building Society v. Stone* [1983] 1 W.L.R. 1242, where none of the above cases was cited. One case before *Re Beddoe* is on its facts to the contrary (*Re Brogden*, above); it turned on its own special facts, and does not lay down a general rule. Cases decided under the system in force before the Judicature Act 1873 are not a safe guide to the modern law on this point.
[59] As should have been done in *Re Craig* [1971] Ch. 95; see at p. 122; and was done in *Re Field* [1971] 1 W.L.R. 555. For other authorities, see *Hayim v. Citibank* [1987] A.C. 730 at pp. 747–748.
[60] Under Ord. 15, r. 4(2); as in *Re Craig* above.
[60a] *Bradstock Trustees Services v. Nabarro Nathanson* [1995] 1 W.L.R. 1405.
[61] See paras. 21–02 and 21–04 above.
[62] *Re Buckton* [1907] 2 Ch. 406 at p. 414.

the rule[63] that costs follow the event is applied; with the exception that personal representatives are entitled to their costs out of the estate, in so far as not recovered from others, unless the personal representatives have acted in substance for their own benefit rather than that of the estate; or they have acted unreasonably.[64] Occasionally in non-hostile proceedings a claimant under a will with a hopeless claim is deprived of costs out of the estate[65]; this is not a risk sufficient to deter such claims.

ALTERNATIVE METHOD OF OBTAINING EFFECTIVE DIRECTIONS

42–23 Agreed Counsel's Opinion. It is not always necessary to incur *court* costs to obtain effective directions on a doubtful or disputed point of law or administration within an estate. When every beneficiary affected is of full capacity, they may agree to resolve their differences by having the personal representatives submit all the papers in the case with copies of all the Opinions of Counsel for those concerned to a named barrister, not in the same chambers as any who have advised in the case; on the basis that his Opinion is to be accepted as a written arbitration on the question; and that the fee for such advice shall fall on the estate.[66]

This course is only open by agreement and is only effective as regards those who agree to it. It cannot be adopted where the facts are not agreed. Its advantages are that it is quicker than having to await a judicial hearing; it is much less expensive in the absence of oral argument and court procedures; and the identity of the person to decide the question can be selected by those concerned (unlike judicial proceedings).

---

[63] Ord. 62, r. 3(3).
[64] Ord. 62, r. 6(2).
[65] *Re Preston* [1951] Ch. 878.
[66] *Re Buckton* above.

43. Friction between and removal of personal representatives; other difficulties arising in the administration of an estate

43–01   Two remedies
43–02   Altering the representation
43–03   Judicial trustee
43–04   Each alternative open
43–05   Costs

43–01   Two remedies.   From time to time, the administration of an estate is obstructed by friction between the personal representatives. The problem can be overcome by one of two judicial remedies, without the need to investigate blame; they are, altering the representation, or appointing a judicial trustee.

43–02   Altering the representation.   The court has statutory power to appoint a new personal representative, or to remove one or more (but not all) the existing personal representatives, and to authorise charging for the services of anyone so appointed.[1] The application is made in the Chancery Division of the High Court, on originating summons, or by summons or motion in a pending action[2]; the evidence is by affidavit.[3]

43–03   Judicial trustee.   An alternative solution is the appointment by the court of a judicial trustee,[4] also on application in the Chancery Division by summons or motion under distinct rules.[5] A judicial

---

[1] A.J.A. 1985, s.50.
[2] R.S.C., Ord. 93, r. 20.
[3] Ord. 38, r. 2(3).
[4] Under the Judicial Trustees Act 1896.
[5] Judicial Trustee Rules 1983; replacing as a result of the Oliver Report the rather cumbersome procedure under previous rules.

311

trustee has somewhat wider powers; and such an appointment is a better solution in a complicated estate. In *Re Ridsdel*[5a], Jenkins J. said at p. 605:

"After all, the object of the Judicial Trustees Act 1896, as I understand it, was to provide a middle course in cases where the administration of the estate by the ordinary trustees had broken down and it was not desired to put the estate to the expense of a full administration [by the court]. In those circumstances, a solution was found in the appointment of a judicial trustee, who acts in close concert with the court and under conditions enabling the court to supervise his transactions."

43–04 Each alternative open. On an application for either form of relief, it is open to the court to award the other form of relief: that is to say, to appoint a judicial trustee when asked to alter the representation[6]; or to alter the representation when asked to appoint a judicial trustee.[7]

43–05 Costs. The personal representatives are entitled to their costs of the application, unless found to have acted unreasonably.[8]

[5a] [1947] Ch. 597.
[6] A.J.A. 1985, s.50(4).
[7] J.T.A. 1896, s.1(7) added by A.J.A. 1985.
[8] Ord. 62, r. 6(2); a finding that is unlikely.

44. The personal representatives' position in hostile litigation outside the estate

44–01 Hostile litigation. This chapter concerns the position of personal representatives when asserting a claim on behalf of the estate or when defending a claim brought against the estate, in relation to the adverse litigant; when the personal representatives have not obtained the protection of an order for general administration.

In an action in England and Wales the personal representatives represent the estate[1]; and so may raise any claim or defence open to the deceased.[2]

When the estate is sufficient to meet the sums and costs awarded against the personal representatives, they indemnify themselves out of the estate. The estate does not always turn out to be sufficient.[3]

44–02 Potential personal liability on a deficiency of assets: the defence of full administration. A plaintiff who obtains judgment against personal representatives for his claim obtains judgment to the

---

[1] R.S.C., Ord. 15, r. 14, applicable in the county court under C.C.A. 1984, s.76. The rules provide for the representation of an estate that has no personal representatives: Ord. 15, rr. 6A, 13 and 15; C.C.R., Ord. 5, rr. 7 and 8.

[2] Law Reform (Miscellaneous Provisions) Act 1934, s.1; with the exceptions, enacted there, of claims by the deceased's estate for: damages for bereavement (on a previous death), exemplary damages, damages for loss of income after the death and gains or losses consequent on the death, other than funeral expenses.

[3] For court proceedings within the estate, see Chap. 42.

extent of the estate's assets, present and future. There survives a principle, derived from the system in force before the Judicature Act 1873, that to avoid personal liability (to the extent of any deficiency of assets) personal representatives, when defendants, must *plead* in the action that the estate has been fully administered,[4] or has been fully administered except as to a specified amount[5]; and must then establish that at the trial. In the absence of such a plea (originally or by amendment) personal representatives are treated as having conclusively admitted that they have assets to meet the claim.[6] If there are afterwards found to be insufficient assets in the estate to meet the claim, the personal representatives are treated as having misapplied[7] assets, unless they can show the contrary.[8] It is therefore risky for personal representatives not to defend an action; or to allow their defence to be struck out.[9]

Only one of the modern cases on this point[10] is in the Court of Appeal. The requirement of a *plea* of full administration is a little out of line with the modern approach to pleadings[11]; and is a ground for seeking leave to amend when the plea has been overlooked, if such leave is available.[12] A rule of court that personal representatives shall be treated as not having admitted assets, except to the extent that assets are expressly admitted, is long overdue.

44–03 Relief from liability. Personal representatives who have not duly pleaded full administration, or who cannot prove full administration, may, however, as a matter of discretion, obtain relief from such personal liability under the Trustee Act 1925, s.61 if they satisfy the court that they have "acted honestly and reasonably and ought fairly to be excused."[13]

44–04 Costs of adverse litigants. Costs when awarded against personal representatives have to be paid by them on the standard basis out of the estate or, if necessary, personally. This is a good

---

[4] *Plene administravit.*
[5] *Plene administravit praeter.*
[6] *Thompson v. Clarke* (1901) 17 T.L.R. 455; *Re Marvin* [1905] 2 Ch. 490; *Marsden v. Regan* [1954] 1 W.L.R. 423.
[7] *Devastavit.*
[8] *Batchelor v. Evans* [1939] Ch. 1007; *Marsden v. Regan* above.
[9] *Midland Bank v. Green* [1979] 1 W.L.R. 460, where Oliver J. reviewed the law, on an application after judgment; and see the cases cited in n. 6.
[10] *Marsden v. Regan* above.
[11] *Warner v. Sampson* [1959] 1 Q.B. 297; *Re Gonin* [1979] Ch. 16.
[12] See *Midland Bank v. Green* above; holding that it is not possible to *amend* a defence that had been struck out.
[13] *Marsden v. Regan* above; where such relief was allowed in part and was refused in part on the strange facts of that case.

reason for personal representatives to be cautious about engaging in litigation on behalf of a small estate.[14]

44–05 Legal aid. Personal representatives sue or are sued in a representative capacity. As personal representatives, they may be able to obtain legal aid for the litigation,[15] with the benefits that provides. One of those benefits is a limitation on the liability of a party with legal aid to meet the costs of another party.[16]

44–06 Advantages of an Administration Order. This position has to be accepted when there are only one or two adverse claims; it has only to be compared with the procedure under an Order for General Administration[17] to demonstrate the advantages of an Administration Order.

44–07 No right of retainer. Personal representatives no longer have a right to retain debts due to themselves nor to prefer creditors; A.E.A. 1971, s.10 provides as follows:

> "**10.**—(1) The right of retainer of a personal representative and his right to prefer creditors are hereby abolished.
>   (2) Nevertheless a personal representative—
>   (a) other than one mentioned in paragraph (b) below, who, in good faith and at a time when he has no reason to believe that the deceased's estate is insolvent, pays the debt of any person (including himself) who is a creditor of the estate; or
>   (b) to whom letters of administration had been granted solely by reason of his being a creditor and who, in good faith and at such a time pays the debt of another person who is a creditor of the estate;
>   shall not, if it subsequently appears that the estate is insolvent, be liable to account to a creditor of the same degree as the paid creditor for the sum so paid."

This is unimportant in a solvent estate; it raises difficulties, not yet resolved, when an estate is solvent apart from a disputed debt of which the personal representatives have notice, and that debt, if valid, would render the estate insolvent.[18] In such a case, the personal representatives should apply to the court under R.S.C., Ord. 85, r. 2,[19] for directions about payment of undisputed debts.

---

[14] See para. 42–17 above.
[15] Civil Legal Aid (General) Regulations 1989, reg. 33.
[16] Legal Aid Act 1988, s.17.
[17] See para. 42–07 above.
[18] See Chap. 39.
[19] See Chap. 42.

45. Liability of personal representatives for maladministration ("devastavit")

45–01 Maladministration. Liability for maladministration (known by its Latin name *devastavit*) does not ordinarily arise and is only summarised here.

It is not always clear to those outside the legal profession quite what ought to be done in an administration: "Nothing is more deplorable than the fact that a person, inexperienced in matters in which he is involved, fails to take advice from solicitors, who could clearly have given advice, and have protected that person from the consequences of his rash conduct."[1] Another benefit of consulting a solicitor is that if the solicitor is also wrong, he will have a policy of insurance for negligence that may provide for the incorrectly advised personal representatives' cover on their own claim against him.

Any breach of the personal representatives' obligations may amount to *devastavit*, once they have taken a grant.[2] Examples of this are: (i) failure to get in assets promptly,[3] or to collect rent[4]; (ii)

---

[1] Evershed M.R. in *Marsden v. Regan* [1955] 1 W.L.R. 423 at p. 435.
[2] Delay in obtaining a grant is not maladministration: *Re Stevens* [1898] 1 Ch. 162. This is consistent with the right of beneficiaries to cite executors to take or to refuse probate: see para. 7–04 above.
[3] *Hiddingh Heirs v. de Villiers* (1887) 12 App.Cas. 624.
[4] *Tebbs v. Carpenter* (1816) 1 Madd. 290.

317

failure to invest money[5]; (iii) failure to inspect property (where what was in fact unoccupied and derelict property was charged to the testator, resulting in the loss of the mortgage debt)[6]; (iv) losing or allowing to be destroyed the deceased's title deeds,[7] share certificates or chattels; (v) distributing assets to beneficiaries without paying debts that were due and known to the personal representatives,[8] (but this risk has been reduced by statutory provisions to protect personal representatives by advertisement for creditors,[9] and for protection as regards obligations on a lease[10]); (vi) engaging in self-dealing with the estate of which he is a personal representative[11]; (vii) distributing the estate incorrectly.[12]; (viii) loss caused by not investing correctly, if proved in evidence.[13]

45–02 Measure of liability. The personal liability of personal representatives for maladministration (and of trustees for breach of trust) is to account for the assets received[14]; in addition in case of *devastavit*, personal representatives may be ordered at any stage of an action to account "on the footing of wilful default," both for what they have received and for what they might have received but for their wilful neglect or default.[15] It can be decided at the trial whether an account on the basis of wilful default should be ordered or not; the test is whether the past conduct gives rise to a prima facie inference that there were other breaches not yet known.[16]

45–03 Discovery of maladministration after an order for a general account. Often a general account is ordered without any decision about wilful default; then in taking the account, instances emerge of

---

[5] *Johnson v. Prendergast* (1860) 28 Beav. 480, where money was retained idle for various periods between 229 and 670 days.
[6] *Re Brookes* [1914] 1 Ch. 558, where the defendant had become a trustee.
[7] Even more so (*a fortiori*) from *Reeve v. Palmer* (1858) 5 C.B.N.S. 84.
[8] *Taylor v. Taylor* (1870) 10 Eq. 477.
[9] Trustee Act 1925, s.27; see Chap. 24 above.
[10] s.26; see paras. 25–08 to 29–10 above.
[11] *Holder v. Holder* [1968] Ch. 353 at first instance; see the form of order at p. 377; reversed in the Court of Appeal on account of the special circumstances of that case, where the executor had never acted; but the rule against self-dealing usually applies: see Chap. 34.
[12] *Re Hulkes* (1886) 33 Ch.Div. 552; *National Trustees Co. of Australia v. General Finance Co.* [1905] A.C. 373; *Re Allsop* [1914] 1 Ch. 1, where relief from liability was given.
[13] *Nestle v. National Westminster Bank* [1993] 1 W.L.R. 1260, where such loss was not proved by the evidence.
[14] Trustee Act 1925, s.30(1), with s.68(17); *Re Munton* [1927] 1 Ch. 262; *Bartlett v. Barclays Bank* [1980] Ch. 515 at p. 543, citing *Re Dawson's Settlement* [1966] 2 N.S.W.R. 211 from Underhill, *Trusts* (13th ed.), p. 702, (14th ed.) p. 734.
[15] *Re Symons* (1882) 21 Ch.Div. 757; for the form of order see Seton, *Judgments and Orders* (7th ed.), at p. 1418.
[16] *Re Tebbs* [1976] 1 W.L.R. 924, where an account on that basis was ordered as to one asset only, and a general account of other assets.

devastavit. In such a case, the mere fact that the original order was for a general account does not preclude a beneficiary from claiming restoration of the property and interest.[17]

45–04 Relief from liability. Under the Trustee Act 1925, s.61 (replacing the Judicial Trustees Act 1896, s.3) a personal representative may be relieved from liability by the court wholly or partly when he "has acted honestly and reasonably and ought fairly to be excused for the breach of trust and for omitting to take the directions of the court in the matter in which he committed such breach." All the three requirements must be met.[18] Then it is a matter of discretion for the court whether to grant relief or not; each case depends on its own circumstances and no general principles can be laid down.[19] The numerous reported cases on section 61 accordingly only amount to illustrations of the way that on particular facts a judge has exercised his discretion. A solicitor is less likely to be found to have acted reasonably.[20] A trust corporation is expected to have a high standard of skill and is unlikely to obtain relief under section 61.[21]

There is no jurisdiction under section 61 to relieve against a breach that has not yet occurred.[22]

45–05 Limitation. The limitation periods for a claim against personal representatives are summarised above in paragraph 38–04.

45–06 Other remedies. The court also has power to alter the representation, or to appoint a judicial trustee: these remedies are discussed in Chapter 43 above under the heading "Friction between personal representatives."

45–07 Procedure. Depending on the nature of the dispute,[23] a claim for *devastavit* may be brought if necessary by writ (followed by pleadings, discovery[24] and oral evidence); or by originating

---

[17] *Gordon v. Gonda* [1955] 1 W.L.R. 885, Romer L.J. at pp. 897–898; and see Evershed M.R. at p. 895; to the same effect, *Re Symons* (1882) 21 Ch.Div. 757; and, *obiter*, *Re Stevens* [1898] 1 Ch. 162, Chitty L.J. at p. 172 approved in the Privy Council; *Anguilla v. Estate and Trust Agencies* [1938] A.C. 624 at p. 637.

[18] *National Trustee Co. of Australia v. General Finance Co.* [1905] A.C. 373, where on a similar act, they did not show they ought to be excused; *Re Dive* [1909] 1 Ch. 328, where he had not acted reasonably.

[19] *Re Turner* [1897] 1 Ch. 536, where relief was refused but as between the two executors, a solicitor and a draper, the loss was taken by the solicitor.

[20] *Re Rosenthal* [1972] 1 W.L.R. 1273 at p. 1278E; compare the result in *Re Turner* above.

[21] *National Trustee Co. of Australia v. General Finance* above at p. 381, followed in *Re Pauling* [1964] Ch. 303 at pp. 338–339 (where the defendant was also interested as a banker, so that its interest and its duty were in conflict); *Bartlett v. Barclays Bank* [1980] Ch. 515.

[22] *Re Rosenthal*, above at p. 1278C.

[23] R.S.C., Ord. 5, r. 4.

[24] Ord. 24, r. 2.

summons,[25] when the evidence is by affidavit,[26] with discovery and cross-examination only if so ordered.[27] The costs in hostile litigation usually follow the event[28]; that is to say, are to be paid by the losing party, unless protected by legal aid.[29]

In practice, actions for *devastavit* are often settled once counsel has been instructed on each side.

A question about *devastavit* must be raised in an action brought for that purpose against the personal representatives; it may not be raised incidentally in an action for damages against the deceased's personal representatives for the deceased's negligence causing personal injuries; a claimant is not a creditor before judgment; and so before judgment for such damages, questions about *devastavit* or *plene administravit* do not arise.[30]

---

[25] Ord. 85, r. 4.
[26] Ord. 38, r. 2(3).
[27] Ord. 28, r. 3; Ord. 38, r. 2(3).
[28] Ord. 62, r. 3.
[29] Legal Aid Act 1988, s.17.
[30] *Morris v. Murray* [1991] 2 Q.B. 6 at pp. 17 H and 31 A-B; and see the argument at p. 8 H.

First Appendix: Summary of the legal system in England and Wales affecting the administration of estates

A–01 This Appendix is intended for lawyers outside England and Wales, and others who may be unfamiliar with the legal system here. It is a summary, with omissions, of the legal system applicable to the administration of estates in England and Wales, based[1] on Pugh, *The Administration of Foreign Estates*.

The law in Scotland is different; so is the law in the Channel Islands and the Isle of Man. The law in Northern Ireland is similar to the law of England, but not identical. The law and practice in relation to succession in England is rather different from that in some countries with close ties with England.

---

[1] With kind permission.

A–02 Legal authorities. The source of authoritative law in England is not always similar to what it might be in countries with a different system of law.

Statutes. Acts of Parliament, "statutes," are law; the courts can only interpret them.[2] There are two types of Act of Parliament, known as Public Acts (enacted to make the law for all concerned) and Private Acts (enacted, after an inquiry before a parliamentary committee, to give the force of law to what is sought by a corporation or individuals and cannot otherwise be achieved). The courts here (unlike those in the United States and elsewhere) will not hear an objection to an Act of Parliament as unconstitutional or in breach of an international convention binding this country[3]; and will not even hear a claim by a landowner that a nationalised Board had obtained a Private Act of Parliament adversely affecting his rights by making false representations to a parliamentary committee.[4] The only exception to the overriding power of an Act of Parliament is that the courts in England must give precedence over English statutes to the law, if different and applicable, of the European Community.[5]

Statutes concerning wills and succession. The basic law of wills was enacted by the Wills Act 1837; amended by a number of subsequent Acts. The law of real property (land) has historical roots back to the statute *Quia Emptores* 1290 which remains "one of the pillars of the law of real property."[6] After various other enactments, the law was varied by far-reaching Acts of Parliament (statutes) passed in 1925[7]; which have since been amended in various ways. It is fruitless to search the statutes themselves; they should be read reprinted as in force now.[8]

Reported cases. The judges sit in public to decide cases (with a few exceptions, cases heard in private, "in chambers" or "in camera"). Most cases heard in public only concern the parties. When a case

---

[2] By a striking departure from the previous constitutional position, the court may refer now to parliamentary statements on a Bill, if clear, when construing ambiguous or obscure statutes or ones that lead to absurdity: *Pepper v. Hart* [1993] A.C. 593.

[3] *Cheney v. Conn* [1968] 1 W.L.R. 242 at p. 247; *Manuel v. Att.-Gen.* [1983] Ch. 77; even when that leads to absurd or unjust results: *Re James* [1977] Ch. 41 (where an alleged debtor escaped payment because an Act of Parliament had denied validity to the judicial system then operating in Rhodesia).

[4] *Pickin v. British Railways Board* [1974] A.C. 765.

[5] European Communities Act 1972, s.2, *R. v. Transport Secretary, ex p. Factortame (No. 2)* [1990] 3 W.L.R. 818.

[6] See Megarry & Wade, *The Law of Real Property* (5th ed.), pp. 29–30.

[7] S.L.A. 1925, T.A. 1925, L.P.A. 1925, L.R.A. 1925, A.E.A. 1925.

[8] See Sweet & Maxwell's *Property Statutes* (5th ed.) (1988). For the text with a commentary see Wolstenholme & Cherry, *Conveyancing Statutes* (13th ed.) (1972); but this authoritative commentary lacks Acts passed subsequently, which occupy approximately 100 pages in *Property Statutes*.

decides a point of law or a point of construction of general application or lays down a new practice, the judgments are reported in one or more of the law reports. Reported decisions are authoritative (as mentioned below). Accordingly the law is largely to be found in reported decisions, which establish many principles not found in statutes; and may disclose that a statute has in law a meaning not apparent from reading its text.

Authority of reported cases. The binding effect of the reasons for a decision (*ratio decidendi*) is as follows. All courts are bound by the reasons for a decision in the Appellate Committee of the House of Lords[9]; and, when on appeal from a part of the former British Empire where the law was similar, will follow the reasons of the Judicial Committee of the Privy Council.[10] All courts, including the Court of Appeal itself, are bound by the reasons for a decision in the Court of Appeal. The reasons for a decision at first instance of the High Court (usually one judge)[11] are normally followed by any other judge at first instance; but are not technically binding in the High Court, if the judge can be persuaded that the reasons for the former decision were clearly wrong (a difficult task). Decisions of the High Court at first instance do not bind the Court of Appeal nor the Appellate Committee of the House of Lords; but when they have stood for some time as the law they tend to be approved in appellate courts. Perplexing problems arise on the rare occasions when reported decisions are, or appear to be, in conflict.

Parker-Tweedale v. Dunbar Bank (No. 2) [1991] Ch. 26 (on a mortgage point) illustrates the well established judicial reluctance to overrule settled practice; the following are two extracts from the judgement of the Court of Appeal at pages 37–38:

> "It is not therefore especially helpful to ask whether the exception to the general rule is illogical or even wrong in principle. We ought rather to ask ourselves whether any good reason has been shown for disturbing a practice of this court which has been settled for more than a century and a quarter, a practice espoused and approved by judges experienced in conveyancing matters and of a wisdom superior to our own."
>
> "Illogicality, if such there be, is no good reason [to overrrule a case decided in 1859 by Page Wood V.-C., afterwards Lord Hatherley L.C.]."

---

[9] Except that they alone have a power to depart from a previous decision there and to overrule it.

[10] Being the same Law Lords, sitting on appeal from places outside the U.K.

[11] County court decisions are not binding in other cases and are not reported.

Obiter dicta. Remarks in a reported judgment made in passing (*obiter dicta*) that are not part of the reason for the decision, are not binding; but are in any subsequent case given the weight that the judge or judges think right.

Commonwealth reports. Reported Commonwealth decisions may be cited and, when based on the same principles as the law of England or on a similar statute, are highly persuasive (especially when decided in appellate courts); they are likely to be followed, although not binding; unless clearly contrary to binding United Kingdom decisions.

Textbooks. Textbooks may be cited, but are not of authority. Lord Wilberforce, disapproving a passage in a well-known textbook, often relied on, said "this passage is almost a perfect illustration of the dangers, well perceived by our predecessors but tending to be neglected in modern times, of placing reliance on textbook authority for an analysis of judicial decisions."[12] Some 10 years before that, Megarry J. had said of the textbook of which he was a co-author that an author "no doubt has the benefit of a broad and comprehensive survey of his chosen subject as a whole, together with a lengthy period of gestation, and intermittent opportunities for reconsideration. But he is exposed to the perils of yielding to preconceptions, and he lacks the advantage of that impact and sharpening of focus which the detailed facts of a particular case bring to the judge. Above all, he has to form his ideas without the purifying ordeal of skilled argument on the specific facts of a contested case. Argued law is tough law."[13]

A–03 Registration of death. Deaths must be registered. Unusual or suspicious deaths are investigated, with or without a formal hearing before a judicial officer known as the coroner. Special authority is needed to take a body abroad for disposal.

A–04 Making a will. Anyone over the age of 18 years may make a valid will of his or her property, if done freely and with full capacity. Making a will does not require a lawyer. A will must be duly attested by two witnesses, as required by the Wills Act 1837 as amended; their attestation disables the witnesses and their husband or wife from benefiting under the will. Those on active military service may make a valid will without attestation. The law of England recognises an international will.[14]

---

[12] *Johnson v. Agnew* [1980] A.C. 367 at p. 395; a case on sale of land.
[13] *Cordell v. Second Clanfield Properties* [1969] 2 Ch. 9 at p. 16, on a right of way referring to Megarry & Wade, *The Law of Real Property* (3rd ed.).
[14] A.J.A. 1982, giving effect to the Convention on Uniform Law on the Form of an International Will.

The Court of Protection (which has jurisdiction over those with mental illness) has power to make a valid will on behalf of its patients, while living; and frequently does so.

A–05 Revocation and variation of a will. A will may be revoked by its deliberate physical tearing or destruction by the person who made it (the testator, or testatrix); or by another will; and, to some extent, by marriage. It may be varied by a document known as a codicil executed in the same manner as a will. It is varied too by a decree of divorce or of nullity.

When a will that was in the deceased's custody is not found after the death, the assumption ("presumption") will usually be that the deceased destroyed it meaning to revoke it; rather than that someone else wrongfully destroyed it. That assumption is not always certainly correct; and so wills of living persons are best deposited either with the Probate Registry, or with a bank or solicitor.

A–06 Intestacy. In the absence of a will, or as far as a will does not extend, property devolves on those entitled on intestacy under the amended Administration of Estates Act 1925; a surviving husband or wife obtains a large share. The others who may take on intestacy include those related by blood (including those not born in marriage), and those related as adopted and legitimated children.

A–07 Right to provision on death. There is in England (unlike many continental countries) no specified share to which a spouse or relative is entitled. A surviving spouse or member of the deceased's family and his dependants may claim that there was not reasonable provision for them and apply to the court for an order to make "reasonable provision" for them.[15] The way that this jurisdiction is exercised is rather unpredictable: it depends on the view of the particular case of the district judge or judge who hears it: such claims are frequently compromised. It has been extended to lovers after two years residence.

A–08 Applicable system of law. According to the English view of international law, a deceased person's movable property (everything except land and buildings) devolves under the system of law of the deceased's last "domicile," meaning his or her last permanent home; and the deceased's immovable property (land and buildings) devolves under the law of the place where it was. This simple rule creates problems when English law refers the devolution of property of a British subject to another system that returns the succession to the law of the deceased's nationality ("renvoi"). These problems are

---

[15] Inheritance (Provision for Family and Dependants) Act 1975.

likely to increase in number and complexity with the removal of barriers within the European Community.

A–09 Grant of representation. It is unlawful to administer the estate of a deceased person without proper authority. Anyone doing so is called an executor *de son tort* (a person wrongfully acting as executor), and incurs liabilities. An executor appointed by the deceased's will may administer the estate as from the death; but he must obtain from the Probate Registry, a document, known as a grant of probate, recognising the will. Where there is no executor (either because there was no will or because the will appointed no executor or no executor willing to act) the Probate Registry issues a grant of letters of administration to an administrator or to more than one administrator. If necessary, a temporary grant of letters of administration may be made to an accountant, a solicitor, or a bank to look after the estate on a temporary basis.

The personal representatives (being either the executor/s or the administrator/s) must to the extent of the deceased's available assets meet his liabilities and then distribute the estate.

There are procedures for determining in court what was the true last will (if any) of the deceased and to whom a grant should be made. Depending on the nature of the question it may be determined before a Probate district judge (with limited judicial powers) or a judge. It may be determined on written evidence (affidavits) where the facts are not in dispute; or, when necessary, on oral evidence.

A–10 Grants are public. Once a grant of representation has been made, the grant and any will or codicil are open to public inspection.

A–11 Variation of the devolution by will or on intestacy. It is frequently desirable after a death to vary the devolution of the estate. If that is done within two years after the death, inheritance tax (death duty) is levied as if the varied provision had been effected by the deceased. This is a valuable concession in large estates.

Persons of full capacity can decide what to agree to. The court can make an order authorising such an agreement on behalf of those without full capacity such as minors or persons suffering from mental illness.

A–12 The legal profession. The legal profession is divided into two branches.

Solicitors.[16] Practise in firms in partnership[17]; and tend to act in almost all legal fields. A client in the first place consults a solicitor. In

---

[16] Approximately 55,000 in number.
[17] A solicitor may be a sole practitioner.

litigation, the solicitor sees to the preparation of the court documents; but only occasionally presents the client's case to the judge (a position that it is sought to alter under the Courts and Legal Services Act 1990).

Barristers ("Counsel"). They are fewer in number.[18] A barrister usually specialises in one or two areas of law; and advises and conducts cases in court on that part of the law. Barristers practise together in sets of chambers (but not in partnership). The lay public cannot directly consult a barrister: a barrister only accepts cases from solicitors and from members of various professional bodies[19]; or from foreign lawyers.

It is one of the bases of a free society that those who conduct cases in court as advocates may not refuse to act for someone, however unpopular the client is or however bad the client's conduct; but may only refuse to act on specified grounds (such as having previously advised another party, or having a personal connection with the dispute).

Q.C.s. Some experienced barristers are, on application, appointed to be Queen's Counsel[20]; they only undertake to appear in or to advise on complicated cases; usually with another barrister, not a Q.C., known as a "junior" however senior he or she is.

Judges. The judges of the High Court[21] are appointed from successful Q.C.s and from juniors who have appeared in court largely for the government; occasionally a county court judge is promoted to the High Court. The judges of the Court of Appeal[22] and of the House of Lords[23] are promoted from the High Court. County court judges[24] are appointed from Q.C.s and juniors; and from solicitors.

A–13 Courts. The civil courts and the criminal courts (not dealt with here) constitute separate systems. For example, it might be found in a civil court that a will was a forgery; although the crime of forgery might not be proved in a criminal court.

There are two tiers of civil court: the High Court and the county court. The High Court is divided into three Divisions; the subject-matter of estates is within the jurisdiction of the Chancery Division. The Chancery Division also has jurisdiction over contentious

---

[18] 8,498 in all; of whom 5,621 practise in London. Annual Report of the General Council of the Bar 1995.

[19] Listed on pp. 15 to 16 of Direct Professional Access, Chancery Bar Association.

[20] Q.C., or "silk" from the custom of wearing a silk gown in court. They are 891 in number: Annual Report of the General Council of the Bar 1995.

[21] 85 in number.

[22] 26 in number.

[23] 11 in number.

[24] Known as circuit judges; there are 435 as at January 1991. The number of judges reflects the fact that almost all of them also sit in criminal courts.

questions in the High Court about whether a document is the deceased's valid last will. For historical reasons grants of probate or of letters of administration are, however, made in the Family Division, where non-contentious matters about representation are decided. Larger cases must be brought in the High Court.[25] The county court[26] is for other cases; the county court is in theory quicker and cheaper than the High Court; the county court is, however, not always cheaper or quicker in practice, at any rate in relation to the administration of estates; the subject-matter is less familiar in the county court than in the High Court.[27]

In practice there is often more delay in the County Court, which is over-loaded with work. A reported example of delay there, though not concerning the administration of estates, is *National Westminster Bank v. Powney* [1991] Ch. 339; where the Court of Appeal said at pp. 361–362:

> "The pressure of business upon county courts, and the consequent delays for those who seek justice, are well known. In this case they were aggravated by a snowstorm, a motor accident, a gale and difficulties over legal aid. In the result it took two years and ten months for the Norwich County Court to determine an application to set aside a warrant for possession."

The Chancery Division of the High Court, when available, is a better forum; such an application is determined there as a motion without delay: see paragraph 14 and note 29.

Both in the High Court and in the county court, interlocutory matters and some final decisions may be dealt with by a judicial officer below the rank of judge.[28]

A–14 Litigation. Litigation is decided on a final hearing, called the *trial*, conducted orally after due exchange of documents between the parties' solicitors.

---

[25] Where the judges are styled "Mr Justice [Smith]" written Smith J. and addressed in court as "my lord". There are also deputy judges, appointed to hear certain cases.

[26] Where the judges are styled "Judge [Jones]" and addressed in court as "your honour." There are also deputy judges.

[27] Another reason is that the practice in the High Court is for a judge who has begun to hear a case to continue it each successive day until the trial is concluded. If the trial takes longer than expected one of the other judges in the High Court hears whatever that judge had been going to hear. Each county court has, however, only a few judges; and so, when a case takes longer than expected, it may have to be adjourned for some time.

[28] Known as the Master (even if female), or as a district judge (formerly registrar). The office of registrar was renamed "district judge": Courts and Legal Services Act 1990, s.74. A district judge exercising this jurisdiction should not be confused with a circuit judge, who sits as a judge in a county court; but probably will be.

Pending trial, interlocutory relief is readily available to either party by injunction to preserve the current position. In the Chancery Division, an application for an injunction may be heard at a few days' notice.[29] The decision on an interlocutory application may decide the entire case.

The rules of court provide for the representation of those interested who cannot themselves give instructions: minors, those with mental illness, estates of persons who have died without there being a grant of representation; and classes of persons. The Crown,[30] in the name of the Attorney General, represents the interests under a will of charity generally: charitable gifts are frequently made by will.

A special characteristic of litigation in England is "Discovery": each party has, through his solicitor, to disclose to the other party, through his solicitor, all the relevant documents, with limited exceptions such as legal advice to that party. At that stage, the likely outcome of the case may be clarified, so that it can be settled.

Litigation taken to trial is costly, and to the costs of legal services there is added V.A.T. at 17.5 per cent. The losing party often has to pay the winning party's legal costs, as well, of course, as his own. Most cases are settled by agreement, once they reach the barrister on each side; with the consent of the court on behalf of any party without legal capacity.

Those with limited means are entitled to legal aid, that is to say to have their solicitors' and barristers' costs met out of the legal aid fund; provided that a committee considers there is a proper case for litigation.[31] But their actual costs are deducted from anything won in the case.

A–15 Taking the court's directions. Apart from litigation (see last above) it is open to executors or to administrators to apply to the court for directions how they should act. This procedure is not contentious litigation; and seems to have no counterpart outside countries based on the English system of law. Such an application is heard in the Chancery Division of the High Court[32] by specialist judges; it provides a swift and comparatively inexpensive solution to difficulties or doubts.

There is a similar procedure for the court to consent to a compromise or other arrangement on behalf of minors (being under the age of 18 years) and of beneficiaries not yet born or not yet

---

[29] At least one judge sits each day to hear such applications, called "motions."

[30] For the legal meaning of the expression "the Crown", see para. 5–10, note 15.

[31] These committees of lawyers meet in large numbers and deal with such applications speedily; subject to an appeal to the Area Committee against a refusal of a certificate.

[32] The county court jurisdiction is little used.

ascertained. An example is a gift by will to grandchildren of the testator, including grandchildren who have not yet been born.

A–16 Appeals. Appeals from the High Court or from the county court are brought to the Court of Appeal,[33] consisting of three judges (or in some cases only two judges). The Court of Appeal reviews the decision appealed from and the law applied, but does not rehear the case from the outset. Appeals are comparatively infrequent. On cases of general importance, there is, with leave, a further appeal from the Court of Appeal (or sometimes direct from a judge of the High Court) to the highest court, the Appellate Committee of the House of Lords; heard by a panel of Law Lords,[34] usually five.

A–17 Need for legal advice. Even what looks a simple point may conceal legal problems; personal representatives should always seek legal advice: "nothing is more deplorable than the fact that a person inexperienced in matters in which he is involved fails to take advice from solicitors, who could clearly have given advice, and have protected that person from the consequences of his rash conduct."[35]

A–18 The Courts and Legal Services Act 1990. On paper, the Courts and Legal Services Act 1990 made fundamental changes to the system of justice in England; enlarging the work that may be done by solicitors to include much that has hitherto been done by barristers; and enabling banks, insurance companies and building societies to do much work hitherto done by solicitors: including obtaining grants of representation to the estates of deceased persons. It is too early to say how much practical effect it will have: one result may be to increase the number of errors in the administration of estates and the claims resulting from them.

In the debates in the House of Lords on the Bill, Law Lords expressed apprehension about the likely effects of the Bill, now the Act.

An important change is the power under section 4 of the Act for a court to order wasted costs to be paid by a member of the legal

---

[33] Where the judges are styled "Lord Justice [Brown]"; written, Brown L.J. and addressed in court as "my lord." Judges with other historical titles sit, or may sit, in the Court of Appeal: namely, the Lord Chancellor ("L.C."), who has not sat there for many years; the Lord Chief Justice ("L.C.J."), who in practice is fully occupied with the criminal law; the Master of the Rolls ("M.R.") who presides in one division of the Court of Appeal; the President ("P.") of the Family Division; and the Vice-Chancellor ("V.-C.") of the Chancery Division. Sometimes retired judges sit in the Court of Appeal.

[34] Styled "Lord [Atkin]"; they are not to be confused with the members of the Court of Appeal; see the previous footnote.

[35] Evershed M.R. in *Marsden v. Regan* [1954] 1 W.L.R. 423 at p. 435.

profession who is guilty of "any improper unreasonable or negligent act or omission". Such an order is not easily obtained.[36]

As regards probate and the administration of estates, a far-reaching change has been made by paragraph 3 of the *Practice Direction* [1995] 1 W.L.R. 508; it provides:

> "3. Unless otherwise ordered, every witness statement shall stand as the evidence in chief of the witness concerned."

Before this Direction was made, an unmeritorious claim or defence was apt to fail because of the manner in which the witnesses gave their oral evidence in chief. This exposure of incorrect evidence is far more effective than cross-examination. Under the Direction, witnesses can however rely in chief on written statements drafted for them; and this protection to the other side is removed.

---

[36] See *Ridehalgh v. Horsefield* [1994] 3 W.L.R. 462, C.A.

Second Appendix: Suggested alterations in the law

INDEX

References are to paragraph numbers

Abatement,
  meaning, 29–01
  specific legacies, 29–09
Abroad,
  blocked assets, 20–13
  grant of representation. *See*
    Grant of Representation.
  polygamous marriages, 27–19
Acceptance of grant,
  contract with deceased, 5–03
  debtor to estate, when, 5–11
  deceased, contract with, 5–03
  executor, deceased was, 5–08
  generally, 5–01
  limitation defence, 5–11
  remuneration, 5–09
  renunciation. *See*
    Renunciation of grant.
  self-dealing, rule against,
    5–02
  tax risks, 5–10
  tort, subsisting claims, 5–04
Access to proved wills,
  avoiding, 9–03
  inspection right, 9–01
  Royal Family, 9–02
Accounts,
  advice, duty to disclose,
    36–06
  agreement of, 38–01
  copies, 36–01
  disclosure of advice, 36–06
  duty, 36–01
  failure to furnish, 42–14
  intestacy, on,
    partial, 31–19

Accounts—*cont.*
  intestacy, on—*cont.*
    total, 31–13, 31–14
  inventory compared, 36–03
  maladministration appearing
    on, 36–05, 45–02
  order for, 36–04
  personal representatives'
    duty, 36–01
  remedies, as, 36–02, 36–04
  wilful default, 36–05
Accumulation of income, 27–31
Accumulation and maintenance
  trust,
  deed of variation, 16–10
  "exit charge" exemption,
    16–10
  inheritance tax, 4–04
  variation of will, 16–10
Ad colligenda bona grant, 2–11
Ad litem grant, 2–11
Ademption,
  general legacies, 29–07
  meaning, 29–01, 29–07
  "portion", subsequent gift of,
    29–12
  specific legacies, 29–07
Administration of estate,
  bankruptcy, in, 39–03, 39–04
  completion of. *See*
    Completion of
    Administration.
  court, by, 39–04
  dissatisfaction of beneficiary,
    33–15
  insolvent estates, 39–02. *See*
    also Insolvent Estates.

Appeals,
  grant of representation,
    amendment/revocation
      of, 6–02n
  summary of law, A–16
Applicable law,
  summary of law, A–08
Appointment, power of,
  general,
    devolution of property
      subject to, 20–35,
        22–12
    incidence of liability when,
      26–08, 26–11
    meaning, 20–34
    release, 20–35
  hybrid,
    devolution of property
      subject to, 20–37,
        22–12
    examples, 20–34n
    meaning, 20–34
  intermediate, 20–34
  joint, 20–34
  limited, 20–32
  meaning, 20–34
  property subject to,
    general power, 20–35
    hybrid power, 20–37
    special power, 20–36
  right to create, 20–34
  settled land, 22–12
  special,
    devolution of property
      subject to, 20–36,
        22–12
    meaning, 20–34
Apportionment of assets, 20–38
Appropriation,
  assent, power to, 33–07
  binding, 33–04
  common law power, 33–04
  conditions for, 33–04
  consent, 33–04
  exercise of power, 33–05
  personal representatives', to,
    33–06

Appropriation—cont.
  power of, 33–04
  property, treatment of, 33–04
  tax consequences, 33–04
  valuation, 33–04
  will, in, 33–04
Armed forces,
  Inheritance tax exemption,
    4–02
  military will. See Military
    will.
  registration of death of
    member of, 1–01n
Artificial insemination, 24–01n,
  27–12
Assent,
  dissatisfied beneficiary,
    remedies of, 33–15
  effect, 33–08
  form of, 33–09
  land, of, 33–10
  other property, 33–11
  overseas property, 33–13
  power to, 33–07
  precedents, 33–09
  requirements for, 33–09
  shares, company,
    gifts of, 33–13
    transfer of, 33–12
Assets,
  animals, 20–11
  appointment, property
    subject to. See
      Appointment, power of.
  apportionment at death,
    20–38
  blocked assets abroad, 20–13
  chattels, 20–12
  company shares, 20–08
  converting, 20–01
  following, 38–05
  getting in,
    animals, 20–11
    appointment, property
      subject to. See
        Appointment, Power
        of.

337

Liabilities—*cont.*
  incidence of—*cont.*
    nominated property, 26–12
    residuary gifts, 26–08
    testamentary option, 26–12
    undisposed property in will,
      26–07
    will, order of application
      varied by, 26–06
  known future, 25–11
  leases, under, 25–09
  maladministration. *See*
    Maladministration.
  personal representatives,
    conditional, 25–11, 25–12
    contingent, 25–11, 25–12
    decree, distributing without
      knowledge of, 14–08
    definite liabilities, 25–12
    future liabilities, 25–08
    insolvency of estate, 39–03,
      39–04
    known future liabilities,
      25–11
    leases, under, 25–09, 25–10
    practice of court, 25–12
    unasserted liabilities, 25–05
  potential personal liability of
    personal representative,
    25–11
  unasserted, 25–05
Lien,
  administration order, effect
    on solicitors', 42–09
  will, over, 15–08
Life interests,
  grant of administration, 2–11
  intestacy, redemption on,
    31–08
Lifetime gift,
  donatio mortis causa, 22–04,
    22–05
  estate, effect on, 22–01
  imperfect. *See* Gifts.
Limitation,
  debts barred by, 25–04

Limitation—*cont.*
  executor *de son tort*, claim for
    amount against, 40–05
  maladministration claim,
    45–05
Limitation defence, 5–11
Litigation,
  adverse litigant as
    beneficiary, 42–19
  authorising litigation,
    charities, 42–16
    cost of estate, at, 42–17
    hostile proceedings, 42–16
    principles applied, 42–17
  Beddoe Order, 42–18
  beneficiary, adverse litigant
    as, 42–19
  defendant's position, 42–18
  directions application,
    adverse litigant as
      beneficiary, 42–19
    costs, 42–22
    defendant's position, 42–18
    hostile proceedings, 42–16
    outside England and
      Wales, litigation
      outside, 42–21
    principles applied, 42–17
    unwilling personal
      representatives', 42–20
  estate, at cost of, 42–17
  hostile,
    outside estate,
      Administration Order,
        advantages of, 44–06
      deficiency of assets,
        44–02
      full administration
        defence, 44–02
      generally, 44–01
      potential personal
        liability, 44–02
      relief from liability,
        44–03
      retainer, right of, 44–07
    within estate, 42–16

Quick succession relief, 4–06

Ramsay doctrine, 18–04
Receiver,
  appointment, 2–12
Rectification of will,
  clerical error as ground for,
    17–04
  Inheritance (Provision for
    Family and Dependants)
    Act 1975, 17–06. *See also*
    Family Provision.
  inheritance tax implications,
    18–03
  jurisdiction, 17–04
  mistake as ground for, 17–04
  power, 17–04
  standard of proof required,
    17–05
  statutory conditions, 17–04
Registrar. *See* Probate Registry.
Registration of title, 20–05
Registry. *See* Probate Registry.
Religion,
  disposal of body, views
    about, 1–02, 1–03
Remedies,
  following assets, 38–05
Remuneration,
  acceptance of grant, 5–09
  personal representatives',
    authority for,
      beneficiaries', 37–09
      court's authority, 37–10,
        37–11
    beneficiaries'authority,
      37–09
    court's authority for, 37–10,
      37–11
    exceptional services, for,
      37–12
    general position, 37–08
    subsequent court authority,
      37–12
    will not authorising, 37–08
  solicitor's. *See* Solicitor.

Renunciation of grant,
  administrator, person entitled
    to become, 5–13
  contract with deceased, 5–03
  debtor to estate, when, 5–11
  disability from, 5–12n
  documents in possession,
    5–13
  effect, 5–13
  executor,
    deceased was, 5–08
    renunciation by, 5–13
  formalities, 5–12
  insolvency, 5–07
  method, 5–12
  partnerships, 5–05
  self-dealing rule, 5–02
  sole trader, deceased as, 5–07
  tort claim, subsisting, 5–04
  trustees, 5–06
  withdrawal, 5–14
Renvoi, 11–02n
Representation, grant of. *See*
  Grant of Representation.
Residuary gifts,
  construction of words in will,
    30–01
  disclaimer, 16–02
  failed share, 30–03
  hazardous investments, 30–05
  Howe v. Dartmouth, rule in
    30–05
  incidence of liabilities, 26–08
  intestacy. *See* Intestacy.
  investments,
    hazardous, 30–05
    unauthorised, 30–05
    unprofitable, 30–05
    wasting, 30–05
  meaning, 30–01
  money, 30–01
  operation of, 30–02
  revoked share, 30–03
  settled,
    Allhusen v. Whittell, rule
      in, 30–04